Taking SIDES

Clashing Views on
Controversial Issues in
Business Ethics
and Society

Fifth Edition

Edited, Selected, and with Introductions by

Lisa H. Newton
Fairfield University
and
Maureen M. Ford
Fairfield University

Dushkin/McGraw-Hill
A Division of The McGraw-Hill Companies

To our husbands—Victor J. Newton, Jr., and James H. L. Ford, Jr.

Photo Acknowledgments

Cover image: © 1998 by PhotoDisc, Inc.

Cover Art Acknowledgment

Charles Vitelli

Manufactured in the United States of America

Fifth Edition

10   9   8   7   6   5   4   3   2   1

Library of Congress Cataloging-in-Publication Data

Main entry under title:
 Taking sides: clashing views on controversial issues in business ethics and society/edited, selected, and with introductions by Lisa H. Newton and Maureen M. Ford.—5th ed.
 Includes bibliographical references and index.
 1. Business ethics. I. Newton, Lisa H., *comp.* II. Ford, Maureen M., *comp.*

174.4

0-697-39108-6

Printed on Recycled Paper

PREFACE

*From the very beginning of critical thought, we find the distinction between top-
ics susceptible of certain knowledge and topics about which uncertain opinions
are available. The dawn of this distinction, explicitly entertained, is the dawn of
modern mentality. It introduces criticism.*

—Alfred North Whitehead
Adventures of Ideas (1933)

This volume contains 38 selections, presented in a pro and con format, that
debate a total of 19 different controversial issues in business ethics. In this
book we ask you, the reader, to examine the accepted practices of business in
light of justice, right, and human dignity. We ask you to consider what moral
imperatives and values should be at work in the conduct of business.

This method of presenting opposing views on an issue grows out of the
ancient learning method of *dialogue*. Two presumptions lead us to seek the
truth in a dialogue between opposed positions: The first presumption is that
the truth is really out there and that it is important to find it. The second is
that no one of us has all of it (the truth). The way to reach the truth is to form
our initial opinions on a subject and give voice to them in public. Then we let
others with differing opinions reply, and while they are doing so, we listen
carefully. The truth that comes into being in the public space of the dialogue
becomes part of our opinion—now a more informed opinion, and now based
on the reasoning that emerged in the course of the airing of opposing views.

Each issue in this volume has an issue *introduction*, which sets the stage for
the debate as it is argued in the YES and NO selections. Each issue concludes
with a *postscript* that makes some final observations and points the way to
other questions related to the issue. The introductions and postscripts do not
preempt what is the reader's own task: to achieve a critical and informed view
of the issue at stake. In reading an issue and forming your own opinion, you
should not feel confined to adopt one or the other of the positions presented.
There are positions in between the given views, or totally outside of them,
and the *suggestions for further reading* that appear in each issue postscript
should help you to continue your study of the subject. At the back of the
book is a listing of all the *contributors to this volume*, which will give you
information on the philosophers, business professors, businesspeople, and
business commentators whose views are debated here.

Changes to this edition   This edition represents a considerable revision. There are 7 completely new issues: *Does Ethics Matter in Business?* (Issue 3); *Does the Market Teach Us Virtue?* (Issue 4); *Are Multinational Corporations Free from Moral Obligations?* (Issue 14); *Does NAFTA Make Life Better for Americans?* (Issue 15); *Are Sweatshops Necessarily Evil?* (Issue 16); *Should the Industrial Use of Chlorine Be Phased Out?* (Issue 18); and *Can Green Marketing Save Tropical Rain Forests?* (Issue 19). In all, there are 14 new selections.

A word to the instructor   An *Instructor's Manual With Test Questions* (multiple-choice and essay) is available through the publisher for the instructor using *Taking Sides* in the classroom. And a general guidebook, *Using Taking Sides in the Classroom,* which discusses methods and techniques for integrating the pro-con approach into any classroom setting, is also available. An online version of *Using Taking Sides in the Classroom* and a correspondence service for *Taking Sides* adopters can be found at www.cybsol. com/usingtakingsides/. For students, we offer a field guide to analyzing argumentative essays, *Analyzing Controversy: An Introductory Guide,* with exercises and techniques to help them to decipher genuine controversies.

Taking Sides: Clashing Views on Controversial Issues in Business Ethics and Society is only one title in the Taking Sides series. If you are interested in seeing the table of contents for any of the other titles, please visit the Taking Sides Web site at http://www.dushkin.com/takingsides/.

Acknowledgments   Praise and thanks are due to our families, without whose patience and support this volume would never have been completed. Special thanks go to those who responded to the questionnaire with specific suggestions for the fifth edition:

Kenneth Bond
Humboldt State University

Lance Brouthers
University of Texas at San
    Antonio

David Cartano
University of Miami

Terrel Gallaway
Colorado State University

Frank L. Kahl
Ohlone College

Andrew Kampiziones
Florence Darlington Technical
    College

William F. Knowles
Lewis–Clark State College

Gene Laczniak
Marquette University

Louis Manza
Lebanon Valley College

Kim Milbrandt
University of Sioux Falls

Glenn Moots
Northwood University

Eric Mount
Centre College of
Kentucky

Dalin Phillips
Utah State University

Mark Sheldon
Indiana University–
Northwest

Harlan M. Smith
University of Minnesota

Eddie C. Sturgeon
National University

Lisa H. Newton
Fairfield University

Maureen M. Ford
Fairfield University

CONTENTS IN BRIEF

**PART 1   CAPITALISM AND CORPORATIONS IN THEORY
AND PRACTICE   1**

Issue 1.   Classic Dialogue: Is Capitalism the Best Route to Human
Happiness?   **2**

Issue 2.   Are Corporate Codes of Ethics Just for Show?   **22**

Issue 3.   Does Ethics Matter in Business?   **38**

Issue 4.   Does the Market Teach Us Virtue?   **54**

PART 2   CURRENT ISSUES IN BUSINESS   77

Issue 5.   Are Business and Medicine Ethically Incompatible?   **78**

Issue 6.   Are Pharmaceutical Price Controls Justifiable?   **100**

Issue 7.   Should Casino Gambling Be Prohibited?   **118**

Issue 8.   Are Financial Derivative Instruments Always a Gamble?   **140**

**PART 3   HUMAN RESOURCES: THE CORPORATION AND
THE EMPLOYEE   159**

Issue 9.   Should Women Have the Same Right to Work as Men?   **160**

Issue 10.   Does Blowing the Whistle Violate Company Loyalty?   **178**

Issue 11.   Should Concern for Drug Abuse Overrule Concerns for
Employee Privacy?   **194**

**PART 4   MOVING THE PRODUCT: MARKETING AND
CONSUMER DILEMMAS   213**

Issue 12.   Is Advertising Fundamentally Deceptive?   **214**

Issue 13.   Should Tobacco Advertising Be Banned?   **236**

Issue 14.   Are Multinational Corporations Free from Moral
Obligations?   **252**

Issue 15.   Does NAFTA Make Life Better for Americans?   **264**

Issue 16.   Are Sweatshops Necessarily Evil?   **276**

**PART 5   ENVIRONMENTAL POLICY AND CORPORATE
RESPONSIBILITY   287**

Issue 17.   Should Property Rights Prevail Over Environmental
Protection?   **288**

Issue 18.   Should the Industrial Use of Chlorine Be Phased Out?   **298**

Issue 19.   Can Green Marketing Save Tropical Rain Forests?   **324**

CONTENTS

Preface   **i**

Introduction: The Study of Business Ethics: Ethics, Economics, Law
and the Corporation   **xiv**

PART 1   *CAPITALISM AND CORPORATIONS IN THEORY
AND PRACTICE*   **1**

ISSUE 1.   **Classic Dialogue: Is Capitalism the Best Route to
Human Happiness?**   **2**

YES: **Adam Smith,** from *An Inquiry into the Nature and Causes of the
Wealth of Nations, vols. 1 and 2*   **4**

NO: **Karl Marx and Friedrich Engels,** from *The Communist Manifesto*   **12**

Free-market economist Adam Smith (1723–1790) argues that if self-interested
people are left alone to seek their own economic advantage, the result, unintended by any one of them, will be greater advantage for all. German
philosopher Karl Marx (1818–1883) and German sociologist Friedrich Engels
(1820–1895) argue that if people are left to their own self-interested devices,
those who own the means of production will rapidly reduce everyone else to
virtual slaves.

ISSUE 2.   **Are Corporate Codes of Ethics Just for Show?**   **22**

YES: **LaRue Tone Hosmer,** from *The Ethics of Management*   **24**

NO: **Lisa H. Newton,** from "The Many Faces of the Corporate
Code," in *The Corporate Code of Ethics: The Perspective of the Humanities,*
Proceedings of the Conference on Corporate Visions and Values   **29**

LaRue Tone Hosmer, a professor of corporate strategies, argues that codes of
ethics are ineffective in bringing about more ethical behavior on the part of
employees. Professor of philosophy Lisa H. Newton holds that the formation
and adoption of corporate codes are valuable processes.

ISSUE 3.   **Does Ethics Matter in Business?**   **38**

YES: **Manuel Velasquez,** from "Why Ethics Matters: A Defense of
Ethics in Business Organizations," *Business Ethics Quarterly*   **40**

NO: **David M. Messick,** from "Why Ethics Is Not the Only Thing
That Matters," *Business Ethics Quarterly*   **49**

Professor of business ethics Manuel Velasquez argues that ethical behavior and the development of the virtues that result in ethical behavior are the best predictors of profit in business organizations. David M. Messick, a professor of ethics and decision in management, asserts that actual behavior, in business and in other areas of life, tends to be a nuanced combination of egotistical and justice-oriented profit-maximizing actions.

ISSUE 4. Does the Market Teach Us Virtue?   54

YES: Ian Maitland, from "Virtuous Markets: The Market as School of the Virtues," *Business Ethics Quarterly*   56

NO: Bill Shaw, from "Sources of Virtue: The Market and the Community," *Business Ethics Quarterly*   64

Ian Maitland, a senior fellow at the Center of the American Experiment, argues that the market reinforces and rewards certain standard virtues and may therefore be regarded as an institution that improves the moral level of the people. Bill Shaw, editor of the *American Business Law Journal*, argues that Maitland has neglected the historic anchors of "the virtues": the society that generated and reinforced the virtues, the theory of the person that made them possible, and the conception of "the Good" upon which the notion of virtue hangs.

PART 2   CURRENT ISSUES IN BUSINESS   77

ISSUE 5. Are Business and Medicine Ethically Incompatible?   78

YES: Arnold S. Relman, from "What Market Values Are Doing to Medicine," *The Atlantic Monthly*   80

NO: Andrew C. Wicks, from "Albert Schweitzer or Ivan Boesky? Why We Should Reject the Dichotomy Between Medicine and Business," *Journal of Business Ethics*   89

Professor of medicine Arnold S. Relman argues that financial and technological pressures are forcing doctors to act like businessmen, with deleterious consequences for patients. Andrew C. Wicks, an assistant professor at the University of Washington School of Business, asserts that there are fundamental similarities between physician ethics and business ethics.

ISSUE 6. Are Pharmaceutical Price Controls Justifiable?   100

YES: Richard A. Spinello, from "Ethics, Pricing and the Pharmaceutical Industry," *Journal of Business Ethics*   102

NO: Pharmaceutical Manufacturers Association, from "Price
Controls in the Economy and the Health Sector," *Backgrounder*   **110**

Philosopher Richard A. Spinello argues that the pharmaceutical industry
should regulate its prices in accordance with the principles of distributive
justice. The Pharmaceutical Manufacturers Association, an association of 93
manufacturers of pharmaceutical and biological products, argues that price
controls are counterproductive in providing scarce goods for the consumer.

ISSUE 7.   Should Casino Gambling Be Prohibited?   **118**

YES: Citizens' Research Education Network, from *The Other Side of
the Coin: A Casino's Impact in Hartford*   **120**

NO: William R. Eadington, from "The Proliferation of Commercial
Gaming in America," *The Sovereign Citizen*   **129**

The Citizens' Research Education Network, formed to evaluate the effects
of Connecticut's rapidly growing enthusiasm for casino gambling, concludes
that casinos are harmful to cities. Professor of economics William R. Eadington
argues that commercial gambling can promote the welfare of areas that host
casinos.

**ISSUE 8.   Are Financial Derivative Instruments Always a
            Gamble?**   **140**

YES: J. Patrick Raines and Charles G. Leathers, from "Financial
Derivative Instruments and Social Ethics," *Journal of Business Ethics*   **142**

NO: Timothy Middleton, from "The 'D' Word: Derivatives Are Best
Left to Qualified Professionals," *Nest Egg*   **152**

Associate professor of economics J. Patrick Raines and professor of economics
Charles G. Leathers argue that trading in financial derivatives amounts to
speculation and gambling in financial markets. Timothy Middleton, a contributing editor for *Nest Egg*, asserts that financial derivatives are regularly
used by responsible investment professionals for a variety of risk-reducing
purposes.

PART 3   *HUMAN RESOURCES: THE CORPORATION AND*   159
            THE EMPLOYEE

ISSUE 9.   **Should Women Have the Same Right to Work as Men?**   160

YES: George J. Annas, from "Fetal Protection and Employment
Discrimination—The *Johnson Controls* Case," *The New England Journal
of Medicine*   162

NO: Hugh M. Finneran, from "Title VII and Restrictions on
Employment of Fertile Women," *Labor Law Journal*   168

George J. Annas, a professor of law and medicine, argues that women may not
be legally excluded from traditionally male jobs without some real relation of
gender to job performance. Hugh M. Finneran, former senior labor counsel for
PPG Industries, Inc., holds that women should be excluded from industries
involving substances that can deform or destroy a growing embryo.

ISSUE 10.   **Does Blowing the Whistle Violate Company Loyalty?**   178

YES: Sissela Bok, from "Whistleblowing and Professional
Responsibility," *New York University Education Quarterly*   180

NO: Robert A. Larmer, from "Whistleblowing and Employee
Loyalty," *Journal of Business Ethics*   187

Philosopher Sissela Bok asserts that blowing the whistle involves a breach of
loyalty to the employer. Philosopher Robert A. Larmer argues that attempting
to stop unethical company activities exemplifies company loyalty.

ISSUE 11.   **Should Concern for Drug Abuse Overrule Concerns for**
               Employee Privacy?   194

YES: Michael A. Verespej, from "Drug Users—Not Testing—Anger
Workers," *Industry Week*   196

NO: Jennifer Moore, from "Drug Testing and Corporate
Responsibility: The 'Ought Implies Can' Argument," *Journal of
Business Ethics*   199

Michael A. Verespej, a writer for *Industry Week,* argues that a majority of employees are tolerant of drug testing. Jennifer Moore, a researcher of business
ethics and business law, asserts that employers' concerns about drug abuse
should not override employees' right to dignity and privacy.

PART 4   MOVING THE PRODUCT: MARKETING AND CONSUMER DILEMMAS   213

ISSUE 12.   Is Advertising Fundamentally Deceptive?   214

YES: **Roger Crisp**, from "Persuasive Advertising, Autonomy, and the Creation of Desire," *Journal of Business Ethics*   216

NO: **John O'Toole**, from *The Trouble With Advertising*   224

Philosopher Roger Crisp argues that advertising removes decision-making power by manipulating consumers without their knowledge. John O'Toole, president of the American Association of Advertising Agencies, argues that advertising is no more coercive than an ordinary salesperson.

ISSUE 13.   Should Tobacco Advertising Be Banned?   236

YES: **Mark Green**, from "Luring Kids to Light Up," *Business and Society Review*   238

NO: **John C. Luik**, from "Tobacco Advertising Bans and the Dark Face of Government Paternalism," *International Journal of Advertising*   243

Mark Green, the commissioner of Consumer Affairs in New York City, attacks a popular cigarette advertising campaign that seems to be aimed directly at children. Professor of philosophy John Luik argues that restricting the freedom of speech cannot be justified unless it is shown to be absolutely necessary to avoid certain harm, which has not been done in this case.

ISSUE 14.   Are Multinational Corporations Free from Moral Obligations?   252

YES: **Manuel Velasquez**, from "International Business, Morality and the Common Good," *Business Ethics Quarterly*   254

NO: **John E. Fleming**, from "Alternative Approaches and Assumptions: Comments on Manuel Velasquez," *Business Ethics Quarterly*   260

Professor of business ethics Manuel Velasquez argues that since any business that tried to conform to moral rules in the absence of enforcement would cease to be competitive, moral strictures cannot be binding on such companies. Professor emeritus John E. Fleming asserts that multinational corporations tend to deal with long-term customers and suppliers in the goldfish bowl of international media and must therefore adhere to moral standards or lose business.

ISSUE 15.   Does NAFTA Make Life Better for Americans?   264

YES: Catherine Houghton, from "American Firms Are Doing Well
in Canada Under NAFTA: Small Companies Land Canadian
Government Contracts," *Business America*   266

NO: Dan McGraw, from "Happily Ever NAFTA?" *U.S. News and
World Report*   270

Catherine Houghton, an officer of the U.S. Commerical Service, states that
the North American Free Trade Agreement (NAFTA) has been good for small
American companies, especially in high-tech areas. Dan McGraw, senior editor of *U.S. News and World Report*, surveys a few of the companies impacted
most by NAFTA and finds that where Mexico and the United States make
similar products, Mexican products can sell for significantly less in the market
because of lower labor costs.

ISSUE 16.   Are Sweatshops Necessarily Evil?   276

YES: Susan S. Black, from "Ante Up," *Bobbin*   278

NO: Allen R. Myerson, from "In Principle, a Case for More
'Sweatshops,'" *The New York Times*   281

Susan S. Black, publisher of *Bobbin*, argues that customers will not tolerate
goods made by slave labor, children, or women working in inhumane conditions. She maintains that customers are willing to pay more to make sure that
the goods they buy were not made in sweatshops. Allen R. Myerson, a writer
for the *New York Times*, looks at the economies of less developed countries
and finds that allowing their citizens to work in sweatshops may be the only
option these nations have to accumulate capital.

PART 5   *ENVIRONMENTAL POLICY AND CORPORATE
          RESPONSIBILITY*   287

ISSUE 17.   Should Property Rights Prevail Over Environmental
          Protection?   288

YES: Richard Epstein, from "Property Rights and Environmental
Protection," *Cato Policy Report*   290

NO: John Echeverria, from "Property Rights and Environmental
Protection," *Cato Policy Report*   294

Professor of law Richard Epstein argues that if a law is passed that robs an
individual's property of all value, he or she should be compensated for it.
John Echeverria, a legal counsel to the National Audubon Society, argues that
environmental regulations do not violate a right to one's property.

ISSUE 18. Should the Industrial Use of Chlorine Be Phased Out?   **298**

YES: Joe Thornton, from "Chlorine: Can't Live With It, Can Live Without It," Speech Prepared for the Chlorine-Free Debate Held in Conjunction With the International Joint Commission Seventh Biennial Meeting, Windsor, Ontario, Canada   **300**

NO: Ivan Amato, from "The Crusade to Ban Chlorine," *Garbage: The Independent Environmental Quarterly*   **312**

Greenpeace research coordinator Joe Thornton argues that a systematic phase-out of chlorinated organic compounds is the only effective means of protecting humans and animals from the toxic effects of these chemicals. Science writer Ivan Amato argues that only a few chlorinated compounds are proven health threats and that Greenpeace's claims that substitutes exist are misleading.

ISSUE 19. Can Green Marketing Save Tropical Rain Forests?   **324**

YES: Thomas A. Carr, Heather L. Pedersen, and Sunder Ramaswamy, from "Rain Forest Entrepreneurs: Cashing in on Conservation," *Environment*   **326**

NO: Jon Entine, from "Let Them Eat Brazil Nuts: The 'Rainforest Harvest' and Other Myths of Green Marketing," *Dollars and Sense*   **335**

Economics professors Thomas A. Carr and Sunder Ramaswamy and mathematics teacher Heather L. Pedersen describe three projects to promote sustainable use of rain forest products, which they argue help to preserve the forest and support the local economy. Investigative reporter Jon Entine asserts that most green marketing programs do nothing to slow forest destruction and, moreover, frequently result in the mistreatment of employees, vendors, and customers.

Contributors   **344**

Index   **350**

INTRODUCTION

The Study of Business Ethics: Ethics, Economics, Law and the Corporation

Lisa H. Newton
Maureen M. Ford

This book is aimed at an audience of students who expect to be in business, who know that there are knotty ethical problems out there, and who want a chance to confront them ahead of time. The method of confronting them is an invitation to join in a debate, a contest of contrary facts and conflicting values in many of the major issues of the day. This introductory essay should make it easier to join in the arguments. Managing ethical policy problems in a company requires a wide background—in ethics, economics, law, and the social sciences—which this book cannot hope to provide. But since some background assumptions in these fields are relevant to several of the problems we examine in this volume, we will sketch out very briefly the major understandings that control them. There is ultimately no substitute for thorough study of the rules of the game and years of experience and practice; but an overview of the playing field may at least make it easier for you to understand the object and limitations of the standard plays.

ETHICS

"Business ethics" is sometimes considered to be an oxymoron (a term that contradicts itself). Business and ethics have often been treated as mutually exclusive. But ethics is an issue of growing concern and importance to businesses, and we believe that many share our conviction that value questions are never absent from business decisions, that moral responsibility is the first characteristic demanded of a manager in any business, and that a thorough grounding in ethical reasoning is the best preparation for a career in business. The first imperative of business ethics is that it be taken seriously.

This book will not supply the substance of a course in ethics. For that you are directed to any of several excellent texts in business ethics or to any general text in ethics (see the list of suggested readings at the end of this introduction). *Taking Sides: Clashing Views on Controversial Issues in Business Ethics and Society* teaches ethics from the issue upward, rather than from the principle downward. You will, however, come upon much of the terminology of ethical reasoning in the course of considering these cases. For your reference, a brief summary of the ethical principles and forms of reasoning most used in this book is found in Table 1.

Table 1

Fundamental Duties

	Beneficence—promoting human welfare	Justice—acknowledging human equality	Respect for Persons—honoring individual freedom
Basic fact about human nature that grounds the duty	Humans are animals, with vulnerable bodies and urgent physical needs, capable of suffering.	Humans are social animals who must live in communities and therefore must adopt social structures to maintain communities.	Humans are rational, free—able to make their own choices, foresee the consequences, and take responsibility.
Value realized in performance of the duty	Human welfare; happiness.	Human equality.	Human dignity; autonomy.
Working out of the duty in ethical theory	Best modern example is utilitarianism, from Jeremy Bentham and John Stuart Mill, who saw morality as that which produced the greatest happiness for the greatest number. Reasoning is consequential, aimed at results.	Best modern example is John Rawls's theory of justice as "fairness"; maintaining equality unless inequality helps everyone. Reasoning is deontological: morality derived from duty, not consequences.	Best modern example is Immanuel Kant's formalism, where morality is seen as the working out of the categorical imperative. Reasoning is deontological.
Samples of implementation of the duty in business	Protecting safety of employees; maintaining pleasant working conditions; contributing funds to the local community.	Obedience to law; enforcing fair rules; nondiscrimination; no favoritism; giving credit where credit is due.	Respect for employee rights; treating employees as persons, not just as tools; respecting differences of opinion.

ECONOMICS

Adam Smith

Capitalism as we know it is the product of the thought of Adam Smith (1723–1790), a Scottish philosopher and economist, and a small number of his European contemporaries. The fundamental capitalist act is the *voluntary exchange:* two adults of sound mind and clear purposes meet in the marketplace, to which each repairs in order to satisfy some felt need. They discover that each has that which will satisfy the other's need—the housewife needs flour, the miller needs cash—and they exchange at a price such that the exchange furthers the interest of each. To the participant in the free market, the *marginal utility* of the thing acquired must exceed that of the thing traded, or else why make the deal? So each party to the voluntary exchange walks away from it richer.

Adding to the value of the exchange is the *competition* of dealers and buyers; because there are many purveyors of each good in the marketplace, the customer is not forced to pay exorbitant prices for things needed. (It is a sad fact of economics that to the starving man, the marginal value of a loaf of bread is very large, and a single merchant could become unjustly rich.) Conversely, competition among the customers (typified by an auction) makes sure that the available goods end up in the hands of those to whom they are worth the most. So at the end of the market day, everyone goes home not only richer (in real terms) than when they came—the voluntariness of the exchange ensures that—but also as rich as they could possibly be, since each had available all possible options of goods or services to buy and all possible purchasers of the goods or services brought to the marketplace for sale.

Sellers and buyers win the competition through *efficiency;* that is, through producing the best quality goods at the lowest possible price or through allotting their scarce resources toward the most valuable of the choices presented to them. It is to the advantage of all participants in the market, then, to strive for efficiency (i.e., to keep the cost of goods for sale as low as possible while keeping the quality as high as possible). Adam Smith's most memorable accomplishment was to recognize that the general effect of all this self-interested scrambling would be to make the most possible goods of the best possible quality available at the least possible price. Meanwhile, sellers and buyers alike must keep an eye on the market as a whole, adjusting production and purchasing to take advantage of fluctuations in *supply and demand*. Short supply will make goods more valuable, raising the price, and that will bring more suppliers into the market, whose competition will lower the price to just above the cost of manufacture for the most efficient producers. Increased demand for any reason will have the same effect. Should supply exceed demand, the price will fall to a point where the goods will be bought. Putting this all together, Smith realized that in a system of free enterprise, you have demonstrably the best possible chance of finding for sale what you want, in good quantity and quality and at a reasonable price. Forget benevolent monarchs ordering things for our own good, Smith suggested; in this system, we are led as by an *invisible hand* of enlightened self-interest to achieve the common good, even as we think we are being most selfish.

Adam Smith's theory of economic enterprise emerged in the natural law tradition of the eighteenth century. As was the fashion for that period, Smith presented his conclusions as a series of laws: the law of supply and demand, which links supply, demand, and price; the law that links efficiency with success; and, ultimately, the laws that link the absolute freedom of the market with the absolute growth of the wealth of the free-market country.

To these laws were added others, specifying the conditions under which business enterprise would be conducted in capitalist countries. The laws of *population* formulated by English clergyman and economist Thomas Malthus (1766–1834) concluded that population would always outstrip food production, ensuring that the bulk of humanity would always live at the subsistence level. Since Smith had already postulated that employers would purchase labor at the lowest possible price, it was a one-step derivation for English economist David Ricardo (1772–1823) to conclude that workers' *wages* would never exceed the subsistence level, no matter how prosperous industrial enterprise should become. From these capitalist theorists proceeded the nineteenth-century assumption that society would inevitably divide into two classes, a minority of fabulous wealth and a majority of subsistence-level workers.

These laws, like the laws of physics advanced at that time by Sir Isaac Newton (1642–1727) and the laws of psychology and government advanced at that time by John Locke (1632–1704), were held to be immutable facts of nature, true forever and not subject to change. No concept of progress, or of the historical fitness of a system to society at a point in time, was contemplated.

Karl Marx

Only within the last century and a half have we learned to think "historically." The notion of progress, the vision of a better future, and even the very idea that we might modify that future, in part by the discernment of historical trends, were unknown to the ancients and of no interest to medieval chroniclers. For Western political philosophy, history emerged as a factor in our understanding only with the work of the nineteenth-century German philosopher G. W. F. Hegel (1770–1831), who traced the history of the Western world as an ordered series of ideal forms, evolving one from another in logical sequence toward an ideal future. A young German student of Hegel's, Karl Marx (1818–1883), concluded from his study of philosophy and economics that Hegel had to be wrong: the phases of history were ruled not by ideas but by the *material conditions* of life, and their evolution one from another came about as the ruling class of each age generated its own revolutionary overthrow.

Marx's theory, especially as it applies to the evolution of capitalism, is enormously complex; for the purposes of this unit, it can be summarized simply. According to Marx, the *ruling class* in every age is the group that *owns the means of production* of the age's product. Throughout the seventeenth century, the product was almost exclusively agricultural, and the means of production was almost exclusively agricultural land: landowners were the aristocrats and rulers. With the coming of commerce and industry, the owners of the factories joined the ruling class and eventually dominated it. It was in the nature of such capital-intensive industry to concentrate within itself more capital: as Adam Smith had proved, its greater efficiency would drive all smaller labor-intensive industry out of business, and its enormous income would be put to work as more capital, expanding the domain of the factory and the machine indefinitely (at the expense of the cottage industry and the human being). Thus would the wealth of society concentrate in fewer and fewer hands, as the owners of the factories expanded their enterprises without limit into mighty industrial empires, dominated by machines and by the greed of their owners.

Meanwhile, all this wealth was being produced by a new class of workers, the unskilled factory workers. Taken from the ranks of the obsolete peasantry, artisans, and craftsmen, this new working class, the *proletariat*, expanded in numbers with the gigantic mills, whose "hands" they were. Work on the assembly line demanded no education or skills, so the workers could never make themselves valuable enough to command a living wage on the open market. They survived as a vast underclass, interchangeable with the unemployed workers (recently displaced by more machines) who gathered around the factory gates looking for jobs—*their* jobs. As Ricardo had demonstrated, they could never bargain for any wage above the subsistence level—just enough to keep them alive. As capitalism and its factories expanded, the entire population, except the wealthy capitalist families, sank into this hopeless, pauperized class.

So Marx saw Western society under capitalism as one that ultimately would be divided into a small group of fabulously wealthy capitalists and a mass of paupers, mostly factory workers. The minority would keep the majority in strict control through its hired thugs (the state—the army and the police), control rendered easier by thought control (the schools and the churches). The purpose of the ideology taught by the schools and the churches—the value structure of capitalism—was to show both classes that the capitalists had a right to their wealth (through the sham of liberty, free enterprise, and the utilitarian benefits of the free market) and a perfect right to govern everyone else. Thus, the capitalists could enjoy their wealth in good conscience and the poor would understand their moral obligation to accept the oppression of the ruling class with good cheer.

Marx foresaw, and in his writings attempted to help bring about, the disillusionment of the workers: there would come a point when the workers would suddenly ask, *Why* should we accept oppression all our lives? Their search for answers to this question would show them the history of their situation, expose the falsehood of the ideology and the false consciousness of those who believe it, show them their own strength, and lead them directly to the solution that would usher in the new age of socialism—the revolutionary overthrow of the capitalist regime. Why, after all, should they not undertake such a revolution? People are restrained from violence against oppression only by the prospect of losing something valuable, and, as Marx concluded, the industrialized workers of the world had nothing to lose but their chains.

As feudalism had been swept away, then, by the "iron broom" of the French Revolution, so capitalism would be swept away by the revolt of the masses, the irresistible uprising of the vast majority of the people against the minority of industrial overlords and their terrified minions—the armed forces, the state, and the church. After the first rebellions, Marx foresaw no lengthy problem of divided loyalties in the industrialized countries of the world. Once the scales had fallen from their eyes, the working-class hirelings of the army and police would quickly turn their guns on their masters and join their natural allies in the proletariat to create the new world.

After the revolution, Marx predicted, there would be a temporary "dictatorship of the proletariat," during which the last vestiges of capitalism would be eradicated and the authority to run the industrial establishment would be returned to the workers of each industry. Once the economy had been decentralized, to turn each factory into an industrial commune run by its own workers and each landed estate into an agricultural commune run by its farmers, the state as such would simply wither away. Some central authority would certainly continue to exist, to coordinate and facilitate the exchange of goods within the country (one imagines a giant computer, taking note of where goods are demanded, where goods are available, and where the railroad cars to take the goods from one place to the other are). But with no ruling class to serve and no oppression to carry out, there will be no need of the state to rule *people*; what is left will be confined to the administration of *things*.

Even as he wrote, just in time for the revolutions in Europe of 1848, Marx expected the end of capitalism as a system. Not that capitalism was evil in itself; Marx did not presume to make moral judgments on history. Indeed, capitalism was necessary as an economic system to concentrate the wealth of the country into the industries of the modern age. So, in Marx's judgment, capitalism had a respectable past and would still be necessary for awhile in the developing countries to launch their industries. But that task completed, it had no further role in history, and the longer it stayed around, the more the workers would suffer and the more violent the revolution would be when it came. The sooner the revolution, the better; the future belonged to communism.

As the collapse of the communist governments in Eastern Europe demonstrates (if demonstration were needed), the course of history has not proceeded quite as Marx predicted in 1848. In fairness, it might be pointed out that no other prophets of the time had any more luck with prognostications about the twentieth century. In any case, since Marx wrote, all participants in the debate on the nature and future of capitalism have had to respond to his judgments and predictions.

LAW: RECOVERING FOR DAMAGES SUSTAINED

Life is full of misfortune. Ordinarily, if you suffer misfortune, you must put up with it and find the resources to deal with it. If your misfortune is my fault, however, the law may step in and make me pay for those damages, one way or another.

Through *criminal law*, the public steps in and demands punishment for an offense that is serious enough to outrage public feeling and endanger public welfare. If I knock you on the head and take your wallet, the police will find me, restore your wallet to you, and imprison or otherwise punish me for the crime.

Through *civil law*, if I do you damage through some action of mine, you may take me to civil court and ask a judge (and jury) to determine whether or not I have damaged you, if so by how much, and how I should pay you back for that damage. There are a number of forms of action under which you may make your claim; the most common for business purposes are *contract* and *torts*. If you and I agree to (or "contract for") some undertaking, and I back out of it after you have relied on our agreement to commit your resources to the undertaking, you have a right to recover what you have lost. In torts, if I simply injure you in some way, hurting you in health, life, or limb, or destroying your property, I have done you a wrong (*tort*, in French), and I must pay for the damage I have done. How much I will have to pay will depend (as the jury will determine) on (1) the amount of the damage that has been caused, (2) the extent to which I knew or should have known that my action or neglect to act would cause damage (my *culpability*), and (3) the extent to which *you* contributed to the damage, beyond whatever I did (*contributory negligence*).

Another kind of suit at law alleges *negligence*, which is a tort, on the part of a company, in that it made and put up for sale a product known to be defective and that the defect injured its users. To establish negligence, civil or criminal, four elements must be demonstrated: First, there must have been a *duty*—the party accused of negligence must have had a preexisting duty to the plaintiff. Second, there must have been a *breach of*, or failure to fulfill, that duty. Third, the plaintiff must have suffered an *injury*. And fourth, the breach of the duty must have been the *proximate cause* of the injury, or the thing that actually brought the injury about. Where negligence is alleged in a product liability case, it must be established that the manufacturer had a duty to make a product that could not do certain sorts of harm, that the duty was breached and the harm was caused, that nothing else was to blame, and that the manufacturer therefore must compensate the victim for the damage done.

Should companies ultimately be responsible for any harm that comes from the use of the products they profitably market and sell? Or should consumers be content to bear the responsibility for risks that they freely accept? Our ambivalence on this question as a society mirrors, and proceeds from, the ambivalence of the individual at the two poles of materialization of risk: when we are in a hurry, short of cash, or in need of a cigarette, then risky behavior looks to us to be our right, and we are resentful of the busybodies who would always have us play it safe. But when the risk materializes— when the accident or the disease happens—the perception of that risk (and the direction of that resentment) changes drastically. From the perspective of the hospital bed, it is crystal clear that the behavior was not worth the risk, that we never realized the behavior was risky, that we should have been warned, and that it was someone's duty to warn us. In that instantaneous change of perspective, three elements of negligence come into view: duty, breach, and injury. No wonder product liability suits are so common.

Yet the suit is a relatively recent phenomenon because of a peculiarity in the law. Until the twentieth century, a judge faced with a consumer who had been injured by a product (physically or financially) applied the principle of *caveat emptor*—"let the buyer beware"—and could ask the seller to pay damages only to the original buyer, and only if the exact defect in the product could be proven. For example, a defective kerosene lamp might explode and burn five people, but the exact defect (broken seam or shoddy wick) had to be brought into court or the case would be thrown out. In addition, the buyer could sue only the seller, not the manufacturer or designer, because the right to collect damages rested on the law of *contract*, not torts, and on the warrant of merchantability implied in the contractual relationship between buyer and seller. The cause of the action was understood to be a breach in that contract.

There matters stood until 1916, when an American judge allowed a buyer to sue the manufacturer of a product. A Mr. MacPherson had been injured when his car collapsed under him due to a defect in the wood used to build one of the wheels, and MacPherson went to court against the Buick Motor Company. The judge reasoned that the action was in torts, specifically "negligence," and not in contract, for a manufacturer is under a duty to make carefully any product that could be expected to endanger life, and this duty existed irrespective of any contract. So if MacPherson, or any future user of the product, was injured because the product was badly made, he could collect damages even if he had never dealt with the manufacturer in any way.

In the 1960s the automobile was still center stage in the arguments over the duties of manufacturers. Consumer advocate Ralph Nader's book *Unsafe at Any Speed* (1966) spearheaded the consumer rights movement with its scathing attack on General Motors and its exposé of the dangerous design of the Corvair. In response to the consumer activism resulting from that movement, Congress passed the Consumer Product Safety Act in 1972 and empowered the Consumer Product Safety Commission, an independent federal agency, to set safety standards, require warning labels, and order recalls of hazardous products. When three girls died in a Ford Pinto in 1978, the foundations of consumer rights against careless manufacturers were well established. What was new in the Ford Motor Company case was the allegation of *criminal* negligence—in effect, criminal homicide.

At present, product liability suits are major uncharted reefs in the navigational plans of American business. If a number of people die in a fire in a hotel, for instance, their families will often sue not only the hotel, for culpable negligence, but the manufacturers of the furniture that burned, alleging that it should have been fire-retardant; the manufacturers of the cushions on the furniture, alleging that they gave off toxic fumes in the fire; and the manufacturers of the chemicals that went into those cushions, alleging that there was no warning to the consumers on the toxicity of those chemicals in fire conditions. The settlements that can be obtained are used to finance the suit and the law firm that is managing it for the years that it will take to exhaust all the appeals. This phenomenon of unlimited litigation is relatively new on the American scene, and we are not quite sure how to respond to it.

THE CORPORATION

The human being is a social animal. We exist in the herd and depend for our lives on the cooperation of those around us. Who are they? Anthropologists tell us that originally we traveled in extended families, then settled down into villages of intensely interlocked groups of families. With the advent of the modern era, we have found our identities in family, village, church, and nation. Yet, in the great transformation of the obligations of the Western world (see Henry Maine [1822–1888], *From Status to Contract*), we have abandoned the old family-oriented care systems and thrown ourselves upon the mercy of secondary organizations: club, corporation, and state. The French sociologist Emile Durkheim (1858–1917), in his classic work *Suicide*, suggested that following the collapse of the family and the church, the corporation would be the association in the future that would supply the social support that every individual needs to maintain a moral life.

Can the corporation do that? Or is the corporation merely the organization that implements Adam Smith's self-interested pursuit of the dollar, with no purpose but to maximize return on investment to the investors while protecting them from unlimited liability?

On the other hand, once formed, and having become a major community figure and employer, does the corporation have a right to exist that transcends at least the immediate pursuit of money? The issue of so-called hostile takeovers sends us back to the purpose and foundation of business enterprise in America. Let us review: When an entrepreneur gets a bright idea for how to make money, he or she secures the capital necessary to run the business from investors (venture capitalists); uses that capital to buy the land, buildings, and machinery needed to see the project through; hires the labor needed to do the work; and goes into production. As the income from the enterprise comes in, the entrepreneur pays the suppliers of raw materials; pays the workers; pays the taxes, rent, mortgages, and utility bills; keeps some of the money for him- or herself (salary); and then divides up the rest of the income (profit) among the investors (probably including him- or herself) in proportion to the capital they invested. Motives of all parties are presupposed: the entrepreneur wants money; the laborers and the landlords want money; and the investors, who are the shareholders in the company, want money. The investors thought that this enterprise would yield them a higher return on their capital than any other investment available to them at the time; that is why they invested. However, this is a free country, and people can move around. If the workers see better jobs, they will take them; if a landlord can rent for more, the lease will be terminated; and if the investors see a better place to put their capital, they will move it. The determiner of the flow of capital is the rate of return, no more and no less. Loyalty to the company, faithfulness to the corporation for the sake of the association itself, is not on anyone's agenda—not on the worker's, certainly not on the landlord's, and *most* certainly not on the shareholder's.

The shareholders are represented by a board of directors elected by them to see that the company is run efficiently; that is, that costs are kept down and income up to yield the highest possible return. The board of directors hires management—the cadre of corporate officers headed by the president and/or chief executive officer to do the actual running of the company. The corporate officers thus stand in a *fiduciary* relationship to the shareholders; that is, they are forbidden by the understandings on which the corporation is founded to do anything at all except that which will protect and enhance the interests of the shareholders. That goes for all the normal business decisions made by the management; even the decision not to break the law can be seen as a prudent estimate of the financial costs of lawbreaking.

Yet our dealings with the business world, as citizens and as consumers, have always turned on recognition and support of the huge reliable corporations in established industries; not just coal and steel, which had certain natural limitations built into their consumption of natural resources, but the automobile companies, the airlines, the consumer products companies, and even the banks. Companies had "reputations" and "integrity," and they cultivated (and bought and sold) "good will." Consumers cooperated with the companies that catered to them in developing "brand loyalty." And, most important, those working in business cooperated with their employers in developing "company loyalty," which became a part of their lives, just as loyalty to one's tribe or nation was part of the lives of their ancestors. Is the company that sought our loyalty—and got it—just a scrap of paper, to disappear as soon as return on investment falls below the nearest competition? What part do we want corporations to play in our associative lives? If we want them to be any more than profit maximizers for the investors, what sorts of protections would we have to offer them, and what sorts of limitations should we put on their extra-profit-making activities?

CURRENT ISSUES

Business ethics ultimately rests on a base of political philosophy, economics, and philosophical ethics. As these underlying fields change, new topics and approaches will surface in business ethics. For example, hostile takeovers did not take place very often in the regulatory climate that existed prior to the Reagan administration. The change in political philosophy introduced by his administration resulted in new business practices, which resulted in new ethical problems. Also, the work of John Rawls, a professor of philosophy at Harvard University, profoundly influenced our understanding of distributive justice and, therefore, our understanding of acceptable economic distribution in the society. The work currently being done in postmodern philosophy will change the way we see human beings generally and, hence, the activity of business.

No single work can cover all the issues of ethical practice in business in all their range and particularity, especially since, as above, we are dealing with a moving target. Our task here is much more limited. The purpose of this book is to allow you to grapple with some of the ethical issues of current business practice in the safety of the classroom, before they come up on the job where human rights and careers are at stake and legal action looms outside the boardroom or factory door. We think that rational consideration of these issues now will help you prepare for a lifetime of the types of problems that naturally arise in a complex and pluralistic society. You will find here no dogmas, no settled solutions to memorize. These problems do not have preset answers but require that you use your mind to balance the values in conflict and to work out acceptable policies in each issue. To employ business ethics, you must learn to think critically, to look beyond short-term advantages and traditional ways of doing things, and to become an innovator. The exercise provided by these debates should help you in this learning.

There is no doubt that businesspeople think that ethics is important. Sometimes the reasons why they think ethics is important have to do only with the long-run profitability of a business enterprise. There is no doubt that greater employee honesty and diligence would improve the bottom line or that strict attention to environmental and employee health laws is necessary to protect the company from expensive lawsuits and fines. But ethics goes well beyond profitability, to the lives that we live and the persons we want to be. What the bottom line has taught us is that the working day is not apart from life. We must bring the same integrity and care to the contexts of the factory and the office that we are used to showing at home and among our friends. An imperative of business ethics is to make of your business life an opportunity to become, and remain, the person that you know you ought to be—and as far as it is within your capability, to extend that opportunity to others.

In this book, we attempt to present in good debatable form some of the issues that raise the big questions—of justice, of rights, of the common good —in order to build bridges between the workaday world of employment and the ageless world of morality. If you will enter into these dialogues with an open mind, a willingness to have it changed, and a determination to master the skills of critical thinking that will enable you to make responsible decisions in difficult situations, you may be able to help build the bridges for the new ethical issues that will emerge in the next century. At the least, that is our hope.

SUGGESTED READINGS

Tom L. Beauchamp and Norman E. Bowie, *Ethical Theory and Business*, 3d ed. (Prentice Hall, 1988).

John Matthews, Kenneth Goodpaster, and Laura Nash, *Policies and Persons: A Casebook in Business Ethics*, 2d ed. (McGraw-Hill, 1991).

Manuel Velasquez, *Business Ethics: Concepts and Cases*, 2d ed. (Prentice Hall, 1987).

On the Internet . . .

http://www.dushkin.com

Business Ethics Resources on WWW

Sponsored by the Centre for Applied Ethics, this page of business ethics resources links to corporate codes of ethics, business ethics institutions and organizations, and on-line papers and publications, as well as other elements.
http://www.ethics.ubc.ca/resources/business/

Critical Thinking Across the Curriculum Project

This site, sponsored by Longview Community College in Lee's Summit, Missouri, links to resources in critical thinking. They are divided into the core resources and discipline-specific resources.
http://www.kcmetro.cc.mo.us/longview/ctac/toc.htm

Ethics on the World Wide Web

This site links to associations, organizations, and institutes that focus on the various aspects of ethics, including the Global Ethic Project and the Center for the Study of The Great Ideas.
http://www5.fullerton.edu/les/associations.html

International Business Ethics Institute

The International Business Ethics Institute offers professional services to organizations interested in implementing, expanding, or modifying business ethics and corporate responsibility programs. Its mission is to foster global business practices that promote equitable economic development, resource sustainability, and democratic forms of government.
http://www.business-ethics.org/

PART 1

Capitalism and Corporations in Theory and Practice

The nations of the Western European tradition tend to regard business as central to their citizens' lives and the meaning of their national life. But does business always represent what we want our countries to be about? This first section initially explores business theory. Should societies choose capitalism over other economic systems? Does ethics matter in business? Does virtue have a place in the business world?

■ Classic Dialogue: Is Capitalism the Best Route to Human Happiness?

■ Are Corporate Codes of Ethics Just for Show?

■ Does Ethics Matter in Business?

■ Does the Market Teach Us Virtue?

ISSUE 1

Classic Dialogue: Is Capitalism the Best Route to Human Happiness?

YES: Adam Smith, from *An Inquiry into the Nature and Causes of the Wealth of Nations, vols. 1 and 2* (1869)

NO: Karl Marx and Friedrich Engels, from *The Communist Manifesto* (1848)

ISSUE SUMMARY

YES: Free-market economist Adam Smith (1723–1790) argues that if self-interested people are left alone to seek their own economic advantage, the result, unintended by any one of them, will be greater advantage for all. He maintains that government interference is not necessary to protect the general welfare.

NO: German philosopher Karl Marx (1818–1883) and German sociologist Friedrich Engels (1820–1895) argue that if people are left to their own self-interested devices, those who own the means of production will rapidly reduce everyone else to virtual slaves. Although the few may be fabulously happy, all others would live in misery.

The rationale of capitalism is that an unintended coordination of self-interested actions will lead to the production of the greatest welfare of the whole. The logic proceeds thusly: As a natural result of free competition in a free market, quality will improve and prices will decline without limit, thereby raising the real standard of living of every buyer; to protect themselves in competition, sellers will be forced to innovate by discovering new products and new markets, thereby raising the real wealth of the society as a whole. Products improve without limit, wealth increases without limit, and society prospers.

But how does the common man—the "least advantaged" member of society —fare under capitalism? Not very well. The most efficient factories are those that hire workers at the lowest cost. And if all industry is accomplished by essentially unskilled labor and every worker can therefore be replaced by any other, then there is no reason to pay any worker beyond the subsistence wage. Therefore, only when free competition *fails* because the economy is expanding so rapidly that it runs out of labor can the working man's wages rise in a free market. According to capitalist theory, however, such a market imbalance—too few workers and therefore "artificially" high wages—will rapidly disappear because greater prosperity allows more of the working-class babies to survive to adulthood and enter into the workforce. Eighteenth-century economists Adam Smith, Thomas Malthus, and David Ricardo all agreed that as the society as a whole approaches maximum efficiency, all except the capitalists (the owners) approach the subsistence level of survival. So most of the accumulated wealth of the nation actually ends up in the hands of the employers, who enjoy the low prices of bread themselves while saving the money they would need to spend to keep their workers alive if the bread were more expensive.

This is where Karl Marx comes in. He focused not on the making of the wealth but on how the wealth is distributed—who gets it and who gets to enjoy it when it has been generated by the capitalist process. Marx found it unreasonable for the bulk of society's wealth to be languishing in the bank accounts of the super-rich. He argued that the welfare of the nation as a whole would be vastly increased if it could be shared systematically with the workers, which would allow them to join their employers as consumers of the manufactured goods of society. Lord John Maynard Keynes would later point out that such distribution would be an enormous spur to the economy; Marx, however, was more concerned that it would be a great gain in justice.

One empirical question that surrounds the issue of social justice in a free-market society is this: If the controllers of the wealth—the capitalists—are required to share it with the workers who produced it, will they not lose motivation to put their money at risk in productive enterprises? Other questions concern entitlement (aren't those who control the capital entitled to the entire return on it?) and the relative importance of liberty and equality as political values. As you read the following selections by Adam Smith and by Marx and Friedrich Engels, keep in mind that the debate is not bound by the historical controversies of Marx and his opponents; it goes to the core of contemporary notions of entitlement and justice.

YES

Adam Smith

AN INQUIRY INTO THE NATURE AND CAUSES OF THE WEALTH OF NATIONS

OF THE DIVISION OF LABOUR

The greatest improvement in the productive powers of labour, and the greater part of the skill, dexterity, and judgment with which it is anywhere directed or applied, seem to have been the effect of the division of labour.

The effects of the division of labour, in the general business of society, will be more easily understood by considering in what manner it operates in some particular manufactures. It is commonly supposed to be carried furthest in some very trifling ones; not perhaps that it really is carried further in them than in others of more importance: but in those trifling manufactures which are destined to supply the small wants of but a small number of people, the whole number of workmen must necessarily be small; and those employed in every different branch of the work can often be collected into the same workhouse, and placed at once under the view of the spectator. In those great manufactures, on the contrary, which are destined to supply the great wants of the great body of the people, every different branch of the work employs so great a number of workmen, that it is impossible to collect them all into the same workhouse. We can seldom see more, at one time, than those employed in one single branch. Though in such manufactures, therefore, the work may really be divided into a much greater number of parts than in those of a more trifling nature, the division is not near so obvious, and has accordingly been much less observed.

To take an example, therefore, from a very trifling manufacture, but one in which the division of labour has been very often taken notice of, the trade of the pin-maker; a workman not educated to this business (which the division of labour has rendered a distinct trade), nor acquainted with the use of the machinery employed in it (to the invention of which the same division of labour has probably given occasion), could scarce, perhaps, with his utmost industry, make one pin in a day, and certainly could not make twenty. But

From Adam Smith, *An Inquiry into the Nature and Causes of the Wealth of Nations, vols 1 and 2* (1869). Notes omitted.

in the way in which this business is now carried on, not only the whole work is a peculiar trade, but it is divided into a number of branches, of which the greater part are likewise peculiar trades. One man draws out the wire, another straights it, a third cuts it, a fourth points it, a fifth grinds it at the top for receiving the head; to make the head requires two or three distinct operations; to put it on is a peculiar business, to whiten the pins is another; it is even a trade by itself to put them into the paper; and the important business of making a pin is, in this manner, divided into about eighteen distinct operations, which in some manufactories are all performed by distinct hands, though in others the same man will sometimes perform two or three of them. I have seen a small manufactory of this kind where ten men only were employed, and where some of them consequently performed two or three distinct operations. But though they were very poor, and therefore but indifferently accommodated with the necessary machinery, they could, when they exerted themselves, make among them about twelve pounds of pins in a day. There are in a pound upwards of four thousand pins of a middling size. Those ten persons, therefore, could make among them upwards of forty-eight thousand pins in a day. Each person, therefore, making a tenth part of forty-eight thousand pins, might be considered as making four thousand eight hundred pins in a day. But if they had all wrought separately and independently, and without any of them having been educated to this peculiar business, they certainly could not each of them have made twenty, perhaps not one pin in a day; that is, certainly, not the two hundred and fortieth, perhaps

not the four thousand eight hundredth part of what they are at present capable of performing, in consequence of a proper division and combination of their different operations....

This great increase of the quantity of work, which, in consequence of the division of labour, the same number of people are capable of performing, is owning to three different circumstances: first, to the increase of dexterity in every particular workman; secondly, to the saving of the time which is commonly lost in passing from one species of work to another; and lastly, to the invention of a great number of machines which facilitate and abridge labour, and enable one man to do the work of many....

It is the great multiplication of the productions of all the different arts, in consequence of the division of labour, which occasions, in a well-governed society, that universal opulence which extends itself to the lowest ranks of the people. Every workman has a great quantity of his own work to dispose of beyond what he himself has occasion for: and every other workman being exactly in the same situation, he is enabled to exchange a great quantity of his own goods for a great quantity, or, what comes to the same thing, for the price of a great quantity of theirs. He supplies them abundantly with what they have occasion for, and they accommodate him as amply with what he has occasion for, and a general plenty diffuses itself through all the different ranks of the society.

Observe the accommodation of the most common artificer or day-labourer in a civilised and thriving country, and you will perceive that the number of people of whose industry a part, though but a small part, has been employed in procuring him this accommodation exceeds all computation. The woollen coat, for example, which covers the day-labourer, as coarse and rough as it may appear, is the produce of the joint labour of a great multitude of workmen. The shepherd, the sorter of the wool, the wool-comber or carder, the dyer, the scribbler, the spinner, the weaver, the fuller, the dresser, with many others, must all join their different arts in order to complete even this homely production. How many merchants and carriers, besides, must have been employed in transporting the materials from some of those workmen to others who often live in a very distant part of the country! How much commerce and navigation in particular, how many ship-builders, sailors, sail-makers, rope-makers, must have been employed in order to bring together the different drugs made use of by the dyer, which often come from the remotest corners of the world! What a variety of labour too is necessary in order to produce the tools of the meanest of those workmen! To say nothing of such complicated machines as the ship of the sailor, the mill of the fuller, or even the loom of the weaver, let us consider only what a variety of labour is requisite in order to form that very simple machine, the shears with which the shepherd clips the wool. The miner, the builder of the furnace for smelting the ore, the feller of the timber, the burner of the charcoal to be made use of in the smelting-house, the brickmaker, the bricklayer, the workmen who attend the furnace, the mill-wright, the forger, the smith, must all of them join their different arts in order to produce them. Were we to examine, in the same manner, all the different parts of his dress and household furniture, the coarse linen shirt which he wears next his skin, the shoes which cover his feet, the bed which he lies on, and all the different parts which compose it, the kitchen-grate at which he prepares his victuals, the coals which he makes use of for that purpose, dug from the bowels of the earth, and brought to him perhaps by a long sea and a long land carriage, all the other utensils of his kitchen, all the furniture of his table, the knives and forks, the earthen or pewter plates upon which he serves up and divides his victuals, the different hands employed in preparing his bread and his beer, the glass window which lets in the heat and the light and keeps out the wind and the rain, with all the knowledge and art requisite for preparing that beautiful and happy invention, without which these northern parts of the world could scarce have afforded a very comfortable habitation, together with the tools of all the different workmen employed in producing those different conveniences; if we examine, I say, all these things, and consider what a variety of labour is employed about each of them, we shall be sensible that without the assistance and co-operation of many thousands, the very meanest person in a civilised country could not be provided, even according to, what we very falsely imagine, the easy and simple manner in which he is commonly accommodated. Compared, indeed, with the more extravagant luxury of the great, his accommodation must no doubt appear extremely simple and easy; and yet it may be true, perhaps, that the accommodation of an European prince does not always so much exceed that of an industrious and frugal peasant, as the accommodation of the latter exceeds that of many an African king, the absolute master of the lives and liberties of ten thousand naked savages.

OF THE PRINCIPLE WHICH GIVES OCCASION TO THE DIVISION OF LABOUR

This division of labour, from which so many advantages are derived, is not originally the effect of any human wisdom, which foresees and intends that general opulence to which it gives occasion. It is the necessary, though very slow and gradual consequence of a certain propensity in human nature which has in view no such extensive utility; the propensity to truck, barter, and exchange one thing for another.

Whether this propensity be one of those original principles in human nature, of which no further account can be given; or whether, as seems more probable, it be the necessary consequence of the faculties of reason and speech, it belongs not to our present subject to inquire. It is common to all men, and to be found in no other race of animals, which seem to know neither this nor any other species of contracts.... But man has almost constant occasion for the help of his brethren, and it is in vain for him to expect it from their benevolence only. He will be more likely to prevail if he can interest their self-love in his favour, and show them that it is for their own advantage to do for him what he requires of them. Whoever offers to another a bargain of any kind, proposes to do this. Give me that which I want, and you shall have this which you want, is the meaning of every such offer; and it is in this manner that we obtain from one another the far greater part of those good offices which we stand in need of. It is not from the benevolence of the butcher, the brewer, or the baker, that we expect our dinner, but from their regard to their own interest. We address ourselves, not to their humanity but to their self-love, and never talk to them of our own necessities but of their advantages. Nobody but a beggar chooses to depend chiefly upon the benevolence of his fellow-citizens. Even a beggar does not depend upon it entirely. The charity of well-disposed people, indeed, supplies him with the whole fund of his subsistence. But though this principle ultimately provides him with all the necessaries of life which he has occasion for, it neither does nor can provide him with them as he has occasion for them. The greater part of his occasional wants are supplied in the same manner as those of other people, by treaty, by barter, and by purchase. With the money which one man gives him he purchases food. The old clothes which another bestows upon him he exchanges for other old clothes which suit him better, or for lodging, or for food, or for money, with which he can buy either food, clothes, or lodging, as he has occasion.

... Each animal is still obliged to support and defend itself, separately and independently, and derives no sort of advantage from that variety of talents with which nature has distinguished its fellows. Among men, on the contrary, the most dissimilar geniuses are of use to one another; the different produces of their respective talents, by the general disposition to truck, barter, and exchange, being brought, as it were, into a common stock, where every man may purchase whatever part of the produce of other men's talents he has occasion for....

OF RESTRAINTS UPON THE IMPORTATION FROM FOREIGN COUNTRIES OF SUCH GOODS AS CAN BE PRODUCED AT HOME

... The general industry of the society never can exceed what the capital of the society can employ. As the number of workmen that can be kept in employment by any particular person must bear a certain proportion to his capital, so the number of those that can be continually employed by all the members of a great society, must bear a certain proportion to the whole capital of that society, and never can exceed that proportion. No regulation of commerce can increase the quantity of industry in any society beyond what its capital can maintain. It can only divert a part of it into a direction into which it might not otherwise have gone; and it is by no means certain that this artificial direction is likely to be more advantageous to the society than that into which it would have gone of its own accord.

Every individual is continually exerting himself to find out the most advantageous employment for whatever capital he can demand. It is his own advantage, indeed, and not that of the society, which he has in view. But the study of his own advantage naturally, or rather necessarily, leads him to prefer that employment which is most advantageous to the society.

First, every individual endeavours to employ his capital as near home as he can, and consequently as much as he can in the support of domestic industry; provided always that he can thereby obtain the ordinary, or not a great deal less than the ordinary, profits of stock.

Thus, upon equal or nearly equal profits, every wholesale merchant naturally prefers the home trade to the foreign trade of consumption, and the foreign trade of consumption to the carrying trade. In the home trade his capital is never so long out of his sight as it frequently is in the foreign trade of consumption. He can know better the char-

acter and situation of the persons whom he trusts, and, if he should happen to be deceived, he knows better the laws of the country from which he must seek redress. In the carrying trade, the capital of the merchant is, as it were, divided between two foreign countries, and no part of it is ever necessarily brought home, or placed under his own immediate view and command. The capital which an Amsterdam merchant employs in carrying corn from Konigsberg to Lisbon, and fruit and wine from Lisbon to Konigsberg, must generally be the one half of it at Konigsberg and the other half at Lisbon. No part of it need ever come to Amsterdam. The natural residence of such a merchant should either be at Konigsberg or Lisbon, and it can only be some very particular circumstance which can make him prefer the residence of Amsterdam. The uneasiness, however, which he feels at being separated so far from his capital, generally determines him to bring part both of the Konigsberg goods which he destines for the market of Lisbon, and of the Lisbon goods which he destines for that of Konigsberg, to Amsterdam; and though this necessarily subjects him to a double charge of loading and unloading, as well as to the payment of some duties and customs, yet for the sake of having some part of his capital always under his own view and command, he willingly submits to this extraordinary charge; and it is in this manner that every country which has any considerable share of the carrying trade, becomes always the emporium, or general market, for the goods of all the different countries whose trade it carries on. The merchant, in order to save a second loading and unloading, endeavours always to sell in the home market as much of the goods of all those different countries as he can, and thus, so far as he can, to convert his carrying trade into a foreign trade of consumption. A merchant, in the same manner, who is engaged in the foreign trade of consumption, when he collects goods for foreign markets, will always be glad, upon equal or nearly equal profits, to sell as great a part of them at home as he can. He saves himself the risk and trouble of exportation, when, so far as he can, he thus converts his foreign trade of consumption into a home trade. Home is in this manner the centre, if I may say so, round which the capitals of the inhabitants of every country are continually circulating, and towards which they are always tending, though by particular causes they may sometimes be driven off and repelled from it towards more distant employments. But a capital employed in the home trade, it has already been shown, necessarily puts into motion a greater quantity of domestic industry, and gives revenue and employment to a greater number of the inhabitants of the country, than an equal capital employed in the foreign trade of consumption; and one employed in the foreign trade of consumption has the same advantage over an equal capital employed in the carrying trade. Upon equal, or only nearly equal profits, therefore, every individual naturally inclines to employ his capital in the manner in which it is likely to afford the greatest support to domestic industry, and to give revenue and employment to the greatest number of people of his own country.

Secondly, every individual who employs his capital in the support of domestic industry, necessarily endeavours so to direct that industry, that its produce may be of the greatest possible value.

The produce of industry is what it adds to the subject or materials upon which it is employed. In proportion as the value of this produce is great or small, so will likewise be the profits of the employer. But it is only for the sake of profit that any man employs a capital in the support of industry; and he will always, therefore, endeavour to employ it in the support of that industry of which the produce is likely to be of the greatest value, or to exchange for the greatest quantity either of money or of other goods.

But the annual revenue of every society is always precisely equal to the exchangeable value of the whole annual produce of its industry, or rather is precisely the same thing with that exchangeable value. As every individual, therefore, endeavours as much as he can both to employ his capital in the support of domestic industry, and so to direct that industry that its produce may be of the greatest value, every individual necessarily labours to render the annual revenue of the society as great as he can. He generally, indeed, neither intends to promote the public interest, nor knows how much he is promoting it. By preferring the support of domestic to that of foreign industry, he intends only his own security; and by directing that industry in such a manner as its produce may be of the greatest value, he intends only his own gain, and he is in this, as in many other cases, led by an invisible hand to promote an end which was no part of his intention. Nor is it always the worse for the society that it was no part of it. By pursuing his own interest he frequently promotes that of the society more effectually than when he really intends to promote it. I have never known much good done by those who affected to trade for the public good. It is an affectation, indeed, not very common among merchants, and very few words need be employed in dissuading them from it.

What is the species of domestic industry which his capital can employ, and of which the produce is likely to be of the greatest value, every individual, it is evident, can, in his local situation, judge much better than any statesman or lawgiver can do for him. The statesman, who should attempt to direct private people in what manner they ought to employ their capitals, would not only load himself with a most unnecessary attention, but assume an authority which could safely be trusted, not only to no single person, but to no council or senate whatever, and which would nowhere be so dangerous as in the hands of a man who had folly and presumption enough to fancy himself fit to exercise it.

To give the monopoly of the home market to the produce of domestic industry, in any particular art or manufacture, is in some measure to direct private people in what manner they ought to employ their capitals, and must, in almost all cases, be either a useless or a hurtful regulation. If the produce of domestic can be brought there as cheap as that of foreign industry, the regulation is evidently useless. If it cannot, it must generally be hurtful. It is the maxim of every prudent master of a family, never to attempt to make at home what it will cost him more to make than to buy. The tailor does not attempt to make his own shoes, but buys them of the shoemaker. The shoemaker does not attempt to make his own clothes, but employs a tailor. The farmer attempts to make neither the one nor the other, but employs those different artificers. All of them find it for their interest to employ their whole industry in a way in which they have some advantage over their neighbours, and to purchase with a part of its produce, or, what is the same thing, with the price of a part of it, whatever else they have occasion for.

What is prudence in the conduct of every private family, can scarce be folly in that of a great kingdom. If a foreign country can supply us with a commodity cheaper than we ourselves can make it, better buy it of them with some part of the produce of our own industry, employed in a way in which we have some advantage. The general industry of the country, being always in proportion to the capital which employs it, will not thereby be diminished, no more than that of the above-mentioned artificers, but only left to find out the way in which it can be employed with the greatest advantage. It is certainly not employed to the greatest advantage, when it is thus directed towards an object which it can buy cheaper than it can make. The value of its annual produce is certainly more or less diminished, when it is thus turned away from producing commodities evidently of more value than the commodity which it is directed to produce. According to the supposition, that commodity could be purchased from foreign countries cheaper than it can be made at home. It could, therefore, have been purchased with a part only of the commodities, or, what is the same thing, with a part only of the price of the commodities, which the industry employed by an equal capital would have produced at home, had it been left to follow its natural course. The industry of the country, therefore, is, thus turned away from a more to a less advantageous employment, and the exchangeable value of its annual produce, instead of being increased, according to the intention of the lawgiver, must necessarily be diminished by every such regulation.

By means of such regulations, indeed, a particular manufacture may sometimes be acquired sooner than it could have been otherwise, and after a certain time may be made at home as cheap or cheaper than in the foreign country. But though the industry of the society may be thus carried with advantage into a particular channel sooner than it could have been otherwise, it will by no means follow that the sum total, either of its industry or of its revenue, can ever be augmented by any such regulation. The industry of the society can augment only in proportion as its capital augments, and its capital can augment only in proportion to what can be gradually saved out of its revenue. But the immediate effect of every such regulation is to diminish its revenue, and what diminishes its revenue is certainly not very likely to augment its capital faster than it would have augmented of its own accord, had both capital and industry been left to find out their natural employments.

Though for want of such regulations the society should never acquire the proposed manufacture, it would not, upon that account, necessarily be the poorer in any one period of its duration. In every period of its duration its whole capital and industry might still have been employed, though upon different objects, in the manner that was most advantageous at the time. In every period its revenue might have been the greatest which its capital could afford, and both capital and revenue might have been augmented with the greatest possible rapidity.

The natural advantages which one country has over another in producing particular commodities are sometimes so great, that it is acknowledged by all the world to be in vain to struggle with them. By means of glasses, hot-beds, and hot-walls, very good grapes can be raised in Scotland, and very good wine too can be made of them, at about thirty times the expense for which at least equally good can be brought from foreign countries. Would it be a reasonable law to prohibit the importation of all foreign wines, merely to encourage the making of claret and burgundy in Scotland? But if there would be a manifest absurdity in turning towards any employment thirty times more of the capital and industry of the country than would be necessary to purchase from foreign countries an equal quantity of the commodities wanted, there must be an absurdity, though not altogether so glaring, yet exactly of the same kind, in turning towards any such employment a thirtieth or even a three-hundredth part more of either. Whether the advantages which one country has over another be natural or acquired, is in this respect of no consequence. As long as the one country has those advantages and the other wants them, it will always be more advantageous for the latter rather to buy of the former than to make. It is an acquired advantage only which one artificer has over his neighbour who exercises another trade; and yet they both find it more advantageous to buy of one another than to make what does not belong to their particular trades.

NO   Karl Marx and Friedrich Engels

MANIFESTO OF THE COMMUNIST PARTY

A spectre is haunting Europe—the spectre of Communism. All the powers of old Europe have entered into a holy alliance to exorcise this spectre; Pope and Czar, Metternich and Guizot, French Radicals and German police-spies.

Where is the party in opposition that has not been decried as communistic by its opponents in power? Where the opposition that has not hurled back the branding reproach of Communism, against the more advanced opposition parties, as well as against its reactionary adversaries?

Two things result from this fact.

I. Communism is already acknowledged by all European Powers to be itself a Power.

II. It is high time that Communists should openly, in the face of the whole world, publish their views, their aims, their tendencies, and meet this nursery tale of the Spectre of Communism with a Manifesto of the party itself.

To this end, Communists of various nationalities have assembled in London, and sketched the following manifesto, to be published in the English, French, German, Italian, Flemish and Danish languages.

BOURGEOIS AND PROLETARIANS

The history of all hitherto existing society is the history of class struggles.

Freeman and slave, patrician and plebeian, lord and serf, guild-master and journeyman, in a word; oppressor and oppressed, stood in constant opposition to one another, carried on an uninterrupted, now hidden, now open fight, a fight that each time ended, either in a revolutionary re-constitution of society at large, or in the common ruin of the contending classes.

In the early epochs of history, we find almost everywhere a complicated arrangement of society into various orders, a manifold graduation of social rank. In ancient Rome we have patricians, knights, plebeians, slaves; in the Middle Ages, feudal lords, vassals, guild-masters, journeymen, apprentices, serfs; in almost all of these classes, again, subordinate gradations.

The modern bourgeois society that has sprouted from the ruins of feudal society, has not done away with class antagonisms. It has but established new

From Karl Marx and Friedrich Engels, *The Communist Manifesto* (1848).

classes, new conditions of oppression, new forms of struggle in place of the old ones.

Our epoch, the epoch of the bourgeoisie, possesses, however, this distinctive feature; it has simplified the class antagonisms. Society as a whole is more and more splitting up into two great hostile camps, into two great classes directly facing each other: Bourgeoisie and Proletariat.

From the serfs of the Middle Ages sprang the chartered burghers of the earliest towns. From this burgesses the first elements of the bourgeoisie were developed.

The discovery of America, the rounding of the Cape, opened up fresh ground for the rising bourgeoisie. The East-Indian and Chinese markets, the colonization of America, trade with the colonies, the increase in the means of exchange in commodities, generally, gave to commerce, to navigation, to industry, an impulse never before known, and thereby, to the revolutionary element in the tottering feudal society, a rapid development.

The feudal system of industry, under which industrial production was monopolized by closed guilds, now no longer sufficed for the growing wants of the new markets. The manufacturing system took its place. The guild-masters were pushed on one side by the manufacturing middle-class; division of labor between the different corporate guilds vanished in the face of division of labor in each single workshop.

Meantime the markets kept ever growing, the demand, ever rising. Even manufacturing no longer sufficed. Thereupon, steam and machinery revolutionized industrial production. The place of manufacture was taken by the giant, Modern Industry, the place of the industrial middle-class, by industrial millionaires, the leaders of whole industrial armies, the modern bourgeoisie.

Modern Industry has established the world-market, for which the discovery of America paved the way. This market has given an immense development to commerce, to navigation, to communication by land. This development has, in its turn, reacted on the extension of industry; and in proportion as industry, commerce, navigation, railways extended in the same proportion the bourgeoisie developed, increased its capital, and pushed into the background every class handed down from the Middle Ages.

We see, therefore, how the modern bourgeoisie is itself the product of a long course of development, of a series of revolutions in the modes of production and of exchange.

Each step in the development of the bourgeoisie was accompanied by a corresponding political advance of that class. An oppressed class under the sway of the feudal nobility, an armed and self-governing association in the medieval commune, here independent urban republic (as in Italy and Germany), there taxable "third estate" of the monarchy (as in France), afterwards, in the period of manufacturing proper, serving either the semi-feudal or the absolute monarchy as a counterpoise against the nobility, and in fact, cornerstone of the great monarchies in general, the bourgeoisie has at last, since the establishment of Modern Industry and of the world-market, conquered for itself, in a modern representative State, exclusive political sway. The executive of the modern State is but a committee for managing the common affairs of the whole bourgeoisie.

The bourgeoisie, historically, has played a most revolutionary part.

The bourgeoisie, wherever it has got the upper hand, has put an end to all feudal, patriarchal, idyllic relations. It has pitilessly torn asunder the motley feudal ties that bound man to his "natural superiors," and has left remaining no other nexus between man and man than naked self-interest, than callous "cash payment." It has drowned the most heavenly ecstasies of religious fervor, of chivalrous enthusiasm, of philistine sentimentalism, in the icy water of egotistical calculation. It has resolved personal worth into exchange value, and in place of the numberless indefeasible chartered freedoms, has set up that single, unconscionable freedom—Free Trade. In one word, for exploitation, veiled by religious and political illusions, it has substituted naked, shameless, direct, brutal exploitation.

The bourgeoisie has stripped of its halo every occupation hitherto honored and looked up to with reverent awe. It has converted the physician, the lawyer, the priest, the poet, the man of science, into its paid wage-laborers.

The bourgeoisie has torn away from the family its sentimental veil, and has reduced the family relation to a mere money relation.

The bourgeoisie has disclosed how it came to pass that the brutal display of vigor in the Middle Ages, which Reactionists so much admire, found its fitting complement in the most slothful indolence. It has been the first to show what man's activity can bring about. It has accomplished wonders far surpassing Egyptian pyramids, Roman aqueducts, and Gothic cathedrals; it has conducted expeditions that put in the shade all former Exoduses of nations and crusades.

The bourgeoisie cannot exist without constantly revolutionizing the instruments of production, and thereby the relations of production, and with them the whole relations of society. Conservation of the old modes of production in unaltered form, was, on the contrary, the first condition of existence for all earlier industrial classes. Constant revolutionizing of production, uninterrupted disturbance of all social conditions, everlasting uncertainty and agitation distinguish the bourgeois epoch from all earlier ones. All fixed, fast-frozen relations, with their train of ancient and venerable prejudices and opinions, are swept away, all newly-formed ones become antiquated before they can ossify. All that is solid melts into air, all that is holy is profaned, and man is at last compelled to face with sober senses, his real conditions of life, and his relations with his kind.

The need of a constantly expanding market for its products chases the bourgeoisie over the whole surface of the globe. It must nestle everywhere, settle everywhere, establish connections everywhere.

The bourgeoisie has through its exploitation of the world-market given a cosmopolitan character to production and consumption in every country. To the great chagrin of Reactionists, it has drawn from under the feet of industry the national ground on which it stood. All old-established national industries have been destroyed or are daily being destroyed. They are dislodged by new industries, whose introduction becomes a life and death question for all civilized nations, by industries that no longer work up indigenous raw material, but raw material drawn from the remotest zones; industries whose products are consumed, not only at home, but in every quarter of the globe. In place of the old wants, satisfied by the productions of the country, we find new wants, requiring for their satisfaction the products of distant lands and climes. In place of the old local and national seclusion and self-sufficiency, we have intercourse in every direction, universal inter-dependence of nations. And as in material, so also in intellectual production. The intellectual creations of individual nations become common property. National one-sidedness and narrow-mindedness become more and more impossible, and from the numerous national and local literatures there arises a world-literature.

The bourgeoisie, by the rapid improvement of all instruments of production, by the immensely facilitated means of communication, draws all, even the most barbarian, nations into civilization. The cheap prices of its commodities are the heavy artillery with which it batters down all Chinese walls, with which it forces the barbarians' intensely obstinate hatred of foreigners to capitulate. It compels all nations, on pain of extinction, to adopt the bourgeois mode of production; it compels them to introduce what it calls civilization into their midst, i.e., to become bourgeois themselves. In a word, it creates a world after its own image.

The bourgeoisie has subjected the country to the rule of the towns. It has created enormous cities, has greatly increased the urban population as compared with the rural, and has thus rescued a considerable part of the population from the idiocy of rural life. Just as it has made the country dependent on the towns, so it has made barbarian and semibarbarian countries dependent on the civilized ones, nations of peasants on nations of bourgeois, the East on the West.

The bourgeoisie keeps more and more doing away with the scattered state of the population, of the means of production, and of property. It has agglomerated population, centralized means of production, and has concentrated property in a few hands. The necessary consequence of this was political centralization. Independent, or but loosely connected provinces, with separate interests, laws, governments and systems of taxation, became lumped together in one nation, with one government, one code of laws, one national class-interest, one frontier and one customs-tariff.

The bourgeoisie, during its rule of scarce one hundred years, has created more massive and more colossal productive forces than have all preceding generations together. Subjection of Nature's forces to man, machinery, application of chemistry to industry and agriculture, steam-navigation, railways, electric telegraphs, clearing of whole continents for cultivation, canalization of rivers, whole populations conjured out of the ground—what earlier century had even a presentiment that such productive forces slumbered in the lap of social labor?

We see then: the means of production and of exchange on whose foundations the bourgeoisie built itself up, were generated in feudal society. At a certain stage in the development of these means of production and of exchange, the conditions under which feudal society produced and exchanged, the feudal organization of agriculture and manufacturing industry, in one word, the feudal relations of property became no longer compatible with the already developed productive forces; they became so many fetters. They had to be burst asunder; they were burst asunder.

Into their places stepped free competition, accompanied by a social and political constitution adapted to it, and by the economical and political sway of the bourgeois class.

A similar movement is going on before our own eyes. Modern bourgeois society with its relations of production, of exchange and of property, a society that has conjured up such gigantic means of production and of exchange, is like the sorcerer, who is no longer able to control the powers of the nether world whom he has called up by his spells. For many a decade past the history of industry and commerce is but the history of the revolt of modern productive forces against modern conditions of production, against the property relations that are the condition for the existence of the bourgeoisie and of its rule. It is enough to mention the commercial crises that by their periodical return put on trial, each time more threateningly, the existence of the entire bourgeois society. In these crises a great part not only of the existing products, but also of the previously created productive forces, are periodically destroyed. In these crises there breaks out an epidemic that, in all earlier epochs, would have seemed an absurdity—the epidemic of overproduction. Society suddenly finds itself put back into a state of momentary barbarism; it appears as if a famine, a universal war of devastation had cut off the supply of every means of subsistence; industry and commerce seem to be destroyed; and why? Because there is too much civilization, too much means of subsistence, too much industry, too much commerce. The productive forces at the disposal of society no longer tend to further the development of the conditions of bourgeois property; on the contrary, they have become too powerful for these conditions, by which they are fettered, and so soon as they overcome these fetters, they bring disorder into the whole of bourgeois society, endangering the existence of bourgeois property. The conditions of bourgeois society are too narrow to comprise the wealth created by them. And how does the bourgeoisie get over these crises? On the one hand by enforced destruction of a mass of productive forces; on the other, by the conquest of new markets, and by the more thorough exploitation of the old ones. That is to say, by paving the way for more extensive and more destructive crises, and by diminishing the means whereby crises are prevented.

The weapons with which the bourgeoisie felled feudalism to the ground are now turned against the bourgeoisie itself.

But not only has the bourgeoisie forged the weapons that bring death to itself; it has also called into existence the men who are to wield those weapons—the modern working-class—the proletarians.

In proportion as the bourgeoisie, i.e., capital, is developed, in the same proportion is the proletariat, the modern working-class, developed, a class of laborers, who live only so long as they find work, and who find work only so long as their labor increases capital. These laborers, who must sell themselves piecemeal, are a commodity, like every other article of commerce, and are consequently exposed to all the vicissitudes of competition, to all the fluctuations of the market.

Owing to the extensive use of machinery and to division of labor, the work of the proletarians has lost all individual character, and, consequently, all charm for the workman. He becomes an appendage of the machine, and it is only the most simple, most monotonous, and most easily acquired knack that is required of him. Hence, the cost of production of a workman is restricted, almost entirely, to the means of subsistence that he requires for his maintenance, and for the propagation of his race. But the price of a commodity, and also of labor, is equal to its cost of production. In proportion, therefore, as the repulsiveness of the work increases, the wage decreases. Nay more, in proportion as the use of machinery and division of labor increases, in the same proportion the burden of toil also increases, whether by prolongation of the working hours, by increase of the work enacted in a given time, or by increased speed of the machinery, etc.

Modern Industry has converted the little workshop of the patriarchal master into the great factory of the industrial capitalist. Masses of laborers, crowded into the factory, are organized like soldiers. As privates of the industrial army they are placed under the command of a perfect hierarchy of officers and sergeants. Not only are they the slaves of the bourgeois class, and of the bourgeois State, they are daily and hourly enslaved by the machine, by the over-looker, and, above all, by the individual bourgeois manufacturer himself. The more openly this despotism proclaims gain to be its end and aim, the more petty, the more hateful and the more embittering it is.

The less the skill and exertion or strength implied in manual labor, in other words, the more modern industry becomes developed, the more is the labor of men superseded by that of women. Differences of age and sex have no longer any distinctive social validity for the working class. All are instruments of labor, more or less expensive to use, according to their age and sex.

No sooner is the exploitation of the laborer by the manufacturer so far at an end, that he receives his wages in cash, than he is set upon by the other portions of the bourgeoisie, the landlord, the shopkeeper, the pawnbroker, etc.

The low strata of the middle class —the small trades-people, shopkeepers, and retired tradesmen generally, the handicraftsmen and peasants—all these sink gradually into the proletariat, partly because their diminutive capital does not suffice for the scale on which Modern Industry is carried on, and is swamped in the competition with the large capitalists, partly because their specialized skill is rendered worthless by new methods of production. Thus the proletariat is recruited from all classes of the population.

The proletariat goes through various stages of development. With its birth begins its struggle with the bourgeoisie. At first the contest is carried on by individual laborers, then by the workpeople of a factory, then by the operatives of one trade, in one locality, against the individual bourgeois who directly exploits them. They direct their attacks not against the bourgeois conditions of production, but against the instruments of production themselves; they destroy imported wares that compete with their labor, they smash to pieces machinery, they set factories ablaze, they seek to restore by force the vanished status of the workman of the Middle Ages.

At this stage the laborers still form an incoherent mass scattered over the whole country, and broken up by their mutual competition. If anywhere they unite to form more compact bodies, this is not yet the consequence of their own active union, but of the union of bourgeoisie, which class, in order to attain its own political ends, is compelled to set the whole proletariat in motion, and is moreover yet, for a time, able to do so. At this stage, therefore, the proletarians do not fight their enemies, but the enemies of their enemies, the remnants of absolute monarchy, the landowners, the non-industrial bourgeoisie, the petty bourgeoisie. Thus the whole historical movement is concentrated in the hands of the bourgeoisie; every victory so obtained is a victory for the bourgeoisie.

But with the development of industry the proletariat not only increases in number, it becomes concentrated in great masses, its strength grows, and it feels that strength more. The various interests and conditions of life within the ranks of the proletariat are more and more equalized, in proportion as machinery obliterates all distinction of labor, and nearly everywhere reduces wages to the same low level. The growing competition among the bourgeoisie, and the resulting commercial crises, make the wages of the worker ever more fluctuating. The unceasing improvement of machinery, ever more rapidly developing, makes their livelihood more and more precarious, the collisions between individual workmen and individual bourgeois take more and more the character of collision between two classes. Thereupon the workers begin to form combinations (Trades Unions) against the bourgeoisie; they club together in order to keep up the rate of wages; they found permanent associations in order to make provision beforehand for these occasional revolts. Here and there the contest breaks out into riots.

Now and then the workers are victorious, but only for a time. The real fruits of their battles lie, not in the immediate result, but in the ever expanding union of the workers. This union is helped on by the improved means of communication that are created by modern industry, and that place the workers of different localities in contact with one another. It was just this contact that was needed to centralize the numerous local struggles, all of the same character, into one national struggle between classes. But every class struggle is a political struggle. And that union, to attain which the burghers of the Middle Ages, with their miserable highways, required centuries, the modern proletarians, thanks to railways, achieve in a few years.

This organization of the proletarians into a class, and consequently into a political party, is continually being upset again by the competition between the workers themselves. But it ever rises up again, stronger, firmer, mightier. It compels legislative recognition of particular interests of the workers, by taking advantage of the divisions among the bourgeoisie itself. Thus the ten-hour bill in England was carried.

Altogether collisions between the classes of the old society further, in many ways, the course of development of the proletariat. The bourgeoisie finds itself involved in a constant battle. At first with the aristocracy; later on, with those portions of the bourgeoisie itself, whose interests have become antagonistic to the progress of industry; at all times, with the bourgeoisie of foreign countries. In all these battles it sees itself compelled to appeal to the proletariat, to ask for its help, and thus, to drag it into the political arena. The bourgeoisie itself, therefore, supplies the proletariat with its own elements of political and general education, in other words, it furnishes the proletariat with weapons for fighting the bourgeoisie.

Further, as we have already seen, entire sections of the ruling classes are, by the advance of industry, precipitated into the proletariat, or are at least threatened in their conditions of existence. These also supply the proletariat with fresh elements of enlightenment and progress.

Finally, in times when the class-struggle nears the decisive hour, the process of dissolution going on within the ruling class, in fact, within the whole range of old society, assumes such a violent, glaring character, that a small section of the ruling class cuts itself adrift, and joins the revolutionary class, the class that holds the future in its hands. Just as, therefore, at an earlier period, a section of the nobility went over to the bourgeoisie, so now a portion of the bourgeoisie goes over to the proletariat, and in particular, a portion of the bourgeois ideologists, who have raised themselves to the level of comprehending theoretically the historical movements as a whole.

Of all the classes that stand face to face with the bourgeoisie today, the proletariat alone is a really revolutionary class. The other classes decay and finally disappear in the face of Modern Industry; the proletariat is its special and essential product....

In the conditions of the proletariat, those of old society at large are already virtually swamped. The proletarian is without property; his relation to his wife and children has no longer anything in common with the bourgeois family-relations; modern industrial labor, modern subjugation to capital, the same in England as in France, in America as in Germany, has stripped him of every trace of national character. Law, morality, religion, are to him so many bourgeois prejudices, behind which lurk in ambush just as many bourgeois interests.

All the preceding classes that got the upper hand, sought to fortify their al-ready acquired status by subjecting society at large to their conditions of appropriation. The proletarians cannot become masters of the productive forces of society, except by abolishing their own previous mode of appropriation, and thereby also every other previous mode of appropriation. They have nothing of their own to secure and to fortify; their mission is to destroy all previous securities for, and insurances of, individual property.

All previous historical movements were movements of minorities, or in the interests of minorities. The proletarian movement is the self-conscious, independent movement of the immense majority, in the interest of the immense majority. The proletariat, the lowest stratum of our present society, cannot stir, cannot raise itself up, without the whole superincumbent strata of official society being sprung into the air.

Though not in substance, yet in form, the struggle of the proletariat with the bourgeoisie is at first a national struggle. The proletariat of each country must, of course, first of all settle matters with its own bourgeoisie.

In depicting the most general phases of the development of the proletariat, we traced the more or less veiled civil war, raging within existing society, up to the point where that war breaks out into open revolution, and where the violent overthrow of the bourgeoisie lays the foundation for the sway of the proletariat.

Hitherto, every form of society has been based, as we have already seen, on the antagonism of oppressing and oppressed classes. But in order to oppress a class, certain conditions must be assured to it under which it can, at least, continue its slavish existence. The serf, in the period of serfdom, raised himself to membership in the commune, just as the petty bourgeois, under the yoke of feudal absolutism, managed to develop into a bourgeois.

The modern laborer, on the contrary, instead of rising with the progress of industry, sinks deeper and deeper below the conditions of existence of his own class. He becomes a pauper, and pauperism develops more rapidly than population and wealth. And here it becomes evident that the bourgeoisie is unfit any longer to be the ruling class in society, and to impose its conditions of existence upon society as an overriding law. It is unfit to rule, because it is incompetent to assure an existence to its slave within his slavery, because it cannot help letting him sink into such a state that it has to feed him, instead of being fed by him. Society can no longer live under this bourgeoisie, in other words, its existence is no longer compatible with society.

The essential condition for the existence, and for the sway of the bourgeois class, is the formation and augmentation of capital; the condition for capital is wage-labor. Wage-labor rests exclusively on competition between the laborers. The advance of industry, whose involuntary promoter is the bourgeoisie, replaces the isolation of the laborers, due to competition, by their revolutionary combination, due to association. The development of Modern Industry, therefore, cuts from under its feet the very foundation on which the bourgeoisie produces and appropriates products. What the bourgeoisie therefore produces, above all, are its own grave-diggers. Its fall and the victory of the proletariat are equally inevitable.

POSTSCRIPT

Classic Dialogue: Is Capitalism the Best Route to Human Happiness?

As a society, Americans have always prized liberty over equality. The attitude within the United States seems to be that the wealth of the society as a whole is the only legitimate goal of economic enterprise and that distribution for the sake of equity or charity is a side issue best left to churches and private charities. Americans have resisted attempts to socialize such basic needs as medicine, communications (e.g., the telephone companies), and economic security for the old, young, and infirm. In promoting capitalism, economists point to the failures of socialism in England and Sweden, and they cite the fall of communism in Eastern Europe and Russia.

The United States has built some safety nets: Social Security, Medicare and Medicaid, Aid to Dependent Children, and the like. But these and other elements of the welfare system have become a major political issue. People in the welfare system complain about its failure to provide adequately for those who need the most—babies and the infirm elderly, for example. Meanwhile, conservative members of Congress argue that welfare subsidies are costing the taxpayers too much. Can it be said that capitalism is "working" for people on welfare?

What about the "invisible hand" of Smith's free market; is it operating in the United States? Does America have true capitalism?

The last two decades of economic reform have seen the richest people in America absorbing more and more of the wealth and income while the poorest people have been becoming poorer. Should society strive to redistribute the productive assets of the country?

SUGGESTED READINGS

John D. Bishop, "Adam Smith's Invisible Hand Argument," *Journal of Business Ethics* (March 1995), pp. 165–180.

Keith Bradsher, "As U.S. Urges Free Markets, Its Trade Barriers Are Many," *The New York Times* (February 7, 1992), p. A1.

Richard John Neuhaus, "The Pope Affirms the 'New Capitalism,'" *The Wall Street Journal* (May 2, 1991).

David Schweickart, *Against Capitalism*, rev. ed. (Cambridge University Press, 1993).

"The Search for Keynes: Was He a Keynesian?" *The Economist* (December 26, 1992).

Adam Smith, *The Wealth of Nations* (Clarendon Press, 1976).

ISSUE 2

Are Corporate Codes of Ethics Just for Show?

YES: LaRue Tone Hosmer, from *The Ethics of Management* (Irwin Press, 1987)

NO: Lisa H. Newton, from "The Many Faces of the Corporate Code," in *The Corporate Code of Ethics: The Perspective of the Humanities,* Proceedings of the Conference on Corporate Visions and Values (Fairfield University, 1992)

ISSUE SUMMARY

YES: LaRue Tone Hosmer, a professor of corporate strategies, argues that codes of ethics are really only for show and that they are ineffective in bringing about more ethical behavior on the part of employees.

NO: Professor of philosophy Lisa H. Newton holds that the formation and adoption of corporate codes are valuable processes because they raise corporate awareness of ethical issues and because they can be a valuable part of the corporate action review process.

Business ethics, as an academic discipline and a corporate concern, is the product of the combination of two unlikely companions. Early in the twentieth century, what was called "business ethics" was in reality a set of agreements, created for and by businessmen, concerning the way they did business, and for the most part they were highly *un*ethical. These agreements demanded that you keep your salesman off the other guy's turf; that you refrain from introducing new products in direct competition with other members of the club; that you hire only white males, or at least make sure that only white males made it to the upper echelons of the company; and that you keep secret whatever you might know about your fellow businessmen's adulterated products or fictional tax returns. In short, like the "ethics" of any profession of the period, business ethics were the rules of the in-group—self-protective and self-serving.

Meanwhile, the ethics taught in colleges was linguistic and analytic. Professors taught only terms and their meanings, conversed only with themselves and their students, and were well aware that their teachings were of little use in the real world of business. Business ethics was not seen as a serious discipline.

However, starting in the late 1950s, scandals began to surface: price-fixing, unsafe products, and foreign bribes, for example. In response, the "social responsibility" movement, led primarily by the churches and a few crusading consumer advocates such as Ralph Nader, attempted to make business accountable to the general public for its practices. Businesses were told to get out of South Africa because of apartheid, to ensure product quality and safety, and to take responsibility for the environment. Although the business community's first response was to ignore the activists, some severe consequences —such as jail terms for some highly respected corporate officers, demonstrations, and hostile regulatory legislation—made it clear that some attention would have to be paid to ethics or at least to the *appearance* of ethics.

Businesspeople started thinking seriously about public accountability around the time when the armed conflict in Vietnam brought the ethics professors out of their classrooms and into the public arena. Philosophy developed a new, socially relevant branch of ethics, soon to be called "applied ethics," and by the early 1970s the ethicists of the applied branch were in dialogue with physicians over medical ethics, lawyers on legal ethics, and businesspeople on business ethics. Some familiarity with ethics is now required of most undergraduate business majors.

But does writing and teaching about ethics do any good? In the following selection, LaRue Tone Hosmer says no. He sees a fundamental problem with codes of ethics in that "ethics in management represents a conflict between the economic and the social performance of an organization." Accordingly, codes of ethics must be exercises in futility because they direct the corporation away from its primary function. Lisa H. Newton, arguing the contrary, asserts that the actual code is the least important element in the development of the corporate culture. She argues that the process of code development— principled, comprehensive, and participative—is the most valuable part of the development exercise.

Ask yourself, as you read these selections, is there a conflict between economic and social performance—that is, between business and ethics? Is *business ethics* an oxymoron?

YES

LaRue Tone Hosmer

ETHICAL CODES

Ethical codes are statements of the norms and beliefs of an organization. These norms and beliefs are generally proposed, discussed, and defined by the senior executives in the firm and then published and distributed to all of the members. Norms, of course, are standards of behavior; they are the ways the senior people in the organization want the others to act when confronted with a given situation. An example of a norm in a code of ethics would be, "Employees of this company will not accept personal gifts with a monetary value over $25 in total from any business friend or associate, and they are expected to pay their full share of the costs for meals or other entertainment (concerts, the theatre, sporting events, etc.) that have a value above $25 per person." The norms in an ethical code are generally expressed as a series of negative statements, for it is easier to list the things a person should not do than to be precise about the things a person should do.

The beliefs in an ethical code are standards of thought; they are the ways that the senior people in the organization want others to think. This is not censorship. Instead, the intent is to encourage ways of thinking and patterns of attitudes that will lead towards the wanted behavior. Consequently, the beliefs in an ethical code are generally expressed in a positive form. "Our first responsibility is to our customer" is an example of a positive belief that commonly appears in codes of ethics; another would be "We wish to be good citizens of every community in which we operate." Some company codes of ethics appear in [the two boxes that follow].

Do ethical codes work? Are they helpful in conveying to all employees the moral standards selected by the board of directors and president? Not really. The problem is that it is not possible to state the norms and beliefs of an organization relative to the various constituent groups—employees, customers, suppliers, distributors, stockholders, and the general public—clearly and explicitly, without offending at least one of those groups. It is not possible to say, for example, that a company considers its employees to be more important to the success of the firm than its stockholders, without putting the stockholders on notice that profits and dividends come second. Stockholders, and their agents at trust departments and mutual funds, tend to resent that, just as the employees would if the conditions were reversed. Consequently codes of ethics are usually written in general terms, noting obligations to each of the groups but not stating which takes precedence in any given situation.

The basic difficulty with codes of ethics is that they do not establish priorities between the norms and beliefs. The priorities are the true values of a firm, and they are not included. As an example, let us say that one division in a firm is faced with declining sales and profits; the question is whether to reduce middle-management employment and cut overhead costs—the classic downsizing decision—but the code of ethics says in one section that we respect our employees and in another section that we expect "fair" profits. How do we decide? What is "fair" in this instance? The code of ethics does not tell us.

Let us look at two other examples very briefly. Another division in our company is in a market that has grown very rapidly and has now reached such a large size that direct distribution from the factory to the retail outlets would be much more economical. Our code of ethics says that we will "work closely with our suppliers and distributors, for they too deserve a profit," but perhaps we can reduce our prices to our customers, and gain a competitive advantage for ourselves, if we eliminate the wholesalers and ship directly. The code does not tell us how

to choose between our distributors, our customers, and ourselves.

As a last example, we are fortunate in having within our company another division that also is growing rapidly; it needs to build a new manufacturing plant, but a town in an adjoining state has offered much more substantial tax concessions than the town in which we have operated for 60 years, and in which, let us assume, there is substantial unemployment and need for additional tax revenues. Our code of ethics says that we will be "good citizens" in every community in which we operate, but it does not explain how to choose between communities, or what being a "good citizen" really means.

Ethical dilemmas are conflicts between economic performance and social performance, with the social performance being expressed as obligations to employees, customers, suppliers, distributors, and the general public. Ethical codes can express a general sense of the obligation members of senior management feel towards those groups, but the codes cannot help a middle- or lower-level manager choose between the groups, or between economic and social performance. Should we reduce employment and increase our profits? Should we eliminate our wholesalers and cut our prices? Should we build in another city and reduce our taxes? Should we—and this is the reason I have included the code of ethics of Johnson and Johnson, Inc.—spend over $100 million removing Tylenol from the shelves of every store in the country after the nonprescription drug was found to have been deliberately poisoned in the Chicago area during 1982, causing the deaths of four individuals. James Burke, chairman of Johnson and Johnson, credits that code

THE ETHICS CODE OF JOHNSON AND JOHNSON, "OUR CREDO"

We believe our first responsibility is to the doctors, nurses and patients, to mothers and all others who use our products and services.

In meeting their needs everything we do must be of high quality.

We must constantly strive to reduce our costs in order to maintain reasonable prices.

Customers' orders must be serviced promptly and accurately.

Our suppliers and distributors must have an opportunity to make a fair profit.

⟶ We are responsible to our employees, the men and women who work with us throughout the world.

Everyone must be considered as an individual.

We must respect their dignity and recognize their merit.

They must have a sense of security in their jobs.

Compensation must be fair and adequate, and working conditions clean, orderly and safe.

Employees must feel free to make suggestions and complaints.

There must be equal opportunity for employment, development and advancement for those qualified.

We must provide competent management, and their actions must be just and ethical.

We are responsible to the communities in which we live and work and to the world community as well.

We must be good citizens—support good works and charities and bear our fair share of taxes.

We must encourage civic improvements and better health and education.

We must maintain in good order the property we are privileged to use, protecting the environment and natural resources.

Our final responsibility is to our stockholders.

Business must make a sound profit.

We must experiment with new ideas.

Research must be carried on, innovative programs developed and mistakes paid for.

New equipment must be purchased, new facilities provided and new products launched.

Reserves must be created to provide for adverse times.

When we operate according to these principles, the stockholders should realize a fair return.

Source: Company annual report for 1982, p. 5.

THE ETHICS CODE OF BORG-WARNER CORPORATION, "TO REACH BEYOND THE MINIMAL"

Any business is a member of a social system, entitled to the rights and bound by the responsibilities of that membership. Its freedom to pursue economic goals is constrained by law and channeled by the forces of a free market. But these demands are minimal, requiring only that a business provide wanted goods and services, compete fairly, and cause no obvious harm.

For some companies that is enough. It is not enough for Borg-Warner. We impose upon ourselves an obligation to reach beyond the minimal. We do so convinced that by making a larger contribution to the society that sustains us, we best assure not only its future vitality, but our own.

This is what we believe....

→ We believe in the dignity of the individual. However large and complex a business may be, its work is still done by people dealing with people. Each person involved is a unique human being, with pride, needs, values and innate personal worth. For Borg-Warner to succeed we must operate in a climate of openness and trust, in which each of us freely grants others the same respect, cooperation and decency we seek for ourselves.

We believe in our responsibility to the common good. Because Borg-Warner is both an economic and social force, our responsibilities to the public are large. The spur of competition and the sanctions of the law give strong guidance to our behavior, but alone do not inspire our best. For that we must heed the voice of our natural concern for others. Our challenge is to supply goods and services that are of superior value to those who use them; to create jobs that provide meaning for those who do them; to honor and enhance human life, and to offer our talents and our wealth to help improve the world we share.

Box continued on next page.

with guiding the actions of his company. "This document (the code of ethics) spells out our responsibilities to all our constituencies: consumers, employees, community, and stockholders. It served to guide all of us during the crisis, when hard decisions had to be made in what were often excruciatingly brief periods of time. All of our employees worldwide were able to watch the process of the Tylenol withdrawal and subsequent reintroduction in tamper-resistant packaging, confident of the way in which the decisions would be made. There was a great sense of shared pride in the knowledge that the Credo was being tested... and it worked!" I think that we can agree that the employees of Johnson and Johnson should be proud of the response of their firm, which put consumer safety

We believe in the endless quest for excellence. Though we may be better today than we were yesterday, we are not as good as we must become. Borg-Warner chooses to be a leader—in serving our customers, advancing our technologies, and rewarding all who invest in us their time, money, and trust. None of us can settle for doing less than our best, and we can never stop trying to surpass what already have been achieved.

We believe in continuous renewal. A corporation endures and prospers only by moving forward. The past has given us the present to build on. But to follow our visions to the future, we must see the difference between traditions that give us continuity and strength, and conventions that no longer serve us—and have the course to act on that knowledge. Most can adapt after change has occurred; we must be among the few who anticipate change, shape it to our purpose, and act as its agents.

We believe in the commonwealth of Borg-Warner and its people. Borg-Warner is both a federation of businesses and a community of people. Our goal is to preserve the freedom each of us needs to find personal satisfaction while building the strength that comes from unity. True unity is more than a melding of self-interests; it results when values and ideals are also shared. Some of ours are spelled out in these statements of belief. Others include faith in our political, economic and spiritual heritage; pride in our work and our company; the knowledge that loyalty must flow in many directions; and a conviction that ownership is strongest when shared. We look to the unifying force of these beliefs as a source of energy to brighten the future of our company and all who depend on it.

Source: Company booklet, published 1982.

ahead of company profits, but we also have to agree that that response, and that priority ranking, is not unequivocally indicated in the Credo of the company.

NO

Lisa H. Newton

THE MANY FACES OF THE CORPORATE CODE

We seem to be in another of our code-writing phases. Interest in the development of corporate codes of ethics—by which term we encompass corporate Aspirations, Beliefs, Creeds, Guidelines and so on through the alphabet—has continued to rise since the 1970's, in tandem with the interest in the teaching and taking of ethics, in colleges and workplaces alike. In what follows, I take on some of the dominant themes in the codes of ethics literature, in an attempt to give a partial overview of the state of the art in the formulation of the corporate code.

The attempt turns out to be a study in multiple function. The much-recommended "corporate code of ethics" serves a diversity of functions, and must avoid a similar diversity of pitfalls. Some of these we will survey; to anticipate the end, we will discover that for maximum effectiveness and ethical validity, each code ought to meet three specifications:

1. In its *development and promulgation*, the code must enjoy the maximum participation of the officers and employees of the corporation (the principle of *participation*);
2. In its *content*, the code must be coherent with general ethical principles and the dictates of conscience (the principle of *validity*);
3. In its *implementation*, the code must be, and must be seen to be, coherent with the lived commitments of the company's officers (the principle of *authenticity*).

CLEAR AND PRESENT NEED

Businesses ought to have codes of ethics, if for no other reason than to allay real doubts that businessmen are capable of morality at all. Leonard Brooks has recently taken note of the "... crisis of confidence about corporate activity. Many corporate representations or claims have low credibility, including those made regarding financial dealings and disclosure, environmental protection, health and safety disclosures related to both employees and customers, and questionable payments." That is quite a list of things to

From Lisa H. Newton, "The Many Faces of the Corporate Code," in *The Corporate Code of Ethics: The Perspective of the Humanities,* proceedings of the Conference on Corporate Visions and Values, sponsored by the Connecticut Humanities Council and Wright Investors' Service (Fairfield University, 1992). Copyright © 1992 by Lisa H. Newton. Reprinted by permission.

be distrusted about. If we were looking for a blanket indictment of business, that one ought to cover the ballpark.[1] Or as Michael Hoffman and Jennifer Moore put it somewhat more concisely, it is the opinion of many of our wiser heads that "... business faces a true crisis of legitimacy."[2]

We cannot, *pace* Milton Friedman, leave the governance of the corporation to the forces of the market. While the market may bring about economic efficiency, Gerald Cavanagh points out, it cannot guarantee that corporate performance will be ethically and socially sensitive. Here the responsibility lies with the Board of Directors and top management, and it is "essential that board and management step up to the task," ascertain the ethical climate already prevailing and guide policy and decision in ethical directions. He adds as a final qualification that "while codes, structures and monitoring can encourage ethical decisions, it is even more important to have ethical people in the firm who want to make ethical judgments, know how to, and are not afraid to do so."[3] This is surely true: there is no structure or device in the universe, let alone within the capability of the American business community, that will keep people moral if they are determined to be immoral. But most people, at least most businesspeople, it seems are really neither one nor the other; they are prepared to be either, depending on the prevailing culture, and that is where the code can help.

There is nothing new in the aspiration to ethical codes. As early as 1961, Fr. Raymond Baumhart's survey of 2,000 business managers showed two-thirds of them interested in developing codes of ethics, which they thought would improve the ethical level of business

practice.[4] By the seventies, public attention reinforced that view. George Benson traces the current effort on codes to the revelations on foreign and domestic bribery in government investigations 1973–1976, leading to the Foreign Corrupt Practices Act of 1977.[5] In the mid-seventies, W. Michael Blumenthal, then CEO of Bendix, went so far as to propose that the business executives of America organize a professional association to develop a comprehensive code of ethics for business with a review panel to enforce it. The idea died at the time, but might be worth following up at some point.[6] To this day, the most highly placed businessmen support the development of codes of ethics. In a survey conducted by Touche Ross in October, 1987, 1,082 respondents concluded that the most effective way to encourage ethical business behavior was the adoption of a code of ethics—outscoring the adoption of further legislation by 19%.[7] Nor is this support surprising. Ethics pays, not just in public relations but in company work. As the Business Roundtable, an association of Chief Executive Officers of major U.S. companies, concluded in 1988,

> It may come as a surprise to some that... corporate ethics programs are not mounted primarily to improve the reputation of business. Instead, many executives believe that a culture in which ethical concern permeates the whole organization is necessary to the self-interest of the company.... In the view of the top executives represented in this study, there is no conflict between ethical practices and acceptable profits. Indeed, the first is a necessary precondition for the second.[8]

To be sure, we can, at least in theory, behave like saints without a code to describe how we are behaving. But a written document reinforces an intention to be ethical—as a reminder, as a guide, and as a focus for the solidarity of the corporate officers in their attempts to run the company along the lines it lays down. And beyond this, there is the first concern mentioned: that the public is, probably justifiably, concerned over the proclivities of the business community and interested in seeing tangible proof of its intention to behave.

So a public commitment to ethics serves at least two functions: it addresses the concerns of the public and it reinforces (and clarifies) a bottom-line-justified interest in ethical behavior on the part of the officers. A third reason to take ethics seriously, address the subject explicitly, and articulate provisions to enforce it, is simple realism. As Freeman and Gilbert point out, as long as organizations are composed of human beings, no organizational task can proceed, nor can any cogent corporate strategy be formulated, without recognizing that these human beings have values. Their "First Axiom of Corporate Strategy," "Corporate strategy must reflect an understanding of the values of organizational members and stakeholders," is derived directly from the discovery that the human players in the corporate enterprise very often act in accordance with personal and cultural ethical imperatives, and that the corporation relegates itself to irrelevance if it fails to recognize this fact. Their second Axiom, "Corporate strategy must reflect an understanding of the ethical nature of strategic choice," acknowledges the interaction between corporate direction and private value. It is essential that the choices made by management in strategic planning meet the ethical standards implicit in the stakeholders' values.[9] The authors note the current fashion for describing strategy formulation as if persons did not exist, and point out at some length the errors of such attempts.[10]

WHY CODES FAIL

We sometimes take note of "widespread skepticism" as to the effectiveness of codes and the motivation behind their development. That skepticism bears some examination. Oddly, the doubts do not seem to have their roots in the business community, whose opinions are captured above. It seems to originate in the academic community of the business schools, possibly due to misunderstandings on the nature of valid corporate codes. LaRue Tone Hosmer states well the prevailing error:

> Ethical codes are statements of the norms and beliefs of an organization. These norms and beliefs are generally proposed, discussed, and defined by the senior executives in the firm and then published and distributed to all of the members. Norms, of course, are standards of behavior; they are the ways the senior people in the organization want the others to act when confronted with a given situation.[11]

Again,

> The beliefs in an ethical code are standards of thought; they are the ways that the senior people in the organization want others to think.[12]

With that understanding, no wonder that he must immediately insist that "[t]his is not censorship"! Although that insistence is hardly reinforced with his following, "the intent is to encourage ways of thinking and patterns of attitudes that will lead towards the wanted behavior."

And with both of those understandings in place, again it is not surprising that his evaluation of codes is negative: "Do ethical codes work? Are they helpful in conveying to all employees the moral standards selected by the board of directors and president? Not really."[13] The problem with the code he describes is not only that it is not effective—taking no essential account of the nature of the business, let alone the pre-existing commitments of the people to whom it is supposed to apply, how could it be? —but that it is not ethical. The basis for its norms is, it appears, completely subjective, founded on the whim of whoever happens to be in the executive offices the day that it occurs to a CEO to write a code of ethics; its application is coercive, being conceived by a more powerful group to apply to a less powerful group (but not to themselves); and there is no built-in check to see that it will actually help the company and its employees achieve the ends of the business. In short, it fails by any standards of reasonableness, and why on earth any firm would be interested in such a code is puzzling beyond the norm for such writings. (As Richard DeGeorge points out, we are occasionally willing to allow short lists of rules to be simply imposed on us, as long as the author is reliably known to be God. Senior officers, even CEO's, are not God.)[14]

While we have Hosmer's example before us, we may take the opportunity to extract some more general ethical principles from the critique. The code he describes was brought into existence by a few people in a few remote offices, enlisting the energies of none of the lower-ranking employees of the company. For this reason it fails on any measure of democracy, that understanding of governance that holds participation in policy formulation to be a part of justice; and it fails on any estimate of likely relevance to the situation of those excluded employees. The temptations that beset the stockman and secretary are best known to them, and it is inherently unwise to draw up rules without drawing on their experience. To avoid both sets of failures, it is essential to include as many employees as possible in the development process. This imperative we may call the *principle of participation.*

Second, the content of the code is completely unspecified save by reference to its authors—its provisions are those that strike the CEO and his golfing buddies as good, at the time they write it. Given their understandings of justice (see above and below), we are not inspired to confidence in their intuitions, but that is quite beside the point. Subjective presentations of this type can never qualify as imperatives with the authority of ethics. The provisions of a code must be reasoned, logically consistent, defended by reasoned argument, and coherent with the usual understandings of ethics: they must demonstrate respect for the individual, a commitment to justice, and sensitivity to the rights and interests of all parties affected by corporate action. We may call this requirement the *principle of validity.*

Third, it is assumed that the code is written by the senior officers, but that they themselves are not bound by it, and are therefore by implication perfectly free to ignore it or defy it if that is what they want to do. No liberty could be more destructive. People will do not as they are told, but as it is modeled to them; the company's values are trumpeted in the acts of the highest ranking employees, and need appear nowhere else. Again there is a violation of justice, in the development of a set of rules from which a privileged few shall be exempt, and again there is gross inattention to effectiveness. Whatever we may not know about codes, we know for sure that the real culture of a corporation will be embodied in the behavior of the senior officers, especially the CEO, and that it is imperative to secure the allegiance and the compliance of those persons for a code to be taken seriously; we may call this imperative the *principle of authenticity*. Hosmer's understanding of a corporate code violates all three principles, and condemns itself to ineffectiveness through its violations.

In the limiting case, then, a purported "code" can be no more than some authority's attempt to impose whimsical rules, which are bound to fail. A second type of code that is doomed to failure is the oracular code, confined to bare rules or ideals, no matter how derived or promulgated, with no commentary or explanation grounding the rule in experience.

> The difficulty with many codes is not that they prescribe what is immoral, but that they fail to be truly effective in helping members of the profession or company to act morally. To be moral means not only doing what someone says is right, but also knowing *why* what one does is right, and assuming moral responsibility for the action. How were the provisions of the code arrived at? On what moral bases do the injunctions stand?[15]

The standard instruction at the end of such codes, to discuss any dilemmas with the legal office, won't do it; they don't know morality. Implicit in this objection is a strong suggestion that the code must serve an educational function. This is correct; we will come back to this point.

A third and common way for codes to fail is through failure of the highest executives to take the provisions seriously, not only as they apply to themselves (the principle of authenticity, above), but as they apply to the company's management policies (especially "management by objectives") and other standard procedures. If the CEO honestly believes in the provisions, and takes the lead in modeling and enforcing them, if top management follows suit, and if the company's reward and punishment structure reinforces those provisions consistently, the code may well achieve its purpose even if it fails as a model of logical coherence. If they do not [do] so, there is very little chance that anyone else will either, at least when no one is watching. "Management needs to understand the real dynamics of its own organization. For example, how do people get ahead in the company? What conduct is actually rewarded, what values are really being instilled in employees?"[16] And the modeling and enforcement must be spread throughout the company. As Andy Sigler, CEO of Champion International and initiator of one of the best corporate codes in existence, put it, "Making speeches and sending letters just doesn't do it. You need a culture and peer pressure that spells out what is acceptable and isn't and why. It involves training, education, and follow-up."[17] For example, the institutionalization of any code must include protection from retaliation by supervisors against whistleblowers.[18] Kenneth Arrow would go further, arguing that any effective code must not only be fused into the corporate culture, but "accepted by the significant operating institutions and transmitted from one generation of executives to the next through standard operating procedures [and] through education in business schools."[19]

HOW CODES SUCCEED

The first condition for success is a commitment to the promotion of ethical behavior in a company—not to better public relations, nor to more certain deterrence of Federal inspectors, nor to the terror of an occasional bad apple, but to make the whole company a better and finer employer, producer, resident and citizen. For starters, the business community must take a leaf from the book of the professions, who have seen themselves as moral communities from the outset.[20] Like the professions, the corporation must take its status as a moral agent seriously. (There is almost a note of surprise in Leonard Brooks' observation that nowadays, there is a public expectation that if managers are caught *in flagrante delicto* [in the act of committing a misdeed], as they sometimes are, they will be punished. "This is a significant change because it is signalling that our society no longer regards the interests of the corporation or its shareholders to be paramount in importance. Neither corporate executives nor professionals can operate with impunity any longer, because society now expects them to be accountable.")[21] It certainly does.

From that basic commitment should follow a commitment to a process aimed at gathering that ethos from, and infusing it throughout, the entire company. Our first and third specifications, the principle of participation and the principle of authenticity, are two phases of that process commitment. The whole company (starting from the top) must commit itself to the development of the corporate code; the whole company (including the most junior members) must contribute to the process of deliberation; and the whole company (again, especially the top) must be, and feel, bound to obey and to exemplify it.

The imperative of validity is no more than a remote test of the coherence of the content. In accordance with the examples set by the professions, it is not essential for a cede to be a model of academic ethics. The requirement that the code be in conformity with theory does not mean that the code must explicitly signal the kind of reasoning that validates it. Earlier in this enterprise academicians were perhaps too insistent, and codecrafters too self-conscious, on this point; earlier discussions of the issue of corporate and professional codes were known to break down on the issue of "consequentialist vs. deontological moral reasoning." Both are necessarily included in the development of a corporate ethic. As Robin and Reidenbach point out, maintaining a certain kind of "ethical profile" (e.g. strong customer orientation for a sales-driven industry) is absolutely essential for the bottom line—there is no more utilitarian requirement. Yet the "core values" extracted from that profile (e.g. "Treat customers with respect and honesty,... the way you would want your family treated") can be derived from any system of primary duties, and are deontological in form and function. Any good formulation of a company's creed should be subject to verification by both kinds of moral reasoning.[22]

As Robin and Reidenbach emphasize, the code must be drawn to reflect the aims of the particular set of business practices with which the company is concerned. The ruling ideal of the code might equally be integrity of the practitioners, the excellence of craftsmanship, or the dedication to serve the client/customer, depending on the type of business it is. One of the first principles of "excellence" in the running of any company—the imperative to "stick to the knitting"—entails that a code for one industry, or one kind of company, need not apply with equal force to any others.

Along that line, be it noted that there are many reasons why a code cannot be all things to all people. Critics with certain key areas of interest, for instance, will often discover limits in codes that might not occur to the rest of us. Pat Werhane, for instance, complains that codes "usually tell the employee what he or she is not permitted to do, but they seldom spell out worker rights."[23] She goes on to argue that they tend to turn employees into legalists, obedient to the letter of the regulation but ignorant of its moral spirit.

The solution to both problems may lie in the shift of focus from dead rule to living dialogue. I am inclined to argue that the real value of the code does not lie in the finished product, rules with explanations that all must obey, but in the process by which it came to be. The first call for participation is an invitation to the employee to look into his conscience, discover his own moral commitments, and attempt to prioritize and formulate them. This may be the first time he has ever been asked to take on that job, and the educational value is enormous. The second phase of the participatory process includes the discovery of community consensus, a dialogue in which the employee must test his perceptions against those of others, re-examine and perhaps replace those that do not meet the test, and discover the defenses of those that do. However the code emerges, we will have much more articulate employees at the end of the process than we had at the beginning. And in this articulation is implicit genuine self-awareness: the employee now has his moral beliefs where he can see and get at them, and can be educated to apply them in new and creative ways should the situation around him change.

And it will change. Change was always a fact in the American business community, and very rapid, almost chaotic, change an occasional reality. Now, as Tom Peters points out, partly at his instigation, it has become a conscious policy. The continuation of that dialogue is needed especially as firms radically reorganize themselves, destroying the traditional departmental divisions and job descriptions. In the absence of traditional guides, all members of the corporation will need new and extraordinary norms to govern practice, and there is no substitute for a dialogical process in place as the change happens.[24]

NOTES

1. Leonard J. Brooks, "Corporate Codes of Ethics," *Journal of Business Ethics* 8 (1989):117–129, p. 119.

2. W. Michael Hoffman and Jennifer Mills Moore, *Business Ethics*, second edition. New York: McGraw Hill, 1990, p. 2.

3. Gerald F. Cavanagh, *American Business Values*, second edition. Englewood Cliffs, New Jersey: Prentice-Hall, 1984, p. 159.

4. Raymond C. Baumhart, S. J., "How Ethical Are Businessmen?" *Harvard Business Review* 39 (July–August 1961):166–71.

5. George C. S. Benson, "Codes of Ethics," *Journal of Business* 8 (1989):305–319, p. 306.

6. W. Michael Blumenthal, "New Business Watchdog Needed," *The New York Times*, May 25, 1975, F1; and "R_x for Reducing the Occasion of Corporate Sin," *Advanced Management Journal* 42 (Winter 1977):4–13.

7. Touche Ross, *Ethics in American Business: An Opinion Survey of Key Business Leaders on Ethical Standards and Behavior*. New York: Touche Ross, 1988, p. 14. The sample included only chief

executive officers of companies with S500 million or more in annual sales, deans of business schools and members of Congress.

8. *Corporate Ethics: A Prime Business Asset.* New York: The Business Roundtable, 1988, p. 9.

9. R. Edward Freeman and Daniel R. Gilbert, Jr., *Corporate Strategy and the Search for Ethics.* Englewood Cliffs, New Jersey: Prentice-Hall, 1988, pp. 6–7.

10. *Loc. cit.* See also p. 138, and p. 197, n.25.

11. LaRue Tone Hosmer, *The Ethics of Management.* Homewood, Illinois: Irwin, 1987, p. 153.

12. *Ibid.* p. 154.

13. *Loc. cit.* p. 154.

14. Richard T. DeGeorge, *Business Ethics*, third edition. New York, Macmillan, 1990, p. 390.

15. DeGeorge, *op. cit.* p. 391.

16. William H. Shaw, *Business Ethics.* Belmont, California: Wadsworth Publishing Company, 1991, p. 175.

17. Andrew Sigler, CEO of Champion International, cited in "Businesses Are Signing Up for Ethics 101," *Business Week,* February 15, 1988, p. 56.

18. Leonard J. Brooks, "Corporate Codes of Ethics," *Journal of Business Ethics* 8 (1989):117–129, p. 124.

19. Kenneth J. Arrow, "Social Responsibility and Economic Efficiency," *Public Policy* 21 (Summer 1973):42.

20. Mark S. Frankel, "Professional Codes: Why, How, and With What Impact?" *Journal of Business Ethics* 8 (1989):109–115, p. 110.

21. Brooks, *op. cit.* p. 119.

22. Donald P. Robin and R. Eric Reidenbach, *Business Ethics: Where Profits Meet Value Systems.* Englewood Cliffs, New Jersey: Prentice-Hall, 1989, pp. 94–95.

23. Patricia H. Werhane, *Persons, Rights and Corporations.* Englewood Cliffs, New Jersey: Prentice-Hall, Inc. 1985, p. 159.

24. See Tom Peters, "Get Innovative or Get Dead (part one)," *California Management Review* 33 (Fall 1990):9–26.

POSTSCRIPT

Are Corporate Codes of Ethics Just for Show?

Why might a corporation's management decide to develop a corporate code of ethics, to sponsor or join lectures and workshops on ethics, or to hire consultants to run "ethics training programs" for their middle managers? There are numerous possible answers to this question: The company may be in the headlines again for falsifying time sheets for government projects, and management wishes to project a righteous image before sentencing; employees may be stealing supplies and the employers want to make their people more moral in order to cut costs; or managers may simply believe that ethics as a principle is important to the company.

There may be no single answer to that question in any given case. Surely, given the fiduciary obligations of management to the shareholders, and given the expectations of the community, the managers will stress different motivations for community service at shareholders' meetings. This is probably as it should be; people are complex beings and operate from mixed motivations in most areas of life. There may be no need to insist on purity of motive before an ethics project begins. Motives, after all, come immediately under scrutiny in any consideration of ethics, and it is natural to search for ulterior ones. Whatever the motivation, are efforts to improve corporate behavior often successful? Should we promote the adoption of corporate codes of ethics in all, some, or no companies?

SUGGESTED READINGS

Peter Drucker, "What is Business Ethics?" *The Public Interest* (Spring 1981).

Catherine C. Langlois and Bodo B. Schlegelmilch, "Do Corporate Codes of Ethics Reflect National Character? Evidence from Europe and the United States," *Journal of International Business Studies* (November 1990).

Maurica Lefebvre and Jang B. Singh, "The Content and Focus of Canadian Corporate Codes of Ethics," *Journal of Business Ethics* (October 1992).

Robert Solomon and Kristine Hanson, *It's Good Business* (Atheneum, 1985).

ISSUE 3

Does Ethics Matter in Business?

YES: Manuel Velasquez, from "Why Ethics Matters: A Defense of Ethics in Business Organizations," *Business Ethics Quarterly* (April 1996)

NO: David M. Messick, from "Why Ethics Is Not the Only Thing That Matters," *Business Ethics Quarterly* (April 1996)

ISSUE SUMMARY

YES: Professor of business ethics Manuel Velasquez argues that ethical behavior is more profitable, more rational, and more intrinsically valuable than unethical behavior. Following a line of argument pioneered by Plato and updated by game theorist Robert Axelrod and economist Robert Frank, Velasquez posits that ethical behavior and the development of the virtues that result in ethical behavior are the best predictors of profit in business organizations.

NO: David M. Messick, a professor of ethics and decision in management, argues that Velasquez's conclusions are oversimplified if they aim to predict that the rational businessperson will regularly follow ethical rules of conduct. He asserts that actual behavior, in business and in other areas of life, tends to be a nuanced combination of egotistical and justice-oriented profit-maximizing actions.

The first complete work of philosophy ever written for the instruction of a nonprofessional audience was Plato's *Republic,* and its argument bears repeating: People ought to treat each other with justice and kindness, never taking advantage of another even when they are sure that the other can do nothing to retaliate, never seeking an unfair profit even when they know that they can get away with it. They ought to do this not for the sake of duty, for God, nor out of concern for the welfare of another. On the contrary, people should act virtuously out of concern for their own happiness and the welfare of their own souls. Plato claims that the worst misery comes from enslavement to the passions and that the passions are stirred into action mostly by the prospect of unjust gain or spiteful triumph. Therefore, to live a happy life, a person should live a life of justice and benevolence to others, not for the sake of the material rewards, but for the sake of the order of the soul—what one might call inner peace.

The twentieth century produced a Plato "rerun" in the form of the "prisoner's dilemma," a central construction of game theory. Game theory investigates paths to the maximization of advantage in structured adversarial situations, producing, for instance, the "war games" of the cold war era. In a prisoner's dilemma (explained more fully in the following selection by Manuel Velasquez), two parties are asked to make simultaneous moves in a situation where they cannot observe each other and where disturbingly familiar consequences follow from the wrong moves. If they "cooperate," agree upon and stick to the same story, they both win; if party A sticks to the agreement but party B defects, A loses big and B loses a little; if B sticks to the agreement and A defects, the rewards are reversed; if both defect, they both lose, but nowhere near as badly as the one who cooperates loses if the other defects. So when weighing the chances, each prisoner might conclude that she or he is better off defecting—at least that avoids the worst losses. The game is of infinite interest to strategists, for it mimics disarmament agreements on the international scene and all environmental agreements, national or international. (For instance, if all fishermen agree to use "dolphin-safe" methods of catching tuna, the price of all tuna will go up a little, but the dolphin will be saved, and the consumer, who likes dolphins, will not complain. But if one company decides to abandon these methods, it will be able to sell its tuna a little cheaper. Faced with a choice between more and less expensive tuna on the shelf, in the knowledge that saving the dolphins is now a lost cause since the less expensive tuna will surely crowd out the more expensive tuna, the consumer will take the less expensive, and those who stick by the agreement will lose market share.) When Robert Axelrod proved that cooperation—sticking to an agreement—maximizes interests of both parties in any realistic situation, philosophers took heart and hoped for a better future.

On the negative side, as David M. Messick asserts in the second selection, such proofs of rational behavior do not automatically control behavior, and the practicing corporate officer should not subject business decisions to such a rigorous, long-term formula. Many things other than that rational outcome matter, and evidence of "judgmental incoherence" in undergraduate choices is common in the field, as well as a good predictor of judgmental incoherence in careers to come. In short, people are messier than Plato or Axelrod ever dreamed.

As you read the following selections, remember that both authors are talking about choices that are made every day but that change the directions of lives and corporations. What sorts of calculations are uppermost in your mind as you choose—actions, careers, or lives?

YES

Manuel Velasquez

WHY ETHICS MATTERS: A DEFENSE OF ETHICS IN BUSINESS ORGANIZATIONS

In an article in the *Harvard Business Review* Amar Bhide and Howard H. Stevenson write that "Treachery, we found, can pay," and "There is no compelling economic reason to tell the truth or keep one's word."[1] Bhide and Stevenson are not the first to suggest that unethical behavior may be more profitable than ethical behavior. Over two thousand years ago, exactly the same claim was made by Thrasymachus, a character in Plato's *Republic* who concluded that while justice is for the simpleton, injustice is for the wise.

... Bhide and Stevenson are on the side of Thrasymachus. They assert that their claims are based on the empirical data provided by "extensive interviews." It is unclear just what this data is supposed to be, since they do not bother to provide it in their article. Perhaps they think that the readers of the *Harvard Business Review* might not be up to plowing through tables of numbers and statistics. Instead, what they provide are anecdotes and snippets of conversations taken, apparently, from their interviews with a variety of business people. These business people describe incidents where dishonesty or broken promises paid off and several are quoted as saying that many businesses "cavalierly break promises" yet suffer no sanctions. What Bhide and Stevenson's interviews clearly demonstrate is that many business people feel that unethical behavior in business often pays off.

But it is difficult to see what more we are supposed to learn from these stories and quotations since they seem to tell us what we already knew: that wrongdoing sometimes pays and that the good sometimes suffer. The real issue, however, and the issue that Plato's *Republic* addresses is this: is there any kind of systematic advantage to ethical behavior or any kind of systematic disadvantage to unethical behavior? That Platonic question is the issue I here want to address. In particular, I want to ask, is there any kind of systematic advantage that a business organization or business person has to gain from just behavior or is injustice truly more profitable? Like Bhide and Stevenson, however, I will address this question by appealing to some very unPlatonic empirical data....

RESEARCH ON PRISONERS DILEMMAS

In a crucial passage in the *Republic*, one of Plato's characters suggests that norms of justice can be thought of as the outcome of a cooperative agreement among people. In a society that lacks norms of justice, he suggests, people inflict injustices on each other. People quickly conclude that they will be better off if everyone adheres to norms of justice. People consequently agree to cooperate in mutual adherence to norms of justice. However, each individual knows that he would be better off if he personally defected from following the norms that everyone else is following, "For no man who is worthy to be called a man would ever submit to such an agreement if he were able to resist; he would be mad if he did."

In this account, justice is characterized as creating the kind of situation that contemporary game theory calls a "prisoners dilemma." Prisoner's dilemmas are situations in which two parties are faced with a choice between two options: to cooperate in some course of action, or to not cooperate, that is, to defect. If both cooperate, they will both gain some benefit. If both defect, neither gets the benefit. If one cooperates while the other defects, the one who cooperates suffers a loss, while the one who defects gains a benefit. . . .

The prisoner's dilemma gets its name from a story that is supposed to illustrate the kind of situation it represents. The story goes like this: Two thieves arrested for a crime vow not to betray each other. But the police put them in separate rooms, and tell each thief the same thing: "If your partner confesses and you keep silent, he goes free and you get 5 years in prison; if you confess and he keeps silent, you go free and he gets 5 years in prison. If you both confess, then you both get 3 years in prison. If you both keep silent, then we'll give you each 1 year in prison on a lesser charge."

The best outcome in a prisoner's dilemma is for both parties to cooperate. Mutual cooperation will leave them better off than if both defect. However, as early inquiries in game theory showed, if the parties are rational and self-interested, they will both choose to defect. Each party will reason as follows: "The other party will either cooperate or defect. If the other party cooperates, I will gain more by defecting than by cooperating; and, if the other party defects, I will also gain more by defecting than by cooperating. In either case, I will be better off by defecting than by cooperating." Since both parties reason in this self-interested way both end up defecting, and thus both end up losing out. Prisoner's dilemmas, in short, are situations in which the self-interested behavior of two parties leaves both worse off than cooperative behavior would.

Although prisoner's dilemmas technically involve only two parties, their lessons can be generalized to what are more accurately called "social dilemmas," situations in which several parties each face a prisoner's dilemma situation with respect to the other parties. The members of a commodity cartel, for example, will all benefit if all charge an agreed-upon high price for the commodity. But each member knows that if the others stick to the agreement, he has more to gain by selling the commodity at a lower price, while if the others do not stick to the agreement, he will also be better off selling at a lower price. Since all will reason this way, the cartel breaks down, prices fall, and all the members of the cartel end up worse off than if they had cooperated in the agreement. Studies have indicated that large groups in a social dilemma are rarely able to secure cooperation, especially if they expect not to interact frequently.

Prisoners dilemmas, in the form of social dilemmas, mirror many of the kinds of social situations with which our lives are filled, i.e., situations in which several people have a choice between cooperation or non-cooperation and in which the self-interested pursuit of non-cooperation leaves all worst off than cooperation. In addition to cartels, such situations include contracts and agreements or promises, honor systems, market competition, military arms races, the game of chicken, the provision of public goods, the "NIMBY" ("Not In My Back Yard") syndrome, the consumption of unowned resources, the free rider phenomenon, and, of course, ethics. Ethical norms can be interpreted as norms that put us in a prisoners' dilemma situation. For example, when two individuals talk with each other, they have a choice of cooperating in the norm of telling the truth, or they can try to take advantage of each other by lying to each other. When two individuals make an agreement, they have a choice of cooperating in the norm of keeping their word, or they can try to take advantage of each other by breaking the agreement. When individuals who each own a piece of property interact, they have a choice of cooperating in the norm against theft, or they can try to take advantage of each other by stealing each other's property. Being ethical, then, can be thought of as a kind of cooperation between individuals: it is cooperating in the moral norms that sustain our fundamental institutions such as the institution of language, of contract, and of property, and, more generally, the social conditions that make an orderly and flourishing human life possible. Being unethical, on the other hand, can be conceptualized as an attempt to take advantage of others by breaking the moral norms that others are following.

Seeing ethics in terms of the prisoner's dilemma suggests an explanation for two common observations business people make about ethics. First, business people often acknowledge that the business world would be a better place if everyone behaved ethically. This is what the prisoner's dilemma analysis of ethics would suggest since mutual cooperation in the norms of ethics is mutually beneficial; in particular we all gain the benefit of stable social institutions and an orderly and flourishing society if everyone cooperates in the moral norms that sustain these. But, secondly, business people just as often suggest, as Plato's Thrasymachus did, that ethical behavior in business is for suckers. And this, again, is what the prisoner's dilemma suggests since the person who sticks to ethics will lose out when she encounters a person who takes advantage of her by being unethical. The ethical person, then, is in a prisoner's dilemma and so appears to be at a disadvantage when dealing with an unethical one.

And, as a matter of fact, the central lesson of the prisoner's dilemma is that when individuals deal with each other in a prisoners dilemma situation, it is in each person's individual interest not to cooperate but to try to take advantage of the cooperation of the other party. Why, then, are people ever ethical? If, as Thrasymachus suggests, injustice pays off, why are people ever just? The Prisoner's Dilemma analysis raises in very stark form the question with which we began: why be ethical if getting away with being unethical pays better than being ethical?

Part of the explanation for why ethics matters lies in an unreal assumption we have so far been making. We have assumed that the people who meet in a prisoners dilemma interact with each other only once. In fact, as the prisoners dilemma analysis of ethics suggests, unethical behavior will pay off in a one-time meeting when the person who is taken advantage of cannot get back at the person who took advantage of her. This is perhaps the reason why ostensibly unethical behavior emerges in those exchanges in which parties interact only once, such as in the sale of cars or other big-ticket items, or exchanges in which the parties cannot identify each other, such as in freeway driving.

However, the situation is quite different when interactions are iterated and are between individuals who are known to each other; for example, when individuals have to deal with each other repeatedly or have on-going relationships with each other. When individuals can identify each other and have to deal with each other in repeated prisoner's dilemma situations, those who continue to try to take advantage of the other party can be made to suffer sustained losses, while those who learn to cooperate with the other party can make the largest gains.

The crucial factor that is at work when identifiable people deal with each other repeatedly, of course, is that when one party takes advantage of the other in one interaction, the injured party remembers this and can retaliate by doing the same in the next interaction. Through mutual retaliation, the parties can enforce cooperation, and a stable pattern of mutual co-operation can emerge. This phenomenon has been extensively studied in contemporary game theory. [Robert] Axelrod, in particular, has shown that in a series of repeated prisoners' dilemma encounters, the best strategy—called TIT FOR TAT— is for a party to cooperate initially but to retaliate with non-cooperation each subsequent time the other party fails to cooperate. Because of this continuous threat of retaliation, it is more rational for the parties to a series of repeated exchanges to cooperate with each other than to fail to cooperate. And cooperation, of course, brings with it the mutual advantages of mutually beneficial activities. Thus, where individuals have to deal with each other repeatedly, and where the threat of retaliation is present, it is better to cooperate with the other party than to try to take advantage of them.

The implications of the prisoners' dilemmas research for ethics in business are fairly clear. Business interactions with its stakeholders—employees, customers, suppliers, creditors, and stockholders— are usually repetitive and on-going. Consequently, if a business attempts through unethical behavior to take advantage of these or other stakeholders in today's interaction, they can usually find some way to retaliate against the business in tomorrow's interaction. The retaliation can consist of as simple an act as refusing to buy from, work for, or do business with the unethical party; or it may be a more complex form of retaliation such as sabotage, absenteeism, pilferage, organizing boycotts or other forms of getting others to refuse to do business with the unethical party, or getting even by inflicting other kinds of covert or overt injuries. Simply put, it is shortsighted for management to try to take advantage of these groups through unethical behavior. It is possible for a business to sometimes get away with unethical behavior, but in the long run, if interactions between identifiable parties are iterated and retaliation is a realistic option, unethical business behavior tends to be unprofitable and nonrational, while, ethical behavior will reap the rewards of mutual cooperation.

Although the threat of retaliation in repeated interactions goes some way toward explaining why ethics matters in business, still the explanation does not take us very far in making ethics more appealing. This is because the explanation assumes a negative motivation for ethical behavior. In effect it says that ethics is preferable because unethical behavior is punished. This provides a negative incentive for avoiding unethical behavior, but does not show that ethical behavior is itself an attractive option. A more satisfying justification of ethics would show that ethical behavior itself is desirable because it is beneficial. In fact, that was Plato's hope in the *Republic*. Plato aimed to show that ethical behavior was not merely a lesser evil, to be preferred over the greater evils that unethical behavior entailed, but that ethical behavior itself was advantageous.

In fact, a more positive explanation of why justice matters can be found in the work of the economist Robert Frank. Frank's research, like the prisoners' dilemma research, looks at situations in which people have a choice between cooperating with or taking advantage of others. Frank's analysis, however, is aimed at investigating whether it is better for a person to habitually cooperate with others or to habitually take advantage of others, when that person is living in a population of people some of whom habitually cooperate and some of whom habitually take advantage of others.

Since, as I have argued, ethics is a kind of cooperation in the rules that support our fundamental social institutions, the question comes down to this: is it better to be habitually ethical or unethical in a society that consists of both ethical and unethical people? Plato, in the *Republic*, answered this question in the affirmative, arguing that the person who is habitually just will enjoy important reputational benefits.

Frank's studies provide ingenious support for Plato's claim that ethical behavior is itself beneficial. Frank uncovered two important facts about human behavior. First, he found that people send fairly reliable signals to each other regarding whether they habitually cooperate in keeping to rules and agreements, or whether they habitually attempt to take advantage of others. Signals of one's predisposition to be cooperative include visual cues such as facial expressions, auditory cues such as tone of voice, and past history such as is embodied in reports from others and in reputation. Frank's studies showed that people can accurately identify cooperative predispositions about 75 percent of the time, and can accurately identify non-cooperative predispositions about 60 percent of the time.

Secondly, Frank's studies showed that when people interact with each other and can choose the persons with whom they interact, they more often choose to interact with those whom they believe habitually cooperate in the rules of ethics and avoid those whom they believe will try to take advantage of them. That is, people try to avoid those who are unethical, and seek out those who are ethical.

Frank argued that these two factors —the ability to identify ethical and unethical predispositions, and the tendency to seek out those who are ethical and avoid those who are unethical— imply that it is more advantageous to be habitually ethical than unethical. Because ethical people seek each other out and avoid unethical people, they will tend to increase the frequency of their dealings with each other. Ethical people will therefore increase the frequency with which they engage in mutually cooperative and thus mutually beneficial exchanges. On the other hand, unethical people will be avoided by ethical people and so they will be forced to deal with other unethical people. As a result, unethical people will tend to increase the frequency of their dealings with each other, and in these dealings each will try to take advantage of the other in a mutually destructive exchange. Frank's conclusion is that habitually ethical people will more often have mutually advantageous relationships with other ethical people while habitually unethical people will more often have mutually destructive relationships with other unethical people. In the long run, it turns out that habitually ethical people end up with larger gains than habitually unethical people.

Frank's research has clear implications for ethics in business. His findings imply that employees, for example, have fairly reliable ways of discovering whether a manager or even a team of managers is habitually ethical or unethical. His research implies, further, that given the choice ethical employees will tend to seek to deal more with those whom they identify as ethical than with those who are unethical: that is, ethical employees will tend not to enter or to exit organizations when they learn those organizations are staffed by managers who deal unethically with their employees, and they will tend to enter and remain loyal to organizations staffed by ethical managers. Unethical managers, on the other hand, will be left with the unethical remainder. Consequently, over the long run and for the most part, ethical managers will tend to have mutually cooperative interactions with ethically reliable employees and together with them will create mutually beneficial corporate enterprises, while unethical managers will more often tend to find themselves in mutually destructive interactions with unethical employees and together with them create dysfunctional enterprises. Habitually ethical management is more advantageous over the long run, than habitually unethical management.

The prisoners' dilemma research is thus fairly supportive of the Platonic view that adherence to other-regarding norms of ethics confers benefits on the agent. First, adherence to other-regarding norms avoids injurious retaliation in ongoing relationships with customers, employees, suppliers, and creditors. Second, habitual adherence to other-regarding norms will increase the frequency with which managers will find themselves in mutually beneficial interactions with ethical employees, while habitually unethical behavior will increase the frequency with which managers will find themselves in mutually destructive relationships with unethical employees....

The research on distributive justice [the fairness of the way in which benefits and burdens are distributed among the members of a group] suggests that people desire distributive justice for itself and not merely for its external advantages and that this desire is a powerful motivating force, often, but not always, even overriding personal advantage. This conclusion has important implications for profit-oriented business organizations, particularly insofar as the research shows that people's desire for justice will motivate them to take steps to ensure that justice prevails, even when this means foregoing advantages to themselves. It must matter to businesses, for example, that employees seek distributive justice in compensation and work assignments, and will take steps to ensure that work burdens are justly proportionate to compensation. In particular, if employees believe they are not being paid enough for the work they are doing in comparison to others, they will likely adjust their work output downward, perhaps by putting forth less effort, perhaps by taking days off from work, or perhaps by otherwise lowering their productivity. People outside a business will also react negatively to violations of distributive justice in ways that must matter to a business. Customers, for example, will turn against a company if they believe that it is unjustly charging more than it should for a product, as may happen, for example, when an essential commodity is in very short supply. Finally, it must matter to business that task performance is affected by the kind of distributive justice that prevails in an organization: compensation systems based on the principle of contribution create a competitive atmosphere in which resources and information are not shared, while compensation systems based on the principle of equality encourage cooperation and the sharing of resources and information. Clearly, then, distributive justice is intrinsically valuable to the employees, customers, and others with whom businesses deal, and for this reason it has to matter to businesses....

The first studies on procedural justice found that dispute resolution processes in which the parties to a dispute are allowed to provide their own input into the process are seen as fairer than processes that deny parties any direct input. These studies also indicated that when processes embodied procedural justice, the institutions or processes themselves were respected and valued by the participants. Indicative of this was the fact that when decisions were made through processes that allowed for direct input, the decisions that emerged from the process were embraced and accepted as legitimate by the affected parties, to an extent not present when exactly the same decisions were made through processes that did not allow such input. Moreover, subsequent studies in a variety of social contexts showed that decision-making processes and institutions that allow affected parties direct input into the process, are judged to be more just than those which don't, and that such just processes and institutions, as well as the decisions reached through them are more likely to be accepted by affected parties, more likely to be seen as legitimate by the parties involved, and more likely to be complied with by the parties involved. Studies of workers, for example, have shown that when a system of employee evaluation allows workers to express their viewpoints and feelings and to communicate information about themselves and their work, they judge it to be more fair and are more likely to be satisfied with the process and more acceptant of their final evaluations regardless of whether the evaluations are low or high. Other studies have shown that employee evaluation systems are also judged as fair and valued when they are consistent and they communicate and rely on accurate information, factors that also contribute to acceptance of, and compliance with, processes and their outcomes. Some experimental models have suggested that the fairness of procedures is further determined by the extent to which they provide: adequate methods of selecting decision-makers, adequate procedures for setting and communicating the ground rules that will determine rewards, suitable methods of gathering and communicating the information on the basis of which the rules are applied, suitable decision-making mechanisms in the application of rules, safeguards against the abuse of power, procedures for appeals, and mechanisms for change that can represent the concerns of all participants.

The research on procedural justice has provided a number of additional indications that organizational participants respect and attribute intrinsic value to processes that are just. One set of studies showed that when employees feel that an organization's decision-making processes are just they exhibit lower levels of turnover and absenteeism, and higher levels of trust and commitment to the organization and to its management. And when employees believe an organization's decision-making processes and procedures are just, they are more willing to follow organizational leaders, more willing to do what they say and more willing to see their leadership as legitimate. In short, employees become committed to the just organization and remain loyal to it and willing to accept and follow its leaders. On the other hand, employees are repelled by the unjust organization and respond to organizational injustice with disaffection, disloyalty, and resistance to organizational leaders and their commands.

Organizations constituted of decision-making processes that are just, then, are valued by participants and endowed with respect. But is there any direct empirical evidence that just organizational procedures are valued for themselves instead of merely for the benefits they instrumentally provide their members? This is an extremely difficult question to answer with certainty, since it is possible that people value just processes because at some level they believe that just processes are likely to provide them with larger rewards than unjust ones. Nevertheless, there are some studies that indicate that people place some value on just procedures that is independent of the extent to which such procedures personally benefit them. Although certain studies have shown that just procedures have instrumental value for their participants, these same studies have demonstrated that just procedures are also imbued with noninstrumental or intrinsic value. For example, in one study, two groups of workers were both allowed to say what they thought would be an appropriate amount of work to perform in a given time. But while the amount of work for one group was adjusted in accordance with their input, the other group was told that although their input was being solicited, the amount of work they had to do had already been decided and their input would have no effect on the amount of work they would be asked to perform. A third, control group, was not allowed even to say what they thought would be an appropriate amount of work, and their work was simply assigned to them. Not surprisingly, this third group did not judge this process to be particularly fair. But the other two groups, even those who knew their input would have no effect on the outcome, rated the process as fair. Thus, procedures are judged to be fair, and so are desired, even apart from their instrumental value. It has been suggested, in fact, that procedural justice is desirable not for its instrumental value, but because it communicates that those who are treated justly (for example, those whose opinion or "voice" is solicited) are valued, respected, and accorded dignity. The empirical evidence we have, then, suggests that Plato was entirely right: justice is intrinsically desirable because it creates an intrinsically desirable organizational order, an order that communicates value, respect, and dignity, and so an order which elicits trust, organizational commitment and loyalty, which leads participants to attribute legitimacy to the organization's leaders and their decisions, and which leads participants to accept and implement organizational decisions. When an organization is constituted of processes that are seen as just, participants in the organization cleave to the organization itself: they embrace it, respect it, and are intensely loyal to it and its leadership....

CONCLUSION

We have argued, then, that Plato was right: justice is more profitable, more rational, and more intrinsically valuable than injustice, even in business. The research on prisoners' dilemmas shows that ethical behavior is more profitable and more rational than unethical behavior in terms of both the negative sanctions on unethical behavior and the positive rewards of ethical behavior; and the psychological research on justice shows that justice is intrinsically valuable, both from an outcome and from a process perspective, and so crucial for business organizations, particularly in terms of organizational effectiveness. There is, undoubtedly, much more to be said for ethics and justice in organizations. There is reason, for example, to suspect that the just organization is one in which morale is high and in which members are motivated to work harder and more productively at achieving organizational goals, and reason to suspect that the justice of an organization bears some significant relationship to its stability, i.e., its ability to maintain its essential functions though periods of stress and in turbulent environments. But enough has been said to show that Plato was correct and that Thrasymachus and his modern counterparts are wrong. Ethics in general and justice in particular matter tremendously for the profit-oriented self-interested business organization.

NOTES

1. Amar Bhide and Howard H. Stevenson, "Why be Honest if Honesty Doesn't Pay," *Harvard Business Review* (September-October 1990), pp. 121–29.

NO

David M. Messick

WHY ETHICS IS NOT THE ONLY THING THAT MATTERS

Abstract: Ethics surely matters to people, but to ignore the fact that other things matter as well is to oversimplify human motivation and behavior. Human action is often the ungainly resolution of conflicts between ethical and egotistical impulses, and the challenge for moral psychology is to understand these conflicts and their resolution.

Professor [Manuel] Velasquez has written an eloquent essay defending the importance of ethics in business organizations. Much of his defense draws on the famous prisoner's dilemma and on psychological research dealing with distributive and procedural justice. His conclusion, that justice matters to people, in business organizations and elsewhere, is firmly supported by decades of psychological research.

But people are complex. While I agree with Professor Velasquez' conclusion, I must add that the story is more complicated than he implies. Ethics does matter to people, but so do a lot of other things including success, friendship, sex, money, prestige, love, power, and authority. Human motivation is a tumult of goals and desires that are often mutually incompatible. Psychologists and other behavioral scientists make a living by trying to understand how these potentially conflicting impulses get expressed in people's thoughts and deeds. Let me offer three illustrations of how ethics matters along with money, and, at the same time, illustrate how one might study the psychological processes that govern the conflicts between competing impulses.

1. For his dissertation research, van Avemaet (1974) conducted a study in which he had undergraduates perform a task that involved filling out questionnaires. The task was undertaken in a psychological laboratory with a purported second person whom the subjects never saw.

The subjects worked for either 45 or 90 minutes and completed either 6 or 3 questionnaires in this time period. When the subject had finished the questionnaires, the experimenter entered the room and stated that the other subject had had to leave immediately and was gone. The experimenter had $7.00 to pay the subjects, he continued, and had hoped to have the two

From David M. Messick, "Why Ethics Is Not the Only Thing That Matters," *Business Ethics Quarterly,* vol. 6, no. 2 (April 1996). Copyright © 1996 by The Society for Business Ethics. Reprinted by permission. References omitted.

students decide between themselves how to make the allocation. Now that the other had left, the pair could no longer make a joint decision, and the experimenter also had an appointment in just a few minutes and could not wait. Thus, the experimenter suggested that the subject take the entire $7.00, along with an envelope addressed to the other subject, and keep the amount of money to which he or she was entitled, and send the remainder to the other person.

Before giving the money (in 6 one dollar bills and change) and the envelope to the subject, the experimenter reminded the student of the amount of time he or she had spent and of the number of questionnaires completed. He also told the subject how much time and how many questionnaires the other person had logged. The crucial independent variable in this experiment was the information that was given to the subject about his and the others' accomplishments. The subject found out that he worked longer, shorter, or the same length of time as the other person, and that he completed more, fewer, or the same number of questionnaires.

The address on the envelope was actually the experimenter's apartment. What van Avemaet measured in the study was how much of the $7.00 that the subject sent to the other person in each experimental condition. The results can be summarized briefly as follows: When subjects had a claim to more that half the money *either* because they had worked longer or because they filled out more questionnaires, they kept most of the money. When the subjects had *no* claim to more than half and the other person did have on one or both dimensions, the subjects kept half the money. Clearly this pattern is unjust in that it displays a bias in favor of the subject. For instance, when subjects worked longer *and* did more than the other, they kept $4.68, on average. When the other did more and worked longer than the subject, the subjects kept $3.33 (not the $2.32 that they sent to the other in the symmetrical situation). The pattern of data displays a clear self-serving or egocentric bias that seems to imply that justice is irrelevant.

But not so fast. Of the 92 subjects who took the money and left the laboratory with it, 90 sent *some* money. Only 2 percent of the subjects, at most, adopted the purely selfish strategy of keeping all the $7 and forgetting about the other person. The data display a pattern of greed tempered by justice, or justice contorted by greed. The violations of justice are self-serving and predictable as are the deviations from simple greed. Greed and justice fuse into an ungainly shape that resists explanation by one principle alone.

2. One of the benefits of ethics that Professor Velasquez cites is the value of having an ethical reputation. Such a reputation evokes trust and attracts potential employees for whom trust and ethics matter. If these employees are better, in the sense of being cheaper, more honest, or more loyal than potential employees who do not value trust and ethics, then this is an economic advantage for being ethical (or for having the reputation of being ethical).

There may be more to it than this. Frank (forthcoming) presents evidence that less socially responsible firms must pay higher salaries than more socially responsible firms to attract employees. Frank's argument is that employees value social responsibility and view this quality as substitutable for salary. Thus, when asked if they would prefer a $30,000 per year job writing ads for Camel Cigarettes or for the American Cancer Society, 88% of the Cornell University seniors responding chose the latter. When asked how much they would have to be paid to switch jobs, the average pay differential was more than $24,000. These seniors claim that they would have to be paid 80% more, on average, to sell cigarettes than to sell health. This is the good news. The bad news is that there is a price for which most would be willing to switch. Again, what we witness is a trade-off that says that justice is important, but not supreme.

At least Frank's research suggests that it may be possible to put a price on ethics, to determine the economic value of a good reputation.

3. Research by Bazerman, Schroth, Shah, Diekmann, & Tenbrunsel (1994) indicates that this possibility may be an illusion. These investigators were interested in the value MBA students placed on procedural justice in comparison to salary, an issue obviously related to Frank's concern. The MBA students were asked to imagine that they were on the job market and that they were evaluating six offers of employment. Some of the subjects were instructed to evaluate the offers alone. Their task was merely to say whether they would accept the job or not. The other subjects had the offers presented in three pairs. Each pair contained one job that paid more but provided less procedural justice than the other. For example, part of the procedural justice instructions for the higher paying ($75,000) job of one of the pairs reads as follows:

Decisions involving company policies such as training and job objectives are made by senior management. In general, new associates are not encouraged to voice their opinions or objections.

Instructions for the lower paying job ($60,000), with better procedural justice qualities, containing the following sentence:

The firm encourages all consultants, both junior and senior, to voice their opinions for changes and improvements to the company's policies.

One of the firms provided an opportunity for junior associates to have a voice in policy making, whereas the other firm did not. Voice is a crucial ingredient in many theories of procedural justice, including those of Lind & Tyler (1988) and Thibaut & Walker (1975). The other two pairs varied the fairness of the firms' grievance procedures and interactional justice (Bies & Moag, 1986), respectively.

Two features of the results of this study are pertinent. There is evidence to support Velasquez' contention that ethics matters. Many students selected the lower paying job over the higher paying one, presumably because they valued procedural justice more than the salary difference. However, the strength of this preference depended on whether the students were evaluating the jobs singly or in pairs. Singly, 59% of the students said that they would accept the lower paying job in which they would have some voice, and only 36% said that they would accept the higher paying job without voice. When the jobs were offered in pairs, however, 55% of the students said they would take the higher paying job (without voice), only 33% said they would take the lower paying job (with voice), and 12% said they would accept neither. When evaluating the options singly, it appears that justice matters more than the salary difference; when evaluating pairs of jobs, it appears that the money matters more than justice. So how do we measure the economic value of justice?

This type of judgmental incoherence is not uncommon in psychological research. In fact much recent work has shown that the incoherence is systematic and lawful (Tversky, Sattah, & Slovic, 1988; Payne, Bettman, & Johnson, 1994). This work suggests that efforts to measure the value of justice may be ill-fated. Money matters as well as ethics and there may not be a simple answer to the question about how these two interests combine or trade off against each other.

Our last illustration and much other recent psychological research suggests that the expression of different, possibly conflicting interests and values in people's actions and judgments is highly context dependent. Whether need, equity, or equality is considered most important in a specific problem will hang on the details of the problem. One person's (perceived) justice may be another's wrong.

If we agree that ethics matters, along with a variety of other, occasionally incompatible interests, we may see some wisdom in the view that unethical actions may occur not because ethics does not matter, but because other factors matter more, or because mistakes are made. An understanding of how the psychology of judgment and decision making plays into ethics in organizations (Messick & Bazerman, in press) may complicate, but at the same time deepen our understanding of the ways in which ethics matters.

POSTSCRIPT

Does Ethics Matter in Business?

Shall I live a moral life? This is not the kind of question one can answer in a day, or a week, after reading some contrary views on the subject. It may be that the less we think about it, the more definitively it will be answered by our actions.

Corporations often develop "codes of conduct" or "vision statements," affirming a fundamental recognition of the importance of ethical behavior in business. Often it is unclear whether the code is intended to help people live more ethical lives, is a public relations ploy to impress neighbors and regulators in order to get more favorable treatment, or is designed as a legal lever to enable corporate executives to fire employees whose aggressive business practices become counterproductive. Some claim that corporate executives extol moral life only to keep the lowest-paid workers honest.

SUGGESTED READINGS

Amar Bhide and Howard H. Stevenson, "Why Be Honest If Honesty Doesn't Pay?" *Harvard Business Review* (September–October 1990).

R. Murray Lindsay, Linda M. Lindsay, and V. Bruce Irvine, "Instilling Ethical Behavior in Organizations: A Survey of Canadian Companies," *Journal of Business Ethics* (April 1996).

David M. Messick and Max H. Bazerman, "Ethics for the Twenty-First Century: A Decision Making Perspective," *Sloan Management Review* (1996).

James C. Wimbusch, Jon M. Shepard, and Steven E. Markham, "An Empirical Examination of the Relationship Between Ethical Climate and Ethical Behavior from Multiple Levels of Analysis," *Journal of Business Ethics* (December 1997).

ISSUE 4

Does the Market Teach Us Virtue?

YES: Ian Maitland, from "Virtuous Markets: The Market as School of the Virtues," *Business Ethics Quarterly* (January 1997)

NO: Bill Shaw, from "Sources of Virtue: The Market and the Community," *Business Ethics Quarterly* (January 1997)

ISSUE SUMMARY

YES: Ian Maitland, a senior fellow at the Center of the American Experiment, argues that the market reinforces and rewards certain standard virtues and may therefore be regarded as an institution that improves the moral level of the people. Furthermore, the market carries on Aristotle's agenda—linking the good human being and the good society.

NO: Bill Shaw, editor of the *American Business Law Journal*, argues that Maitland has neglected the historic anchors of "the virtues": the society that generated and reinforced the virtues, the theory of the person that made them possible, and the conception of "the Good" upon which the notion of virtue hangs. Shaw also asserts that Maitland has not established the connection between the operation of the market and virtue in Aristotelian terms.

For starters, what *is* virtue? Virtue is traditionally defined as the condition of anything in which it best fulfills its function. Given this definition, what counts as a virtuous person depends at least in part on the function that person fulfills. In that sense, does the practice of business make one a good person or a bad person? Before undertaking any discussion of this question, you should be aware of a powerful current in Western thought that insists that business is fit only for bad people and that business makes bad people worse.

It seems that as often as someone suggests that the image of the scoundrelly businessperson was a creation of philosophers and novelists, a scandal surfaces from the canyons of Wall Street showing corporate operators reaping millions for manipulating advertising images, sacrificing product quality, downsizing employees, or increasing stock prices. Is it true that bad people go into business or that business (and the fixation on the "bottom line") makes people bad?

This concept goes back to Aristotle, who, reflecting the social class structure of his time, divided occupations into two categories, "worthy" and "unworthy." Among the worthy occupations were hunting, farming, herding, military activities on land and sea, and ruling (participating in government). All commercial activities, especially retail trade, were considered unworthy, for they concerned money, which was thought of as an "unnatural substance" that destroyed one's character. Aristotle reserved his strongest condemnations for the bankers who charged interest on loans—"as if lifeless metal should beget offspring!" And in the category of "hunting" (a worthy profession) he included piracy—preying on merchant ships with armed force—as if the employees and property of the merchants were simply wild game to be taken at will. In the view of Aristotle's society, all right came from inheritance, and for the nobility, a contract really had no binding force.

It is important to note that Aristotle was not describing the society in which he lived and prospered. By Aristotle's time, the noncommercial aristocratic society was a distant memory. Athens was a cosmopolitan seaport, and the luxuries enjoyed by the nobility were the products of the East brought to Greek tables by some of the most astute merchants the world has ever known. Nevertheless, the seed of anticommercialism was sown. The Italian philosopher Saint Thomas Aquinas, following Aristotle, lent his authority to the Church's prohibition against the taking of interest on loans—"usury"—and it was not until the Protestant Reformation that commerce could begin in earnest and the grip of the landowners was broken.

In literature and philosophy there is a historical hostility to business as corrupting of the character. The English philosopher John Locke would have reestablished a landed gentry in America; the English novelist Charles Dickens portrayed the businessmen of his day as slimy characters who would gladly eat widows and orphans for breakfast; and a stream of utopian literature condemns capitalism and business for the misdirection of humans from their native goodness to their present benighted state.

There was a countertrend to this adverse view of business, beginning in the Enlightenment of the eighteenth century and centered in the United States. An indigenous American philosophy, emerging from the colonial experience and culminating in pragmatism, was rooted in the practical work experience of small tradesmen and farmers, who were considered entrepreneurs (as opposed to traditional European peasants). Benjamin Franklin was the forefather of this philosophy, preaching an ethic of prudence, honesty, responsibility, moderation, kindness, and industry entirely appropriate to small trade in a small town, yet echoing Aristotle's teachings on the virtuous life of the citizen.

As you read the following selections, consider whether we depend on a notion of "the Good" to generate a notion of the virtuous person or whether we need a picture of an entire society to discern appropriate functions. Can virtue be only a series of dispositions to behavior that lead to productive functioning in the market? Or is the whole virtue of the human being at stake? Do we have the right to expect our institutions, especially our economic institutions, to help us become better people?

YES
Ian Maitland

VIRTUOUS MARKETS: THE MARKET AS SCHOOL OF THE VIRTUES

Adam Smith said that in a commercial society "every man becomes in some measure a merchant." If Smith is right, what implications does that have for the character of the society? Economists are often charged with neglecting the fact that economic arrangements not only produce goods and services; they also produce certain types of people. In this paper I address the character forming effects of the market. Specifically, I look at the impact of the market on the "virtues." By that I mean the qualities of character or disposition or intellect that enable a person to lead a virtuous life or to act in an ethically appropriate manner.

According to virtue theorists, the success of our political institutions depends not simply on how artfully contrived they are, but also on the presence of civic virtues among the citizenry. Similarly, the effective functioning of the economy is not the automatic result of the operation of the hidden hand of the market, but instead depends critically on the moral virtues that economic actors bring to the marketplace. If the viability of our political system and our economy depends on the presence of certain virtues among the citizenry, then it becomes vital to inquire into where these virtues come from. The result has been a renewed interest among philosophers in the socializing effects of family, school, community, religion, civic associations, and the like, as agencies for inculcating the virtues.

Conspicuous by its absence from this list is one of the major institutions of our society—the market. There is a long tradition, going back to Aristotle, of viewing commerce as hostile to the virtues. (I will call the adherents of this tradition the "pessimists"). In this view, the market is held to have legitimated the pursuit of narrow self-interest at the expense of social and civic obligations and moral restraints. But ... many Enlightenment moralists saw commercial society as a moralizing force. (I will call the Enlightenment and its heirs the "optimists"). Which view is right? Does the market subvert or strengthen the virtues which it depends on for its own smooth functioning? What sort of character traits does the market reward—and so, presumably, reinforce and diffuse through society? Do these traits undermine or support the operation of the market and liberal political institutions?

THE MARKET ACCORDING TO THE PESSIMISTS

For pessimists on both the left and the right, the market has long been an object of suspicion. One recurring concern is that the market frees individual acquisitiveness from moral, social and/or religious constraints. While this acquisitiveness can be a source of great energy and creativity, it is also a turbulent, disruptive, and potentially disintegrative force. Moreover, the market is believed to contain an expansionary dynamic, so that unless it is contained it progressively invades and colonizes other spheres of our social lives. The charges against the market are almost as old as capitalism itself, if not older.

- It releases self-interest from moral restraints.
- It erodes all social ties other than purely economic ones and/or converts social relationships into instrumental ones ("commodifies" them).
- It promotes a preoccupation with narrow individual advantage at the expense of responsibility to the community or social obligations.
- It substitutes competition for voluntary cooperation.
- It favors materialistic or hedonistic values.

In the past, various social institutions have served to restrain the expression of self-interest, and to direct it into socially constructive channels. But most of these institutions—the Protestant ethic, religious belief, the bourgeois virtues, a social morality, etc.—have become enfeebled or are being systematically weakened by the spread of the market. The upshot is, in Alasdair MacIntyre's memorable phrase, that "Modern society is indeed often, at least in surface appearance, nothing but a collection of strangers, each pursuing his or her own interests under minimal constraints."

Part of the reason for the revival of interest in the virtues may be the perceived need for some counterweight to the disintegrating effects of the market. On this view, the function of the virtues is to counteract the disruptive effects of the market on society and economy. They moderate the expression of self-interest, mark its boundaries, exact respect for the legitimate interests of others, harness it to serve collective ends, propose a range of legitimate aspirations and goals for it, mitigate its results in the interests of fairness, insist on standards of fair-dealing, teach self-restraint, and so on. In short, the virtues civilize or domesticate the turbulent passion of self-interest.

However, the more completely a society has come to be dominated by market relations, the weaker will be its capacity to foster the virtues. So it is necessary to carve out sanctuaries from the market—such as family, school, church, community—where the virtues can be nurtured. A representative statement of this view is Gertrude Himmelfarb's: "In Britain and America, more and more conservatives are returning to an older Burkean tradition, which appreciates the material advantages of a free market economy (Edmund Burke himself was a disciple of Adam Smith) but also recognizes that such an economy does not automatically produce the moral and social goods that they value—that it may even subvert those goods. For the promotion of moral values, conservatives have always looked to individuals, families, churches, communities, and all the other voluntary associations [Alexis de] Tocqueville saw as the genius of American society."

THE SELF-DESTRUCTION THESIS

It is not just the moral foundations of the *good society* that are undermined by the market; so are the moral foundations of the *market* itself. This is the thesis of Fred Hirsch's influential book *Social Limits to Growth*. For Hirsch, the efficient working of the market itself depends on certain aspects of social morality, but this social morality—which is a legacy of an earlier pre-industrial culture—is being weakened by what he calls "the full permeation of an individualistic calculus. As it becomes more socially respectable to pursue one's own individual self-interest, so it becomes increasingly difficult to persuade people that they should exercise restraint for the collective good.

What are the contents of this social morality? Hirsch identifies several "social virtues" which, he says, play a central role in the functioning of an individualistic, contractual economy: They are truth, trust, acceptance, restraint and obligation. Take the role played by trust. Without a well-founded expectation that others will voluntarily keep their promises the modern economy would grind to a halt. It rests on a foundation of trust, credit, handshakes, mutual confidence, and implicit commitments. Almost every transaction, even the most basic one, requires a degree of trust in the other party. "To put the matter in its simplest form,"

says Kenneth Arrow, "in almost every transaction, somebody gives up his valuable asset before he gets the other's; either the goods are given before the money or the money is given before the goods." Reliance on third-party enforcement (e.g., through the courts) to guarantee that promises are kept would simply be prohibitively expensive. In Arrow's words, "much business is done on the basis of verbal assurance. It would be too elaborate to try to get written commitments on every possible point."

This much is uncontroversial. But how do we ensure the supply of the requisite level of trust—and other virtues—to lubricate the workings of the market? While the virtues are functional for the system as a whole, they may put the individual who practices them at a disadvantage. Take R. M. Hare's hypothetical example of the baker who short-weights his loaves:

> It is to the individual trader's advantage to file a bit off his "pound" weight, provided that he can get away with it; and this will be so whatever the others do. If they remain honest, he will get more money for less bread; but if they do the same as he has, he will still get more money for less bread than if he had not filed down his "pound" weight. If everybody does it, or even just a few people, the market will start operating inefficiently and all will suffer. But all the same the dishonest will suffer less than the honest. How then are we to set about avoiding this decline of the market?

As Arrow says, "an ethical code, however much it may be in the interest of all, is ... not in the interest of any one firm. The code may be of value to the running of the system as a whole, it may be of value to all firms if all firms maintain it, and yet it will be to the advantage of any one firm to cheat....." Social cooperation makes everyone better off than they would be if everyone pursued his narrow self-interest; but each individual stands to benefit most if he is selfish while everyone else is virtuous.

In the language of the prisoner's dilemma, the virtuous actor gets the "sucker's payoff," or—to stick with our example of a moment ago—the "honest baker's payoff." (Actually, since virtue is supposed to be its own reward, the real payoff comes in the form of a warm glow of pleasure at having done the right thing). If the virtues are "dispositions that lead one to act in accordance with collective goals and in opposition to one's narrow self-interest," then (by our definition) being virtuous means passing up unethical opportunities for private gain. Other things equal, a firm (or individual) that is burdened by such scruples is presumably at a competitive disadvantage in the marketplace compared with a rival not laboring under such a burden. According to MacIntyre, it is notorious that "the cultivation of trustfulness, justice and courage will often, the world being what it contingently is, bar us from being rich or famous or powerful."

The result is that the normal operation of the market offers people powerful inducements to desert the virtues. If not by inclination, then in self defense, people find themselves compelled to conform to market norms of behavior. Truthfulness is subordinated to the single-minded pursuit of individual gain. Self-control is weakened by the lifting of the constraints of traditional morality, by the market's sanctioning of the pursuit of material rewards and gratification, and by the weakening of social ties that might discipline or temper the pursuit of

narrow self-interest. Concern for others is weakened by the market's legitimation of absorption with self and with selfish preoccupations, and then it is further diminished by the market's emphasis on competition. And so on.

In this way, the virtues that support the operation of the market are progressively being eroded by the operation of the market. To the extent that we can still rely on virtuous behavior to help the market work, that behavior is presumably the residue of an older, pre-capitalist moral and religious tradition. On this view, the market is living on borrowed time—and on borrowed virtues. In due course, the string will run out, the ethical capital will be depleted, and the moral foundations of the market will have been hollowed out. This view has been the source of repeated predictions of the collapse of capitalism under weight of its own contradictions.

THE MARKET ACCORDING TO THE OPTIMISTS

But is it in fact the case that the market depletes rather than replenishes its stock of virtues? ... [T]he claim that the virtues are eroded by contact with market society has not always been the dominant view. Eighteenth century observers expected market society to "generate as a by-product, or external economy, a more 'polished' human type—more honest, reliable, orderly, and disciplined, as well as more friendly and helpful, ever ready to find solutions to conflicts and a middle ground for opposed opinions." The virtues necessary for the functioning of the market "were confidently expected to be *generated*, rather than eroded, by the market, its practices and incentives."

How might the market generate or replenish its stock of virtues? One possibility that pessimists appear to have overlooked (or defined away) is that the virtues may not only be socially beneficial, but they may be a source of private economic benefits as well. Those who cultivate the virtues may be more successful in the marketplace. To the extent that is true, the normal operation of the market rewards—and so reinforces—the virtues. The pessimists appear to have ruled out this possibility by narrowly defining virtue as the disposition to act in the public interest and, if necessary, *against* one's own individual interest. Apparently, if a disposition to act in a particular way can be shown to be a source of private benefits, then it does not qualify as virtuous. The optimists don't set the bar so high. For them, honesty and fairness count as virtues irrespective of their consequences for those who practice them.

PUBLIC VIRTUES, PRIVATE BENEFITS?

Can the virtues be a source of private economic benefit? Or must they by their nature be a hindrance to worldly success? In the rest of this paper, I examine the case for optimism. I begin with two of the virtues that Fred Hirsch identified as critical to the functioning of the market, namely honesty (which I will call trustworthiness) and self-control. Then I add two others to the list, namely, sympathy and fairness. (I pass over a number of other virtues: Industry and inventiveness because there is general agreement that they are fostered by the market, and justice because even partisans of the market are divided over whether it generates just outcomes.) Are these virtues, that lubricate the workings of a market economy, moral "inputs" from extra-capitalist sources? Or are they endogenous to the market?

Trustworthiness: Why do people keep their promises? According to Hirsch, "[t]he point is that conventional, mutual standards of honesty and trust are public goods that are necessary inputs for much of economic output." But, two centuries earlier, Adam Smith located the source of promise keeping squarely in self-interest, and he provided the classic explanation of how it is generated:

> This is not at all to be imputed to national character as some pretend. It is far more reducible to self-interest, that general principle that regulates the action of every man, and which leads men to act in a certain manner from views of advantage.... Where people seldom deal with one another, we find that they are somewhat disposed to cheat, because they can gain more by a smart trick than they can lose by the injury which it does to their character [i.e., reputation]... Whenever dealings are frequent a man does not expect to gain so much by any one contract as by probity and punctuality in the whole, and a prudent dealer, who is sensible of his real interest, would rather choose to lose what he has a right to than give any ground for suspicion...

On this account, then, we do not need to have recourse to a supposed moral legacy, etc., to explain the prevalence of trustworthiness in market economies. The principal sanction that holds dishonesty in check is not a residue of pre-capitalist morality, nor is it any penalty the courts might exact. Instead, it is the loss of business that would follow the damage to the business person's reputation. A reputation for being trustworthy will create business opportunities;

conversely, even a whiff of suspicion of untrustworthiness may cut off such opportunities. People will seek out persons with a reputation for honesty because the alternative—writing contracts comprehensive enough to protect their rights in all conceivable states of the world, and then monitoring compliance with the terms of the contracts—is prohibitively expensive.

If the pessimists were right, we would expect to see a secular decline in the general level of trust, as the religious belief in which it is rooted has grown weaker under the relentless pressure of the market. But there is no evidence of any such trend. Trust is pervasive in our business culture, despite occasional well-publicized violations of the norm. Every year brokers trade some $40 trillion worth of securities on the basis of telephone calls, with very little fraud or cheating. Indeed, as Adam Smith noted in another famous passage, trustworthiness is a distinctively bourgeois virtue, rather than a legacy from the pre-market era: "Wherever commerce is introduced in any country probity and punctuality always accompany it.... When the greater part of people are merchants they always bring probity and punctuality into fashion, and these are the principal virtues of commercial nations." Far from being inherited from feudal times, care in the timely payment of debts and loyalty to superiors were both "points of striking weakness in the aristocratic code."

Self-Control: Trustworthiness, in its turn, presupposes another virtue that enlightenment thinkers associated with the market—self control. What, after all, is promise-keeping if not the ability or disposition to pass up an immediate advantage or pleasure or gratification?

That explains why, for Adam Smith, "self-command is not only itself a great virtue, but from it all the other virtues seem to derive their principal lustre." Self-control does not involve a trade-off between self-interest and the public interest. Rather from the individual's point of view, the trade-off is strictly one between short-term self-interest and long-term self-interest. We teach our children self-control knowing that it is critical to their own success and happiness and personal adjustment. Even opportunists tacitly acknowledge the truth of this proposition. As Robert Frank points out, they let their own children be taught moral values. "Why don't they instead teach them to cooperate only when it is in their narrow interests, and to behave opportunistically otherwise?," he wonders.

Sympathy: In a market, the fortunes or livelihoods of economic agents depend on successfully meeting the needs of others. To the extent that what Adam Smith called "sympathy"—or what we might call empathy—helps us to anticipate those needs, it contributes to economic success. "It is in a firm's interest to avoid putting features into a produce which are not regarded as useful by customers." Firms make huge investments in trying to forecast how other people will react to new product features, stock offerings, pricing or styling changes, etc. Smith knew, as Patricia Werhane notes, that "sympathy is indirectly linked to self-interest because it might be in our self-interest to understand the passions of others." Accordingly, while sympathy may not be *reducible* to self-interest or selfishness, it is likely that participation in the market develops and reinforces the capacity to share the feelings or emotions of others. Moreover, even where sympathy is lacking, repeated personal contacts are likely to generate some minimal level of courtesy between the parties—to soften or polish manners: "The market promotes civility because commercial success depends on the courteous treatment of people who have the option of taking their business elsewhere."

Fairness: Like the other virtues we have considered, a reputation for fairness is likely to create business opportunities. Since it is next to impossible to regulate a complex, ongoing transaction by means of a written contract, parties will prefer to restrict their business to others whom they can rely on not to take advantage of them if circumstances change drastically. By limiting their business to such people, they can realize considerable savings in transaction costs. They are spared the costs of attorneys, auditors and inspectors, and others. As Stewart Macaulay puts it, based on his observation of actual business practice, disputes between businesses "are frequently settled without reference to the contract or potential or actual legal sanctions. There is a hesitancy to speak of legal rights or to threaten to sue in these negotiations...." Or, as one businessman put it, "You can settle any dispute if you keep the lawyers and the accountants out of it. They just do not understand the give-and-take needed in business."

On this account, the virtues are not (just) public goods—that is, unrequited gifts to society—but are a source of private advantage in the marketplace. And, as Robert Solomon has pointed out, "[t]he virtues on which one prides oneself in one's 'personal' life are essentially the same as those essential to good business."

...[S]elf-interest and virtue are closely intertwined, but they are not the same thing. Self-interest may provide the initial impetus to the (conscious or unconscious) choice to cultivate a virtue, and it may provide subsequent reinforcement in the form of the economic returns to that investment. But in due course much of the satisfaction from exercising the virtue is intrinsic: "Virtue is not learned by precept,... it is learned by the regular repetition of the right actions. We are induced to do the right thing with respect to small matters, and in time we persist in doing the right thing because now we have come to take pleasure in it." Tocqueville's account of the process can't be improved upon:

> The principle of self-interest rightly understood produces no great acts of self-sacrifice, but it suggests daily small acts of self-denial. By itself it cannot suffice to make a man virtuous; but it disciplines a number of persons in habits of regularity, temperance, foresight, self-command; and if it does not lead men straight to virtue by the will, it gradually draws them in that direction by their habits. If the principle of interest rightly understood were to sway the whole moral world, extraordinary virtues would doubtful be more rare; but I think that gross depravity would then also be less common.

CONCLUSION

Typically we view institutions like family, church, community, and school itself, as schools of the virtues; we are unaccustomed to thinking of the market that way. If anything, the marketplace is seen as a source of the snares and delusions that threaten to tempt people to stray from the straight and narrow path of the virtues.

In contrast, I have suggested that many of the character traits that we commonly call virtues are rewarded by the market. Therefore participation in the market may inculcate values and dispositions that make us better citizens—as well as better colleagues, suppliers, employers or employees, and so on. By reinforcing these character traits, the market (as it were by a hidden hand) strengthens its own foundations and reproduces a moral culture that is functional to its own needs.

NO

Bill Shaw

SOURCES OF VIRTUE: THE MARKET AND THE COMMUNITY

INTRODUCTION

Virtue is understood in the Aristotelian tradition that claims "happiness" to be the chief good, and excellence of character to be both a component of the good and a means of obtaining it over a lifetime.

The Aristotelian notion of virtue is not the only such notion alive and well in the world. There is nothing to preclude utilitarians from claiming that virtue is the propensity to advance "the greatest good for the greatest number," or Kantians from collapsing virtue into the habit of rule obedience. Some speak of patrician, plebeian, and mercantile or bourgeois virtues, and there is no particularly good reason why these writers can't give virtue their own unique spin.

I want to say, however, that I have in mind none of those conceptions of virtue. I think of virtue in the tradition of Aristotle, that is, in the tradition that claims "happiness" to be the chief good, and excellence of character to be both a component of that good and a means of achieving it over a lifetime. This project, then, examines behaviors that some writers advance as "market virtues" and asks whether they are in any unique or meaningful sense "generated" by the market. It concludes that certain traditional virtues are consistent with the market, but that these virtues are not "market generated."

THE MARKET AND THE GOOD

This section attempts to convey an understanding of the "good for mankind" in a way that encompasses the "market;" to warn that an overemphasis on the market/material wealth as a guide fosters opportunism; and to question Professor [Ian] Maitland's thesis that the market generates virtue.

As a preliminary inquiry, one may ask, "Why bother with the virtues or virtue ethics theory, if there is no definitive sense of the good for the virtues to rally around?" After all, happiness, flourishing, fulfillment—the telos, or the aim and objective of Aristotelian virtue—are capable of being interpreted

From Bill Shaw, "Sources of Virtue: The Market and the Community," *Business Ethics Quarterly* (January 1997). Copyright © 1997 by The Society for Business Ethics. Reprinted by permission. Notes omitted.

in different ways and of being achieved in different ways. If the components of the good can't be nailed down, or advanced with compelling reasons, how are we to know what's virtue and what's a vice?

To put it another way, if the aim and attributes of baseball were to disappear, what would be the virtue in strategy or team play? Roger Clemens could still hurl a fastball in the high 90's, but so what? A machine, if anyone was interested, could do it even faster. There would, of course, be a place in the new world order for throwing a baseball, and running from 3rd to home. We all need some form of exercise, but it wouldn't be quite the same. We'd look back nostalgically at the pastimes of our grandparents, but we'd have other pastimes, "cyber-pastimes."

Consider a different example. What if the values associated with marriage and family were to evaporate? Would loyalty, trust, sharing and caring be virtues? If we said good-bye to marriage, we could still have kids and raise them, but something important would be different. We wouldn't have those bonds of marriage. We'd have freedom, and we could use that freedom to create new bonds, or not, as we chose.

Out with the old, in with the new! Out with the old order—the classical, aristocratic, Aristotelian order that held sway through St. Thomas and the medieval period. In with the new, the modern, the now!

An important component of the new, as we understand it today, is the market. Virtue ethicists clearly acknowledge that reality, and understand it to be a component of the good. Adam Smith, a virtue ethicist himself, would be justly proud of the successes that the market has registered. At the same time he might show some concern that the "propensity

to truck, bargain, and exchange" has gotten the better of us, or at least of those characterized by the dominant economic paradigm as "O's," "opportunists" or "self-interested preference maximizers."

These "O's," for purposes of this essay, will represent single dimensioned, rational "choosers" who evaluate all decisions on the way in which those decisions foster the choosers' interests. This paradigm flourishes most efficiently in an atmosphere of maximal freedom, or one in which external, social restraints do not greatly diminish the range of the individual chooser's preferences. This loosening, if not loss, of community ties is what concerns "pessimists" the most.

Economists are constrained from linking this model with the social ties of trust, friendliness, and sociability that characterize a strong sense of community because of their affection for the ideal market, for "perfect competition."

> The economists' claims of allocative efficiency and all-round welfare maximization are strictly valid only for this market. Involving large numbers of price-taking anonymous buyers and sellers supplied with perfect information, such markets function without any prolonged human or social contact among or between the parties. Under perfect competition there is no room for bargaining, negotiations, remonstration or mutual adjustment and the various operators that contract together need not enter into recurrent or continuing relationships as a result of which they would get to know each other well.

For a different set of reasons, Aristotle had little appreciation for economics or for wealth producing merchants, bankers, and people of commerce. But at least he recognized them as real people, people with hopes and dreams and human failings that go along with that sort of thing—not a single "O" among them. Adam Smith wrote in the post-Enlightenment era, and there are few things about his culture that resemble the polis of Aristotle's day, but Smith also thought and wrote about real flesh-and-blood people, people with "moral sentiments."

In any event, economic exchange in a free global market is regarded today as a good, though not an unmixed good. This makes it of special interest because the market produces particular kinds of people as well as particular kinds of goods. What, then, are the implications for virtue ethics? Shall we speak now of "market virtues," and, if so, what is the relation of these virtues to the Aristotelian tradition.

In "Virtuous Markets: The Market As School of the Virtues," Professor Ian Maitland finds the market to be a creator of virtue, and he criticizes a collection of modern "pessimists" who see the market as something of a parasite that feeds upon a pre-capitalist accumulation of virtue.

[T]he virtues that support the operation of the market are progressively being eroded by the operation of the market. To the extent that we can still rely on virtuous behavior to help the market work, that behavior is presumably the residue of an older moral and religious tradition. On this view, the market is living on borrowed time—and on borrowed virtues. In due course, the string will run out, the ethical capital will be depleted, and the moral foundations hollowed out.

Professor Maitland might also have linked Adam Smith to that collection of pessimists. In Smith's view, we draw goods from a pool of "happinesses" that is the product of our religious tradition.

This essay re-examines the Maitland thesis. In doing to I will assume that he attributes to the market some unique role in generating virtue, that is, something beyond merely saying that "on the road of life, we learn from our experiences." This paper concludes that virtues will foster economic well being, though not the efficiency-bent, wealth-maximizing economy that some theorists envision. Virtue stems from an internal source, that is, from the excellence of character that has long been acknowledged as the distinctive feature of virtue in the Aristotelian tradition. Not all efficiency-producing behaviors are virtuous. The reason is that virtuous behavior is identified with, and advances, a balanced and coherent notion of the good, and economic well being is only part of that good, not its entirety. If follows, then, that virtuous behavior may advance some non-material aspect of the good even though that behavior is not efficient in an economic sense. For example, the virtue of justice may impede or prohibit certain ways of producing material goods....

THE IMPACT OF THE MARKET ON VIRTUE ETHICS

This section reviews some of the reasons that virtue ethics gave way to rule-based ethics during the Enlightenment and the emergence of the free market.

If the Enlightenment, and the recognition of human freedom and self-consciousness, can be said to begin with Descartes (1596–1650), then the initial stages of the Industrial Revolution must be linked with James Watt's steam engine, 1755, and classical economics with the publication of Adam Smith's great work, *The Wealth of Nations*, 1776. One need not even mention the great impetus that the

American and French revolutions gave to these liberating events to convey the sense that the last 300 years have been busily about the task of removing obstacles set upon the emergence of human freedom by the Church, the State, and related cultural institutions and beliefs.

In retrospect, then, it comes as no shock to learn that the ethical tone of the middle years—the ethics of the Scholastics who expanded upon St. Thomas's interpretation of Aristotle—was deemed scarcely fitting in temper or in spirit for the modern era. Nor is it surprising that Enlightenment observers would expect, or at least hope for, a market society that would produce.

[A] more "polished" human type—more honest, reliable, orderly, and disciplined, as well as more friendly and helpful, ever ready to find solutions to conflicts and a middle ground for opposed opinions.

Professor Maitland's position is consistent with Hirschman on this point, and that is true as well for his view that virtues "were confidently expected to be generated, rather than eroded, by the market, its practices and incentives." Given the deprivations of the middle period—the poverty, the plagues, and the pettiness of Popes and monarchs—why shouldn't they look forward with hope? The question is whether the market delivered on these hopes, and if it did not, why not?

Kant, and later Mill, were the principal Enlightenment voices of freedom and morality. An ethics of duty, articulated by Kant, launched the view that human reason revealed a basic moral touchstone (the categorical imperative) and that the moral worth of one's intentions and efforts were to be judged in accordance with this standard.

By contrast, Mill, in rough agreement with Bentham, imagined the world populated by sensible creatures under the twin forces of pleasure and pain. Mill and Bentham were not in accord with one another on the components of pleasure/pain, and that continues to be one of the troubling features of utilitarianism, but they did advance the view that a person should act in such a way as to produce, in the aggregate, "the greatest good for the greatest number."

Freedom, then, was the hallmark of the Enlightenment, and with that freedom, moral responsibility. One must be guided by a sense of duty, or by a commitment to produce outcomes that optimize utility. In contrast with virtue ethics, you cannot help but notice, neither of these approaches require a morally virtuous person to be at the helm. In other words, one does not have to be a person of excellent moral character to act on the basis of the categorical imperative or to act in a way that optimizes utility.

Virtue ethics is more complete in this regard. It represents a way of living one's life rather than a way of resolving moral dilemmas. Living one's life requires decisions and choices and judgments to be made, so virtue ethics has that mental element, but it is not solely an intellectual enterprise. It fuses the rational and emotional elements of one's being. The rational keeps the emotional elements within proper bounds, and the emotions support and reinforce the rational elements with the appropriate attitude towards one's project and the appropriate stability for reflection and judgment.

For example, the emotion of anger, focused on some acknowledged evil (fraud and other intentional wrongdoing, reckless and negligent conduct), but kept within bounds by reason, can set the proper attitude toward that evil, and fuel the determination to combat it. This attitude, this level-headedness, fosters rational reflection and judgment and, maybe, success in one's project.

Be that as it may, from the Enlightenment to the Modern area, and for reasons suggested above, virtue ethics lost its hold on the mainstream. Not all of the reasons for this were economic in nature, but many of them were. Rules—rules based on duty or on utility—were the order of the day. And it is principally obedience to these rules, rules identified with certain behavioral norms, that Professor Maitland characterizes as virtues. A close reading of his text will support this conclusion.

MAITLAND AND MARKET VIRTUES

This section examines Professor Maitland's view on trustworthiness, self-control, sympathy, and fairness.

Professor Maitland attributes to undesignated, but pessimistic, writes the view that a disposition or propensity does not qualify as virtuous if it is shown to be a source of private benefit. He continues,

> "The pessimists have ruled out this possibility [the possibility of a virtue resulting in a private benefit] by narrowly defining virtue as the disposition to act in the public interest and against one's own personal interest."

Ironically, Adam Smith, upon whom Professor Maitland relies quite heavily in the development of his thesis, had something quite different to say about the sacrifice of one's personal interest:

> "[T]he wise and virtuous man is at all times willing that his own private interest be sacrificed to the public interest of his own particular order or society."

Pessimism may well be the attitude of the writers that Professor Maitland has in mind, but observe how far that position is from the Aristotelian tradition that links (in a sense even fuses) social and personal interests. Aristotle characterizes our species as "social animals," and claims that the full potential of individuals so constituted can only be reached in a community with good laws. The various roles that are taken on by citizens of such a community, and the excellences or virtues that advance a person's performance of those roles, may on occasion call for the sacrifice of personal well being, but that is a far cry from putting self and social interest into a state of conflict or turmoil.

For the most part, the intense personal interest and satisfaction in doing one's job well, or performing one's role in an exemplary manner, is exactly in accord with the social or community interest. There may be times in the lives of some military people, members of the clergy, physicians, public servants, and, of course, of some parents, where unusual sacrifices are called for, but that does not dominate the day-to-day unfolding of their lives. It may even be the case that the challenges of those roles are the very "spice" that attracts certain people to choose them. If that is the case, it is clearly in the Aristotelian tradition of linking the public and the private, the social and the personal.

If Professor Maitland is to chide anyone for narrowly defining virtue, he should proceed with extreme caution on this point. It is, after all, Professor Maitland himself who is linking favored behaviors with the efficient production of material goods, and calling those behaviors virtues. He does this even though those behaviors may not induce, or instill, the excellence of character that is historically identified with virtue, and even though economic good is not the whole of good.

The behaviors he applauds are applaudable for their productivity enhancing features. From an economics perspective, these behaviors reduce transaction costs, support voluntary compliance with promises, and produce efficiency. But there is not evidence at all that they are done for their own sake, or that they advance anything other than a narrow, material conception of the good, or that they would be done at all except for the economic pay-off. This is not an argument that virtuous activity must be in opposition to market efficiency; it is an argument that a reduction of the good too a single focus on market efficiency will not generate virtue as Professor Maitland supposes.

Professor Maitland's essay examines trustworthiness, self-control, sympathy, and fairness, in that order. I will revisit his arguments on trustworthiness and critique them in some detail. For reasons that I will subsequently relate to you, I do not believe that he has proved his case. As it turns out, the position I take in opposition to Professor Maitland as he develops his thesis on self-control, sympathy, and fairness will be variations on my original argument, so my response will be brief but, I hope, equally compelling.

Trustworthiness: The first of the four advanced by Professor Maitland is anchored by a source no less eminent than Adam Smith. In this view, trustworthiness and promise keeping are strongly linked to self-interest, though not to the virulent self-interest of the opportunist. Self-interest in Smith is mediated and contained by "fellow-feeling", "sympathy." This amounts to the capacity to swap places with the other guy, to tune-in on another's wave-length, and, in some sense, to be directed and guided by that imaginative experience.

Smith is not making the empirical claim that business people are in fact trustworthy or do keep their promises. If that were the case, you would have to wonder about the grounds that would support such a claim, particularly in view of the fact that the market he put such great confidence in was not yet a reality. Giving credit where credit is due, however, it looks as if Adam Smith anticipated the positive effects of extended game-plays, that is, repeated plays of the "prisoner's dilemma." Trustworthiness or promise keeping is

> [r]educible to self-interest, that general principle that regulates the action of every man, and which leads men to act in a certain manner from views of advantage.... Where people seldom deal with one another, we find that they are somewhat disposed to cheat, because they can gain more by a smart trick than they can lose by the injury which it does to their character.... Whenever dealings are frequent a man does not expect to gain so much by any one contract as by probity and punctuality in the whole, and a prudent dealer, who is sensible of his real interest, would rather choose to lose what he has a right to than give any ground for suspicion....

There is not much question that games can teach virtue. In fact, that may be the most frequent and effective way of doing it. Games can teach friendliness, fairness, cooperativeness, loyalty, reliability and probably many other virtues. But that doesn't mean that successful game players are necessarily virtuous. A person has to want the right things, for the right reasons, and to their right degree to be virtuous.

A prudent game player, one successful at repeated plays of the "prisoner's dilemma," may learn no more about cooperation than that it's the only way to get what he wants. "Tit-for-tat," the most successful strategy one can employ in this endeavor, is no more than that . . . a successful strategy. It's a rule that anyone can follow. And it's a rule that a person will follow if that person is prudent in the sense that Professor Maitland here employs.

In the Aristotelian tradition, virtues can't be reduced to rules like that. Game players such as those above would be regarded as merely "clever."

> Prudence is not to be confused with a simple faculty for seeing what means will bring about a given end. Aristotle denominates that particular faculty cleverness and holds that it is morally neutral, since it is of equal use to the man who pursues praiseworthy and to the man who pursues blameworthy ends.

Virtue ethics focused on excellence, specifically, on excellence of character as a means of fostering the good. A prudent person, one who deliberates well, would have in mind not only one's own good, but that of others as well. And for reasons sufficient to a person like that, "tit-for-tat" may be judged to be an awful way of teaching virtue, a terrible way of fostering the good. Certain game strategies may result in high profits, but that profit need not be seen by the virtuous person as the best way of advancing the good.

There is no way just now of exposing all of the reasons a person may have for thinking that, but one of those reasons could be that money and material success just aren't that important. Maybe being a good character, being a role model, being an example or a mentor is more important than maximizing material outcomes.

To turn that around just a little bit, who is to say that being a good character is not more important than being clever, more important than maximizing profit, or more important than being prudent in the game playing sense? Or, one might productively speculate, what would it take to show that it is not reasonable to elevate character above these other considerations? Or, what would serve as a compelling basis for the view that "tit-for-tat" should be employed even on those occasions when some other response is a better way of producing virtue and the good?

In the "prudent dealer/prisoner's dilemma" passage above, Professor Maitland identifies Adam Smith's notion of prudence with rule-following. Alasdair MacIntyre does the same, and so, evidently, does Adam Smith himself, "The man who acts according to the rules of perfect prudence, of strict justice, and of proper benevolence, may be said to be perfectly virtuous." This doesn't mean that prudence is not a virtue as Adam Smith defines virtue, it only means that, in the Smithian sense, and in the sense adopted by Professor Maitland, it is not a particularly noble or uplifting one.

Quite aside from that, however, has Professor Maitland advanced his thesis that the market generates virtue? If all he has to demonstrate is the self-evident proposition that "a good reputation is good business," then I think the point would be too uninteresting to dwell upon. It seems he would have to show that the reputation is solid and well earned, that it is the product of the engagement in market transactions (as opposed, for example, to an Aristotelian description of a good upbringing, good family, school, laws and so forth), and, finally, that he has not left us with a "Gyges Ring" illusion in which the reputation is a pure fabrication, and good in the "Madison Avenue" sense only.

For whatever reasons, though perhaps in light of some of these considerations, Professor Maitland has reduced his claim to a minimum. In place of a stronger thesis, for example, that honesty per se is rewarded by the market, he claims only that "In most cases being honest is good business. In that case, trustworthiness... is a source of private advantage in the marketplace."

In those cases in which being honest and trustworthy would not be a source of private advantage, he emphatically does not mean to imply that one is entitled to violate those norms.... But the alternative is that one must sacrifice "private advantage" in order to remain honest, and that would involve him in a contradiction. He would then have to join those much-belittled "pessimists," the very group that he has undertaken to rebut because, as you will recall, pessimists (including Adam Smith) define "virtue as the disposition to act in the public interest and against one's own individual interest."

Too much virtue...? Professor Maitland introduces us to a piece of evidence that seems hardly capable of supporting its own weight.

The market seems to be as threatened by a surplus of trust as it is by a deficit of it. Too much trust—in the wrong hands—may just as easily subvert the workings of the market.

Price fixing, conspiracy, bribery, collusion, and inside trading are then named as the downside of too much trust. People who fit this description come closer to resembling felons, or at the least opportunists, than any other human profile I can imagine. If, indeed, there is "honor among thieves", then such behavior is not recognized as virtuous in the Aristotelian tradition. To the contrary, base things cannot be done virtuously.

Finally, Professor Maitland scarcely helps his case by citing the securities industry as good evidence that the market generates virtue. Even if the excesses of the 1980's could be put out of mind, and if we could start with an unbiased perspective, there is no way to "factor out" the force of law, and to conclude with any degree of confidence, that legal compliance is not mainly attributable to the threat of criminal sanctions rather than to the internal generation of market virtue. In any event, I regard this as an empirical question, and, having no way at hand to test the matter, I leave it to Professor Maitland to go forward with his proofs.

Self-control: My observations upon Professor Maitland's characterization of self-control as a virtue is simply that his claim is unsupported. "Trustworthiness," he relates, "presupposes another virtue that enlightenment thinkers associated with the market—self control.... That explains why, for Adam Smith 'self-command is not only itself a great virtue, but from it all the other virtues seem to derive their principal lustre.' "

Smith added self-command in the 6th edition of *The Theory of Moral Sentiments* shortly before his death in 1790.

It is that trait of discipline and order that controls these passions that tend either toward excessive fear and anger... or toward excessive ease, pleasure, applause, and self-gratification. In short, self-command is that personal quality of strength of mind and temperance that one relies upon to regulate the selfish passions.

The Smithian virtue of self-command counsels one to forego the easiest and most tempting short-cut to some pleasurable objective, and face up to the task of "paying one's dues." "How do you get to Carniege Hall? Practice, practice, practice." Again, the questions for Professor Maitland are "does the market teach this, and, if it does, where is the evidence?"

In the previous section, I represented that Professor Maitland was not forthcoming with evidence that the market taught prudence, and I find myself repeating that allegation. Perhaps I should give evidence of my own that the market does not generate virtue as he claims. The Journal of Business Ethics recently published the results of the Treadway Commission (headed by James Treadway, former SEC commissioner) study, and reported in The Wall Street Journal.

After getting nearly 400 people (more than 85% of them men) over the past seven years to play the role of a fictional exec... 47% of the top executives, 41% of the controllers, and 76% of the graduate level business students... were willing to commit fraud by understating write-offs that cut into their companies' profits.

Such behavior isn't just the stuff of academic experiments. Failure to properly report write-offs is one of the most common types of fraud investigated by the SEC... [It was] ruled late last year that the Bank of Boston had neglected to write down its deteriorating real-estate loan portfolio, making its earnings look better than they were.

University of Texas at Austin Management professor Janet Dukerich, one of the four researchers, believes the results of the study may be conservative rather than overstated. Participants in the study "didn't really have their jobs on the line," she observed. The implication being, if jobs were on the line, the results could look much worse.

Now then, I don't offer this study to prove that business people can never learn virtue from their experiences in business, but that Professor Maitland has yet to show that business experience offers something unique in this regard.

Sympathy: If sympathy is to be counted as a virtue, it is not one that Professor Maitland will be able to ground in Aristotle or in Adam Smith. After citing Werhane for the proposition that "sympathy is indirectly linked to self-interest," he might also have noted her extended elaboration on the same page.

But... Smith makes clear in the *Theory of Moral Sentiments* that sympathy entails genuine fellow feeling not connected with selfishness or self-interest or, indeed, with any passion at all. Thus he would not want to derive sympathy from self-interest, and such a move would be contrary to his criticism of Hobbes for making a similar suggestion.

...Werhane further details her view of Smith.

When we sympathize we place ourselves in another's situation, not because of how that situation might affect us, but, rather, as if we were that person in that situation. We truly project ourselves into another's experience... in order to understand—although not experience—what another person is feeling rather than merely to relate that situation to our own. Sympathy is the comprehension of what another feels or might feel in a situation, but it is not an experiential or sentimental identification with that feeling. With the help of imagination, sympathy is the means through which we place ourselves in another's situation and conceive of what another feels, experiences, or is capable of feeling in a particular situation or set of circumstances.

Rather than a virtue, then, sympathy is a capacity, something comparable to a method or procedure, that allows one to exercise the imaginative ability to put oneself in another's position.

This is not an argument that the display toward others of genuine sympathy, contrasted with some postured or hypocritical version, won't gain one some kind of economic advantage. Further, it is not an argument that Professor Maitland can't characterize sympathy as a virtue if he wants to. It is, however, a reminder that there is no support for sympathy as a virtue in Adam Smith's practically-oriented, living in the world virtues, or in Aristotle's excellencies focused on achieving his projected telos, the good for mankind.

Fairness: Professor Maitland doesn't advance any grounds at all for fairness as a virtue or show how the market might generate it. It goes without saying, and I certainly don't disagree, that "a reputation for fairness is likely to create business opportunities." But one may as well say that life presents a number of trials and tribulations and

that a reputation for fairness, deserved or underserved, will help one to overcome those problems. However, if the market does not possess some unique capacity for developing virtue, if it doesn't provide some special training ground, or offer challenges of a nature that cannot be found or replicated in any other setting, then Professor Maitland has hardly advanced his case that the market generates virtue.

Professor Maitland does bring to one's attention the observation that a reputation for fairness may produce a savings in transaction costs, and that further savings might ensue if "lawyers and accountants" can be kept out of disputes. If that correlation is valid, one could build an argument that a hard-earned reputation for fairness is sort of a "waste-saving device," that it advances efficiency in the production of material goods, that material goods are an important component of the good for mankind, and that by serving as good role models in the business community, men and women of excellent character can actually teach virtue by example, and that, over time, this will actually produce virtue in the Aristotelian sense.

If these things follow, then Professor Maitland must be credited with suggesting the groundwork for their development. It remains for him to demonstrate, however, how the market is unique in this regard. After all, waste and inefficiency are scarcely valued in any endeavor, whether it be running a household, a school, theater, a military, or a government.

CONCLUSION

Professor Maitland has not shown that the market creates virtue as that concept is understood in the Aristotelian tradition.

In fairness to Professor Maitland, he has persuasively argued that there are certain rules of behavior—an ethical bottom line—that must be observed if the market is to function efficiently. Further, if he wants to call these behavior virtues, then he can do that.

However, if he wanted to argue that these behaviors were virtues in the Aristotelian tradition, he would have to show much more than he has shown in his essay, "Virtuous Markets: The Market as School of the Virtues." He would have to show the importance of material well-being to a conception of the good, and further that a market economy is a viable means of generating material goods, that material goods do not automatically "trump" non-material goods, that the relative importance and distribution of material and non-material goods is determined by the values and traditions of a particular society, that certain excellencies of character (virtues) habituate or incline people to foster material and non-material goods, and, in doing so, these virtues bring about the sort of fulfillment, flourishing, happiness that is understood to constitute the whole of the good.

On reflection, then, it does not appear that he has demonstrated his thesis, namely, that the market is a school of the virtues. This doesn't mean that he couldn't do it, and he is certainly on the right track as he closes his essay with an observation consistent with the Aristotelian tradition, "Virtue is not learned by precept... it is learned by the regular repetition of the right actions."

POSTSCRIPT
Does the Market Teach Us Virtue?

The traditional approach to ensuring ethical behavior in business is the imposition of regulations aimed at compelling business to act in the public interest. This approach, known as "command and control," is very expensive because it requires recruiting a whole team of bureaucrats to enforce it. Is there a better way? Some writers have tried to enlist the Aristotelian notion of virtue in the search for answers to the problems of recurrent ethical failure. Can corporations be persuaded to encourage goodness amongst themselves and their employees? Should they?

SUGGESTED READINGS

Robert Axelrod, *The Evolution of Cooperation* (Basic Books, 1984).
Daniel Bell, *The Cultural Contradictions of Capitalism* (Basic Books, 1976).
Sumantra Ghoshal and Peter Moran, "Bad for Practice: A Critique of the Transaction Cost Theory," *Academy of Management Review* (vol. 21, 1996).
Gertrude Himmelfarb, "A De-moralized Society," *The Public Interest* (no. 117, 1994).
Albert O. Hirschman, *Rival Views of Market Society and Other Recent Essays* (Harvard University Press, 1992).
Irving Kristol, *Two Cheers for Capitalism* (Basic Books, 1978).
Alasdair MacIntyre, *After Virtue* (Notre Dame Press, 1981).
Donald McClosdey, "Bourgeois Virtue," *The American Scholar* (vol. 63, 1994).
Jerry Z. Muller, *Adam Smith in His Time and Ours* (Free Press, 1993).
Paul Rubin, *Managing Business Transactions* (Free Press, 1990).
Bill Shaw and Janet McCracken, "Virtue Ethics and Contractarianism: Towards a Reconciliation," *Business Ethics Quarterly* (vol. 5, 1995).
Robert C. Solomon, *Ethics and Excellence* (Oxford University Press, 1992).

On the Internet . . .

http://www.dushkin.com

Institute for Business and Professional Ethics

In addition to providing information about the institute itself, this site also offers ethics links, professional resources, an online journal of ethics, and an ethics calendar. *http://www.depaul.edu/ethics/*

STAT-USA/Internet

This site, a service of the U.S. Department of Commerce, provides one-stop Internet browsing for business, trade, and economic information. It contains daily economic news, frequently requested statistical releases, information on export and international trade, domestic economic news and statistical series, and databases. *http://www.stat-usa.gov/stat-usa.html*

PART 2

Current Issues in Business

This section explores four topical issues in business, including two relatively new enterprises for business: the rapidly expanding medical field and the proliferation of casino gambling. The section closes with an issue on investing.

■ Are Business and Medicine Ethically Incompatible?

■ Are Pharmaceutical Price Controls Justifiable?

■ Should Casino Gambling Be Prohibited?

■ Are Financial Derivative Instruments Always a Gamble?

ISSUE 5

Are Business and Medicine Ethically Incompatible?

YES: Arnold S. Relman, from "What Market Values Are Doing to Medicine," *The Atlantic Monthly* (March 1992)

NO: Andrew C. Wicks, from "Albert Schweitzer or Ivan Boesky? Why We Should Reject the Dichotomy Between Medicine and Business," *Journal of Business Ethics* (vol. 14, 1995)

ISSUE SUMMARY

YES: Professor of medicine Arnold S. Relman argues that although doctors should not be businessmen, financial and technological pressures are forcing them to act like businessmen, with deleterious consequences for patients and for society as a whole.

NO: Andrew C. Wicks, an assistant professor at the University of Washington School of Business, challenges the perceived contrast between physician ethics and business ethics and suggests that a closer look will reveal fundamental similarities.

The heart of this issue may lie with the confusion between the two types of ethics involved: the *professional ethic* and the *market ethic*. The *professional,* or *fiduciary,* ethic, applicable to all professional-client relationships and all commercial fiduciary-beneficiary relationships, requires that the active party (professional or trustee) act *only in the interests of the other.* For example, doctors must act only in the interests of their patients, lawyers for their clients, pastors for their congregations (individually and collectively), and the managers of funds and trusts for those who have entrusted funds to them. By this ethic, boards of directors of publicly owned corporations must act only in the interests of the shareholders in the corporation.

The *market* ethic, in contrast, requires that each party protect *its own interests,* abstaining only from force and fraud as means to achieving an agreement. This adversarial ethic, best seen in labor negotiations and proceedings in a court of law, underlies the "voluntary transaction" on which the free market is based. The free market assumes a universe of rational free agents, each acting to maximize self-interest within a legal framework designed to protect the rights of all. Not all people fit that assumption—especially the very young, very old, sick, or disabled, or simply those who are very far away from the dealings—which is why there are fiduciary relationships.

The professional ethic of the physician is brief and simple, and it is reflected in the Hippocratic oath that is generally taken by those about to begin a medical practice:

> In whatsoever houses I enter, I will enter to help the sick, and I will abstain from all intentional wrongdoing and harm.... And whatsoever I shall see or hear in the course of my profession in my intercourse with men, if it be what should not be published abroad, I will never divulge, holding such things to be holy secrets. Now if I carry out this oath, and break it not, may I gain forever reputation among all men for my life and for my art.

There is much more to the oath than this, but the essence of the oath is as applicable now as it was 2,500 years ago when Hippocrates first established it; the essence is that the physician acts only for the benefit of the patient, attending to the patient's illnesses, comforting and reassuring him or her, tailoring diets and advice to the patient's particular case, and keeping her or his secrets in absolute confidence.

The relationship between the physician and the patient remained the same in the period between 500 B.C. and A.D. 1900. Sick people sought out healers, trusted their advice, often were helped by their ministrations, and, to the extent the patients were able, paid them for their services. In the twentieth century however, medicine began to be "professionalized": Licensing laws were established to eliminate quacks; legislation was enacted requiring licensed professionals to supervise a required professional education; professional organizations active in advancing the state of the art and protecting the professional image surfaced; and, generally, higher rates of reimbursement were charged by the physicians. Rapid advances in medical technology at midcentury sent medical costs beyond the reach of people with ordinary incomes and savings; third-party reimbursement—first from private insurers and then from the federal government (in the form of Medicare and Medicaid)—was introduced at the third quarter of the century and helped relieve the extraordinary burden on patients, but it also allowed the medical profession to prescribe ever more expensive technological cures, which sent health care costs through the roof.

As the twentieth century draws to a close, the consequences of these costs for the economy as a whole are becoming clear. "Cost-containment" measures that take medical care decisions out of the physician's private office and put them into the hands of corporate boards of health maintenance organizations (HMOs) and hospitals dominate medical progress at this point. But how does this affect the privacy aspect of the patient-physician relationship?

As you read these selections, ask yourself whether or not business is incompatible with the physician's ethic, as Arnold S. Relman seems to understand it. Does the reformulation proposed by Andrew C. Wicks make sense? Or do both writers miss the point? What do you see in the future for medical care in America?

YES

Arnold S. Relman

WHAT MARKET VALUES ARE DOING TO MEDICINE

From its earliest origins the profession of medicine has steadfastly held that physicians' responsibility to their patients takes precedence over their own economic interests. Thus the oath of Hippocrates enjoins physicians to serve only "for the benefit of the sick," and the oft-recited prayer attributed to Moses Maimonides, a revered physician of the twelfth century, asks God not to allow "thirst for profit" or "ambition for renown" to interfere with the physician's practice of his profession. In modern times this theme has figured prominently in many medical codes of ethics. The International Code of the World Medical Organization, for example, says that "a doctor must practice his profession uninfluenced by motives of profit." And in 1957, in its newly revised Principles of Medical Ethics, the American Medical Association [AMA] declared that "the principal objective of the medical profession is to render service to humanity." It went on to say, "In the practice of medicine a physician should limit the source of his professional income to medical services actually rendered by him, or under his supervision, to his patients."

Such lofty pronouncements notwithstanding, the medical profession has never been immune to knavery and profiteering. And, particularly in the days before biomedical science began to establish a rational basis for the practice of medicine, the profession has had its share of charlatans and quacks. Still, the highest aspiration of the medical profession—sometimes honored in the breach, to be sure—has always been to serve the needs of the sick. And that has been the basis of a de facto contract between modern society and the profession.

What are the terms of this contract? In this country, state governments grant physicians a licensed monopoly to practice their profession and allow them considerable autonomy in setting their educational and professional standards and their working conditions. The professional education of physicians is heavily subsidized, because tuition, even in the private medical schools, does not nearly cover the costs of educating medical students. Furthermore, the information, tools, and techniques that physicians use to practice their profession are usually developed through publicly supported research. Finally, hospitals provide physicians with the facilities and personnel and often even the specialized equipment they need to treat their hospitalized patients, thus relieving doctors of many of the kinds of overhead costs that businessmen must pay. Physicians have enjoyed a privileged position in our society, virtually assuring them of high social status and a good living. They have been accorded these privileges in the expectation that they will remain competent and trustworthy and will faithfully discharge the fiduciary responsibility to patients proclaimed in their ethical codes.

THE DISTINCTIONS BETWEEN MEDICAL PRACTICE AND COMMERCE

Now, if this description of a contract between society and the medical profession is even approximately correct, then clearly there are important distinctions to be made between what society has a right to expect of practicing physicians and what it expects of people in business. Both are expected to earn their living from their occupation, but the relation between physicians and patients is supposed to be quite different from that between businessmen and customers. Patients depend on their physicians to be altruistic and committed in advising them on their health-care needs and providing necessary medical services. Most patients do not have the expertise to evaluate their own need for medical care. The quality of life and sometimes life itself are at stake, and price is of relatively little importance, not only because of the unique value of the services rendered but also because patients usually do not pay out of pocket for services at the time they are received. Although most physicians

are paid (usually by the government or an insurance company) for each service they provide, the assumption is that they are acting in the best interests of patients rather than of themselves. A fact that underscores the centrality of the patient's interests is that advertising and marketing in medical practice were until very recently considered unethical.

In contrast, in a commercial market multiple providers of goods and services try to induce customers to buy. That's the whole point. Competing with one another, businesses rely heavily on marketing and advertising to generate demand for services or products, regardless of whether they are needed, because each provider's primary concern is to increase his sales and thereby maximize his income. Although commercial vendors have an obligation to produce a good product and advertise it without deception, they have no responsibility to consider the consumer's interests—to advise the consumer which product, if any, is really needed, or to worry about those who cannot afford to buy any of the vendors' products. Markets may be effective mechanisms for distributing goods and services according to consumers' desires and ability to pay, but they have no interest in consumers' needs, or in achieving universal access.

In a commercial market, consumers are expected to fend for themselves in judging what they can afford and want to buy. *"Caveat emptor"* ["Let the buyer beware"] is the rule. According to classical market theory, when well-informed consumers and competing suppliers are free to seek their own objectives, the best interests of both groups are likely to be served. Thus, in commerce, market competition is relied upon to protect the interests of consumers. This is quite different from the situation in health care, where the provider of services protects the patient's interests by acting as ad-vocate and counselor. Unlike the inde-pendent shoppers envisioned by market theory, sick and worried patients can-not adequately look after their own in-terests, nor do they usually want to. Per-sonal medical service does not come in standardized packages and in different grades for the consumer's comparison and selection. Moreover, a sick patient often does not have the option of defer-ring his purchase of medical care or shop-ping around for the best buy. A patient with seizures and severe headache who is told that he has a brain tumor requir-ing surgery, or a patient with intractable angina and high-grade obstruction of a coronary artery who is advised to have a coronary bypass, does not look for the "best buy" or consider whether he really needs "top-of-the-line" surgical quality. If he does not trust the judgment and com-petence of the first surgeon he consults, he may seek the opinion of another, but he will very shortly have to trust someone to act as his beneficent counselor, and he will surely want the best care available, regardless of how much or how little his insurance will pay the doctor.

Some skeptics have always looked askance at the physician's double role as purveyor of services and patients' advocate. They have questioned whether doctors paid on a fee-for-service basis can really give advice to patients that is free of economic self-interest. One of the most caustic critiques of private fee-for-service medical practice was written early in this century by George Bernard Shaw, in his preface to *The Doctor's Dilemma*. It begins,

It is not the fault of our doctors that the medical service of the community, as at present provided for, is a murderous absurdity. That any sane nation, having observed that you could provide for the supply of bread by giving bakers a pecuniary interest in baking for you, should go on to give a surgeon a pecuniary interest in cutting off your leg, is enough to make one despair of political humanity. But that is precisely what we have done. And the more appalling the mutilation the more the mutilator is paid....

Scandalized voices murmur that... operations are necessary. They may be. It may also be necessary to hang a man or pull down a house. But we take good care not to make the hangman and the housebreaker the judges of that. If we did, no man's neck would be safe and no man's house stable.

Some contemporary defenders of fee-for-service evidently see no need to answer attacks like Shaw's. They reject the distinctions I have drawn between business and medical practice, claiming that medicine is just another market —admittedly with more imperfections than most, but a market nevertheless. They profess not to see much difference between medical care and any other important economic commodity, such as food, clothing, or housing. Such critics dismiss the notion of a de facto social contract in medical care. They assert that physicians and private hospitals owe nothing to society and should be free to sell or otherwise dispose of their services in any lawful manner they choose.

THE MEDICAL-INDUSTRIAL COMPLEX

Until recently such views had little in-fluence. Most people considered medical care to be a social good, not a commodity, and physicians usually acted as if they agreed. Physicians were not impervious to economic pressures, but the pressures were relatively weak and the tradition of professionalism was relatively strong.

This situation is now rapidly changing. In the past two decades or so health care has become commercialized as never before, and professionalism in medicine seems to be giving way to entrepreneurialism. The health-care system is now widely regarded as an industry, and medical practice as a competitive business. Let me try briefly to explain the origins and describe the scope of this transformation.

First, the past few decades have witnessed a rapid expansion of medical facilities and personnel, leading to an unprecedented degree of competition for paying patients. Our once too few and overcrowded hospitals are now too numerous and on average less than 70 percent occupied. Physicians, formerly in short supply and very busy, now abound everywhere (except in city slums and isolated rural areas), and many are not as busy as they would like to be. Professionalism among self-employed private practitioners thrives when there is more than enough to do. When there isn't, competition for patients and worry about income tend to undermine professional values and influence professional judgment. Many of today's young physicians have to worry not only about getting themselves established in practice but also about paying off the considerable debt they have accumulated in medical school. High tuition levels make new graduates feel that they have paid a lot for an education that must now begin to pay them back—handsomely. This undoubtedly influences the choice of specialty many graduates make and

conditions their attitudes toward the economics of medical practice.

Along with the expansion of health care has come a great increase in specialization and technological sophistication, which has raised the price of services and made the economic rewards of medicine far greater than before. With insurance available to pay the bills, physicians have powerful economic incentives to recruit patients and provide expensive services. In an earlier and less technologically sophisticated era most physicians were generalists rather than specialists. They had mainly their time and counsel to offer, commodities that commanded only modest prices. Now a multitude of tests and procedures provide lucrative opportunities for extra income. This inevitably encourages an entrepreneurial approach to medical practice and an overuse of services.

Another major factor in the transformation of the system has been the appearance of investor-owned health-care businesses. Attracted by opportunities for profit resulting from the expansion of private and public health insurance, these new businesses (which I call the medical-industrial complex) have built and operated chains of hospitals, clinics, nursing homes, diagnostic laboratories, and many other kinds of health facilities. Recent growth has been mainly in ambulatory and home services and in specialized inpatient facilities other than acute-care general hospitals, in part because most government efforts to control health-care costs and the construction of new facilities have been focused on hospitals. Nevertheless, the growth of the medical-industrial complex continues unabated. There are no reliable data, but I would guess that at least a third of all non-public health-care facilities are now operated by investor-owned businesses. For example, most nursing homes, private psychiatric hospitals, and free-standing therapeutic or diagnostic facilities are investor-owned. So are nearly two thirds of the so-called health-maintenance organizations, which now provide comprehensive prepaid medical care to nearly 35 million members.

EFFECTS ON PROVIDERS

This corporatization of health care, coupled with increasingly hostile and cost-conscious policies by private insurance companies and government, has had a powerful and pervasive effect on the attitudes of health-care providers—including those in the not-for-profit sector. Not-for-profit, nonpublic hospitals ("voluntary hospitals"), which constitute more than three quarters of the non-public acute-care general hospitals in the country, originally were philanthropic social institutions, with the primary mission of serving the health-care needs of their communities. Now, forced to compete with investor-owned hospitals and a rapidly growing number of for-profit ambulatory facilities, and struggling to maintain their economic viability in the face of sharp reductions in third-party payments, they increasingly see themselves as beleaguered businesses, and they act accordingly. Altruistic concerns are being distorted in many voluntary hospitals by a concern for the bottom line. Management decisions are now often based more on considerations of profit than on the health needs of the community. Many voluntary hospitals seek to avoid or to limit services to the poor. They actively promote their profitable services to insured patients, they advertise themselves, they establish health-related businesses, and they make deals with physicians to generate more revenue. Avoiding uninsured patients simply adds to the problems of our underserved indigent population and widens the gap in medical care between rich and poor. Promoting elective care for insured patients leads to overuse of medical services and runs up the national health-care bill.

Physicians are reacting similarly as they struggle to maintain their income in an increasingly competitive economic climate. Like hospitals, practicing physicians have begun to use advertising, marketing, and public-relations techniques to attract more patients. Until recently most medical professional societies considered self-promotion of this kind to be unethical, but attitudes have changed, and now competition among physicians is viewed as a necessary, even beneficial, feature of the new medical marketplace.

Many financially attractive opportunities now exist for physicians to invest in health-care facilities to which they can then refer their patients, and a growing number of doctors have become limited partners in such enterprises—for example, for-profit diagnostic laboratories and MRI [magnetic resonance imaging] centers, to which they refer their patients but over which they can exercise no professional supervision. Surgeons invest in ambulatory-surgery facilities that are owned and managed by businesses or hospitals, and in which they perform surgery on their patients. Thus they both are paid for their professional services and share in the profits resulting from the referral of their patients to a particular facility. A recent study in Florida revealed that approximately 40 percent of all physicians practicing in that state had financial interests in facilities to which they referred patients. The AMA, however, estimates that nationwide the figure is about 10 percent.

In other kinds of entrepreneurial arrangements, office-based practitioners make deals with wholesalers of prescription drugs and sell those drugs to their patients at a profit, or buy prostheses from manufacturers at reduced rates and sell them at a profit—in addition to the fees they receive for implanting the prostheses. In entering into these and similar business arrangements, physicians are trading on their patients' trust. This is a clear violation of the traditional ethical rule against earning professional income by referring patients to others or by investing in the goods and services recommended to patients. Such arrangements create conflicts of interest that go far beyond the economic conflict of interest in the fee-for-service system, and they blur the distinction between business and the medical profession.

Not only practitioners but also physicians doing clinical research at teaching hospitals are joining the entrepreneurial trend. Manufacturers of new drugs, devices, and clinical tests are entering into financial arrangements with clinicians engaged in testing their products—and the results of those studies may have an important effect on the commercial success of the product. Clinical investigators may own equity interest in the company that produces the product or may serve as paid consultants and scientific advisers, thus calling into question their ability to act as rigorously impartial evaluators. Harvard Medical School has wisely taken a stand against such arrangements, but unfortunately this obvious conflict of interest has so far been ignored, or at least tolerated, in many other institutions.

Business arrangements of this kind are also common in postgraduate education.

Respected academic clinicians are frequently hired by drug firms to give lectures or write articles about the manufacturers' new products. The assumption, of course, is that these experts are expressing honest and dispassionate opinions about the relative merits of competing products, but such an assumption is strained by the realization that an expert is being handsomely paid by the manufacturer of one particular product in a market that is often highly competitive.

Similarly, drug manufacturers offer inducements to practicing physicians to attend seminars at which their products are touted, and even to institute treatment with a particular drug. In the former case the ostensible justification is furtherance of postgraduate education; in the latter it is the gathering of post-marketing information about a new drug. The embarrassing transparency of these subterfuges has recently caused pharmaceutical manufacturers to agree with the AMA that such practices should be curtailed.

In short, at every turn in the road physicians both in practice and in academic institutions are being attracted by financial arrangements that can compromise their professional independence.

ANTITRUST MEDICINE

The courts have significantly contributed to the change in atmosphere. For many years the legal and medical professions enjoyed immunity from antitrust law because it was generally believed that they were not engaged in the kind of commercial activity that the Sherman Act and the Federal Trade Commission Act were designed to regulate. In 1975 the Supreme Court ended this immunity (*Goldfarb v. Virginia State Bar*). It decided that the reach of antitrust law extended to the professions. Since then numerous legal actions have been taken against individual physicians or physicians' organizations to curb what government has perceived to be "anti-competitive" practices. Thus the courts and the Federal Trade Commission have prevented medical societies in recent years from prohibiting commercial advertising or marketing and from taking any action that might influence professional fees or legal business ventures by physicians.

Concerns about possible antitrust liability have caused the AMA to retreat from many of the anti-commercial recommendations in its 1957 code of ethics. The latest revisions of the ethical code say that advertising is permissible so long as it is not deceptive. Investments in healthcare facilities are also permissible, provided that they are allowed by law and disclosed to patients, and provided also that they do not interfere with the physician's primary duty to his or her patients. Reflecting the new economic spirit, a statement has been added that competition is "not only ethical but is encouraged." Indeed, the AMA goes even further, declaring that "ethical medical practice thrives best under free market conditions when prospective patients have adequate information and opportunity to choose freely between and among competing physicians and alternate systems of medical care." Thus an earlier forthright stand by organized medicine against the commercialization of medical practice has now been replaced by an uneasy ambivalence.

Very recently, however, the AMA seems to have reconsidered its position, at least with respect to some kinds of entrepreneurial activity. At its last meeting it adopted a resolution advising physicians not to refer patients to an outside facility in which the physician has an ownership interest—except when the facility was built in response to a demonstrated need and alternative financing for its construction was not available. It remains to be seen whether this advice will be heeded and whether the AMA will take a similar position on other commercial practices. It will also be interesting to see what response this modest stand in defense of professional ethics will elicit from the Federal Trade Commission.

THE GOVERNMENT'S RESPONSE

Government policy has also been ambivalent. The Reagan and Bush Administrations have staunchly supported competition and free markets in medicine under the delusion that this is a way to limit expenditures. The White House has therefore supported the Federal Trade Commission's antitrust policies and until recently has resisted all proposals for curbing entrepreneurial initiatives in health care. But expenditures are not likely to be limited in a market lacking the restraints ordinarily imposed by cost-conscious consumers who must pay for what they want and can afford. And if the competing providers in such a market have great power to determine what is to be purchased, then their competition inevitably drives up expenditures and the total size of the market. In business, success is measured in terms of increasing sales volume and revenues —the last thing we want to see in the health-care system. Despite its preference for market mechanisms, however, the Bush Administration recently abandoned ideology and supported legislation to regulate physicians' fees and to prevent physicians from referring their Medicare patients to diagnostic laboratories in which they have a financial interest. Regulations and new legislation to provide even stricter limits on physicians' investments in health-care facilities are currently under consideration in several states—not for ethical reasons but simply as measures to limit health-care spending. Clearly, cost control is now the highest priority in public policy.

Despite its recent willingness to intervene in limited ways to control costs generated by some of the entrepreneurial activities of physicians, the government has as yet shown little interest in interfering with the spreading commercialization of our health-care system. That should not be surprising, because private enterprise is now widely heralded as the answer to most economic problems. We hear much these days about the privatization of schools, highways, airports, jails, national parks, the postal service, and many other aspects of our society—and by this is meant not simply removal from government control but transfer to investor ownership. Business, it is said, can do a much better job of running most of these things than government, so why not turn them over to private enterprise? I do not want to debate this general proposition here, but medical care, I suggest, is in many ways uniquely unsuited to private enterprise. It is an essential social service, requiring the involvement of the community and the commitment of health-care professionals. It flourishes best in the private sector but it needs public support, and it cannot meet its responsibilities to society if it is dominated by business interests.

WHY SHOULD THE PUBLIC CARE?

If government is not concerned about the loss of social and professional values in our health-care system, should the American public care? I think it must. The quality and effectiveness of our medical care depend critically on the values and the behavior of its providers. If health care is not a business, then we should encourage our physicians to stand by their traditional fiduciary obligations, and we should enable, if not require, our voluntary hospitals to honor their commitments to the community.

If most of our physicians become entrepreneurs and most of our hospitals and health-care facilities become businesses, paying patients will get more care than they need and poor patients will get less. In a commercialized system the cost of health care will continue to escalate and yet we will not be assured of getting the kind of care we really need. In such a system we will no longer be able to trust our physicians, because the bond of fiduciary responsibility will have been broken. To control costs, government will be driven to adopt increasingly stringent regulations. Ultimately health care will have to be regulated like a public utility, and much greater constraints will be placed on physicians and hospitals than are now in place or even contemplated.

Our health-care system is inequitable, inefficient, and too expensive. It badly needs reform. The task will be arduous and the solution is far from clear, but I believe that the first step must be to gain a firm consensus on what we value in health care and what kind of a medical profession we want. The medical profession has held a privileged position in American society, based on the expectation that it will serve society's needs first of all. How can it hope to continue in that position if it loses the trust of the public? We cannot expect to solve our health-care problems unless we can count on the basic altruism of the profession and its sense of responsibility to patients and the general public welfare. American society and the medical profession need to reaffirm their de facto contract, because they will have to depend on each other as the United States painfully gropes its way toward a better system of health care.

Physicians have the power to make health-care reform possible. They know the system better than anyone, and if they want to, they can use its resources more prudently than they do now without any loss of medical effectiveness. It is primarily their decisions that determine what medical services will be provided in each case, and therefore what the aggregate expenditure for health care will be. If physicians remain free of conflicting economic ties, and if they act in a truly professional manner, medical facilities will probably be used more appropriately, regardless of their ownership or organization. In any case, no proposed reforms in the health-care system can ultimately be successful without a properly motivated medical profession. But if physicians continue to allow themselves to be drawn along the path of private entrepreneurship, they will increasingly be seen as self-interested businessmen and will lose many of the privileges they now enjoy as fiduciaries and trusted professionals. They will also lose the opportunity to play a constructive role in shaping the major reforms that are surely coming.

The medical profession is not likely to change its direction without help. The incentives that now encourage—indeed, in many cases require—physicians to act primarily as businessmen will have to be changed, and probably so will the configurations in which most physicians practice. In my opinion, a greater reliance on group practice and more emphasis on medical insurance that prepays providers at a fixed annual rate offer the best chance of solving the economic problems of health care, because these arrangements put physicians in the most favorable position to act as prudent advocates for their patients, rather than as entrepreneurial vendors of services. However, regardless of what structural changes in the health-care system are ultimately adopted, physicians hold the key. The sooner they join with government and the public in reaffirming the medical profession's ethical contract with society, the easier will be the task of reform and the greater the chance of its success.

NO

Andrew C. Wicks

ALBERT SCHWEITZER OR IVAN BOESKY? WHY WE SHOULD REJECT THE DICHOTOMY BETWEEN MEDICINE AND BUSINESS

As we contemplate the profound changes the Clinton administration will propose for health care, it is not surprising that numerous passionate and conflicting views exist on what direction to take. While investigating the full range of such perspectives is a task nearly as imposing as restructuring our ailing health care system, I do want to explore some key assumptions that frame how many people think about health care reform. These assumptions are tied to a broader sense that medicine and business are, and should remain, polar opposites—things which ought never to be mixed together or confused for fear that the results could be disastrous. More specifically, many scholars in medicine and medical ethics lament that medicine is increasingly becoming a business, and that the ethos of business will inevitably erode the moral identity of health care workers and dominate the physician-patient relationship.

... While I share much of the concern that is raised here, I will argue that this conceptualization of the issues is overly simplistic and that a more nuanced analysis is necessary. To make my argument I want to explore three questions:

1. What specific changes in medicine reflect the introduction of "business" thinking and are these changes desirable from an ethical standpoint?
2. How substantial are the differences between the ethics of medicine and the ethics of business?
3. Can the two ethical models, or aspects of them, be combined in a positive way?

As a vehicle to address these questions, I will focus on how we think about the models of medicine and business, specifically the ways in which ethical imperatives shape the activities of their respective practitioners and the missions of their institutions....

From Andrew C. Wicks, "Albert Schweitzer or Ivan Boesky? Why We Should Reject the Dichotomy Between Medicine and Business," *Journal of Business Ethics*, vol. 14 (1995), pp. 339–349. Copyright © 1995 by D. Reidel Publishing Co., Dordrecht, Holland, and Boston, U.S.A. Reprinted by permission of Kluwer Academic Publishers. Notes omitted.

My approach to these issues will be that of an ethicist, trained to reflect on normative issues. I will not offer or defend specific policies or institutional arrangements, although my arguments will have direct relevance to the sorts of practical proposals that are being considered for health care. My underlying goal is to help reconceptualize how we think about both medicine and business, and in so doing, reshape how we approach the "American health care crisis."

THE COSTS OF COMMERCIALISM

Among the more significant concerns that the commercialization of medicine raises are the following:

1. The market model doesn't "fit" medicine. Patients are vulnerable, they lack the knowledge to operate as effective consumers under a "caveat emptor" ["let the buyer beware"] model, and health care is an overridingly important good whose availability ought not to be determined by one's income or ability to pay.
2. The business model creates conflicts of interest in medicine, particularly between physicians and patients.
3. Allowing the market model to direct consumption is unacceptable: care would be focused on what pays rather than what is needed; market-thinking validates and supports the idea of "creating" needs rather than just meeting them; there would be incentive to overconsume which could possibly increase overall health care costs.
4. Thinking about health care as a business erodes the basis of a right to health care. That is, by thinking about health care as a commodity, rather than as a basic human right or special set of goods, it becomes more fitting to leave allocation and purchasing to market forces and individual ability to pay.
5. The growing ethos of commercialism erodes, or perhaps even renders inept, the Hippocratic tradition. By teaching physicians that they are business people we legitimate their self-interested aspirations, make patients equivalent to "customers" and, in so doing, undermine the sacred moral calling of physicians.

While I highlight these concerns and suggest they have merit, I also will argue that they create an overly simplistic picture. My strategy will be to expose some dubious assumptions which cloud our thinking on these matters. Among the assumptions embedded in the thinking of critics, such as Relman and Dougherty, are the following:

1. Medicine and business are ethically opposed and incompatible.
2. There can be no substantial mixture and/or balancing of the ethics of medicine and business [opening the door to commercialism and business will inevitably lead to its dominance over medicine].
3. The ethical problems associated with "medicine as a business" can be remedied only by rejecting the business framework.

The conceptions of business and medicine that are tied to these assumptions depict medicine as fundamentally about caring and healing. Physicians and other health care workers are compassionate, put the interests of their patients above their own, and are altruistic—i.e. there is a clear moral, perhaps even an "ultra" moral, content which defines their identity and shapes their activity. In contrast, business people are thought of as self-interested to the point of excluding any concern other than profit in their activities—i.e. they pursue only activities which serve their interest and maximize profits. The quintessential business person is greedy and driven by bottom line "business" considerations. Talk of concern for others or morality would, at best, be an after-thought, and at worst, only confuse the pursuit of their larger raison d'etre. As such, business activity is fundamentally amoral.

Let us examine these assumptions in turn. I will condense my critique of this reading of the two fields into four separate arguments.

Overestimating charity and altruism in health care workers.

This position makes too much of the charitable and altruistic nature of health care professionals. My purpose in saying this is not to question the integrity of the profession, or the extremely valuable moral traditions of medicine, but rather to temper the level of esteem in which we hold physicians. Due to the nature of the physician-patient relationship under a fee-for-service arrangement, it is in the self-interest of the physician not only to apply beneficial therapies, but to be overzealous. Providing aggressive and even excessive care to patients actually benefits the physician financially—to this extent, the well-being of the patient and the self-interest of the physician point generally in the same direction. One can also look to the stance of the majority of physicians and the AMA [American Medical Association] on such issues as HMO's, Medicare and

Medicaid, and wholesale reform of the health care system to provide access for more patients as further evidence to question the degree to which physicians are self-effacing and charitable. Finally, one can point to the relatively high and rising salaries of physicians, the growth of medical specialists, the decline in indigent care, and the geographic maldistribution of physicians towards wealthier areas as further confirmation that we should be skeptical of imagining Albert Schweitzer or Mother Teresa when we call to mind the ordinary physician. Again, this is not to malign physicians or question their moral charge, rather, it is to give it a more sober and balanced interpretation.

The moral problems of introducing "business" into medicine aren't qualitatively different from those that currently exist in the "medical" model.

As I have already argued, the conflicts of interest which have been attached to the business model as areas of great concern, are present in the current system of health care delivery. The only difference is that while the "medical" model creates incentives to overtreat, the "business" model would lead physicians to undertreat. Even though both scenarios contain obvious conflicts many would argue that the former arrangement is clearly preferable to the latter. Yet, it has been persuasively argued that such a conclusion is far from obvious. First of all, there are substantial risks and harms which go along with overtreatment. Extra office visits may only hurt one's pocketbook, but unnecessary surgery, x-rays, or other invasive procedures can pose more serious physical harms to patients with little or no benefit. A recent report on the periodic use of unnecessary cesarean sections provides a disturbing reminder of just how common a phenomenon this may be. In addition, there are costs to society and third parties from overtreatment in the form of higher overall medical costs and fewer resources to offer more beneficial treatments to patients with clear and compelling needs. Finally, in this era of de facto rationing and fiscal scarcity, there is an implicit and indirect trade-off being made. When treatments are offered, others are being denied such that we must remember the harms of overtreatment are not simply to the patient and to society, but to other particular patients who have pressing medical needs that may not be met....

Talking in grand metaphors/paradigms oversimplifies the problem.

Although I direct the next criticism at the commentators whom I challenge, it is also a criticism of my paper. By talking about "medicine" and "business" in global and unified models, we risk imposing a singular framework or paradigm onto a complex set of institutions and relationships. "Health care" and "medicine" include the interaction of patients with physicians, nurses, and nurse practitioners; it refers to interactions which take place in free clinics,—emergency rooms, private hospitals, public teaching hospitals, individual physician practices and HMO's; and it also connects with medical supply companies, pharmaceutical companies, insurance companies, and a range of other public and private institutions which play a variety of direct and indirect roles in the availability and delivery of health care. Talk of models is important and helps clarify a range of problems, yet it can also create new and less visible ones. The oppositional model of medicine and business tends to reinforce the idea of a singularity of norms and ideals, of context and organizational structure. Without tempering this image and accounting for the subtle and significant differences across these realms, such modeling can create arrangements which are not only inappropriate but dangerous. Indeed, I would argue that the differences that are encompassed between the various relationships and levels provides evidence that we need a more nuanced and balanced approach. The range of institutions, and the degree to which they are tied to the moral imperatives of medicine, should reinforce the idea that we are better off seeing the two models as on a continuum rather than as opposites.

Practical realities may force a marriage/combination.

Finally, if we are to construct a health care system which best fulfills the range of purposes we have for it, then it must be able to encompass a variety of objectives. A number of these objectives seem to require applying to medicine the skills, wisdom, and reflection of "business." There is a need to cut costs, reduce bureaucratic waste, spur innovation, recognize scarcity and turn what are now defacto trade-offs into conscious choices. We need to avoid the replication of services and expensive technologies across hospitals and research centers in close proximity; we need to educate physicians—at some level—to be more active gate-keepers of health services; and finally, we not only want to create greater access with reasonable cost, we want to temper public expectations and consumptive behavior—a key factor in the increased use and overall cost of health care. While this list is far from exhaustive, it illustrates the need for combining and perhaps even integrating the two models as well as the skills, wisdom, and imperatives of each. There are a number of ways to realize the ethical goals in practice, and we may be able to continue to keep the "business" and "medical" tasks distinct, but it seems clear that the two activities (and the ethics which emerge from them) can no longer be separated to the degree that they have been. In fact, one could argue that one of the key sources of this health care crisis is a failure to connect these two models, and more specifically, to ask the hard questions raised by fiscal scarcity.

IN SEARCH OF A BETTER MODEL FOR BUSINESS

So far I have challenged the validity of the oppositional model based on practical limitations and reasons internal to the model itself. I want next to extend the argument by offering an alternative way of conceptualizing the ethics of medicine and business. I begin with a reconsideration and reconstruction of business ethics. In so doing, I seek to challenge how we think about the content of the terms "business" and "ethics", and as a result, how we think about medical ethics.

I take the description of business in the oppositional model outlined above as an accurate description of how many, and perhaps most, Americans approach the subject of business ethics. It is a model that economists have done a great deal to create and perpetuate. Business is about the pursuit of profit and self-interest—or more accurately, any form of self-beneficial activity that allows one to make a profit. Egoism and the valorization of greed drive business activity such that ethical considerations have no meaningful place, except as outside constraints

placed on firms by consumers and the public (e.g. as boycotts, laws and regulations). This is not because people want businesses to ignore ethical issues, rather, it is due to the fact that competition, efficiency and the dynamics of the market leave no room for people to hold such ideals—those who do lose out. Why is this the case? In part, it has to do with assumptions about ethics. At its core, many assume ethics to be about altruism, about being kinder and gentler, about being charitable. Many associate ethical activity with looking out for others, putting their needs above one's own, doing the right thing for the right reasons. Ethics, we tend to think, requires denying self-interest. Thus, ethics and business cannot fit together: one activity upholds self-interest, while the other rejects it. In such a context, business ethics is necessarily an oxymoron and capitalism becomes all of the disturbing things that the movie *Wall Street* and the many narratives on the "Decade of Greed" made it out to be.

I want to challenge this viewpoint for a variety of reasons, many of which have been articulated by others. To do so, I will draw on examples of corporate activity, and specifically, one particular problem faced by Merck & Co., a prominent American pharmaceutical firm.

One obvious and common criticism is that this model gives us an extreme and unrealistic account of human beings. Few people are as greedy or purely self-interested as we assume Ivan Boesky, Michael Milken and others to have been. Human action stems from a variety of impulses and norms that have to do with our acculturation, sense of propriety, and other moral and social values. Self-interest is clearly one such impulse, and an important feature of human behavior, but its influence is far more complex as it is both shaped and balanced by a variety of other features. At the same time, few people are as pure of heart and single-mindedly self-effacing as Mother Teresa or Albert Schweitzer. Even when we perform the most apparently selfless acts, there is usually some element of "impure" motivation for selfish gain that accompanies it. Most human activity takes place in the realm in between, where there are a variety of motives and where practices have elements of both self-interest and regard for others. This is true for business as it is for other spheres or practices. The "self-interest" model should be rejected because it forces us to make crude and unrealistic assumptions about how people behave, glossing over the most interesting and complex part of life.

Second, the two realms problem sets the content of both ethics and business in ways which profoundly limit our ability to fit the two together. While economists have used some of Adam Smith's writings to argue for self-interest —better described as egoism or greed— as the crucial driving force of capitalism, their slant on the concept is defective. I have no argument against self-interest, but I would maintain that there is a vast difference between self-interest and selfishness or greed. The former allows room for consideration of the interests of others and competing moral interests (indeed, when it is constrained by other relevant moral values and virtues, we may call self-interest a moral concept). The same cannot be said for greed or selfishness, as the content of these notions is premised on rejecting any moral limits and competing norms. Thus, on this rehabilitated account, we can agree that self-interest has a prominent role in business, but only when it is

constructed as a moral value which is shaped and limited by a variety of other moral considerations. Indeed, on this view, there is nothing odd about connecting or integrating self-interest with a range of other moral purposes for the organization or the individual.

It is equally important that we offer a more compelling account of ethics. Rather than highlighting altruism and charity, it would be more appropriate to focus on aspects of the moral life as respect for others, decency, trust, and justice or fair play. These concepts are arguably more relevant and appropriate concepts to use for interaction among strangers or for public and professional life. They are also less directly opposed to self-interest (particularly in the context of my rehabilitated definition). Indeed, on my redescription, not only is there nothing morally illegitimate about the pursuit of self-interest or financial gain, it may be described as a limited virtue. Thus, by taking a closer look at the content of both business and ethics it is apparent that how the terms are defined has a lot to do with the account of business ethics which emerges. When we use a more balanced and careful approach, ethics and business seem to fit together quite well.

Finally, I draw attention to particular corporations to illustrate the differences generated by this revised interpretation of business ethics. Consider the much publicized dilemma faced by Merck & Co. as they decided whether or not to develop and distribute a treatment for river blindness, a horrible illness which afflicted scores of people in the third world (particularly in parts of Africa, Central and South America).

A Merck scientist discovered that a drug the company had developed to fight parasites in farm animals could possibly be adapted to kill the parasite which caused river blindness. The parasites, which grew to almost two feet in length once they entered the body via an insect bite, began as a relatively benign but offensive presence in nodules just under the skin. However, once they reproduced, creating millions of microscopic worms, victims experienced severe suffering that started with itching so terrible that some victims opted to commit suicide rather than continue to endure the pain. As the organisms spread, they often infiltrate the eyes, causing blindness. The idea of creating a drug to treat an illness that was so awful and affected so many was wonderful, except for the fact that none of the potential customers could pay for the drug. Merck faced the dilemma of whether to invest millions of dollars to develop the drug when there was little in the way of potential financial return. Its best case scenario involved gaining financial support from various private and public sources to help offset costs and to deliver the drugs, but such assistance had not been obtained. A key component of this situation is Merck's corporate philosophy:

> We try never to forget that medicine is for the people. It is not for the profits. The profits follow, and if we have remembered that, they have never failed to appear. The better we have remembered it, the larger they have been.

The company had assembled a world-class collection of scientists and workers who were not only among the most technically capable, but who were highly motivated. This motivation can be traced to their commitment to Merck's corporate philosophy, a credo which they took quite seriously and which they believed the company did as well. The drug development proved a success, but Merck's extensive efforts to get support for development and distribution failed. Transporting the drug was a further problem—sufferers lived in the bush where there were no established transportation networks. Thus, even if they opted to give the drug away, it would cost them roughly $20 million per year to get it to those in need. What should Merck do? Merck decided to give the drug away and pay to transport it to all countries who wanted the drug—forever.

While this is an extraordinary decision in itself, what is more important for our purposes is how we describe or interpret the situation. Under the "self-interest" model, the dilemma becomes a question of charity. Merck either pursues its larger goal of profit maximization and refuses to develop the drug because it won't generate enough income or good will to pay for the costs, or it decides to undertake a charitable activity. I would argue that this is a poor way to look at this case. A more constructive (and probably more accurate) way to look at it is as a test of Merck's mission statement. Just as their corporate mission statement exploded the dichotomy between business and ethics, so too was their decision a question of whether the company stood for the particular mixture of ethical and business imperatives that made up that philosophy. This is my final reason for dropping the "self-interest" model —because firms like Merck, and many others, reject it. These firms are finding ways to mix values and self-interest: starting with a commitment to serving a moral goal (e.g. patients, customers, or a variety of other "stakeholder" groups, i.e. those groups who can affect or who are affected by the activities of the corporation). Firms are finding that they can shape their guiding philosophy in terms of moral commitments, what many are calling value-driven management, and still have financially successful firms.

... Organizations don't have to be "charitable" or non-profit to undertake important communal projects or to serve moral ends. Ethics doesn't have to be about altruism or a singularity of intention to "do the right thing." Scientists at Merck and physicians in medical practice both display a moral commitment to a mission which we would be wrong to describe as largely "altruistic" or "charitable" because of the extent to which they benefit in the process, but it remains an important moral mission nonetheless. Indeed, I want to argue that it is vital that we distinguish this sort of activity (and the importance of the moral purposes served) from the endeavors of "greed" which the public has attributed to business's profit maximization philosophy. Within the prevailing profit maximization philosophy, moral concerns are, at best, seen as largely irrelevant to the purposes and activities of the firm and at worst, opposed to pursuing their "business" interests. Failure to draw such distinctions reinforces the idea that moral concerns are the domain of government or private citizens and have no place in "business". It leads us to perpetuate a world where corporations focus exclusively on one goal—the wealth, the material gain of its economic activity—while excluding virtually all others. It turns business into an activity which is more destructive and oppressive than creative and uplifting....

FROM OPPOSITION TO CONTINUUM: THE CORE SIMILARITIES OF BUSINESS ETHICS AND MEDICAL ETHICS

I have now set the groundwork for pressing a larger argument about the similarity of business and medical ethics: both in terms of a larger mission or strategic statement of purpose, as well as the moral requirements of practitioners (i.e. physicians and managers respectively). While some have emphasized the altruism of physicians, I have argued that physicians have operated in a system where they can adopt the mantle of altruism without sacrificing their self-interest. Physicians make a good living caring for their patients, and although many have raised questions about the extent of their compensation, no one has questioned that physicians be well paid for serving their patients. Few people hold many illusions about the "altruism" of corporations, although many have provided vital support to charities, local communities, and other important causes. Thus, while altruism is more typically associated with physicians, it is hard to make a persuasive case for this being a prominent feature of either profession.

At the same time, I have argued that we should reject the other end of the spectrum, the model of business as driven by pure egoism and the unbridled pursuit of self-interest. As stakeholder firms and total quality management firms have found, doing so does not mean sacrificing financial success and firm survival, but can be seen as a key to securing both. A balanced reading of the business model and the content of "business" also lead us to want to reject this extreme as well. Insofar as this problem is not associated with medicine, except to the extent that it has been dominated by "business" thinking, I shall assume that my rejection of the greed model for business is sufficient to discredit this other pole of the oppositional model.

The common ground that emerges by closing off these two extremes and accepting the model I have articulated for business ethics is quite substantial. It is clear that physicians serve important moral goals by proclaiming their allegiance to the interests of patients and the general health of the community. Yet, while this is their "mission" statement, it is also not opposed to financial success and a reasonable standard of living. We argue about whether physicians are doing enough to help the poor, are being paid too much, or are sacrificing certain health needs of the community for their own benefit, but few reject that any viable picture of medicine contains elements of both models. Doctors are not about maximizing profits, but about serving patients—yet, like Merck, they recognize that in serving the patients, they will also be financially successful. The point is not to legitimize all self-regarding activities or collapse them into moral duties that are more other-regarding. Rather, it is to recognize that self-interest is a concept different from selfishness and greed, and that the former is perfectly compatible with serving other moral ends while the latter is not. Combining ethics and self-interest together is also about rehabilitating our view of medical (as well as business) ethics, moving away from the extreme of altruism and charity, and toward a view that makes trust, respect for others, decency, and a sense of fair play central concepts. Embracing this model does not entail watering down our expectations, lowering our standards, or legitimizing unacceptable behavior. Instead,

it offers us a more complex view of the world and a more viable account of human activity that may well, ironically, allow us to have higher expectations of corporations and provide them with the means to meet those standards.

There are also important comparisons that some have drawn at the level of individual practitioners in medicine and business—between managers and physicians. It appears that there is a basic difference between the two fields in that physicians have one basic duty and serve one group, while managers have many duties and serve many groups. Whereas stakeholder theory has created obligations for managers to serve an array of interests, physicians have typically had one overriding duty: to serve the well-being of their patients. Yet, even in its prime, this dyadic model was over-simplistic. There have always been limits to this duty, particularly when there are compelling claims on behalf of communal health, legal constraints, the physician's own conscience, or the well-being of third parties. Further, if we accept Haavi Morreim's argument that the emergence of fiscal scarcity requires that we reject the dyadic model, and that the interests of a number of other groups and interests must be included, the role of physician begins to look a good deal more complex and more akin to that of the business manager in the stakeholder model. In practice, we may want to take steps to ensure that physicians focus primarily on the health and well-being of individual patients, yet they must also use the interests and claims of a wide variety of other stakeholder groups to shape and structure their activity. Just as managers used to think that it was enough to serve stockholders and operate in a role perhaps similar to physicians, the emergence of other compelling moral duties have pressed us to dramatically revise, if not disintegrate entirely, both models....

CONCLUSION

... While this discussion doesn't provide definitive answers, it seems possible to respond to my original three questions. *Is the introduction of "business" thinking creating drastic and/or dangerous changes in the practice of medicine?* First, based on the model I have defended and drawing on numerous scholarly sources and examples, it seems clear that "business" thinking and the business model need not be as corrosive as critics have made it out to be. Indeed, based on the reality of fiscal scarcity and the need to temper care for particular patients with a broader sense of justice, it seems evident that the influence of business may be a positive influence. *How substantial are the differences between the ethics of medicine and the ethics of business?* I have offered a sustained critique of the oppositional model which associated medicine with altruism and business with unmitigated self-interest, arguing that both are exaggerated and indefensible. In addition, I provided an alternative reconstruction of the two models ... which establishes core similarities between the two. This view explodes the oppositional image of medicine and business and places them on a continuum which is structured by these core similarities, but allows for significant differences between them. *Can the two models, or aspects of them, be molded together in a con-structive way?* Not only can they be connected, but given the goals we have for health care, it seems essential that they be combined to construct a more useful system.

... [W]hile I suggest that we should continue to be skeptical about the effects of strict corporate control over the health care system and the willingness of companies to accept the sorts of ethical arguments I have articulated, health care institutions may be an ideal context in which to forge such a marriage. Medicine is an area where such interfaces of business and ethics—concerns about costs, innovation, and economics as well as the needs of particular patients and broader human welfare—can, and perhaps must, be connected in terms of the basic strategic identity of health care institutions if they are to serve our large goals. We may be able to draw on the ethics of medicine and the ethics of business to find a way out of the American health care crisis which avoids the pitfalls of the two "extreme" models with which we began.

Regardless of what one thinks of business ethics, or the ethos that pervades much of corporate America, it is clear that we can no longer entertain such global and simplistic dichotomies between medicine and business. Further discourse and the effort to create a promising direction for our health care system requires a more balanced and complex view of the situation, and acknowledgment that whatever directions we take must have substantial elements of both.

POSTSCRIPT

Are Business and Medicine Ethically Incompatible?

Currently, a variety of means to rein in what many consider to be the excesses of health maintenance organizations (HMOs) are being examined. Stories of medical benefits denied, of personal frustration and exorbitant personal expense, and of dreadful medical effects from unwise insurance dispositions regularly splash across the front pages. In some places, lawsuits have been filed against HMOs in which it is claimed that denial of reimbursement for a medical or surgical procedure that the patient cannot afford to pay for himself amounts to denial of that procedure and that *that* amounts to practicing medicine. Thus, if the HMOs are going to practice medicine, then they can be sued for malpractice when the results are bad. Whether or not these suits are successful will have a great impact on the health care industry.

At the state legislature level, state assemblies are now passing laws forbidding HMOs to deny certain benefits—most famously, a two-day hospital stay for new mothers. On one hand, such legislation clearly satisfies the desires of the constituency, which is outraged at the callous treatment of new mothers (i.e., releasing them shortly after they give birth). On the other hand, if HMOs are not very good at practicing medicine, how good can legislatures be? Medicine is an art and a science, not a political activity. Is there a better way to keep health care humane while keeping costs under control? Should the single-payer system be reexamined?

SUGGESTED READINGS

Daniel Callahan, *What Kind of Life: The Limits of Medical Progress* (Georgetown University Press, 1995).

Daniel Callahan, Ruud ter Meulen, and Eva Topinkova, eds., *A World Growing Old: The Coming Health Care Challenges* (Georgetown University Press, 1995).

Norman Daniels, *Seeking Fair Treatment: From the AIDS Epidemic to National Health Care Reform* (Oxford University Press, 1995).

Haavi Morreim, *Balancing Act: The New Medical Ethics of Medicine's New Economics* (Georgetown University Press, 1995).

Marc A. Rodwin, *Medicine, Money and Morals: Physicians' Conflicts of Interest* (Oxford University Press, 1993).

Diann B. Uustal, *Clinical Ethics and Values: Issues and Insights in a Changing Healthcare Environment* (Educational Resources in Healthcare, 1993).

ISSUE 6

Are Pharmaceutical Price Controls Justifiable?

YES: Richard A. Spinello, from "Ethics, Pricing and the Pharmaceutical Industry," *Journal of Business Ethics* (August 1992)

NO: Pharmaceutical Manufacturers Association, from "Price Controls in the Economy and the Health Sector," *Backgrounder* (April 1993)

ISSUE SUMMARY

YES: Philosopher Richard A. Spinello argues that the pharmaceutical industry should regulate its prices in accordance with the principles of distributive justice, with special attention to the needs of the least advantaged. If it does not, then government-imposed price controls may be necessary.

NO: The Pharmaceutical Manufacturers Association, an association of 93 manufacturers of pharmaceutical and biological products who support high manufacturing standards and ethical business practices, argues that price controls are historically counterproductive in providing scarce goods for the consumer, especially in the health care sector.

How shall we distribute the scarce valuable products of our society? Current economic philosophies offer two alternatives: the free market and public provision. In a free market, tradable goods or money or services are exchanged between buyers and sellers at a rate that is acceptable to both. This system assumes that everyone can bring enough money or goods or services to the exchange to have their needs met. A public commodity, on the other hand, is available to all as needed; police protection is a good example of a public commodity. Where does health care and the products that are essential to health care fall in this division?

Before the 1900s, in the United States, physicians charged fees for visits, which the patient was expected to pay; all pharmaceuticals were sold at essentially what the market would bear; and the industry was profitable. The suffering of those who could not afford health care was occasionally relieved by private charities and by religious orders that set up hospitals for the poor. But on the whole, medical care and all that went with it was a marketable good.

In the twentieth century, several nations began to make health care available to all through public taxation, on the same basis as police and fire protection. The medical treatments available under socialized medicine, as it is called, included most of the treatments that were previously available only to those who could pay for them through the private sector.

The rationale for this extension of benefits was simple enough: we are all dependent for our prosperity on the productivity of the nation—that is, the productivity of its citizens—and that depends upon the national level of health. It makes sense to oppose disease and promote health with the same energy that is spent on opposing enemy armies and promoting sound fiscal policy. Early public health movements financed clean water and universal inoculations at public expense; medical treatments and drugs were a direct extension of this idea.

In nations that have socialized their health care provision, there have always been disputes over the acceptable boundaries of medical coverage: Should cosmetic surgery be covered? What about elaborate reconstructive surgery for the very old? Weight loss treatments? Psychiatric care, not including emergencies? However, treatment of disease—AIDS, for example—is always covered, and here is where the dispute begins.

The United States has never fully subscribed to socialized health care provision (or to socialized anything, for that matter), and there is no tax money allocated to underwrite the cost of manufacturing drugs. As part of its federal police power, the United States does have the legal apparatus to control prices of essential commodities if the lawmakers feel that these prices are unconscionably high. But are price controls to equalize access to essential medications justified?

The dispute centers on two points: First, do pharmaceutical companies have an obligation to take into account the needs of the poorest customers in setting their prices (in accordance with the principles of justice), or may they restrict sales to only those who can pay full price? Second, if price controls were established, would they work in practice to achieve the ends of justice, or would they bring about negative consequences such as the shutting down of drug research?

In the following selections, Richard A. Spinello argues that the principles of distributive justice justify the implementation of price controls. On the opposing side, the Pharmaceutical Manufacturers Association, in a paper prepared by Van Dyk Associates, Inc., a public policy consulting firm in Washington, D.C., reports that past attempts to administer price controls have all failed. As you read these selections, ask yourself what kind of arguments are being deployed by the disputants. Do the moral arguments advanced by Spinello carry enough weight to warrant a practical response? Do the empirical arguments advanced by the Pharmaceutical Manufacturers Association that price controls are ineffective in practice render the theoretical arguments irrelevant?

YES

Richard A. Spinello

ETHICS, PRICING AND THE PHARMACEUTICAL INDUSTRY

INTRODUCTION

A perennial ethical question for the pharmaceutical industry has been the aggressive pricing policies pursued by most large drug companies. Criticism has intensified in recent years over the high cost of new conventional ethical drugs and the steep rise in prices for many drugs already on the market. One result of this public clamor is that the pricing structure of this industry has once again come under intense scrutiny by government agencies, Congress, and the media.

The claim is often advanced that these high prices and the resultant profits are unethical and unreasonable. It is alleged that pharmaceutical companies could easily deliver less expensive products without sacrificing research and development. It is quite difficult to assess, however, what constitutes an unethical price or an unreasonable profit. Where does one draw the line in these nebulous areas? We will consider these questions as they relate to the pharmaceutical industry with the understanding that the normative conclusions reached in this analysis might be applicable to other industries which market *essential* consumer products. Our primary axis of discussion, however, will be the pharmaceutical industry where the issue of pricing is especially complex and controversial.

THE PROBLEM

Beyond any doubt, instances of questionable and excessive drug prices abound. Azidothymide or AZT is one of the most prominent and widely cited examples. This effective medicine is used for treating complications from AIDS. The Burroughs-Wellcome Company has been at the center of a spirited controversy over this drug for establishing such a high price—AZT treatment often costs as much as $6500 a year, which is prohibitively expensive for many AIDS patients, particularly those with inadequate insurance

From Richard A. Spinello, "Ethics, Pricing and the Pharmaceutical Industry," *Journal of Business Ethics*, vol. 11 (August 1992), pp. 617–626. Copyright © 1992 by D. Reidel Publishing Co., Dordrecht, Holland, and Boston, U.S.A. Reprinted by permission of Kluwer Academic Publishers.

coverage. The company has steadfastly refused to explicate how it arrived at this premium pricing level, but industry observers suggest that this important drug was priced to be about the same as expensive cancer therapy.[1] ...

ETHICAL QUESTIONS

The behavior of Burroughs and the tendency of most drug companies to charge premium prices for breakthrough medicines raises serious moral issues which defy easy answers and simple solutions. As Clarence Walton observed, "no other area of managerial activity is more difficult to depict accurately, assess fairly, and prescribe realistically in terms of morality than the domain of price" (1969, p. 209). This difficulty is compounded in the pharmaceutical industry due to the complications involved in ascertaining the true cost of production.

To be sure, every business is certainly entitled to a *reasonable profit* as a reward to its investors and a guarantee of long-term stability. But the difficulty is judging a reasonable profit level. When, if ever, do profits become "unreasonable?" It is even more problematic to determine if that profit is "unethical," especially if it is the result of premium prices.

Obviously, the issue of ethical or fair pricing assumes much greater significance when the product or service in question is not a luxury item but an essential one such as medicine. Few are concerned about the ethics of pricing a BMW or a waterfront condo in Florida. But the matter is quite different when dealing with vital commodities like food, medicine, clothing, housing, and education. Each of these goods has a major impact on our basic well-being and our ability to achieve any genuine self-fulfillment. Given the importance of these products in the lives of all human beings, one must consider how equitably they are priced since pricing will determine their general availability. Along these lines several key questions must be raised. Should free market, competitive forces determine the price of "essential" goods such as pharmaceuticals? Is it morally wrong to charge exceptionally high prices even if the market is willing to pay that price? Is it ethical to profit excessively at the expense of human suffering? Finally, how can we even begin to define what constitutes reasonable profits?

Also, the issue of pricing must be considered in the context of the pharmaceutical industry's lofty performance guidelines for return on assets, return on common equity, and so forth. On what authority are such targets chosen over other goals such as the widest possible distribution of some breakthrough pharmaceutical that can save lives or improve the quality of life? Pharmaceutical companies would undoubtedly contend that this authority emanates from the expectations of shareholders and other key stakeholders such as members of the financial community. In addition, these targets are a result of careful strategic planning that focuses on long-term goals.

But a key question persistently intrudes here. Should *other* viewpoints be considered? Should the concerns and needs of the sick be taken into account, especially in light of the fact that they have such an enormous stake in these issues? In other words, as with many business decisions, there appear to be stark trade-offs between superior financial performance versus humane empathy and fairness. Should corporations consider the "human cost" of their objectives for excellent performance? And what role, if any, should fairness or justice play in pricing decisions? It is only by probing these difficult and complex questions that we can make progress in establishing reasonable norms for the pricing of pharmaceuticals.

... The strategic decisions of large organizations "inevitably involve social as well as economic consequences, inextricably intertwined" (Mintzberg, 1989, p. 173). Thus such firms are social agents whether they like it or not. It is virtually impossible to maintain neutrality on these issues and aspire to some sort of apolitical status. The point for the pharmaceutical industry and the matter of pricing seems clear enough. The refusal to take "non-economic" criteria into account when setting prices is itself a moral and social decision which inevitably affects society. Companies have a choice —either they can explicitly consider the social consequences of their decisions or they can be blind to those consequences, deliberately ignoring them until the damage is perceived and an angry public raises its voice in protest.

If companies do choose, however, to be attentive and *responsible* social agents they must begin to cultivate a broader view of their environment and their obligations. To begin with, they must treat those affected by their decisions as people with an important stake in those decisions. This stakeholder model, which has become quite popular with many executives, allows corporations to link strategic decisions such as pricing with social and ethical concerns. By recognizing the legitimacy of its stakeholders such as consumers and employees, managers will better appreciate all the negative as well as positive consequences of their decisions. Moreover, an honest stakeholder analysis will compel them to explore the financial and human implications of those decisions. This will enable corporations to become more responsible social agents, since explicit attention will be given to the social dimension of their various strategic decisions.

... According to Goodpaster and Matthews, the most effective solution to this and most other moral dilemmas is one "that permits or encourages corporations to exercise independent, non-economic judgment over matters that face them in their short- and long-term plans and operations" (1989, p. 161). In other words, the burden of morality and social responsibility does not lie in the marketplace or in the hand of government regulation but falls directly on the corporation and its managers.

Companies that do aspire to such moral and social responsibility will adopt *the moral point of view*, which commits one to view positively the interest of others, including various stakeholder groups. Moreover, the moral point of view assigns primacy to virtues such as justice, integrity, and respect. Thus, the virtuous corporation is analogous to the virtuous person: each exhibits these moral qualities and acts according to the principle that the single-minded pursuit of one's own selfish interests is a violation of moral standards and an offense to the community. The moral point of view also assumes that both the corporation and the individual thrive in an environment of cooperative interaction which can only be realized when one turns from a narrow self-interest to a wider interest in others.

PRICING POLICIES AND JUSTICE

This brings us back to the specific moral question of fair pricing policies for the pharmaceutical industry. The moral issue at stake here concerns justice and more precisely distributive justice. As we have remarked, justice has always been considered a primary virtue and thus it is an indispensable component of the moral point of view. According to Aristotle, justice "is not a part of virtue but the whole of excellence or virtue" (1962, p. 114). Thus, there can be no virtue without justice. This implies that if corporations are serious about assimilating the moral point of view and exercising their capacity for responsible behavior, they must strive to be just in their dealings with both their internal and external constituencies. Moreover, traditional discussions on justice in the works of philosophers such as Aristotle, Hume, Mill, and Rawls have emphasized distributive justice, which is concerned with the fair distribution of society's benefits and burdens. This seems especially relevant to the matter of ethical pricing policies.

Corporations which control the distribution of essential products such as ethical drugs like AZT can be just or unjust in the way they distribute these products. When premium prices are charged for such goods an artificial scarcity is created, and this gives rise to the question of how equitably this scarce resource is being allocated. The consequence of a premium pricing strategy whose objective is to garner high profits would appear to be an inequitable distribution pattern. As we have seen, due to the expensiveness of AZT and similar drugs they are often not available to the poor and lower middle class unless their insurance plans cover this expense or they can somehow secure government assistance which has not been readily forthcoming. However, if this distribution pattern can be considered unjust, what determines a just distribution policy?

There are, of course, many conceptions of distributive justice which would enable us to answer this question. Some stress individual merit (each according to his ability) while others are more egalitarian and stress an equal distribution of society's goods and services. Given a wide array of different theories on justice, where does the manager turn for some guidance and straightforward insights?

One of the most popular and plausible conceptions of justice is advanced by John Rawls in his well known work, *A Theory of Justice*. A thorough treatment of this complex and prolix work is beyond the scope of this essay. However, a concise summary of Rawls' work should reveal its applicability to the problem of fair pricing. Rawls' conception of justice, which is predicated on the Kantian idea of personhood, properly emphasizes the equal worth and universal dignity of all persons. All rational persons have a dual capacity: they possess the ability to develop a rational plan to pursue their own conception of the good life along with the ability to respect this same capacity of self-determination in others. This Kantian ideal underlies the choice of the two principles of justice in the original position. Furthermore, this choice is based on the assumption that the "protection of Kantian self-determination for all persons depends on certain formal guarantees—the equal rights and liberties of democratic citizenship—plus guaranteed access to certain material resources" (Doppelt, p. 278). In short, the essence of justice as fairness means that persons are entitled to an extensive system of liberties *and* basic material goods.

Unlike pure egalitarian theories, however, Rawls stipulates that inequities are consistent with his conception of justice so long as they are compatible with universal respect for Kantian personhood. This implies that such inequities should not be tolerated if they interfere with the basic rights, liberties, and material benefits all deserve as Kantian persons capable of rational self-determination. In other words, Rawls espouses the detachment of the distribution of primary social goods from one's merit and ability because these goods are absolutely essential for our self-determination and self-fulfillment as rational persons. These primary goods include "rights and liberties, opportunities and power, income and wealth" (Rawls, 1971, p. 92). Whatever one's plan or conception of the good life, these goods are the necessary means to realize that plan, and hence everyone would prefer more rather than less primary goods. Their unequal distribution in a just society should only be allowed if such a distribution would benefit directly the least advantaged of that society (the difference principle).

The key element in Rawls' theory for our purposes is the notion that there are material benefits everyone deserves as Kantian persons. The exercise of one's capacity for free self-determination requires a certain level of material well-being and not just the guarantee of abstract and formal rights such as freedom of expression and equal opportunity. Thus the primary social goods involve some material goods, like income and wealth. To a certain extent health care (including medicine) should be considered as one of the primary social goods since it is obviously necessary for the pursuit of one's rational life plan. Therefore, the distribution of health care should not be contingent upon ability and merit. Also it would

be untenable to justify an inequitable distribution of this good by means of Rawls' difference principle. It is difficult to imagine a scenario in which the unequal distribution of health care in our society would be more beneficial to the least advantaged than a more equal distribution which would assure all consumers access to hospital care, medical treatment, medicines, and so forth. If we assume that the least advantaged (a group which Rawls never clearly defines) are the indigent who are also suffering from certain ailments, there is no advantage to any inequity in the distribution of health care. Unlike other primary goods such as income and wealth it cannot be distributed in such a way that a greater share for certain groups will benefit the least advantaged. In short, this is a zero sum game—if a person is deprived of medical treatment or pharmaceutical products due to premium pricing policies that person has lost a critical opportunity to save his life, cure a disease, reduce suffering, and so on.

Thus, at least according to this Rawlsian view of justice with its Kantian underpinnings, there seems to be little room for the unequal distribution of a vital commodity such as health care in a just society. It follows, then, that the just pharmaceutical corporation must be far more diligent and consider very carefully the implications of pricing policies for an equitable distribution of its products. The alternative is government intervention in this process, and as we have seen, this has the potential to yield gross inefficiencies and ultimately be self-defeating. If these corporations charge premium prices and garner excessive profits from their pharmaceutical products, the end result will be the deprivation of these goods for certain classes of people. Such a pricing pattern systematically worsens the situation of the least advantaged in society, violates the respect due them as Kantian persons, and seriously impairs their capacity for free self-determination.

It should be emphasized, however, that this concern for justice does not imply that pharmaceutical companies should become charities by distributing these drugs free of charge or at prices so low they must sustain meager profits or even losses. To be sure, their survival, long-term stability, and ongoing research are also vital to society and can only be guaranteed through substantial profits. Thus, the demand for justice which we have articulated must be balanced with the need to realize key economic objectives which guarantee the long-term stability of this industry. As Kenneth Goodpaster notes, "the responsible organization aims at congruence between its moral and nonmoral aspirations" (1984, p. 309). In other words, it does not see goals of justice and economic viability as mutually exclusive, but will attempt to manage the joint achievement of both objectives.

We are arguing, then, that pharmaceutical companies should seek to balance their legitimate concern for profit and return on investment with an equal consideration of the crucial importance of distributive justice. There must be an explicit recognition that for the afflicted certain pharmaceutical products are critical for one's well-being; hence they are as important as any primary social good and are deserved by every member of society. As a result these products should be distributed on the widest possible basis, but in a way that permits companies to realize a realistic and reasonable level of profitability.

It is, of course, quite difficult to define a "reasonable level of profitability." In many respects the definition of "reasonable" is the crux of the matter here. Unfortunately, as outsiders to the operations of drug companies we are ill prepared to judge whether development costs for certain drugs are inflated or truly necessary. As a result, these corporations must be trusted to arrive at their own definition of a reasonable profit, given the level of legitimate costs involved in researching and developing the drug in question. But we can look to some case histories for meaningful examples that would serve as a guide to a more general definition. One of the most famous controversies over drug prices concerned the Hoffman-LaRoche corporation and the United Kingdom in which the government's Monopoly Commission alleged that Hoffman-LaRoche was charging excessive prices for valium and librium in order to subsidize its research and preserve its monopoly position. In the course of the prolonged deliberations between the British government and the company reasonable profits were defined as "profits no higher than is necessary to obtain the 'desired' performance of industry from the point of view of the economy as a whole."[2] In general, then, under normal circumstances reasonable profits for a particular product should be consistent with the average return for the industry. Exceptions might be made to this rule of average returns if the risks and costs of development are inordinately and unavoidably high.

Thus, based on this Rawlsian ideal of justice I propose the following thesis regarding ethical pricing for pharmaceutical companies: for those drugs which are truly essential the just corporation will aim to charge prices that will assure the widest possible distribution of these products consistent with a reasonable level of profitability. In other words, these companies will seek to minimize the deprivation of material benefits which are needed by all persons for their self-realization by imposing restraints on their egocentric interests in premium prices and excessive profits.... Moreover, we must present some sort of methodology for reaching this determination.

... The more critical the product and the less likely it will be affordable to certain segments of society, the more prominent should be the consideration given to distributive justice in pricing policy deliberations. Justice cannot be the exclusive concern in these deliberations, but must be given its proportionate weight depending upon the way in which the questions in this framework are addressed. Thus, as pricing decisions duly consider factors such as production and promotion costs, etc., they should also take into account the element of distributive justice. Clearly, however, drugs that are less important for society because they deal with less serious ailments should not be subject to the same demands of justice as those for diseases which are truly life threatening or debilitating. Hence drug companies should have much more flexibility in pricing medicines for these less critical ailments....

This analysis does not by any means eliminate the frustrations regarding ethical pricing which were cited earlier by Walton. We can offer no definitive, quantitative formulae or comprehensive criteria to assure that pricing in this industry will always be fair and just. As with most moral decisions, much will depend on the individual judgment and moral sensitivity of the managers making those decisions.... It seems beyond doubt that responsible and fair pricing in the pharmaceutical industry is a serious moral imperative, since for so many consumers it is a matter of well-being or infirmity and perhaps even life or death.

We might consider once again the wisdom of Aristotle on this topic of justice. In the *Nicomachean Ethics* he writes that "we call those things 'just' which produce and preserve happiness for the social and political community" (1962, p. 113). If corporations respond to the demands of justice for the sake of the common good, it will help promote the elusive goal of a just community and a greater harmony between the corporation and its many concerned stakeholders.

NOTES

1. Holzman, D.: 1988, 'New Wonder Drugs at What Price?', *Insight* (March 21), pp. 54–55. For more recent data on drug prices see 'Maker of Schizophrenia Drug Bows to Pressure to Cut Costs', *The New York Times* (Dec. 6, 1990), pp. A1 and D3.

2. 'F. Hoffman-LaRoche and Company A.G.', Harvard Business School Case Study in Matthews, Goodpaster, Nash (eds.), *Policies and Persons* (McGraw Hill Book Company: N.Y., 1985).

REFERENCES

Aristotle: 1962, *Nicomachean Ethics*, trans. by M. Oswald (Library of Liberal Arts, Bobbs Merrill Company, Inc., Indianapolis).

Doppelt, G.: 1989, 'Beyond Liberalism and Communitarianism: Towards a Critical Theory of Social Justice', *Philosophy and Social Criticism* 14 (No. 3/4).

Goodpaster, K.: 1984, 'The Concept of Corporate Responsibility', in T. Regan (ed.), *Just Business: New Introductory Essays in Business Ethics* (Random House, New York).

Goodpaster, K. and Matthews, J.: 1989, 'Can a Corporation Have a Conscience', in K. Andrews (ed.), *Ethics in Practice* (Harvard Business School Press, Boston).

Mintzberg, H.: 1989, 'The Case for Corporate Social Responsibility', in A. Iannone (ed.), *Contemporary Moral Controversies in Business* (Oxford University Press, New York).

Rawls, J.: 1971, *A Theory of Justice* (Harvard University Press, Cambridge).

Walton, C.: 1969, *Ethos and the Executive* (Prentice Hall, Inc., Englewood Cliffs, N.J.).

NO

Pharmaceutical Manufacturers Association

PRICE CONTROLS IN THE ECONOMY AND THE HEALTH SECTOR

EXECUTIVE SUMMARY

The current national focus on health care reform has revived discussion of price controls as a possible policy instrument.

Such discussion is predictable because health-sector costs consistently have risen faster than the general rate of price inflation and—in part because of unintended inflationary consequences created by health-reform programs of the 1960s—have tended to be resistant to government efforts to date to contain them. If, as anticipated, current contemplated reform includes dramatic expansion of health system access, additional pressures for cost containment will be created.

This brief paper examines experience with price controls historically and, then, since World War II in the U.S. health sector. Major points:

1. Price controls have been attempted in many times and places dating back 40 centuries. Except in those times and places where national unity and consensus made controls easily enforceable—for instance, in World War II Great Britain where the country quite literally was fighting for its survival —they generally have failed. Moreover, when controls have been ended, inflation typically has equalled or exceeded the rate which would have been reached without controls. In the meantime, economic growth has been inhibited.
2. Controls, when applied, quickly create artificial scarcities, resource misallocations, and black markets. Large bureaucratic structures are required for administration. Problems of enforcement and equity arise. Since controls interfere with normal market mechanisms, issues of fairness (both to consumers and producers) quickly present themselves. Public support for controls quickly erodes.
3. In the United States, those government officials who have administered price controls universally counsel against their further use. These judgments are made, typically, on practical as well as theoretical bases.

From Pharmaceutical Manufacturers Association, "Price Controls in the Economy and the Health Sector," *Backgrounder* (April 1993). Copyright © 1993 by The Pharmaceutical Manufacturers Association. Reprinted by permission. Prepared independently for the Pharmaceutical Manufacturers Association by Van Dyk Associates, Inc., Washington, D.C.

4. In the health sector, the federal government has made numerous attempts since World War II to freeze or selectively control costs. None of these efforts has slowed a steady rise in health sector inflation.
5. The experience with overall drug-price controls has been limited in this country to Nixon-era controls. Their effect, however, was the same as with controls generally. Prices rose sharply after their relaxation.
6. Internationally, drug price controls also have proved ineffective. Additionally, they have reduced research into breakthrough drugs in countries where they have been adopted.
7. New health-sector price controls could be expected to create the same effects that prior controls have done. Alternative means of health-sector cost containment are available and already have been applied on a limited basis. All would be felt only over a longer period.

Summary: When faced with near-term general or sectoral inflation, national leaders often have turned to price controls. Such controls create enormous distortions and in the end do not quell inflation. Imperfect but applicable means of cost containment suggest themselves in the current effort toward health care reform. . . .

CLEAR LESSONS FROM THE EXPERIENCE OF THE UNITED STATES AND OTHER NATIONS WITH PRICE CONTROLS

From Hammurabi, Babylonia, and the Roman Empire to the 1970s experiences of the United States, Japan, Canada, and Australia, price controls have been tried. And in every single instance, with the possible exception of wartime Britain, they have been found wanting. They basically did not work. Their only certain result in any country has been to reduce production. And such losses in production usually mean a profit squeeze, less investment in plant and equipment and in R&D [research and development], and less growth in the future.

Another lesson learned: All the great monetary stabilizers of this century have been classical economists who insisted upon balanced budgets and government living within its means at home and abroad, without borrowing from the central bank or printing more paper money of its own.

Not one resorted to price controls because all knew from previous history that price controls, freezes and "rollbacks" simply produced scarcities and artificial distortions.

Treasury Secretary Lloyd Bentsen, while Vice Chairman of the Congressional Joint Economic Committee in 1978, chaired a hearing in which he noted that one of the problems he had seen with wage and price controls was that there were so many ways that they could be evaded. His assessment:

"Mandatory wage and price controls don't stop inflation any more than the Maginot line stopped the defeat of the French Army. And they are not going to protect the American consumer from all of the hurt and the damage of inflation. . . . The Joint Economic Committee . . . found that the mere prospect of controls . . . resulted in a substantial increase to the consumers of this country and additional inflation because of manufacturers increasing prices in anticipation of the wage demands that resulted...."

PRICE CONTROLS IN THE U.S. HEALTH SECTOR

Since World War II the federal government has made several attempts to control health care costs, either by freezing prices across the board or by imposing selective controls on individual sectors such as hospitals or physicians. None of these initiatives has slowed the steady rise in what Americans are paying for health care through taxes, through private insurance, or out of their own pockets.

Throughout this period, any savings achieved by controls in one sector have been offset by increased spending in others. Economies achieved by shorter patient stays in hospitals have been erased by higher payments for nursing home and home health care. Hospitals barred from adding new beds have poured the money into new outpatient facilities and expensive diagnostic equipment. Placing a ceiling on prices that doctors could charge for treatments or office visits simply has produced a larger number of treatments or office visits. Indeed, Medicare administrators drawing up a new "resource-based" schedule of allowable physician fees have factored into their calculations the assumption that doctors automatically would offset half the reduction in their rates of payment by an increase in billings.

No scheme yet tried has produced actual dollars-and-cents savings. No scheme could—short of central government control of all health care costs and spending. And were that attempted, it would produce... shortages, dislocations, and other problems....

This section will examine... health care price controls initiated at the federal level in the last 50 years, and show how and why they failed. (The wage-price stabilization program during the Korean War is not discussed because professional fees, such as doctor bills and hospital charges, were excluded from controls.) It will then sketch alternative cost control initiatives mounted in the private sector, often with government support, that offer more hope for moderating health care inflation than does price regulation....

The Steady Expansion of Federally-Funded Health Services

... [I]n the U.S. experience, price controls have not stemmed the growth of health care spending. As a government program, price controls necessarily exist in a political environment where other pressures are operating in the direction of greater spending. Each year, Congressional budgetmakers make significant cuts in Administration Medicare and Medicaid requests—almost always through cuts to providers. Yet each year, actual payments increase.

Why is it that, despite the "success" of PPS [Prospective Payment System] in halving the growth of inpatient hospital costs (the single largest segment of the Medicare program), total spending for hospital care by Medicare and Medicaid has doubled in the seven years after PPS over the seven years before—from $230 billion to $460 billion?

Why has total federal spending for Medicaid increased by 73 percent in just the last two years while Medicare spending was rising far less rapidly?

The answer: At the same time the government was administering its price controls, it was taking other actions that raised its health care costs. Example:

- In the same legislation in which Congress froze physician fees, it required Medicaid to cover more children and more low income pregnant women and extended Medicare to mammographies.
- At the same time it reduced provider fees for Medicare, it was mandating states to cover expensive and medically-questionable treatments under Medicaid, for which it provides half the funds.
- At the same time it was implementing the RVS fee schedule [a revised payment system for Medicare physicians, begun in 1992], Congress significantly extended Medicare benefits for nursing homes, home health and hospice care.

The same political thinking that makes price controls attractive to them makes it hard for policymakers to restrain themselves from sweetening government health benefits packages to enlist Congressional and interest-group support. This bit of history is instructive in view of the declared objective of the Clinton Administration to extend health insurance to the 37 million uninsured while at the same time reducing health care costs.

PRICE CONTROLS ON PHARMACEUTICALS

Conclusions about the wisdom of price controls in the pharmaceutical sector must be drawn primarily from the experience of other countries. The United States has had only one experience with such controls—during the wage-price freeze of the Nixon Administration. Most other industrialized countries have long tried to regulate drug prices and outlays as part of their broader programs of national health insurance. Only the United States and Denmark leave pricing to the competitive marketplace.

The U.S. Experience

The Nixon Administration Wage and Price Stabilization programs tried to control drug prices, with these results:

- In the three years prior to the program, the drug component of the Consumer Price Index had risen only 3 percent, considerably less than health care cost inflation generally.
- During the period of controls (April, 1971 through October, 1974) the Index increased by only 1.5 percent.
- As soon as controls were lifted, however, the typical "catch-up" effect was seen. Between 1975 and 1977, drug prices rose almost 12 percent. When the last impacts of price controls had faded from the economy, prices were probably higher than they would have been without controls.

Controls also were ineffective in curbing spending on drugs.

In the three years before they were instituted, patient drug costs rose by an average of $378 million a year. During the three control years, they rose $515 million a year. In the three years after, they rose $600 million a year....

Effects of Drug Price Controls Beyond Prices

... [I]t is clear that price controls on drugs in other countries have uniformly failed to accomplish their goal. It also is clear why controls, which are supposed to hold down spending, have had the opposite effect. If government decides for a pharmaceutical company how much it can charge for its products, the company has little incentive to conduct the extremely expensive search for truly innovative and breakthrough therapies. The odds against a drug in development making it to market are 5,000 to 1. Even when a drug advances to where it is actually tested in clinical trials on patients, the odds against its being marketed are 10 to 1. Unless there is pricing freedom, the financial reward is just not worth the risk.

Many firms in nations with strict price controls largely have abandoned the search for breakthrough drugs. Funds that might have been used for research have been shifted to increased promotion and marketing of existing drugs, seeking increased demand as a way of maintaining revenues in the face of controlled prices. Foreign firms also engage in low-risk research and development to come up [with] "new" drugs that are not innovative, and only marginally better than existing therapies, but are nonetheless eligible for higher controlled prices than the older drugs in their inventory.

A study of the French pharmaceutical industry, which was responsible for only 3 world class drugs between 1975 and 1989, concluded that "the calibre of research [has] deteriorated because severe price control has encouraged French companies to give priority to small therapeutic improvements which are useful in price negotiations." Of Japan, Dr. Heinz Redwood, a British researcher and policy analyst, says "There is a pronounced tendency to develop 'Japanese drugs for Japan' rather than for world health care. This is largely the result of the Japanese system of price regulation... which grants very high prices for new drugs, whilst putting heavy pricing pressure on older drugs."

In Italy, the Ruoppolo Commission, created to revamp the price control system to give greater encouragement to innovative activity, reported that:

> "The virtual freezing of the price of old products... has acted as a decisive incentive in the search by companies for new registrations in order to obtain more up-to-date prices; and then, by means of appropriate promotion, induce a prescription shift from the old to the new [drug]."

Were price controls to touch off the same syndrome here, it could have a profound effect not only on the nature of this country's pharmaceutical industry but on world health. The international community depends on innovative U.S. industry to provide it with new medicines. Almost 50 percent of the new drugs effective enough to be marketed globally in the past 20 years have been developed in the U.S. In biotechnology and immunology, it is 70 percent.

What Will Happen If New Price Controls Are Placed on Health Care?

Given previous experience with price controls generally, and on what has happened when they have been imposed in different forms upon the U.S. health care system, it is not difficult to speculate what will happen if federal policymakers impose what have been called "interim cost containment measures" to hold the line on prices for the period—probably several years—that will pass before a new national health insurance system can be passed into law, implemented by regulations, survive the inevitable court challenges, and actually begin to operate throughout the country.

1. Investment funds that would have flowed into the development of new

medical technology, new cures for disease and other advances will be diverted to other, more economically attractive channels.

2. The economic incentive to enter the health care field will decline, eventually leading to a shortage of physicians and other trained personnel.

3. Providers will continue to find ways to "game" the system, reducing hoped-for savings. To counter this, government will impose increasing supervision, restrictions, and paperwork on the activities of health care professionals.

4. The quality of health care will suffer. Physicians will spend less time with patients and there will be fewer drugs in hospital formularies. Shortages and waiting lists will develop as they have in other countries. Those who can afford it will try to preserve their current quality of care by creating a separate, privately-funded privileged system of health care as exists in Britain. This alternative system in turn will draw the best professionals and force the quality of care given the rest of us lower.

5. The inherent contradiction between universal system access and simultaneous cost containment inevitably will lead to de facto rationing of care. The Medicaid experience is instructive here. As Medicaid has become the largest item in their budgets, many states have severely restricted reimbursement under the program. Many doctors have responded by refusing to take Medicaid patients. To expand eligibility for Medicaid, the state of Oregon has had to adopt a rationing system, barring payment for whole categories of treatments. Similarly, Great Britain denies expensive surgery to patients over a certain age.

Alternative to Controls Which Could Contain Costs

Health care costs can be contained without the distortions created by controls.

Most of the measures listed below now are being practiced in the health care system—many with the support and encouragement of government. Others are readily available. Strong incentives to use these measures would occur under "managed competition" schemes for health care reform.

- Expansion of Health Maintenance Organizations, group practice associations, and other organizations under which health care practitioners have no incentives to perform unneeded services.

- Expansion of Preferred Provider Organizations and other arrangements in which physicians give up higher fees for an assured caseload.

- Greater emphasis on prevention, early intervention, wellness, and lifestyle changes to lower the incidence of disease and the necessity for surgery.

- Requiring second opinions before surgery and other expensive services.

- Living wills, which give terminal patients the right to appoint someone to decide when to stop the use of high-cost technology whose only purpose is to prolong life according to its clinical definition.

- Drug utilization review systems, that are consistent with the principles developed by the American Medical Association, the American Pharmaceutical Association, and the Pharmaceutical Manufacturers Association. Such systems detect and correct inappropriate prescribing practices as well as fraud and abuse.

- Encouraging medical innovation, including the development of cost-effective therapies such as drugs as a cure for major diseases and a substitute for surgery.
- Greater research on the "outcomes" of alternative treatments, to spread knowledge among physicians about the most effective treatments and therapies.
- Education of patients so they can work more knowledgeably with their doctors. Patient information should be more widely available on computer networks.
- Tort reform to reduce the practice of "defensive" medicine to avoid malpractice suits which, according to the American Medical Association, costs the health care system $15 billion a year.
- Measures to reduce redundancy of expensive technologies and equipment in the same markets—i.e., where several hospitals and clinics in the same area invest in the same costly technologies whereas demand might justify only one such facility.
- The imposition of substantial deductibles and/or co-payments on the insured so as to require patients to make prudent choices about health expenditures. (A Rand Corporation study has shown that patients, when required to write a check on each physician visit, make visits with less frequency.)
- Voluntary industry measures to limit drug-price increases, with or without

antitrust waivers, with provision for monitoring by credible third-party agency.

None of the above measures, of course, can be expected to produce immediate and dramatic reductions in health-sector inflation—particularly if implemented while health-sector access simultaneously is being dramatically expanded. Nor can they counteract and overcome those factors which plague the U.S. health system more greatly than those of other Western countries: High rates of poverty, violent crime, homelessness, aging, AIDS and drug abuse.

The aforementioned measures are appropriate ways of maintaining quality while reducing costs. Any government involvement should be designed to increase incentives to adopt such measures.

But the government cannot have it both ways by adopting incentives for the marketplace to manage care *and* government price controls on the components of care. To manage care, providers and insurers must invest significant fiscal and human resources into restructuring, expanding and monitoring health care delivery. Why invest when price controls will likely reward those providers who were most inefficient in the old fragmented system? Attempts to solve the data needs equity issues and enforcement rules would further slow enactment of proper incentives.

At the same time, however, it can be predicted with relative certainty that, given past international and U.S. experience, health-sector as well as other price controls—even when applied short-term—lead to distortions and, over time, do not result in net cost reductions.

POSTSCRIPT

Are Pharmaceutical Price Controls Justifiable?

The United States is more committed to the free market than any other developed nation. Consequently, the arguments advanced by the Pharmaceutical Manufacturers Association against pharmaceutical price controls tend to be accepted for all cases: attempts to regulate the market must fail. According to the laws of the market, if we try to support prices (as with the products of American farms), we will drive buyers from the market and tempt inefficient suppliers to stay in, both of which tend to drive prices *down*. Without price supports, prices would likely recover on their own as enthusiastic buyers outbid each other for the reduced amount of product. On the other hand, as in the case of pharmaceuticals, if we try to control prices, we will drive suppliers from the market and truncate the healthy process of competition that would have brought prices down naturally. Meanwhile, the company's reward for, and means for, pursuing research into better drugs would be destroyed.

But the principles of justice, which govern us as surely as the laws of supply and demand, require that we make our economic arrangements keeping in mind the fate of the least advantaged among us. Does the market do that? Which do we hold more dear, the liberty of the market or justice in distribution? As Spinello notes, people who have AIDS are dying. Is it likely that this fact will eventually persuade pharmaceutical manufacturers to accept price controls?

SUGGESTED READINGS

Judy Chaconas, "Providers Offer Prescription for Medicaid Drug-Pricing Law," *Trustee* (December 1991).

Joseph A. DiMasi et al., "The Cost of Innovation in the Pharmaceutical Industry," *Journal of Health Economics* (vol. 10, 1991).

David Hanson, "Report on Drug R & D Fuels Attack on Prices," *Chemical and Engineering News* (March 8, 1993).

Office of Technology Assessment, *Pharmaceutical R & D: Costs, Risks and Rewards* (Government Printing Office, 1993).

David Pryor, "Drugs *Must* Be Made Affordable," *The New York Times* (March 7, 1993), p. F13.

Pamela Zurer, "NIH Weighs Role in Drug Pricing," *Chemical and Engineering News* (December 21, 1992).

ISSUE 7

Should Casino Gambling Be Prohibited?

YES: Citizens' Research Education Network, from *The Other Side of the Coin: A Casino's Impact in Hartford* (December 16, 1992)

NO: William R. Eadington, from "The Proliferation of Commercial Gaming in America," *The Sovereign Citizen* (Fall 1994)

ISSUE SUMMARY

YES: The Citizens' Research Education Network, formed to evaluate the effects of Connecticut's rapidly growing enthusiasm for casino gambling, concludes that casinos are harmful to cities and that other avenues to urban revival should be pursued.

NO: Professor of economics William R. Eadington argues that gambling is a normal extension of commercial activity and that it can promote the welfare of areas that host casinos.

Cities in the United States grew to wealth and splendor with the expansion of heavy manufacturing and America's domination of the world markets following World War II. The cities attracted hundreds of thousands of immigrants in search of jobs, education, and a better life for themselves and their families. While the good times lasted, waves of immigrants educated their children and watched them move up into the mobile middle class and adopt a suburban lifestyle. When the bad times came, the last of those waves (notably the African Americans and Hispanics from the South and from the Caribbean) were left stranded in cities without jobs, without ways up or out, and with little hope for improvement.

In times of growth, the rich cities created and offered to the public an enormous variety of expensive services—medical, cultural, and social support—that were not available in the smaller towns. These services were funded by the high tax revenues from the manufacturers, who were forced to stay in the cities by their need for raw materials and labor—they could only operate where the railroads converged, the ships could dock, and very large numbers of people lived within walking distance of the plants.

Beginning in the 1950s, technological advance led to new forms of transportation for raw materials and made possible new types of factories that employed a fraction of the workforce demanded by the old ones. No longer did the factories have to stay in the cities, and taxes were much lower elsewhere, so they left. The educated middle class also left; they moved to the new suburbs, where they created new country villages with pleasant vistas and low property taxes, and where they could still use the city's resources if they wanted. Left behind, however, were the workers who could not move; the expensive services—the hospitals and universities; and various people who had drifted to the city because they needed those services but had no means by which to leave. The cities were left without a tax base and without any clear direction for an economic future.

Present initiatives to introduce casino gambling to cities, and the issue before us in this debate, result from two facts. First, traditional economic remedies are unlikely to help the cities. The services that the public demands from the cities are too expensive to support with any available enterprise that might choose to locate in a city. Manufacturing has been lost to technology and foreign competition, and the new information industries will not employ the city's poor and undereducated, feed its hungry, or care for its sick.

Second, casino gambling has shown itself to be a highly profitable enterprise. No coercive collection mechanisms are needed to transfer money from private pockets to the public good; people choose freely and happily to spend their money at the gaming tables. Costs are low and revenues are spectacular. For instance, the Mashantucket Pequot Indians in Connecticut set up a casino on their reservation in 1992. The casino now supports and educates every member of the once-destitute tribe with its income; it contributes handsomely to Native American cultural foundations; it employs hundreds of non-Indian residents of the state; and, in addition to what it contributes to the state in taxes, it transfers $130 million each year to Connecticut as quid pro quo for the casino's monopoly on slot machines.

Inner cities are dying for lack of jobs and money; casinos supply both, without adding to the tax burden of the marginal industries and dwindling middle class that remains within the city boundaries. The argument to bring casino gambling into the cities seems compelling. However, critics have expressed concern about the possible relationship between casinos and crime, especially organized crime. Critics also cite the many problems associated with compulsive gambling and the additional drain that impoverished gamblers put on social services.

As you read the following selections, remember that no one can really know for certain how far the market for gaming will continue to expand or what effects casinos will have on aging urban centers.

YES

Citizens' Research
Education Network

THE OTHER SIDE OF THE COIN:
A CASINO'S IMPACT IN HARTFORD

HUMAN COSTS SUMMARY

Casino Supporters' Claims vs. Reality

Neighborhoods

Claims: Casinos will revitalize Hartford.

Reality: Casinos created land speculation in Atlantic City that led to the mass destruction of homes and businesses that served local residents. Nevada has a higher rate of poverty than Connecticut. While jobs are being created in Las Vegas at a high rate, older central neighborhoods do not appear to benefit. Rather, new neighborhoods are being built on the outskirts of the city to house workers who move into Las Vegas from other areas. Las Vegas is not just the exciting, prosperous town casino supporters would have us believe. Riots broke out in sections of Las Vegas following the Rodney King verdict, indicating a high level of frustration and anger in some Las Vegas neighborhoods. There is no evidence that casinos will bring anything to Hartford neighborhoods but dislocation, crime, and traffic.

Gambling Addiction

Claims: Addicted gambling is a small problem.

Reality: Connecticut already has one of the highest levels of gambling addiction measured and studies have shown that casinos are especially inviting to addicted gamblers. Pathological gambling is a growing problem that affects about 160,000 people in Connecticut. Furthermore, it is estimated that for each addicted gambler, 10 to 17 other people (family members, employers, employees, crime victims, creditors) are negatively affected by the addicted gambler's behavior. Addicted gamblers often commit crimes for money to continue gambling and by the time they seek treatment, many

From Citizens' Research Education Network, *The Other Side of the Coin: A Casino's Impact in Hartford* (December 16, 1992). Notes omitted.

have no money, no job, and no insurance. Therefore, the public costs to treat gambling addiction are much higher than other addictions. In addition to crime and addiction treatment, it has been estimated that each addicted gambler costs society $30,000 in "abused money" and lost productivity. It is believed that almost 25% of addicted gamblers attempt suicide.

Youth

Claims: The complex will provide family entertainment. Under-age persons will not be allowed in the casino.

Reality: Gambling addiction is twice as high among youths as adults and casinos have poor records for keeping out underage gamblers. One study of underage college students near Atlantic City found that 40% of them had gambled in a nearby casino. Nearly one-third of high school students in New Jersey reported gambling weekly or more in 1987, more than three times the rate in other states. Among the adult population, problem gamblers are more likely than other gamblers to have started gambling before they were 15 years old. The marketing of casinos as part of a family entertainment complex exposes more children to gambling who may later develop gambling addiction.

HUMAN COSTS OF CASINOS

Residents of Hartford are facing multiple crises in the 1990s. Drug abuse continues to outpace efforts to discourage it; unemployment is high; the schools are struggling to educate children with too little money and support; child abuse and neglect is commonplace; and alcoholism

still destroys families. As businesses close or move away, hope grows dimmer. There is no place for residents to buy groceries at a fair and reasonable price. Child care is difficult to find. Is a casino going to meet any of the real needs of Hartford residents?

CASINOS AND THE NEIGHBORHOODS

While all of Hartford would be affected in some way by the presence of a casino, the proposed location of the casino complex makes its impact especially important to people living in Hartford's north end. The preliminary proposal by Steve Wynn would require the demolition of Barnard-Brown School and the Hartford Graduate Center. Right near the site lie several offices, social service agencies, and apartments. Those will all be affected by the casino complex. The next concern is what kind of development will tend to spring up around the casino and how will that affect the people who live and work in the neighboring community?

The impact of the casino on the nearby neighborhood would depend largely on the legislation controlling its operation. One possibility is that speculative investment in Hartford real estate could destroy residential areas and force businesses that serve Hartford residents to close. This was the case in Atlantic City in large part because the city government gave the impression that it would allow casinos in any part of the city. Although a plan was adopted that limited casinos to specific areas, the city regularly granted exemptions to that restriction. The result was that developers bought property all over the city in hopes that someone else may eventually buy it from them (at a much higher price) to build a casino.

Once speculators owned land, they found it easier to tear down the existing buildings while they waited for a casino developer to come along. By tearing down the buildings, they saved money on property taxes. Needed housing for residents of Atlantic City was thus destroyed, although few of the sites ever became casinos.

The issue comes down to what speculators *believe* is the attitude of city officials regarding further development, not what their attitudes really are. If government leaders appear divided on this issue or speculators believe that new leaders will be elected who will favor further casino development, land speculation and displacement of city residents could result.

Even if speculators believe that no more casinos will ever be allowed in Hartford, the construction of the casino complex and supporting facilities will affect the neighboring area. Virtually all of the visitors to the casino will be arriving by car or bus. Many will use the highways; many may seek shortcuts through the surrounding streets. (Since casinos are generally a 24-hour business, the effect of cars and buses at all hours could be very disturbing to nearby residents.) Roads may have to be widened. Perhaps parking garages will be added. All we really know is that the area will be affected, probably in a way that does not preserve the unique architecture of that neighborhood or benefit the residents or small businesses owners.

The exact location of a Hartford casino is not set in stone, but the question for the people in the neighborhoods near any casino site has to be whether they trust the political process enough to believe that it will prevent destructive speculation and development that displaces current residents and businesses. Hartford has experience with that kind of development: Constitution Plaza replaced a thriving neighborhood that had supported generations of Hartford immigrants; I-84 was built where other neighborhoods had once been, causing the city to lose some wonderful old buildings. True community development happens when people in an area have better housing, better job opportunities, and chances to start their own businesses. The steam-roller style development of Las Vegas casino developers won't benefit the people who live in our communities.

PROBLEM AND PATHOLOGICAL GAMBLING

It is estimated that there are between 43,000 and 94,000 pathological gamblers in Connecticut, plus between 61,000 and 121,000 problem gamblers. Together, that represents about 6.3% of the adult population of Connecticut.

Gambling addiction is a real problem that needs to be carefully considered and addressed. Addicted gamblers are split into two groups by mental health experts. People with the addiction are problem gamblers; those with severe addictions are pathological gamblers.

Pathological gambling has symptoms similar to those of addictions to alcohol or other drugs. Increasing amounts of money are gambled; the gambler becomes obsessed with betting and acts without concern for the impact on himself or others. (Three out of four addicted gamblers are male.) He borrows money to gamble beyond his ability to repay it in hopes that he will get lucky. Many begin to commit crimes in order to get money for gambling. Families suffer as gamblers use money that should be used to pay the rent or buy food. By the time an addicted gambler seeks treatment, he is often unemployed and/or uninsured. Therefore, the costs of treatment need to be paid by the public. Addicted gamblers also have no money to hire attorneys, so if an addicted gambler is charged with a crime, the public defender's office often must provide legal defense. The financial strain on the addicted gambler's family is often severe and the family may need public assistance. The public and personal costs of gambling addiction are, therefore, very high.

Experts on gambling addictions say that the social stigma that was once associated with gambling has been removed. At the same time, while people are bombarded with messages about the dangers of drug or alcohol abuse, no widespread effort exists to educate them about the dangers of gambling. As the State of Connecticut has progressed from charity bingo to the state lottery to pari-mutuel wagering to the daily lotto to casinos, the message is clear that gambling is now an acceptable form of recreation. Thus, more people are more likely to try gambling. Of those who try gambling, a certain percentage will be likely to develop a gambling addiction.

The only national study of gambling concluded that the availability of gambling in Nevada had caused an increase in gambling addiction. In that study, 0.77% of the adult population nationally scored as "probable compulsive gamblers" while 2.62% of Nevada residents scored as such. (People who had moved to Nevada recently or specifically for the gambling opportunities were not counted.) According to the State of Connecticut's consultant regarding gam-

bling, "All subsequent studies of the prevalence of problem gambling, regardless of the methods used, indicate that *casino gambling* is especially appealing to problem and pathological gamblers."

Gambling addiction does not strike all people equally. Rachel Volberg, a specialist in the study of problem gambling, has said, "Certain groups appear to be at greater risk for developing gambling related problems. Minority individuals, African Americans and Hispanics, seem to be at a somewhat greater risk; also, individuals under the age of 30, individuals with low income and low levels of education." ...

Financial Costs of Gambling Addiction
In addition to the pure social impact of gambling addiction, there are financial costs. While the exact costs associated with the high number of addicted gamblers in Connecticut are impossible to measure, estimates can be made. The Task Force on Gambling Addiction in Maryland estimated that the 50,000 pathological gamblers in that state cost "$1.5 billion annually in lost work productivity and embezzled, stolen or otherwise abused dollars." If that cost estimate holds true for Connecticut, **the cost of *pathological* gambling in this state is between $1.3 and $2.8 billion annually.** (This does not include similar costs for problem gamblers.)

Looked at another way, the cost for each addicted gambler is $30,000 per year in lost productivity and "abused" (i.e., embezzled or stolen) money. (This estimate does not include the costs of law enforcement, medical treatment, or family support.) Thus, if 1,000 people develop a gambling addiction as a result of the great access and temptation of a downtown casino, it will cost society $30 million, plus the costs of law enforcement and addiction treatment, which are substantial. Much of this expense will have to be borne by Connecticut taxpayers.

Problem and pathological gambling should not be dismissed lightly. It is an expensive social problem that affects hundreds of thousands of people. Nationally, rates of addictive gambling have increased dramatically over the past two decades, growing right along with the increase in legal gambling options.

CASINOS AND YOUTH

Addictive gambling among high-school age persons is becoming a widely recognized crisis nationally. Although students are constantly exposed to messages about the dangers of drugs and alcohol, they are also told that gambling is a respectable form of entertainment. State sponsored gambling (i.e. the state lottery) strongly sends the message that gambling is acceptable. It is even presented as a virtue because revenues often go to good causes like education or the elderly. Advertising for state lotteries is widespread, misleading, and effective. More kids, therefore, try gambling and more become addicted.

It is estimated that about 5% of high school students have gambling addictions. Many have no trouble buying lottery tickets from careless vendors, and illegal bookies have been known to develop a large business from students. In 1987, almost one-third of the high school students in north, central, and south New Jersey stated that they gambled weekly or more. This is 3–5 times the rate in other states. It is estimated that at least one million minors gamble in Atlantic City casinos each year. One survey of college students at a New Jersey campus near Atlantic City found that 40% of the under-21 students had illegally gambled at a nearby casino.

The cynical view of the current move to "family entertainment" centers in Las Vegas (as well as the complex proposed for Hartford) is that the gamblers of tomorrow are being groomed today. Gambling has left the smoke-filled back room and has become more widely accepted. Casinos are now being marketed as appropriate family vacation destinations. It is not yet known how that will affect the attitudes of children who grow up surrounded by this kind of gambling. Barriers to gambling that traditionally existed are being destroyed and it can be safely assumed that, in the future, more of today's children will gamble more money more often.

CRIME SUMMARY

Casino Supporters' Claims vs. Reality

Regular Crime

Claims: Casinos do not attract crime any more than would a Disney theme park.

Reality: Analysts have concluded that two-thirds of the crime increase expected from a new casino in New Orleans is because it is a casino, not because of the number of new visitors to the city. Casinos simply attract a different kind of customer (and criminal) than would a children's theme park. It is estimated that a 100,000-square foot casino in New Orleans that attracts 5 million visitors a year will cost the city about $5 million in law enforcement and court cost.

Organized Crime

Claims: Casino operators have no connection to organized crime.

Reality:

- Any business that creates the huge cash profits of the casino industry has a tendency to attract organized crime.
- Links between the most respected casino operators and organized crime have been exposed repeatedly. For example, early in 1992, the Las Vegas Police Department released a list of the associates of Charles Meyerson, a long-time friend and employee of Steve Wynn, who have ties to organized crime families. Meyerson's work card was revoked by the city for arranging a free five-night stay at the Mirage for three high-ranking members of the Genovese crime family in July of 1991 and Mr. Meyerson was accused by Las Vegas police of being an associate of Genovese crime boss Anthony "Fat Tony" Solerno. (A vice president and director of Wynn's company resigned his position in 1984 after he was seen by investigators visiting Solerno's headquarters in New York.)
- Traditionally, casinos have been used by organized crime to launder cash. The best way to prevent this is to report large cash transactions to authorities, but the IRS stated in August, 1992, that despite tough new reporting requirements, casino employees are still lax in reporting large cash transactions.
- Law enforcement experts say that organized crime infiltration of casino-related businesses and labor unions

is a very real problem. The United States Senate Permanent Subcommittee on Investigations found in 1984 that organized crime actively involved with the Hotel Employees and Restaurant Employees International Union. The Subcommittee concluded that the union locals in Las Vegas and Atlantic City were controlled by organized crime. In December 1990, the U.S. Justice Department brought a civil action against the Las Vegas local, alleging that it was controlled by the Bruno/Scarfo family of organized crime.

POTENTIAL IMPACT ON CRIME IN HARTFORD

It's a question as old as the casino business itself. Will the introduction of casinos increase the level of crime in the community? Everyone, including casino supporters, will agree that a casino will cause the crime rate to increase. But, the casino supporters also argue that *any attraction* that brings visitors to a city will cause crime. Crime is no more a reason to stop casinos, they argue, than any other tourist development.

Casinos vs. Disney World

Recently, a casino executive stated that the crime rate in Orlando—the home of Disney World—is higher than the crime rate in Atlantic City, even though they both have about 30 million visitors per year. The executive concluded that there is nothing about casinos themselves that attracts criminals.

A common sense way to compare the impact of casinos in Atlantic City with the impact of Disney in Orlando is to look at their reported crimes before and after the opening of these entertainment developments. While Orlando has experienced a disturbing increase in crime over the past 25 years, there is no noticeable jump in criminal activity immediately following the opening of Disney World. Between 1977 [when the first casino opened] and 1982 in Atlantic City, however, crime increased 237% and has stayed high since.

Furthermore, the crime rate increase or decrease each year in Orlando closely mirrors those of all of Florida. The increase in the crime rate in Atlantic City, however, jumped much higher than the crime rate seen in all of New Jersey in 1977.

Casino Crime Separated from Tourist Crime

Analysts at the University of New Orleans, Division of Business and Economic Research, did a study of casino crime to separate the effect of increased visitors from the effect of casino gambling per se.

They compiled data from 80 cities, large and small, and factored into their analysis of crime:

- number of visitors
- personal income
- poverty rates
- racial composition
- unemployment rates
- population density
- police expenditures

By accounting for all these factors that influence crime rates, they were able to separate the impact casino gambling has on crime *from the effect of increased tourism.* What they concluded was that in New Orleans, a 100,000 square foot casino with 4.9 million visitors a year would mean 3,802 additional crimes within the city. *More than two-thirds of those crimes (2,625)*

would be due to gambling, less than one-third (1,177) would be due to increased visitors to the city. They calculated that the new crime caused by the casino would cost the city almost $5 million per year in police and corrections spending, district attorney costs, and court costs. The State of Louisiana would also face the costs of housing additional convicted criminals in prison.

Clearly, casinos are different than other tourist attractions. They create an atmosphere that attracts a different group of people than does a Disney theme park. Hartford needs to take this certain increase in crime into consideration before allowing a casino in the city.

CASINOS AND ORGANIZED CRIME

Experts disagree over the extent that organized crime is involved in the casino gambling industry. Many believe that tight regulation of casinos has driven organized crime away over the past 30 years or so.

Links to the Mob

An in-depth analysis of organized crime and its involvement with casinos is beyond the scope of this analysis. Of particular interest to Hartford, however, may be the legal troubles of Mirage Resorts employees over the years. The *Las Vegas Review-Journal* has published stories detailing links between one long-time Mirage Resorts employee and organized crime. His history of association with organized crime figures (he claims to have not known about their criminal ties) shows the kind of "innocent" trouble casino operators can get into.

Corruption of the unions that staff casinos is also a major problem. The U.S. Senate Permanent Subcommittee on Investigations found in 1984 that organized crime was active in the Hotel Employees and Restaurant Employees International Union and concluded that the union locals in Las Vegas and Atlantic City were controlled by organized crime. In December 1990, the U.S. Justice Department brought a civil action against the Las Vegas local, alleging that it was controlled by the Bruno/Scarfo family of organized crime.

Political Corruption

Any industry with as much wealth as the casino business opens the door to inappropriate political influence. Political corruption has been a problem in Atlantic City both before and after the arrival of the casinos. Three mayors have been convicted of corruption since 1977 and three more have been forced to resign. Political corruption limits any government's ability to regulate or act in the community's best interest. The casino also presents an opportunity to build political patronage. Government officials may have the temptation to use their influence (gained from casino operators in exchange for their legislative support) to get jobs for friends, thereby giving the casino even more power to influence policy decisions.

Money Laundering

Another major drawback of the casino business is some of the customers it attracts. People who make a lot of money and operate on a cash basis (i.e. drug dealers or "mobsters") make excellent casino patrons because they have money to spare and are limited in how they can spend it. Federal regulations have been tightened over the years so that very large cash transactions through casinos have to be reported much as they are through banks, but the casino industry has a long history of looking the other way.

There have been repeated incidents of organized crime figures being associated with major casino hotel executives who claim ignorance of the mob ties.

Organized crime is a serious problem and law enforcement professionals around the country say that the threat of organized crime infiltration of casino-related businesses must be fully considered before allowing a casino in the city.

CONCLUSION

Public officials must look beyond personal gain or even state budget needs to make a determination of what is truly in the public's best interest. Urban casinos do not contribute to the public good, would ultimately harm the city, and should, therefore, not be allowed in Hartford.

Although the casino industry has already entered Connecticut through the Mashantucket Pequot reservation, bringing casinos to the cities of the state will create far more problems than it will solve.

Among the problems identified are:

- casino associated costs (law enforcement, gambling addiction, traffic) that exceed the casino generated public revenue;
- replacement of existing jobs with casino jobs;
- negative impact on non-casino businesses;
- failure to develop a convention or tourism industry in Hartford;
- increased levels of gambling addiction, especially among Hartford residents;
- the creation of a gambling environment in Connecticut that may act to discourage investment by other industries;

- negative influence on Hartford's youth, especially the unmistakable message that gambling is acceptable in light of the high rates of addicted teenage gamblers;
- higher rates of crime; and
- likely attraction of organized crime to Hartford.

Hartford would be best served by devoting its resources to developing and implementing a comprehensive economic development plan designed to create a diversified economy. Dependence on only one or two industries is not in Hartford's best interest.

NO

William R. Eadington

THE PROLIFERATION OF COMMERCIAL GAMING IN AMERICA

Commercial gaming has arrived in America in the 1990s. To understand this, it is worthwhile to begin by examining the phenomenal success of the Foxwood's Casino and High Stakes Bingo in Ledyard, Connecticut. This is an Indian casino, owned by the 260 tribal members of the Mashantuckett Pequot Indian tribe, which opened in February, 1992. The amount of revenue generated by the casino in gaming winnings—customer expenditures on table games—in its first year of operation exceeded $200 million. In their second year of operation, after they negotiated with the Governor of Connecticut for the right to have slot machines and an exclusive franchise on casinos in Connecticut in exchange for a minimum $100 million payment to the State, their gaming winnings will approach $500 million. In their third year of operation—1994—when they have doubled their size, their gross gaming revenues could approach $700 million. At that point, they will be generating almost as much revenue as all the casinos in Reno, Nevada.

For another comparison, if you were to take all the movie theaters in America, the Foxwood's Casino is already generating about 10% as much in revenue as is generated in all ticket sales to all movie theaters in this country. Furthermore, because of its monopoly status in New England, the casino's profit margins are likely to be approximately 50%. That is for a tribe that ten years ago only had three people living on the reservation.

The gaming industry in America is going through an unprecedented proliferation and expansion that carries with it some amazing stories, of which the Ledyard situation is one. It also poses some fascinating and quite complex challenges to public policy, with regard to the impact that gambling is likely to have on society.

We are in the midst of a near total reversal of legal commercial gaming opportunities for American citizens in terms of their presence and accessibility. We are actually in the midst of a phenomenon that is occurring world wide.

From William R. Eadington, "The Proliferation of Commercial Gaming in America," *The Sovereign Citizen*, no. 1 (Fall 1994). Copyright © 1994 by Nichols College Institute for American Values. Reprinted by permission.

I would like to address a number of questions that relate to this phenomenon. Generally the questions are:

- Why is this occurring at this particular point in time?
- What are the dimensions of the gaming industries that are emerging?
- Where are these changes likely to carry us?
- What challenges will society have to confront as gambling becomes more and more present, and more and more pervasive in modern society?

As with many other facets of society, the following axiom is a useful starting point. To understand where we are today, we must first have an understanding of where we have been and how we have evolved to the current situation. Then we must try to see the directions implied by the current momentum to project what the situation will be like over the next couple of decades.

If one looks back as recently as 1910, we could note that gambling In America was virtually illegal almost everywhere. 1910 is interesting because that was the year that Nevada made casinos illegal. It was the year that New York made pari-mutuel wagering and race track wagering illegal. The only legal gambling one could find that year was on race tracks in Kentucky and in parts of Maryland. Everywhere else in America, gambling was illegal.

A half century later, in the year 1960, gambling was still largely prohibited in America. There were, as of yet, no lotteries. Casinos could be found only in Nevada, but Nevada, clearly, in the eyes of the rest of the country, was an outlaw state, which had created an environment to allow outlaws to legitimize themselves in the casino business. Wagering on racing had proliferated to about twenty states. However, people in the racing industry had a tendency to claim they were not in the gambling business; rather, they were in the business of improving the bloodlines and breed stock of thoroughbred horses, and if wagering on horses could be used as a way to subsidize the improvement of the quality of horses in this country, all the better.

That was the extent of legal gaming. There was a lot of illegal gambling, to be sure, but it was often viewed with a very critical eye. It was often cited as being the major source of income for organized crime, and a common view of gambling at the time could be summed up by an article written by Robert Kennedy, soon to become Attorney General of the United States. The article was entitled, "A Two Dollar Bet Means Murder". That seemed to summarize the public attitude towards gambling as late as the 1960s.

Churches, governments and good citizens agreed that gambling was evil, or at least that gambling was not something that should be accepted and brought into society. What were the substantive reasons? It was felt that gambling corrupted officials and law enforcement; it undermined the Protestant ethic of linkages between hard work and reward. And gambling could destroy lives through compulsive gambling, which would also lead to thefts, embezzlement, suicides, or worse. In total, gambling was considered a thoroughly unwholesome activity. That did not mean it was not fun for customers, however.

The contrast with the status of commercial gaming in the 1990s, however, is striking. Lotteries, which did not exist at all in America in 1960, can now be found in thirty-seven states and the District of Columbia. More than eighty percent of Americans can walk down to their local convenience store and purchase a lottery ticket. In 1992 lottery sales in America were over $21 billion, and after payment of prizes to winners, lotteries generated gross revenues of about $10 billion to the various states that had them. Casinos, as late as 1989 still could only be found in two places in the United States, in Nevada and in Atlantic City. Yet only four years later, one could gamble legally casino style in Nevada and Atlantic City, New Jersey; in mining town small stakes casinos in South Dakota and Colorado; on riverboats in Iowa, Illinois and Mississippi, and soon Louisiana, Missouri and Indiana. Or one could go [to] Indian casinos in Connecticut, Michigan, Minnesota, Wisconsin, South Dakota, Washington, Arizona, California, Colorado, New York, and soon in Mississippi, Louisiana, Texas and Rhode Island. All of this has transpired in a period of four years.

There has also been an expansion of non-casino casino style gambling, in the form of slot machines, video poker machines, or—in the euphemistically more acceptable name—video lottery terminals. The spread of gaming devices has been quite rapid, with their introduction into bars and taverns or other age restricted locations in the states of Montana, South Carolina, South Dakota, Oregon, Louisiana, West Virginia and Rhode Island. It has also recently been considered by the legislature of the state of Massachusetts, among others.

What does the casino industry do? How big an industry is casino gaming? And how does it affect peoples lives?

In 1992, the gross winnings for the various gaming industries in the United States, including lotteries, casinos, race tracks, charitable gambling and Indian gaming, were nearly $30 billion. That is the total expenditure of all customers on various gambling products. This also reflects total player losses after payment of winnings, as well as gross revenues on gaming to the various operators and purveyors of gambling services. This is approximately 0.6% of disposable income in the United States; roughly one-dollar out of every $150 spent in America is spent on gambling. This represents about five times as much money as Americans spend on going out to the movies: it represents about the same amount of income that is earned by all stock brokerages and securities firms in America; it represents approximately one-fourth of the gross revenues of all attorneys in America. Gambling is not a small business, it is substantial in its revenues and in its presence in society, and it is in the midst of a phenomenal expansion.

What has happened to social attitudes concerning gambling, and why are we seeing this phenomenon occurring now, at this very point in time?

There have historically been three main arguments in opposition to gambling. All of these arguments have been undermined by trends in the past three decades. The arguments are as follows:

1. Gambling leads to political corruption and brings organized crime into the mainstream of society.

However, as has been discovered time and again, political corruption and the infiltration of organized crime into gambling occurs more often when gambling is illegal, or where it is set up legally with considerable discretion given to public officials who can essentially sell the economic rents from gambling to the highest bidders. Gambling, especially when it is presented with a high degree of competent and professional regulation, can be run without scandal, and it can be run by individuals and organizations who themselves have a high degree of honesty and integrity with regard to their business dealings. It can be run without the kind of corruption that had dominated the quasi-legal or illegal gambling that used to be the major form of gambling in this country.

Lotteries, which have been run predominantly by governments, have had virtually no scandal in the 25 years that they have existed. Indeed, lotteries have also taught Americans how to gamble more than any other single activity, certainly more than such personalities as Jimmy the Greek, and more than casinos. Lotteries have played a very important role in this phenomenon, both by teaching people that gambling can be fun —even though lotteries themselves are far less interesting and entertaining than casino style gambling—but they have also demonstrated that gambling can be run with a high degree of honesty.

In New Jersey, the integrity of the regulatory process and the competence and integrity of the gaming operations has been there almost from the start, with relatively few lapses. Nevada has had a long learning process where its casino industry has gone from one of questionable integrity to one of fairly decent integrity with competent and professional operations and regulation.

2. Gambling is immoral.

Gambling has been considered as sinful by many religions. In earlier times, the church and the state would argue a person should not gamble because it is not good for people; it runs against family values; it undermines a husband's work values and long term objectives of achieving prosperity through hard work and meeting family responsibilities

Why has this changed? In the last thirty years the church and the state have become major purveyors of gambling services. They have co-opted themselves out of the ability to take a strong moral position with regard to gambling. For many churches and charities, gambling— in the form of bingo and pull-tab tickets —have become a major revenue source.

Governments have turned to lotteries as a major revenue generator, arguing, in a world of increasing demand on public services, they cannot increase taxes not without risking their political futures. They also claim gambling is really a free tax. It is a tax that is voluntary because people choose to gamble. Therefore, governments have gone through the process of taking an illegal activity—gambling—legalizing it through lottery, and attempting to hold an exclusive franchise on their gambling monopoly so that they could maximize revenue for the state out of lottery profit. One has to be only slightly cynical to suggest that this may not be the appropriate role of government in preying on the propensities of its citizens to participate in an activity many still consider immoral.

Another factor relating to the moral arguments against gambling is that if one examines the challenges of the modern world, which is characterized by such terrible moral dilemmas and controversies over policy aimed at such things as abortion, AIDS, genocide, homosexuality, homelessness, and drug abuse, the moral questions posed by these broader issues make the morality of gambling seem quaint in comparison, or perhaps even anachronistic.

3. Gambling creates compulsive gamblers.

The third argument against gambling, compulsive gambling, is a real issue. Society is gaining greater understanding over time of this phenomenon. Among those factors that have improved our understanding of compulsive gambling in recent years is that it is an affliction that affects only a small percentage of the population, estimated at between one and five percent of the adult population. It is unclear whether compulsive gambling is a psychological or a physiological phenomenon. It is also unclear whether it is truly an addiction or merely an irresponsibility, an immaturity, on the part of those who are so cursed. But society has chosen more and more to take the attitude that if most people want to gamble, and if most people can do so responsibly, than gambling should not be prohibited for the majority, just to protect a small minority who might be at fault anyway, and for whom prohibition of gambling might not stop them from destroying themselves through gambling or some other vice anyway.

In summary, society has changed its attitude from "gambling is wrong, gambling is a sin", to one of saying "It's ok to gamble". The policy questions have shifted from "Should we gamble or not?" to "Who gets to benefit by being the purveyors of gambling services?" With regard to this point, we have seen the various claimants come forward. The claimants on gambling are the following groups, all of whom are well deserving. Governments have said that they should be the purveyors of gambling services because clearly they must deal with the fiscal crisis that is pervasive throughout this country, and clearly the demands for public services cannot be met through continuing tax increases on the middle class and the poor. So if government gets to run gambling, they can generate important tax revenues, and turn around and spend it in a fashion that is beneficial for society.

A second group of claimants—charities —respond to this argument with the claim that, if we allow government to take the revenues from gambling, it is like throwing it into a black hole. Nothing good seems to come out of government. They can absorb as much income as they can without resolving their crises. Rather, society should let charities be the purveyors of gambling services. Charities throughout Canada, and charities in certain states in the United States such as North Dakota or Minnesota, have become major purveyors of gambling services. In Minnesota, for example—a state of about four million people—charitable organizations and not-for-profit organizations in 1990 grossed about $250 million from their legal charitable gambling, after payment of prizes. They certainly are in the gambling business, and their argument is, "Let us have the revenues from gambling because we will spend them directly on things of definite and distinct value for the community; as charities, we know how to do good things."

Another set of groups who are purporting to be the legitimate claimants to the right to offer gambling are cities, or regions, in partnership with private sector gambling corporations. We have seen a bit of this in Connecticut, with attempts to legalize casinos in Hartford and Bridgeport, and we have seen legalization of a number of casinos in the Midwest, on the basis that their communities need jobs; their communities need investments; their communities need to stimulate economic development and tourism.

The way they do this is to try to capture the same kinds of economic benefits that have accrued to Nevada and—to a lesser extent—New Jersey. The argument is, if the state would authorize a casino or casinos, private sector firms in partnership with political jurisdictions will create jobs; they will create investments; they will bring in tourists to the area; and everybody will benefit.

The fourth group of claimants are the Indian tribes in America. There is little doubt that, among all the minorities who have been treated in various ways by government programs over time, Indians have probably been the least effectively treated. The worst of the welfare cases in America have been Indian stories. After a combination of the emergence of Indian sovereignty as a well-defined right and a quirky law—the Indian Gaming Regulatory Act of 1988—along with some quite opportunistic situations that evolved for certain tribes, Indian gaming has become the most powerful economic development tool ever to develop for Indian tribes in America. Some tribes—such as the Mashantuckett Pequot of Connecticut—are becoming wealthy beyond their wildest expectations because of being at the right place at the right time with a set of circumstances that could be fully exploited.

Of the various claimants, one should probably concentrate on private sector casino development in league with cities, which is probably going to be the most important one over time. What are the jurisdictions who are legalizing casinos trying to do, and how effective are they likely to be? The motivation for places such as New Orleans, Kansas City, St. Louis, Davenport, Biloxi/Gulfport, Chicago, Bridgeport, Hartford and in Canada, Windsor and Montreal and Winnipeg have been to attempt to capture the economic benefits from casinos in the same manner as Nevada has done. These cities have looked at Las Vegas, which is a very interesting city for a number of reasons. They argue that they should be able to achieve the same successes.

Las Vegas is a city that most people would have claimed in 1960 was "all mobbed up". The common perception outside of Nevada was that Las Vegas was a city run for mobsters, by mobsters, in a very corrupt political system. However, Las Vegas is a city that for each of the last three decades has been among the five fastest growing metropolitan areas in the United States. It is a city that now has the ten largest hotels in the world. In terms of number of rooms, Las Vegas has more hotel rooms than both New York and London. Las Vegas is probably the best large convention city in the world today. They have the ability to accommodate over 100,000 visitors at one time. Las Vegas is also evolving in the same general direction as Orlando, Florida, with the construction of major amusement parks at a number of destination resort casino properties. In fact, the term "Las Orlando", has been used more and more commonly in recent years, and the term is actually getting to the point where one wonders whether the term Las Orlando, is an attempt to describe Las Vegas as a variant of Orlando, or an attempt to describe Orlando as a variant of Las Vegas.

The process of a rush to legalization of gambling has pointed out some very interesting patterns, and indeed, weaknesses in the American system. The first such weakness is that the American political system can be very myopic. It tends to concentrate on a single issue and run with that issue as long as it can. With regard to gambling, the dominant policy consideration used to be organized crime. That was the only point of debate: the concern that gambling inevitably led to involvement by organized crime and consequent political corruption.

If one examines the way that New Jersey wrote its Casino Control Act in 1977, and tries to see what their concerns were as embodied in the Act, it becomes very clear. The concerns of the Casino Control Act were to keep organized crime out of the casino gaming business, because that is its natural tendency. And that was the dominant way of thinking about commercial gaming until the late 1980s, especially with regard to casinos. And then —all of a sudden—concerns about organized crime diminished; they seemed to pass into posterity, into nostalgia. What replaced it was the primacy of economic benefits to be derived from gaming. Gambling's greatest social value is in creating economic benefits; thus, state after state has moved toward the legalization of gambling to capture those economic benefits.

There is a second weakness inherent in the American political system. This is the belief that if legislation works well in one place, it can work just as well in another jurisdiction, even though the safeguards may be slightly more relaxed and the circumstances somewhat different. There has been a very interesting and clear evolution in the legalization of casino style gambling in America. If we examine the third jurisdiction to legalize casinos, after Nevada and Atlantic City, we find it in a little place called Deadwood, South Dakota. Deadwood is about thirty miles from Mount Rushmore, and its population is about 1600 people. It is a small, remote, rural area. Deadwood peaked economically in the 1890s as a mining town, and it has not had much economic stimulus ever since. It is most famous for being the town where Wild Bill Hickock was shot in the back while playing poker, holding a hand of aces and eights, now known as the "dead man's" hand. The tourist attraction of Deadwood was the tomb of Wild Bill in Boot Hill, buried next to Calamity Jane.

In the 1980s, the town of Deadwood was literally falling apart. The city fathers argued the only way Deadwood could be saved would be to create a revenue source that will allow them to put some money aside for historic preservation of Deadwood. They were able to convince the voters of South Dakota in the 1988 election to authorize small stakes limited casino gambling in Deadwood. Five dollar maximum wagers were allowed, and no license could have more than thirty slot machines or table games. In November, 1989, Deadwood opened its first casinos and became the third jurisdiction in America to have casinos. Within a year every business in Deadwood had become a casino, and every other business was pushed out. In one sense, it was phenomenally successful; in another sense it was a disaster. People would travel six or eight hours to get to the slot machines of Deadwood.

Shortly thereafter, Iowa set up constrained riverboat gaming legislation that would allow no more than five dollar maximum wagers, and a person could lose no more than $200 per excursion. There was a belief among the good people of Iowa that the evils of gambling would show up if large wagers were allowed and if people were allowed to lose too much money in any given visit. Therefore, they legislated against it. They also allocated three percent of the gross winnings from their casinos for compulsive treatment programs, so that any social damage created by the casinos would be taken care of. They also mandated that —at least when the river was not frozen —gambling would have to take place on the riverboats while they were floating on the water. The belief—or symbolism —was that if all the sinning from gambling was taking place on the Mississippi River, then those sins, as they work their way back to shore, would be washed pure by the time they reached shore so as to not infect the good people of Iowa.

So Iowa and South Dakota set the tone for responsible, remote, small stakes gambling. But what happened next? Illinois is right across the river from Iowa and so they decided they did not want Iowa to get all the gaming revenues from their citizens, so they passed a riverboat gaming bill as well. However, they failed to put in the maximum wager limitation, or the maximum loss limitation, and they even allowed casino credit about which Iowa would shudder at the thought. Within nine months after Iowa passed its legislation, Illinois had copied it.

Further down the Mississippi River, in the state of Mississippi, the legislature argued that they also should have riverboat gambling; but they carried it one step further. They legislated that their riverboats did not have to go out and sail on the river. Indeed, after the law was passed, the Attorney General of Mississippi offered an opinion that Mississippi gaming boats do not even need to have motors on the boats. Indeed, they did not even have to be boats. A license holder in Mississippi can build a casino as long as it sits over the water. So, in an analogy to Darwinian evolution, we have seen casinos crawl out of the rivers and position themselves on the banks of rivers to become land-based casinos.

By the time riverboats worked their way into Louisiana, not only were the riverboats getting closer to the shore; they were getting closer to the cities. Louisiana, over a period of a little over a year, passed legislation that authorized riverboats within New Orleans, a major metropolitan area. They also passed non-casino gaming legislation that allowed video lottery terminals in bars, taverns, truck stops and off-track betting parlors throughout the state. Then in 1992, they passed legislation for a land-based monopoly casino in the center of New Orleans, right in the heart of its tourism area.

Thus, there has been a very rapid evolution from harmless, distant, remote gambling, to wide-open urban style gambling, bringing for the first time casinos to where many people live. This has been part of a process that has moved very quickly. It is also being copied in a lot of other jurisdictions. Every new jurisdiction, in order to be competitive, takes the position that they have to be more aggressive than the previous competing jurisdiction which legalized. So as legislation has moved one step further each time, casinos and their presence have become less constrained, less remote, less socially responsible.

The Indian gaming issue—which has been more influenced through the courts —accelerates the process of legalization. If Indians have casinos in particular jurisdictions, the entire public policy debate changes, because once Indians have casinos, the debate in the state, as has already occurred in Connecticut, is no longer, "Should we have casinos?" Rather, the important questions shift to "Who should have the casinos?", "Who should benefit from them?", and "Where should they be located?"

So, at this point in time, America confronts a situation where the momentum for the spread of gambling is, in my opinion, still just beginning. The United States casino and gaming market could be characterized as being terribly under-supplied. That under-supply is being addressed in a variety of ways, and at a very rapid pace.

How much growth remains in the gaming industry in America? In the United States, as mentioned earlier, commercial gaming is nearly a $30 billion a year industry. That represents an expenditure of about $110 per capita.

How much can such expenditures grow? To gain some insight into that question, we can examine the experience of New South Wales, Australia, the largest Australian state, home of Sydney, the country's largest city. In many respects, Australia is similar to America. With regard to gambling, there is generally widely available and accessible gambling in New South Wales. Per capita expenditures in New South Wales are about $570, about four times that of America when corrected for exchange rate differences.

How large can the American gaming industry get? It is not unreasonable to project an industry with gross revenues of $100 billion to $125 billion at maturity with current population and current real income. It can expand by a factor of about four or five just by addressing the question of under-supply of gaming facilities in America. If this process continues unconstrained, we could go from about 300,000 slot machines in America, to about three million, within a decade or so.

One of the issues with this type of projection is, could this really occur? The one thing that is working to bring it about is, if one examines the reasons why politicians are legalizing gaming, especially casino style gaming, one sees the rationale shrouded in economic justifications. Legislatures legalize casinos because of jobs. As Mayor Richard Daly of Chicago said, "Why do we want casinos in Chicago? Jobs, jobs, jobs."

POSTSCRIPT

Should Casino Gambling Be Prohibited?

By the end of 1995 the possible introduction of casino gambling into two major cities in Connecticut—Hartford and Bridgeport—had become a hotly debated issue. Thirty-seven states and the District of Columbia currently have lotteries. In 1993 those lotteries sold $25.1 billion in tickets. Many regions have instituted or are considering instituting riverboat casinos or other restricted gaming establishments. Nonprofit institutions have long supported themselves with gambling. Can the private sector be far behind?

Underlying the entire debate is the tension of passing time; the market for gambling cannot be infinite, and each casino that opens draws revenue that the next cannot tap. And video lotteries—essentially, casinos on the Internet—which bring income to no location whatsoever, threaten gambling establishments of all kinds.

Life is a gamble, and risk is a part of daily life. In that sense, the questions before us are not new. But they are certainly more complex, and they will demand attention in the next decade. Cities in the United States need help, and casinos may be the solution. But is this solution worth the potential problems of gambling?

SUGGESTED READINGS

"Canada: A Gamble," *The Economist* (June 18–24, 1994).

Francis X. Clines, "Gambling, Pariah No More, Is Booming Across America," *The New York Times* (December 5, 1993), p. 1.

"Gambling May Yield Revenue Windfall," *Aviation Week and Space Technology* (August 15, 1994), p. 46.

Susan B. Garland, "Clinton vs. the Sin Lobby: All Bark," *Business Week* (July 18, 1994).

Robert Goodman, "Legalized Gambling as a Strategy for Economic Development," *United States Gambling Study* (March 1994).

Dan Parker, "Night Moves—When an Industry Runs Around the Clock (Weekends and Holidays) It Leaves Workers and Families Run-Down and Stressed Out," *The Atlantic City Press* (June 14, 1993).

Timothy P. Ryan, Patricia J. Connor, and Janet F. Speyerer, *The Impact of Casino Gambling in New Orleans*, Division of Business and Economic Research, University of New Orleans, LA (May 1990).

Gerald Slusher, *The Casino Industry and Its Impact on Southern New Jersey*, Division of Economic Development, Atlantic City, NJ (January 1991).

Frank Wolfe, "Inherited Talents," *Forbes Four Hundred* (October 17, 1994).

ISSUE 8

Are Financial Derivative Instruments Always a Gamble?

YES: J. Patrick Raines and Charles G. Leathers, from "Financial Derivative Instruments and Social Ethics," *Journal of Business Ethics* (vol. 13, 1994)

NO: Timothy Middleton, from "The 'D' Word: Derivatives Are Best Left to Qualified Professionals," *Nest Egg* (May/June 1995)

ISSUE SUMMARY

YES: Associate professor of economics J. Patrick Raines and professor of economics Charles G. Leathers argue that trading in financial derivatives amounts to speculation and gambling in financial markets and that an undesirable change in social ethics has reduced opposition to the practice.

NO: Timothy Middleton, a contributing editor for *Nest Egg*, asserts that financial derivatives are regularly used for a variety of risk-reducing purposes by responsible investment professionals.

Derivatives are financial instruments whose returns are linked to the performance of underlying assets such as mortgages, bonds, currencies, or commodities. Although the commodities market has been around a long time and has had its share of criticism, it operates under an agreed contract; derivatives operate without such an agreed contract. They are used to hedge, or to protect from loss, against changes in the marketplace. If you buy futures in eggs, for instance, speculating that the price will go up at some future date, but you forget to sell as the market moves, when your date arrives, so will your eggs. This might become a big problem if you are not in need of a truckload of eggs. This possibility tends to regulate the futures commodities market. That is, the possibility of the commodity being delivered takes buying futures out of the realm of "gambling": the intent of the contract at purchase time (to make a profit through an advantageous trade) is, according to the law, limited by the words of the contract and the existence of a real commodity (in this case, eggs).

While derivatives are linked to the performance of underlying assets, that linkage has nothing to do with the way they operate. Let us take the case of Orange County, California, which is discussed by Timothy Middleton in the second selection. In 1994 Orange County's speculators bought billions of dollars' worth of derivative securities linked to movements in a multiple of the difference between Swiss and U.S. interest rates. As the Swiss and U.S.

interest rates changed, so did the amount of difference between them; as U.S. interest rates moved toward or away from Swiss interest rates, Orange County won or lost money on (a multiple of) the amount of the change. If the interest rates moved in the right direction, the yield on the investment was very high. As it happened, U.S. interest rates were raised by the Federal Reserve to clamp down on inflation during most of 1994 and the first months of 1995. That was the wrong direction for Orange County; the rate hikes sent the value of Orange County's portfolio on a downward spiral (keep in mind that if the yield is high, so are the risks).

What should be done to prevent this type of disaster? Arthur Levitt, the chairman of the Securities and Exchange Commission, has addressed this concern by asking state and local governments to monitor those who manage and invest the taxpayers' money. It is unclear if that request will be sufficient to protect local governments from uninformed or unscrupulous investment advisers. Would it be more effective to restrict the states and counties regarding exactly what they can and cannot buy?

In the selections that follow, J. Patrick Raines and Charles G. Leathers call derivatives trading "speculation" and "gambling," and they decry society's apparent tolerance of it. Middleton suggests that in the hands of capable investors, financial derivative instruments perform a valuable function. What weight should be given the values of freedom and justice in investment activities? Should government curb, with careful regulation, the activities of investment experts who manage public monies (but not necessarily those who speculate for their own profit or for the profit of private clients)? What could or would government regulation of the financial markets do to the choices for investors and the ability to raise money for those who wish to expand or gain from these markets? Can government do a better job of protecting the public till than a well-trained professional who knows the local territory?

As you read the following selections, try to find solutions to these questions: Should pension fund managers, government officials, or financial advisers be allowed to put at risk, for profitable gains or losses, the millions of dollars that the public funds to which they are entrusted contain? The public trusts their investments will grow and be there for them at some future date. If the mandate is to hold such funds for future distributions (retirement or savings), should risk of any sort be allowed? If the government protects these funds, what happens to the ability to optimize profits and growth?

YES

J. Patrick Raines and
Charles G. Leathers

FINANCIAL DERIVATIVE INSTRUMENTS
AND SOCIAL ETHICS

ABSTRACT. Recent finance literature attributes the development of derivative instruments (interest rate futures, stock index futures) to (1) technological advances, and (2) improved mathematical models for predicting option prices. This paper explores the role of social ethics in the acceptance of financial derivatives. The relationship between utilitarian ethical principles and the demise of turn-of-the-century bucket shops is contrasted with modern tolerance of financial derivatives based upon libertarian ethical precepts. Our conclusion is that a change in social ethics also facilitated the growth in trading in modern financial derivatives.

INTRODUCTION

One of the most important recent developments in financial markets has been the rise of financial derivative instruments from a secondary role to a position of dominance (Konishi and Dattatreya, 1991). Financial derivatives are contracts whose values are dependent upon the values of the underlying financial assets which trade separately. Prominent examples include futures contracts on the 30-year Treasury bond and stock index futures and options. Often referred to as "synthetic securities," modern financial derivatives have taken increasingly sophisticated forms and carry such exotic labels as swaptions, collars, caps, and circuses.

In finance literature, the rapid growth of trading in derivative instruments is largely attributed to (1) technological advances in communications and data processing, and (2) the use of sophisticated mathematics in financial theory to determine prices for financial options (Torres, 1991). But from a behavioral perspective, the prominent role of modern financial derivatives reflects changes in social ethics. In the late 1800's and early 1900's, social reformers vigorously lobbied for legislation limiting or prohibiting the relatively unsophisticated derivative instruments of that era. By the ethical precepts then in

From J. Patrick Raines and Charles G. Leathers, "Financial Derivative Instruments and Social Ethics," *Journal of Business Ethics*, vol. 13 (1994), pp. 197–204. Copyright © 1994 by D. Reidel Publishing Co., Dordrecht, Holland, and Boston, U.S.A. Reprinted by permission of Kluwer Academic Publishers.

vogue, speculative trading in commodities futures and options and transactions at bucket shops (mock brokerage houses) were construed as forms of gambling. In this paper, we note that if those ethical precepts still prevailed today, modern financial derivatives would be subject to a similar indictment.

ETHICAL OPPOSITION TO EARLY FINANCIAL DERIVATIVES

Opposition to trading in the early forms of financial derivatives was driven in part by the economic interests of several parties involved, in particular, agricultural producers and processors and officials of organized stock and commodity exchanges. But the popular influence of social precepts relating to gambling and speculation in financial and commodity markets provided the opposition with a fundamental claim to a broader social legitimacy. Even those motivated by pecuniary self-interest recognized the political expediency of couching their arguments in terms of social ethics relating to gambling.

Given the militant anti-gambling sentiment prevailing in the late 19th and early 20th century, moralistic judgements against the early financial derivatives rested on the fundamental principle that contracts settled by simply paying the differences in cash were devices for betting on price changes. This principle was invoked, directly or indirectly, in both the agrarians' campaign against trading in commodity futures (which organized exchanges successfully resisted) and the social reformers' crusades against operation of bucket shops (which the organized exchanges successfully turned to their own advantage).

Opposition to Trading in Commodity Futures

In the late 1800's, the agrarian interests mounted strong organized support for Congressional action aimed at restricting speculation in commodities futures. On purely economic grounds, farmers and millers believed that speculative commodity futures trading created unfavorable market prices. But on social and legal grounds, the argument was advanced that speculative trading in commodity futures constituted gambling because the commodities specified were not actually delivered.

Since the quantities of commodities specified in futures contracts often exceeded the total quantities in storage and production, proponents of anti-futures legislation contended that settlement of the contracts by delivery of actual commodities was physically impossible. The alleged trade in fictitious commodities was captured by the contemptuous term "wind wheat." In 1892, Congress very nearly passed a bill which would have effectively banned speculation in commodities futures by levying prohibitive taxes on "wind wheat" contracts. Since futures contracts involving commodities actually owned would have been exempted from the taxes, opportunities for farmers and millers to hedge against market price fluctuations through the use of commodity futures would not have been affected (Cowing, 1965).

The principle that distinguished legitimate financial contracts from gambling contracts was clearly incorporated in the legal status of options contracts in commodities markets. Under prevailing legal theory, an option "was inescapably a wagering contract because the purchaser could offer no intent other than a desire to profit by a price change. The intent to profit, where no goods were exchanged, was held to be socially unjustifiable" (Cowing, 1965). On that basis, options (which in theory could always be settled in cash) were viewed by the courts as unenforceable contracts.

Ultimately, the efforts to ban speculative trade in commodity futures failed because legal representatives of the organized commodity exchanges were able to draw a crucial distinction between options as gambling contracts and futures contracts. Despite the fact that only about 3 percent of futures contracts were actually settled by delivery of the commodities, the purchaser of a futures contract could demand actual delivery. The *right* to require delivery established an *intent* that was legitimate. Whether that intent was actually carried out into action was deemed to be immaterial (Cowing).

Ethical Opposition to Bucket-Shops

The anti-gambling sentiment prevalent in the early 1900s also manifested in ethical criticism of the stock market. Writing in 1904, Conant quoted a passage from an unnamed source on the ethics of stock exchanges:

> If, instead of betting on something so small as falling dice, one bets on the rise and fall of stocks..., the law will pay not the slightest attention. A gambling house for these larger purposes may be built conspicuously in any city, the sign 'Stock Exchange' may be set over its door, influential men appointed its officers, and the law will protect it and them as it does the churches. How infamous to forbid gambling on a small scale and almost to encourage it on a large! (Conant, 1904).

Conant strongly denied that stock exchanges were gambling houses. While conceding that betting on the rise and fall of stocks is a form of gambling, he asserted that such betting occurred not in the stock market but in bucket shops. Bucket shops, declared Conant, were of no use to the community, destructive to the morals and pocketbooks of young men, and could not be too severely censured (Conant, 1904).

Although a prevalent institution from the late 1800's through the 1920's, bucket shops seem now to be largely forgotten. As Kindleberger (1978) observed: "The term bucket shop has practically disappeared from the language since the Securities and Exchange Commission stamped it out after 1933 as an illegal practice. Nor is it discussed in the economic literature." Consequently, it is not surprising that transactions at bucket shops have not been properly recognized as an early form of financial derivatives whose values derived from the market prices of the underlying securities.

In modern terminology, bucket shops might be described as "simulated" brokerage houses. Transactions at real brokerage houses resulted in the actual buying and selling of securities on organized exchanges which determined the market prices. Bucket shops allowed customers to speculate on changes in those prices without any actual buying and selling taking place. Essentially, both the bucket shop operator and the customers were only pretending to buy or sell stocks (or commodities), but the obligation to pay based on price changes was real. In choosing the shares to be "traded," customers could go "long" or "short". If prices rose, those who had gone "long" realized gains, and if prices fell, those who had gone "short" profited.

Bucket shops provided opportunities to speculate on movements in prices without any ownership of shares being involved. In technical terminology, the expression "to bucket an order" meant that the receiver (the "bucketeer") covered the order himself without entering into a contract with another party or clearing the transaction (Hieronymus, 1971). Most patrons went "long," optimistically expecting prices to rise. This put the bucket shops in chronic short positions, such that if prices did rise the operators would incur losses. Although the odds were naturally in favor of the operators, various types of fraudulent practices were allegedly used to bilk the customers.

The movement to force closure of the bucket shops involved a curious alliance between social reformers motivated by high moral principle and representatives of the organized exchanges. The latter viewed the bucket shops as both irritating competitors and sources of negative public perceptions of the nature of trading in stock and commodities markets. Fraudulent practices by bucket shop operators, e.g., false reporting of stock prices, were widely and sensationally exposed by newspapers and popular magazines, fueling public hostility toward the shops. But the efforts to outlaw bucket shops ultimately rested on the principle that bucket shop transactions were in the nature of gambling contracts since no actual purchase and delivery of stocks or commodities was involved. Under the New York Anti-Bucket Shop Law, for example, the purchase or sale of securities was a penal offence if it was intended that the contract would be settled upon the basis of quotations on any exchange and without intending a bona fide sale, or when such market quotations reached a certain figure without intending a bona fide purchase or sale, or based on the differences in such market quotations at which such securities were bought or sold.

Utilitarian ethical theory provides an explanation for the efforts to abolish the bucket shops. A utilitarian regulatory philosophy was evolving at this time which held that commerce could be regulated to promote social welfare by maximizing societal benefits and minimizing harms. Utilitarian moral theory was manifested in the Interstate Commerce Act (1887), the Sherman Antitrust Act (1890) and, later, in the Clayton Act (1914). Such social legislation was engineered to protect the public from unfair competitive practices, fraud, deception, and dishonesty. Since bucket shop opponents believed gambling losses caused more unhappiness and conflict in society than social good, legislation was necessary to protect the public from the harm of this financial chicanery.

In general, regulation based upon utilitarian principles was supported by the business community and, in this specific instance, by legal stock exchanges because regulation of anticompetitive practices increased investor, consumer and competitor confidence and worked to everyone's advantage.

Despite stringent opposition from social reform groups and officials of organized exchanges, bucket shops proved to be highly resilient until the Securities and Exchange Commission [SEC] was created. Their popularity is not difficult to explain. In some respects, the bucket shops were more democratic than the organized exchanges. Indeed, bucket shop operators responded to attacks from organized exchanges by arguing that their operations provided lower income people the same opportunities to speculate on stock and commodity prices that were available to the privileged few who enjoyed access to the organized exchanges. Bucket shop transactions were not only in small amounts that ordinary people could make but could be made on a very thin margin. And unlike the organized exchanges, bucket shops did not discriminate on basis of race, sex, or age (see Fabian, 1990).

Moreover, despite the alleged frequency of fraudulent practices, e.g., falsifying price quotes, a number of men who later became major figures on the organized exchanges learned to read the ticker tape and developed their investment strategies in bucket shops. Indeed, some of those individuals, e.g., Jesse Livermore, were able to consistently beat the bucket shops (Cowing, 1965; Thomas, 1989).

On the surface, the eventual suppression of bucket shops by the SEC reflected the ability of the organized exchanges to exploit public hostility against the shops. By making the bucket shops the symbol of gambling on stock and commodity prices, the exchanges successfully diverted charges that speculation in commodity futures and in various types of stock market practices also constituted gambling. Speculation on organized exchanges was defended as being necessary to the efficient functioning of the real economy of production and distribution.

But the key factors in the demise of bucket shops were the strong social disapproval of gambling and the identification of bucket shop transactions as a form of gambling because no actual sales of stocks took place. If the only moral objection to bucket shops had been their fraudulent practices, the shops could have simply been regulated and allowed to remain open. Such a policy would certainly have been appropriate under what appears to be the modern ethical perspective on financial derivatives.

MODERN SOCIAL ETHICS AND FINANCIAL DERIVATIVES

While futures trading in commodities has long existed, trading in financial futures began in 1972, when the Chicago Mercantile Exchange (CME) introduced futures contracts in currency through its International Monetary Market division. Subsequently, futures contracts were introduced on Treasury bills, large bank CDs, and Eurodollar deposits. The success of the new "interest rate futures" (so-called because the values of the underlying securities are highly sensitive to changes in the interest rate) led to the introduction of options on those futures (Konishi and Dattatreya, 1991). Equity derivative instruments appeared in 1982 when the CME introduced the S&P 500 stock index futures contract. In the following year, the CME established trading in options on those futures.

Competitive development of new derivative instruments has become a booming high-tech business. The creation of "synthetic securities" which artificially replicate portfolios of the underlying securities can involve highly complex transactions (Crawford and Sihler, 1991). Major securities firms are now using new high-powered computers capable of developing highly sophisticated mathematical programs to create a host of new "synthetics" that can "identify hundreds of never-before-imagined trades in stocks, bonds, and currencies" (Torres, 1991).

As an example, a derivative instrument produced from a combination of Nikkei stock-index futures and exchange-traded stock-index options created a synthetic option that "cost less than the real thing" (Torres, 1991). The incentive for producing and marketing such "synthetics" is indicated by a profit of $500,000 realized by an investment bank on a single trade in one of the newly created options.

Proponents of the growing use of financial derivatives contend that these instruments improve the efficiency of financial markets by providing hedging devices to insure against risk and by increasing the degree of liquidity in the markets. Malkiel (1990), for example, defends derivative instruments on grounds that they "provide important risk-reducing benefits" and "reduce transactions costs since brokerage costs are lower in the futures market than in the stock market." Modern trading strategies, e.g., portfolio insurance and index arbitrage, use index futures to quickly, efficiently, and cheaply trade the "entire market" as if it were a single commodity.

Those trading strategies have generated growing concern over the effects of financial derivatives on the stability of financial markets. Stock index arbitrage (program trading) and portfolio insurance have been blamed for increasing the volatility of stock prices and contributing to stock market crash of 1987. In index arbitrage, speculators seek risk free gains by quickly substituting stock index futures for the stocks represented in those indexes, or vice-versa, using computerized trading systems. When the gap between prices of the indexed stocks in cash markets and the prices of the index futures becomes abnormally large, the higher priced instruments are sold and the lower-price ones are bought. Portfolio insurance involves computerized programs which protect portfolios of stocks by triggering large sales of stock index futures when stock prices begin to fall.

According to Mayer (1988), there was overwhelming evidence that "back-and-forth transactions in derivative instruments and stocks helped drive the market too high and then pushed it down too quickly." Roll (1989), however, argued that "taken as a characteristic in isolation, computer directed trading such as portfolio insurance and index arbitrage, if it had any impact at all, actually helped mitigate the market decline" (p. 57). International financial regulators have recently expressed fears that the global market for financial derivatives "is growing too fast, has too little regulation and is being used by some traders as a speculative arena" (Lipin and Power, 1992; see also, *The Economist* 1992).

In contrast to the publicly expressed concern about the effects of modern financial derivatives on market stability, relatively little has been said about the ethical aspects of modern financial derivatives. The *nature* of financial derivatives as gambling contracts has largely escaped critical attention in the recent literature. Borna and Lowry (1987) only briefly noted the resemblance of futures trading to gambling in arguing that speculative business practices in general should be considered as public gambling. Ethical inquiries instead have focused more on the *use* of financial derivatives. Horrigan (1987), for example, observed that "the world of the New Finance," where investors can adjust immediately to any financial strategy chosen by corporate management with actions that include "clever option positions," is ethically "not a nice place." Similarly, Shriver (1989) briefly cited ethical concerns about the impact of stock index futures on the stability of financial markets.

Yet, the contracts involved in modern derivative trading are fundamentally similar in nature to the commodity futures and bucket shop transactions of a century ago. Certainly, the "wind wheat" case against speculation in commodity futures would apply to modern derivative markets since the volume of trade in derivative instruments often exceeds the underlying assets trading in cash markets. The dollar value of the S&P 500 stock index futures contract, for example, runs about 60 percent more than the value of the actual stocks in that index traded on the New York Stock Exchange (Merrick, 1990).

More importantly, the ethical/legal principle cited in the battle against bucket shops—that contracts settled in cash constituted gambling contracts—would lead to a similar charge against stock index futures. Traditional futures contracts, such as those for gold or Treasury bills, allow final settlement by delivery of the underlying assets. But in stock index futures trading, the underlying securities (the individual stocks themselves) are never actually involved. Instead, stock index futures contracts are settled through cash payments, a deliberate design feature intended to avoid the costs and inconvenience of final settlement through physical delivery. In the case of the S&P 500 contract, for example, actual delivery would require the purchase and delivery of the properly weighted basket of 500 stocks (Merrick, 1990). (While the contracts are often settled by reverse trading before expiration date, over one-third are settled by cash.)

One of the ethical arguments against bucket shops was that the transactions had no effect on the determination of stock prices. According to economic philosophy rooted in ethical considerations of the nature of market prices tracing back to Aristotle, prices play a socially legitimate role by reflecting true values and efficiently allocating resources. Thus, transactions between buyers and

sellers of actual stocks on organized exchanges which produced those prices were deemed to be socially legitimate functions. A double indictment of bucket shops was raised on this point. Transactions by bucket shop patrons not only failed to enter the price determination process. They also interfered with the ability of organized exchanges to establish socially efficient stock prices by diverting funds from those exchanges.

The relationship between trading in modern stock index futures and the determination of stock prices in cash markets, although more complex, is fundamentally not that different. In applying for permission to trade the S&P 500 index future, the Chicago Mercantile Exchange argued that trading in this contract would have no effect on prices in the cash market: "Arbitrage would not be possible because of the difficulty of buying or selling 500 stocks at once" (Mayer, 1988). Thus, there was an explicit intent from the beginning that buying and selling stock index futures contracts would not perform the socially beneficial function of establishing efficient prices of the actual shares of stock being traded in the cash market.

Subsequently, it has been recognized that prices in the index futures markets indirectly influence prices of stocks in the cash market through index arbitrage. That influence has also been recognized as periodically disrupting the ability of the cash markets to establish socially efficient prices. The explicit cash-settlement design of the stock index futures creates a special problem on expiration days when arbitrageurs "unwind" their positions. Arbitrageurs hold offsetting positions in stocks and index futures. At expiration, the futures price equals the price of the actual stocks in the index. The buy or sell orders that arbitrageurs place with the stock specialists on the day of expiration tend to create imbalances between supply and demand which result in temporary price swings. These imbalances occur because stock index futures contracts are settled in cash rather than through actual delivery of stocks.

The indirect effect of the cash settlement feature of stock index futures contracts has drawn critical attention from the SEC's Division of Market Regulation, but only in regard to the effects on price volatility. A staff report of a study of the October 1987 stock market crash recommended requiring physical settlement of index products, i.e., actual delivery of the underlying securities. The cash settlement feature of stock index futures contracts "eliminates the risk that a market participant must liquidate its position prior to the termination of the future or accept delivery (and make payment for) a market basket of stocks" (SEC, 1988). The absence of that risk may encourage institutional investors to assume excessively large positions with "tighter triggers" for selling when prices decline.

Social Ethics and Public Policies

The contrast between the strong ethical concern about the nature of financial derivatives in the early 1900s and the relative lack of such concern today has interesting public policy implications. If the moral perspective had not drawn such an absolute judgement that transactions in the bucket shops constituted gambling, the shops could have been simply regulated to suppress the fraudulent activities. The outcome would have been somewhat similar in effect to the indirect relationship described above between stock index futures and the cash market. As Hieronymus (1971) noted,

operators of bucket shops could have hedged their positions by taking positions in the actual stocks. No record exists of the extent to which bucket shop operators actually laid off their net open positions by trades on the exchanges. While the large brokerage houses attempted to prevent such actions, some brokers apparently were willing to work with the bucket shop operators.

Conversely, if the same social ethics were applied today to stock index futures—the principle that an intent to take delivery of the underlying securities must be explicit to the contract if the gambling charge was to be avoided —social concerns about program trading would disappear as stock index futures would not be permitted. But such a policy would also eliminate opportunities to hedge portfolios and the other benefits attributed to trading in financial futures and options. It is noteworthy that all the reports on the effects of financial derivatives on modern stock markets call for regulations, not prohibitions on use of derivative instruments.

CONCLUDING STATEMENT

The more tolerant attitude toward financial derivatives reflects the extent of change in society's ethical perspective on the relationship between speculative financial trading and gambling. An indication of that change is found in the sensitivity on part of financial writers to terms and analogies that might link trading on organized exchanges to betting. Financial journalists and writers who spoke for the organized exchanges in the early 1900's, e.g., Conant (1904), carefully avoided gambling terminology in their discourses on financial markets. In contrast, modern financial writers frequently (and happily) draw analogies between speculative stock and commodities trading and gambling.

The authors of a leading capital markets textbook, for example, state that "Stock index options can be used to *bet* on the movement of stock prices (speculating)..." (Fabozzi and Modigilani, 1992, emphasis added). The following statement appears in *The Wall Street Journals' Guide to Understanding Money and Markets:* "Speculators may be the highest flying *gamblers* in the financial world" (Wurman *et al.*, 1990, emphasis added). Crawford and Sihler (1991) write about "the new casino of futures and options." Perhaps most revealing is the concession by the editor of *The Journal of Portfolio Management* that the question is no longer as to whether investing in the stock market is a form of gambling but rather what kind of gambling: "The stock market is a lot more like poker and black jack than it is like roulette and craps" (Bernstein, 1990).

Critics of our thesis might argue that social ethics actually have not changed in a substantive fashion. Rather, the degree of ethical concern on part of society may simply vary with the types of participants involved. Social opposition to bucket shop transactions was particularly strong because most of the patrons were individuals who were perceived as being unsophisticated in their knowledge of financial markets and unable to afford the losses. Social indifference as to whether modern financial derivatives are gambling contracts stems from a recognition that the participants are large institutional investors with sufficient knowledge and ability to assume the risks involved. But if the opposition to bucket shops had rested primarily on a public perception that the

patrons needed protection, the more logical approach would have been to impose regulations on the shops to prohibit fraudulent activities. The strong public will to force closure of the shops arose from and was sustained by the perception that the social costs of gambling (economic losses, social disharmony) exceeded the gains to society from investment alternatives. During the 1980's, the prevalent philosophy of regulation was that financial markets were the most efficient method of meeting the needs of a dynamic economy. For example, in 1985 the Securities and Exchange Commission urged government-securities brokers to create a *self-regulating* national organization for the purpose of developing a code of ethics for the unregulated securities market. In hindsight, deregulation and the legendary fraud and abuses that occurred in the securities markets clearly reflects the dominance of ethical egoism and libertarian theories. Modern social reformers have advocated a maximum degree of individual freedom to allow economic agents to pursue their own self-interest in the belief that the public interest will be served. Thus, contemporary social indifference to the gambling characteristics of financial derivatives is rooted in the principle that maximum economic gain will result when self-interested investors have the freedom to assume financial risks and claim pecuniary rewards.

Ethical indifference to the booming trade in modern financial derivatives, which are similar in nature to bucket shop transactions, must therefore be seen as evincing a change in social ethics with regard to speculation and gambling in financial markets.

REFERENCES

Benson, G. C. S.: 1982, *Business Ethics in America* (Lexington Books, Lexington, MA).

Bernstein, P. L.: 1990, 'Of Crap, Black Jack, and Theories of Finance', *Journal of Portfolio Management* Fall, 1.

Borna, S. and J. Lowry: 1987 Apr, 'Gambling and Speculation', *Journal of Business Ethics*, 225–231.

Conant, C. A.: 1904, *Wall Street and the Country* (Greenword Press, New York).

Cowing, C. B.: 1965, *Populists, Plungers and Progressives* (Princeton University Press, Princeton).

Crawford, R. D. and W. W. Sihler: 1991), *The Troubled Money Business* (Harper Business).

Fabian, A.: 1990, *Card Sharps Dream Books and Bucket Shops* (Cornell University Press).

Fabozzi, F. J. and F. Modigliani: 1992, *Capital Markets* (Prentice Hall, Englewood Cliffs).

Gilman, S. P.: 1923, *Stock Exchange Law* (The Ronald Press Company, New York).

Hieronymus, T. A.: 1971, *Economics of Futures Trading* (Commodity Research Bureau, Inc., New York).

Horrigan, J. O.: 1987 Feb, 'The Ethics of the New Finance', *Journal of Business Ethics*, 97–110.

Kindleberger, C. P.: 1978, *Manias, Panics, and Crashes* (Basic Books, New York).

Konishi, A. and R. E. Dattatreya: 1991, *The Handbook of Derivative Instruments* (Probus Publishing Company, Chicago).

Lipin, S. and W. Power: 1992 Mar 24, "Derivatives' Draw Warnings From Speculators', *Wall Street Journal*, C1.

Malkiel, B. C.: 1990, *A Random Walk Down Wall Street* (New York).

Mayer, M.: 1988, *Markets* (W. W. Norton, New York).

Merrick, J.: 1990, 'Fact and Fantasy About Stock Index Futures Program Trading', in D. R. Fraser and P. S. Rose (eds.), *Readings on Financial Institutions and Markets* (Irwin, Homewood), pp. 365–377.

Roll, R. W.: 1989, 'The International Crash of 1987', *Black Monday and the Future of Financial Markets* (Irwin, Homewood).

Shriver, D. W.: 1989, 'Ethical Discipline and Religious Hope in the Investment Industry', in O. Williams *et al.* (eds.), *Ethics and the Investment Industry* (Rowman & Littlefield Publishers, Inc. Savage, MD), pp. 233–250.

The Economist: 1992 May 23, 'Taming the Derivatives Beast', 81–82.

Thomas, D. L.: 1989, *The Plungers and the Peacocks* (Morrow, New York).

Torris, C.: 1991 Oct 18, 'Mathematicians Race to Develop New Kinds of Trading Instruments', *Wall Street Journal*, C1.

U.S. Securities and Exchange Commission, Division of Market Regulation: 1988, *The October 1987 Break* (Commerce Clearing House, Inc., Chicago).

Wurman, R. S., A. Siegel, and K. M. Morris: 1990, *The Wall Street Journal Guide to Understanding Money and Markets* (Prentice Hall Press, New York).

NO

Timothy Middleton

THE "D" WORD: DERIVATIVES ARE BEST LEFT TO QUALIFIED PROFESSIONALS

When it was sold to a West Coast investor two years ago, it sounded too good to be true: a one-year government-guaranteed security paying 17% in interest. And indeed it was. This collateralized mortgage obligation, or CMO, is currently yielding 0.6%, because its maturity mushroomed to 25 years due to higher interest rates. When the investor, who had paid $8,700 for the CMO, tried to sell it recently, he was offered $1,500.

"This guy had no idea what his broker was selling him," says Kenneth R. Hyman, a trader at Associated Securities Corp. in Los Angeles, to whom the hapless investor turned for help. There was nothing Hyman could do. The customer was just another victim of derivatives.

Derivatives became the dirtiest word on Wall Street last year, after Orange County, California, and some income-oriented mutual funds offered by Piper Jaffray were devastated by rising interest rates. Early this year the venerable Barings, one of Britain's oldest banks, collapsed when one of its traders made colossal losing bets in the derivatives market on the direction of the Tokyo Stock Exchange.

While derivatives are centuries old and are used conservatively every day to hedge farmers' crops and investors' stocks, securities artificially carved out of other financial instruments lend themselves to speculation and thus to exploitation by commission-driven brokers.

Referring to the very kind of high-risk derivatives that plunged Orange County into bankruptcy, money manager James I. Midanek warns: "These things are being shown to retail investors by brokers. They say, 'After all, it's backed by an agency of the U.S. government—how wrong can you go?' Well, you can go very wrong."

The lessons of the past two years are clear: Don't touch derivatives unless you understand them thoroughly. As with any other financial product, if their yield is above average, so is their risk.

DECIPHERING DERIVATIVES

While derivatives can be as complicated as the financial objective they are created to carry out, conceptually there are only three kinds: forward-based contracts, such as futures; options; and securities based on assets or liabilities.

Forward contracts often involve interest rates, currencies, or commodities. In a rate agreement, the parties agree on an interest rate to be paid on a principal amount at some future date. The payoff is the difference between the contract rate and the prevailing rate at the time of settlement. The principal itself is never exchanged.

Currency contracts promise to exchange one currency for another at an agreed-upon rate on a future date. Commodities forward contracts are similar, except the underlying asset is a physical commodity, such as gold or pork bellies.

Another type of forward contract is the financial future. Usually tied to interest rates, currencies, or an equity index, such as the Standard & Poor's 500 Index, these contracts are standardized and trade on an organized exchange, whereas forward contracts are often individually negotiated.

Swap contracts are almost infinitely varied, but the basic concept is that the parties agree to exchange something in the future, such as an interest rate. Rate swaps are the commonest such contracts, although they can be pegged to commodity price indexes or currency exchange rates. In a simple interest-rate swap, one party locks in a fixed rate of interest on the principal amount, while the other agrees to pay a variable rate, which starts out lower than the fixed rate but is expected to rise over the period of the contract. The intended effect is for the parties to split the income, with the variable side getting the cash in the early years or months and the fixed side later on. If everything works as designed, the transaction is a wash; only risk has been shared.

Operations are a whole different animal. Here the holder has the right, but not the obligation, to take possession of the underlying security, which usually is a common stock. Call options give the purchaser the right to demand the underlying shares at the agreed price, and they increase in value if the share price exceeds the option amount on the settlement date. Otherwise they are worthless. Put options are the opposite. They increase in value if the share price declines. If it doesn't, they have no value.

Asset- or liability-based derivatives are linked to cash flows of the underlying securities. So-called strips consist of interest-only and principal-only shares in an income security, like a Treasury note. Collateralized mortgage obligations, or CMOs, are similar; a pool of mortgages is sliced into subsets, or tranches, with different risk characteristics. The least risky have low yields and are usually purchased by institutions, such as pension funds. High-yielding CMOs, which by definition are much riskier, are often sold to the public.

THE RISE OF EXOTICS

Money managers are constantly devising new variations on these themes, and these innovations are collectively called "exotic derivatives." There is almost nothing you can't do to a financial security to alter its risk profile, which is often the prime objective of a derivative. By the nature of their rapid evolution, exotics defy definition. Some of those currently operating in world markets include all or nothings (option contracts that only pay if a predetermined trigger point is reached) and inverse floaters (debt instruments whose interest moves the opposite of the underlying index).

"These are not anything that's really new," says Robert Herman, who traded derivatives for eight years before quitting to write about them for Knight-Ridder Financial, a news wire in New York City. "People have made fortunes and gone bust in the rice futures market for hundreds of years." Convertible bonds have a derivative—a stock option— embedded in them, on the same principle as structured notes. Stock warrants in essence are long-term call options. Says Herman, "These are products that have been around for generations and they are a very effective mechanism for transferring risk."

Investment professionals regularly use simple derivatives for a variety of risk-reducing purposes. KPMG Peat Marwick, the accounting firm, uses this example in a booklet, "Solving the Mystery of Derivatives," it published for its clients:

"A pension fund manager bought 100,000 shares of a large company when the price was $40 per share. Since that time the price has moved to $60. Because the fund requires certain cash dividend targets, the pension fund manager decides not to sell the shares despite concluding that the price is more likely to move down than up. In order to protect the existing profit of $20, the fund manager buys a put option on the stock at a strike price of $60, and pays a $2 premium for this right. The fund manager has thereby guaranteed that the combined stock and option value will not fall below $58 per share during the term

of the put option, while continuing to receive the dividend on the stock."

To the extent a derivative reduces risk on one side of the transaction, it magnifies risk on the opposite side. Some investors —actually, speculators—happily assume such risk if they expect outsize rewards as compensation.

This is exactly the trap into which Orange County, California, fell. It purchased billions of dollars of structured notes that produced above-market yields when interest rates were declining. They were inverse floaters, yielding a variable rate that moved the opposite of real interest rates. When interest rates rose, Orange County was ruined.

DERIVATIVES AND MUTUAL FUNDS

"Those guys were gambling not investing," says Andrew M. Hudick, a financial planner in Roanoke, VA, and president of the National Association of Personal Financial Advisors.

When derivatives became Page One news, Hudick received frantic calls from his clients, who hold considerable assets in the form of mutual funds and were worried that their funds contained derivatives. Hudick explained that a great many funds use derivatives all the time to help protect their assets.

"When they're used the way they're supposed to be, in order to hedge a portfolio or protect some profits, then I think they're used appropriately," he says.

Midanek, chief investment officer of Solon Asset Management in Walnut Creek, CA, manages $500 million of fixed-income assets, mostly in the form of mortgage-backed securities. He uses a derivative called puts on U.S. Treasury notes to hedge bonds against possible increases in interest rates. Such a hike would depress the value of his bonds, because their value moves inversely with interest rates, but it would bolster the puts. If rates don't increase, the puts become worthless on their expiration date, and Midanek is out only the cost of the derivatives, which are measured in hundredths of a percentage point.

Midanek, who also manages the Solon Short-Duration Government Bond mutual funds, stresses that derivatives are so complex that trading them requires considerable expertise and numbers-crunching capacity on a computer. "We don't think this is a market for retail investors to use on their own," he says.

If you are confronted by a broker who wants to sell you anything other than straight debt or garden-variety equity, ask for a thorough explanation of ex-actly what the product is intended to accomplish for its issuer and how you're supposed to benefit from that. Collateralized mortgage obligations ultimately serve such government agencies as Fannie Mae and Freddie Mac as a lower-cost form of financing than straight bonds, because they shift risk from themselves to purchasers.

Also ask the salesperson to explain every single assumption underlying the sales pitch. CMOs require numerous assumptions about the outlook for mortgage prepayments as well as interest rates. Press the seller to explain, point by point, what happens if the opposite scenario unfolds.

And remember 1994, when many conservative bond investors saw the value of their capital erode 20%—and investors in many derivatives lost considerably more.

POSTSCRIPT

Are Financial Derivative Instruments Always a Gamble?

Consider the reasons for the stock and commodities markets in the first place, which is to help businesses and farmers to raise cash and also to help investors to make profits. Contrast these reasons with the objectives of public fund management, which tries to ensure security and liquidity. Also remember that investment houses, banks, and financial advisers are all in the business of giving professional advice and selling products to the public. The public in many cases has little or no understanding of the products and the risks involved and therefore depends on professionals to give them good advice.

Are derivatives in large portfolios a safe hedge that can reduce the risks of institutional investors? Is this true for the small investor in a mutual fund that buys derivatives to protect against loss? Or is Raines and Leathers's comparison of derivatives to poker or blackjack games a more accurate description?

Can the Securities and Exchange Commission or the government keep the stock and commodities markets from becoming "casinos" without eliminating the free-market system upon which they operate? Do social ethics change the basic ethical principals regarding financial dealings?

In a free-market economy, is self-regulation effective, or must the government work for the greater good?

SUGGESTED READINGS

Tim W. Ferguson, "The Dynamite and the Derivatives," *The Wall Street Journal* (February 28, 1995), p. A21.

Roger Lowenstein, "Will Orange County Squeeze California?" *The Wall Steet Journal* (June 15, 1995), p. C1.

Suzanne McGee, "Derivatives Could Hedge Career Growth," *The Wall Street Journal* (August 24, 1995), p. C1.

Donald G. Simonson, "Vignettes from the Derivatives 'Crisis,' " *United States Banker* (September 1994), pp. 78–83.

Jeffrey Taylor, "Securities Firms Agree to Set Controls on Derivatives," *The Wall Street Journal* (March 9, 1995), pp. C1, 17.

Richard Saul Wurman, Alan Siegel, and Kenneth M. Morris, *The Wall Street Journal Guide to Understanding Money and Markets* (Access Press, 1990).

On the Internet . . .

http://www.dushkin.com

Employee Incentives and Career Development

This site is dedicated to the proposition that effective employee compensation and career development is an effective tool in obtaining, maintaining, and retaining a productive workforce. It contains links to pay-for-knowledge, incentive systems, career development, wage and salary compensation, and more.
http://www.snc.edu/socsci/chair/336/group1.htm

BLS Employment Projections

The Bureau of Labor Statistics provides figures here about entrants to the labor force by sex, race, and Hispanic origin for the years 1986, 1996, and projected for 2006.
http://stats.bls.gov/emptab3.htm

WorkNet@ILR

The School of Industrial and Labor Relations at Cornell University offers this site consisting of an index of Internet sites relevant to the field of industrial and labor relations; a list of centers, institutes, and affiliated groups; and an electronic archive that contains full-text documents on the glass ceiling, child labor, and more.
http://www.ilr.cornell.edu/workplace.html

U.S. Employment Laws

The Labor Policy Association has assembled this chronological list of U.S. employment laws, starting with the Davis-Bacon Act of 1931. Among the issus addressed by these laws are fair labor standards, work hours, safety standards, age discrimination in employment, equal pay for men and women, job training, disabilities, pregnancy discrimination, and employee retirement income.
http://www.lpa.org/lpa/laws.html

PART 3

Human Resources: The Corporation and the Employee

The workforce is changing. Employees in the United States and Canada, and to a lesser extent elsewhere in the world, are becoming very diverse: many ethnic groups are represented in the workplace, women and men are approaching equality in numbers in most fields, and an array of protected conditions—such as age, ethnicity, disability, and religious persuasion—are making corporate life complicated for employers. Employees are more aware of their rights and more willing to demand that their employers honor them than they have ever been. What can business do to protect the rights of this diverse group while protecting its own economic interests?

■ Should Women Have the Same Right to Work as Men?

■ Does Blowing the Whistle Violate Company Loyalty?

■ Should Concern for Drug Abuse Overrule Concerns for Employee Privacy?

ISSUE 9

Should Women Have the Same Right to Work as Men?

YES: George J. Annas, from "Fetal Protection and Employment Discrimination—The *Johnson Controls* Case," *The New England Journal of Medicine* (September 5, 1991)

NO: Hugh M. Finneran, from "Title VII and Restrictions on Employment of Fertile Women," *Labor Law Journal* (April 1980)

ISSUE SUMMARY

YES: George J. Annas, a professor of law and medicine, argues that women may not be legally excluded from traditionally male jobs without some real relation of gender to job performance. He maintains that health risks to children not yet conceived do not constitute such a relation and that, therefore, women's rights to equal employment cannot be abridged on that rationale.

NO: Hugh M. Finneran, former senior labor counsel for PPG Industries, Inc., holds that preventing women from coming into contact with substances that can deform or destroy a growing embryo is a legitimate excuse for excluding women from certain jobs.

Workplaces often abound with nasty and unpleasant substances, chemical and otherwise. Fortunately, very few of them are really hazardous to health, and of those that are, the worst (such as coal dust, which leads to black lung disease) are well known. Most worrisome are the "quiet hazards," substances that are associated with adverse physical reactions and suspected to be the cause of damage to various organ and physiological systems but that are not surely proven to do any real and lasting damage.

Among the most troubling of these quiet hazards are those that attack the reproductive system. Germ cells, the sperm for men and the ova for women, are both the most carefully segregated of the body's systems—they are almost immune from damage from germs coursing through our blood, for instance —and the most vulnerable to damage, for damage to those cells may pass on, in unpredictable ways, to the next generation.

Reproductive damage is divided into two categories: Some substances directly affect the sperm and ova and cause changes that can damage any child that is conceived by the union of those cells. Such substances are called *mutagens* because they cause mutations in the germ plasma. The second category, called *teratogens*, is even more frightening; they attack the developing embryo in the womb, interfering with the complex physiological reactions and anatomical development of the first several weeks of a human's life, causing deformities of limbs, organs, and the nervous system that are usually, but not always, incompatible with life.

With mutagens, men and women are on equal footing. Mutagens may affect the germ cells of both sexes, so it is equally possible for both sexes to pass adverse effects down to their children. Therefore, women may not be excluded from a work environment in which there is a risk of infection any more than men can. This was the first finding of the *Johnson Controls* case, which is discussed by George J. Annas in the following selection.

The second finding is more controversial: When it is believed that a substance in a workplace is a teratogen, the danger is not to the worker (male or female) but to the developing child in the womb of a female worker. There is no *prima facie* reason to object to a rule excluding children from a workplace that contains a substance that is demonstrably dangerous to children but not to adults. But teratogens do not affect young children, or babies, or (it is believed) even fetuses at the stage where the mother is visibly pregnant. They affect development most at its earliest stages, in the first few weeks after the embryo is implanted in the uterus. But at that stage, the woman herself (let alone her employer) usually does not know that she is pregnant. All the damage has been done by the time she knows that there is an embryo at risk.

It seems that the only practicable way to protect these children is to exclude from that workplace any woman who *might* become pregnant; that is, any woman of childbearing age not provably sterile. It could be argued that the exclusion is not sexist: both male and female embryos (the at-risk groups) are being excluded from the workplace by simply excluding all potential embryo carriers from the workplace. At the same time, it is sexist because although women must be excluded, there is no reason to exclude men. Is this legal? The arbiters of the *Johnson Controls* case say it is not.

Hugh M. Finneran's selection was written before *Johnson Controls*, but the issues that he raises are still ethically significant. Whatever the law says, he argues, in order to protect the new equality for women, we should make special efforts to protect the most vulnerable of workplace participants—especially since there is no way for an embryo to consent to the risk.

As you read these selections, ask yourself whether or not attempts to reach total equality between women and men have gone too far. Are there some aspects of life in which gender equality is impossible? Also ask yourself if society should attempt to maintain some wall of protection for the vulnerable (such as children) that does not exist for the not-so-vulnerable. Should compassion for and protection of weaker persons take precedence over individual rights?

YES

George J. Annas

FETAL PROTECTION AND EMPLOYMENT DISCRIMINATION—THE *JOHNSON CONTROLS* CASE

Employers have historically limited women's access to traditionally male, high-paying jobs.[1] In one famous case early in this century, the U.S. Supreme Court upheld an Oregon law that forbade hiring women for jobs that required more than 10 hours of work a day in factories. The Chief Justice explained that this restriction was reasonable because "healthy mothers are essential to vigorous offspring" and preserving the physical well-being of women helps "preserve the strength and vigor of the race."[2] This rationale was never particularly persuasive, and women's hours have not been limited in traditionally female, low-paid fields of employment, such as nursing. Although such blatant sex discrimination in employment is a thing of the past, the average man continues to earn "almost 50 percent more per hour than does the average woman of the same race, age, and education."[3]

The contemporary legal question has become whether employers can substitute concern for fetal health for concern for women's health as an argument for limiting job opportunities for women. The U.S. Supreme Court decided in March 1991 that the answer is no and that federal law prohibits employers from excluding women from job categories on the basis that they are or might become pregnant.[4] All nine justices agreed that the "fetal-protection policy" adopted by Johnson Controls, Inc., to restrict jobs in the manufacture of batteries to men and sterile women was a violation of law, and six of the nine agreed that federal law prohibits any discrimination solely on the basis of possible or actual pregnancy. The ruling in *International Union* v. *Johnson Controls* applies to all employers engaged in interstate commerce, including hospitals and clinics.

Title VII of the Civil Rights Act of 1964 forbids employers to discriminate on the basis of race, color, religion, sex, or national origin. Explicit discrimination on the basis of religion, sex, or national origin can be justified only

From George J. Annas, "Fetal Protection and Employment Discrimination—The *Johnson Controls* Case," *The New England Journal of Medicine*, vol. 325, no. 10 (September 5, 1991), pp. 740–743. Copyright © 1991 by The Massachusetts Medical Society. Reprinted by permission.

if the characteristic is a "bona fide occupational qualification." The federal Pregnancy Discrimination Act of 1978 made it
clear that sex discrimination includes discrimination "on the basis of pregnancy,
childbirth, or related conditions."[5]

THE FETAL-PROTECTION POLICY OF JOHNSON CONTROLS

Beginning in 1977, Johnson Controls
advised women who expected to have
children not to take jobs involving
exposure to lead, warned women who
took such jobs of the risks entailed in
having a child while being exposed to
lead, and recommended that workers
consult their family doctors for advice.
The risks were said to include a higher
rate of spontaneous abortion as well as
unspecified potential risks to the fetus.
Between 1979 and 1983, eight employees
became pregnant while their blood lead
levels were above 30 µg per deciliter
(1.45 µmol per liter) (a level the Centers
for Disease Control had designated as
excessive for children). Although there
was no evidence of harm due to lead
exposure in any of the children born
to the employees, a medical consultant
for the company said that he thought
hyperactivity in one of the children
"could very well be and probably was
due to the lead he had."[6]

In 1982, apparently after consulting
medical experts about the dangers to the
fetus of exposure to lead, the company
changed its policy from warning to
exclusion:

> ... women who are pregnant or who are
> capable of bearing children will not be
> placed into jobs involving lead exposure
> or which could expose them to lead
> through the exercise of job bidding,
> bumping, transfer, or promotion rights.

The policy defined women capable of
bearing children as all women except
those who "have medical confirmation
that they cannot bear children."

In 1984, a class-action suit was brought
challenging the policy as a violation of Title VII of the Civil Rights Act of 1964. In
1988, a federal district court ruled in favor of Johnson Controls, primarily on the
basis of depositions and affidavits from
physicians and environmental toxicologists regarding the damage that exposure to lead could cause in developing
fetuses, children, adults, and animals.[7]
The U.S. Court of Appeals for the Seventh Circuit affirmed this decision in 1989
in a seven-to-four opinion.[6] The majority
based its opinion primarily on the medical evidence of potential harm to the fetus
and on their view that federal law permitted employers to take this potential harm
into account in developing employment
policies.

THE SUPREME COURT'S DECISION

The U.S. Supreme Court unanimously
reversed the decision in an opinion
written by Justice Harry Blackmun. The
Court had no trouble finding that the
bias in the policy was "obvious," since
"fertile men, but not fertile women, are
given a choice as to whether they wish
to risk their reproductive health for a
particular job."[4] The Court noted that
the company did not seek to protect
all unconceived children, only those of
its female employees. The policy was
based on the potential for pregnancy
and, accordingly, directly in conflict
with the Pregnancy Discrimination Act
of 1978. The key to the case was
determining whether the absence of
pregnancy or the absence of the potential
to become pregnant was a bona fide

occupational qualification for a job in battery manufacturing.

Employment discrimination is permitted "in those certain instances where religion, sex, or national origin is a bona fide occupational qualification reasonably necessary to the normal operation of that particular business or enterprise."[4] The Court's approach was to determine whether Johnson Controls' fetal-protection policy came within the scope of those "certain instances." The statutory language requires that the occupational qualification affect "an employee's ability to do the job."[4] The Court determined that the defense was available only when it went to the "essence of the business" or was "the core of the employee's job performance."[4]

The Court had previously allowed a maximum-security prison for men to refuse to hire women guards because "the employment of a female guard would create real risks of safety to others if violence broke out because the guard was a woman." Thus, sex was seen as reasonably related to the essence of the guard's job: maintaining prison security. Similarly, other courts had permitted airlines to lay off pregnant flight attendants if it was considered necessary to protect the safety of passengers. The Court agreed that protecting the safety or security of customers was related to the essence of the business and was legitimate.

The welfare of unconceived fetuses, however, did not fit into either category of exception. In the Court's words, "No one can disregard the possibility of injury to future children; the BFOQ [bona fide occupational qualification], however, is not so broad that it transforms this deep social concern into an essential aspect of battery making." Limitations involving pregnancy or sex "must relate to ability to perform the duties of the job.... Women as capable of doing their jobs as their male counterparts may not be forced to choose between having a child and having a job." The Court concluded that Congress had left the welfare of the next generation to parents, not employers: "Decisions about the welfare of future children must be left to the parents who conceive, bear, support, and raise them rather than to the employers who hire those parents."[4]

The Court finally addressed potential tort liability should a fetus be injured by its mother's occupational exposure and later sue the company. The Court wrote that since the Occupational Safety and Health Administration (OSHA) had concluded that there was no basis for excluding women of childbearing age from exposure to lead at the minimal levels permitted under its guidelines, the likelihood of fetal injury was slight. And even if injury should occur, the injured child would have to prove that the employer had been negligent. If the employer followed OSHA guidelines and fully informed its workers of the risks involved, the Court concluded that liability seemed "remote at best." Thus, just as speculation about risks to children not yet conceived has nothing to do with job performance, speculation about future tort liability—at least one step further removed from harm to the fetus—is not job-related.

THE CONCURRING OPINIONS

Justice Byron White wrote the main concurring opinion for himself, Chief Justice William Rehnquist, and Justice Anthony Kennedy. Although they agreed with the outcome in this case, they dissented from the bona fide occupational-qualification analysis as it applied to tort liability, and warned that the case could be used to undercut certain privacy rights. These three justices believed that under some circumstances it should be permissible for employers to exclude women from employment on the grounds that their fetuses could be injured and sue the employers (the women themselves could not sue because they would be covered by workers' compensation as their exclusive remedy). Their rationale was that parents cannot waive the right of their children to sue, that the parents' negligence will not be imputed to the children, and that even in the absence of negligence, "it is possible that employers will be held strictly liable, if, for example, their manufacturing process is considered."[4] Avoiding such liability was, in the view of these justices, a safety issue relevant to the bona fide occupational-qualification standard.

The other point made by the three justices was relegated to a footnote, but it is of substantial interest. They argued that the Court's opinion could be read to outlaw considerations of privacy as a justification for employment discrimination on the basis of sex because considerations of privacy would not directly relate to the employees' ability to do the job or to customers' safety. They cited cases in which the privacy-related wishes of some patients to be cared for by nurses and nurses' aides of the same sex had been upheld as a bona fide occupational qualification, including an instance regarding the sex of nurses' aides in a retirement home[8] and a policy excluding male nurses from obstetrical practice in one hospital.[9] The justices in the majority responded to this issue by saying simply, "We have never addressed privacy-based sex discrimination and shall not do so here because the sex-based discrimination at issue today does not involve the privacy interests of Johnson Controls' customers."[4] This issue has been left for another day, but it should be noted that the obstetrical-nurse case rests on outmoded judicial stereotyping of obstetricians as men and nurses as women.[10]

IMPLICATIONS OF THE DECISION

The Court took the language of the Pregnancy Discrimination Act seriously, correctly observing that "concern for a woman's existing or potential offspring historically has been the excuse for denying women equal employment opportunities."[4] The purpose of the act was to end such employment discrimination, and the Court's opinion in *Johnson Controls* holds that recasting sex discrimination in the name of fetal protection is illegal. Johnson Controls had argued that its policy was ethical and socially responsible and that it was meant only to prevent exposing the fetus to avoidable risk. Judge Frank Easterbrook probably had the most articulate response to this concern in his dissent from the appeals-court decision:

> There is a strong correlation between the health of the infant and prenatal medical care; there is also a powerful link between the parents' income and infants' health, for higher income means better nutrition, among other things.... Removing women from well-paying jobs (and the attendant health insurance), or denying women access to these jobs, may reduce the risk from lead while also reducing levels of medical care and quality of nutrition.[6]

Judge Easterbrook argued that ultimately fetal-protection policies cannot require "zero risk" but must be based on reasonable risk. He correctly noted that it is good and reasonable to worry about the health of workers and their future children. But,

> to insist on *zero* risk... is to exclude women from industrial jobs that have been a male preserve. By all means let society lend its energies to improving the prospects of those who come after us. Demanding zero risk produces not progress but paralysis.[6]

The same zero-risk analysis can, of course, be applied to the possibility of tort liability as seen from the industry's perspective. The industry would like its risk to be zero. Six of the nine judges agreed that it is close to zero, or at least remote. As a factual matter, there has been only one recorded case of a child's bringing a lawsuit for injuries suffered while the mother was pregnant and continued to work. In this case, the jury found in favor of the employer, even though there was evidence that the employer had violated OSHA safety standards.[11] Two thirds of the justices on the U.S. Supreme Court think that state tort liability is preempted so long as the employer follows federal law, informs workers of the risks, and is not negligent. Added to this is the extraordinarily difficult issue of causation, even if the employer is negligent. Putting the two together may not eliminate all risk of liability, but the risk is as small as can reasonably be expected.

It has been persuasively suggested that fetal-protection policies that affect only women are based on the view that women are "primarily biologic actors" and not economic ones and that men are only economic actors who have no "biologic connections and responsibilities to their families."[12] The decision in *Johnson Controls* continues the legal and social movement to provide equality of opportunity in the workplace. It does not eliminate the duty to minimize workplace exposure to toxic substances. Indeed, it would be a hollow victory for women to gain the right to be exposed to the same high levels of mutagens and other toxic substances that men are exposed to. The real challenge for public policy remains to turn industry's focus away from new methods of sex discrimination and toward new ways to reduce workplace hazards. In this area, physicians continue to have a prominent role.

Physicians specializing in occupational health should continue to work to reduce exposure to toxic substances in the workplace for all workers (by replacing such agents with other, less toxic substances, reducing their volume, and encouraging the use of protective gear). In addition, all workers should be warned about the health risks of all clinically important exposures that cannot be avoided, and encouraged to be monitored for the early signs of damage. Personal physicians should take a careful occupational history and be sufficiently informed to be able to tell their patients about the risks of exposure to various substances, including what is known about their mutagenicity and teratogenicity.* Armed with this information, workers—both men and women—will be able to make informed decisions about their jobs and the risks they are willing to run to keep them, as well as to pressure management intelligently to make the workplace safer.

Congress and the Court have made a strong statement about the use of fe-

*[Mutagenicity is the capacity to cause mutations; teratogenicity is the capacity to cause developmental malformations.—Eds.]

tal protection as a rationale to control or restrict the activities and decisions of women: the ultimate decision maker must be the worker herself. This policy is consistent with good medical practice as well—as is evident, for instance, in the policy of the American College of Obstetricians and Gynecologists on "maternal–fetal conflicts."[13] To paraphrase Justice Blackmun, it is no more appropriate for physicians to attempt to control women's opportunities and choices on the basis of their reproductive role than it is for the courts or individual employers to do so.

REFERENCES

1. Becker ME. From *Muller v. Oregon* to fetal vulnerability policies, 53 U. Chicago Law Rev. 1219 (1986).
2. Muller v. Oregon, 208 U.S. 412 (1908).
3. Fuchs VR. Sex differences in economic well-being. Science 1986; 232:459–64.
4. International Union v. Johnson Controls, 111 S.CT. 1196 (1991).
5. Pregnancy Discrimination Act of 1978, 92 Stat. 2076, 42 U.S.C. sec 2000e (k).
6. International Union v. Johnson Controls, 886 F.2d 871 (7th Cir. 1989) (en banc).
7. International Union v. Johnson controls, 680 F. Supp. 309 (E.D. Wis. 1988).
8. Fesel v. Masonic Home of Delaware, 447 F. Supp. 1346 (D.Del. 1978).
9. Buckus v. Baptist Medical Center, 510 F. Supp. 1191 (E.D.Ark. 1981).
10. Sex in the delivery room: is the nurse a boy or a girl? In: Annas GJ. Judging medicine. Clifton, N.J.: Humana Press, 1988:53–6.
11. Security National Bank v. Chloride Industrial Battery, 602 F. Supp. 294 (D.Kan. 1985).
12. Becker ME. Can employers exclude women to protect children? JAMA 1990; 264:2113–7.
13. American College of Obstetricians and Gynecologists Committee opinion no. 55, Committee on Ethics. Patient choice: maternal-fetal conflict. Washington, D.C.: American College of Obstetricians and Gynecologists, 1987.

NO

Hugh M. Finneran

TITLE VII AND RESTRICTIONS ON EMPLOYMENT OF FERTILE WOMEN

During the decade of the 1970s, there was a rapid expansion of the female work force accompanied by a simultaneous expansion of scientific knowledge concerning hazards of exposure to toxic substances in the workplace. Health hazards in industry present serious legal, medical, and sociological issues.

Recently, a dramatic awareness of the hazards to the employee's reproductive capacity, i.e., miscarriage, stillbirth, and birth defects, has materialized. The hazard to the reproductive capacity and fetal damage is not a unique problem for female workers. Rather, it is a problem which may impact upon all workers. This article, however, will restrict its analysis to factual situations where the employer considers the problems of exposure to chemicals as uniquely, or primarily, arising out of the female physiology and either restricts or refuses to hire females with childbearing ability. Physical conditions other than chemical substances may also be harmful to the fetus, i.e., radiation, heat stress, vibration, and noise, but will not be treated in this article....

Title VII of the Civil Rights Act of 1964 incorporates two theories of discrimination which must be considered in a legal analysis of restrictions (the term "restriction" includes a refusal to hire) placed on females because of health hazards. These are: disparate treatment and policies, practices, or procedures with disparate impact not justified by business necessity.

Two types of substances will be considered in this article: teratogens and mutagens. Teratogens are substances that can harm the fetus after conception by entering the placenta. Mutagens are substances that can cause a change in the genetic material in living cells.

DISPARATE TREATMENT

The Supreme Court in *International Brotherhood of Teamsters v. United States* stated: "Disparate treatment... is the most easily understood type of discrimination. The employer simply treats some people less favorably than others because of their race, color, religion, sex, or national origin. Proof of discriminatory motive is critical, although it can in some situations be inferred from the mere fact of differences in treatment...."

From Hugh M. Finneran, "Title VII and Restrictions on Employment of Fertile Women," *Labor Law Journal*, vol. 31, no. 4 (April 1980). Published and copyrighted © 1980 by Commerce Clearing House, Inc., 4025 W. Peterson Avenue, Chicago, IL 60646. Reprinted by permission.

The Equal Employment Opportunity Commission and the United States Department of Labor on February 1, 1980, issued, for comment, Interpretive Guidelines on Employment Discrimination and Reproductive Hazards. "An employer/contractor whose work environment involves employee exposure to reproductive hazards shall not discriminate on the basis of sex (including pregnancy or childbearing capacity) in hiring, work assignment, or other conditions of employment."

An employer's policy of protecting female employees from reproductive hazards by depriving them of employment opportunities without any scientific data is a per se violation of Title VII. The Guidelines' position, however, is that the exclusion of women with childbearing ability from the workplace is a per se violation. To arrive at such a conclusion without an analysis of the precise scientific and medical evidence is an erroneous and indefensible legal standard. Thus, an employer's exclusion of females on the basis of their susceptibility to the mutagenic effects of a toxic substance should not be a per se violation but should be analyzed under the rubric of disparate treatment or adverse impact.

One line of inquiry under the disparate treatment analysis would be whether the mutagenic substance has reproductive hazards for male and female employees. If the particular chemical substance has a mutagenic effect on male and female employees, the obvious question is why female workers are treated differently. The answer may be scientifically explained, but it raises the issue of disparate treatment. Indeed, the employer should consider whether there are any other substances in the workplace, other than the substance relied on to exclude the female, which have mutagenic effects on males.

In essence, if the basis for the exclusion is the mutagenic characteristics of a substance, the employer would have to treat all employees, male and female, who are exposed to mutagenic effects in the same manner. The employer may face a serious possibility of a Title VII violation for disparate treatment unless the scientific justification for the differential treatment is very persuasive.

In establishing a prima facie case of sex discrimination, under the principles of *McDonnell Douglas Corp. v. Green* a female must show that: she belongs to a protected class; she applied or was qualified for a job for which the employer was seeking applicants; and despite her qualifications, she was rejected. She also must prove that, after her rejection, the employer continued to seek applicants with her qualifications.

Applying the *McDonnell Douglas* principles to a restriction on female employment, the female could establish a prima facie case of sex discrimination if a chemical substance has a mutagenic effect on the males but only females are excluded from exposure to the hazard by the employer's restrictive policy. In this assumed factual situation, the very basis for the restriction would be applicable to either of sex discrimination, the employer has the burden of proving the existence of a business necessity or a bona fide occupational qualification. Of course, proof of compelling scientific data that the degree or severity of risk was substantially greater might alter the existence of a prima facie case, but the court more likely would consider such evidence as an affirmative defense.

GENDER-BASED CLASSIFICATION

Varying the factual assumptions, let us consider the existence of a work environment in which the chemical substance is a teratogen and an employer restricts the employment of females with childbearing ability. In these circumstances, the employer could argue that the exclusion is based on a neutral health factor rather than sex-based criteria. Since teratogens by definition harm a fetus after conception, the safety hazard is present only for females with childbearing ability and cannot affect males or females without childbearing ability. Thus, a strong argument could be presented that the exclusion of females based upon the teratogenic effect of a chemical substance is a health classification and is not gender based.

In *Geduldig v. Aiello,* the Supreme Court ruled that the exclusion of pregnancy-related disabilities from a state disability system was not sex discrimination but was a distinction based on physical condition "by dividing potential recipients into two groups—pregnant women and non-pregnant persons." Likewise, *General Electric Co. v. Gilbert* viewed pregnancy classifications as not being gender based.

At least one commentator has criticized the relevance of *Gilbert* and *Aiello* to the restriction of female employment in toxic workplaces, because the classification suffers from overinclusiveness since "many women in the excluded class delay or plan to avoid childbearing and thus face no additional risk at all." This contention is small comfort to an employer, however, since women have been known to change their plans and birth-control techniques are not universally effective.

Furthermore, some teratogens are cumulative and remain in the body long after the exposure has ceased. The legal issue is more complex where there is a restriction on the employment of a woman with childbearing ability where teratogens are present but mutagens with adverse reproductive effects present in the workplace affect males on whom no restrictions are placed.

The Pregnancy Disability Amendment to Title VII may have a bearing on the issue of whether the classification is gender based. "The terms 'because of sex' or 'on the basis of sex' include, but are not limited to, because of or on the basis of pregnancy, childbirth, or related medical conditions...."

The Pregnancy Amendment to Title VII does not state expressly that the terms "because of sex" or "on the basis of sex" includes a woman's childbearing ability or potential. The Guidelines, however, interpret "childbearing capacity" as prohibited by the Amendment. Such an interpretation is not without some doubt as to its validity. Nevertheless, if the Guidelines' construction is correct, a distinction based on childbearing ability would be considered gender-based disparate treatment. The practical consequences may be minimal since exclusions or restrictions on the employment of females with childbearing ability has a disparate impact and is best analyzed in this context.

DISPARATE IMPACT

The Supreme Court in *Griggs v. Duke Power Co.* held: "Under the Act, practices, procedures, or tests neutral on their face, and even neutral in terms of intent, cannot be maintained if they operate to 'freeze' the status quo of prior discriminatory employment practices." Thus, *Griggs* ruled that the employer's requirement of a high school diploma or passage of a test as a condition of employment was a prima facie race violation of Title VII, unless these requirements are a "business necessity." "The Act proscribes not only overt discrimination but also practices that are fair in form but discriminatory in operation. The touchstone is business necessity."

In *Dothard v. Rawlinson*, the Supreme Court held that the employer violated Title VII by requiring a minimum height of five feet two inches and a weight of 120 pounds for prison guards since the policy had a disparate impact on women. Likewise, *Nashville Gas Co. v. Satty* is relevant to the issue. In *Satty*, the employer denied accumulated seniority to female employees returning from pregnancy leaves of absence. The Court held that an employer may not "burden female employees in such a way as to deprive them of employment opportunities because of their different role." The conclusion appears inescapable that an employer's restriction on the employment of women with childbearing ability, and this includes restrictions limited to specific jobs, is a prima facie violation of Title VII's proscriptions against sex discrimination under *Griggs*, *Dothard*, and *Satty*.

BONA FIDE OCCUPATIONAL QUALIFICATION

Two affirmative defenses must be considered: bona fide occupational qualification [BFOQ] and business necessity. Title VII provides an affirmative defense to a charge of sex discrimination where sex "is a bona fide occupational qualification reasonably necessary to the normal operation of that particular business or enterprise...."

The Guidelines state: "narrow exception [for BFOQ] pertains only to situations where all or substantially all of the protected class is unable to perform the duties of the job in question. Such cannot be the case in the reproductive hazards setting, where exclusions are based on the premise of danger to the employee or fetus and not on the ability to perform." Under *Weeks v. Southern Bell Telephone & Telegraph Co.*, an employer relying on the bona fide occupational qualification exception "has the burden of proving that he had reasonable cause to believe, that is, a factual basis for believing, that all or substantially all women would be unable to perform safely and efficiently the duties of the job involved."

In the absence of medical evidence to the contrary, an employer's assumption is that all, or substantially all, females have the capacity of bearing children. Thus, the area of controversy will probably center on the issue of whether the safety of the fetus or future generations is reasonably necessary to the normal operation of the employer's business. However, plaintiffs may argue that all or substantially all females are not at risk since not all females plan to have a family.

Courts have sustained decisions by bus companies not to hire drivers over specified ages as being a BFOQ justified by increased safety hazards for third persons. In *Hodgson v. Greyhound Lines, Inc.*, the company refused to consider applications for intercity bus drivers from individuals thirty-five years of age or older. The Seventh Circuit held that the company was not guilty of age discrimination, since its hiring policy was a BFOQ justified by the increased hazards to third persons caused by hiring older drivers. "Greyhound must demonstrate that it has a rational basis in fact to believe that elimination of its maximum hiring age will increase the likelihood of risk of harm to its passengers. Greyhound need only demonstrate however a minimal increase in risk of harm for it is enough to show that elimination of the hiring policy might jeopardize the life of one more person than might otherwise occur under the present hiring practice."

The Fifth Circuit in *Usery v. Tamiami Trail Tours, Inc.*, in upholding the company's refusal to hire bus drivers over forty years of age, found that the policy was a BFOQ. The company had demonstrated "that the passenger-endangering characteristics of over-forty job applicants cannot practically be ascertained by some hiring test other than automatic exclusion on the basis of age."

The language of the BFOQ exception under the Age Discrimination Act is essentially the same as the language of the BFOQ exception under Title VII of the Civil Rights Act. Cases in the airline industry also have considered third-party safety as a sufficient BFOQ in situations involving involuntary pregnancy leaves of absence for flight attendants.

The concept of concern for third parties is sufficiently elastic to include the unborn. It is submitted that society, including employers, has an obligation to avoid action which will have an adverse effect on the health and well-being of future generations. With all the present concerns about the protection of our environment and endangered species, an enlightened judiciary should not callously turn its back on generations unborn. Indeed, on the more mundane and pragmatic basis, it is of the essence of a business venture to operate safely in a manner which avoids costly tort liability.

BUSINESS NECESSITY

The business necessity defense may also justify the exclusionary or restrictive practice. In order to prove this defense, the employer has the burden of establishing that: the practice is necessary to the safe and efficient operation of the business; the purpose must be sufficiently compelling to override the adverse impact; and the practice must carry out the business purpose. The employer also must establish that there are not acceptable alternative policies or practices which would better accomplish the business purpose or accomplish it with lesser adverse impact on the protected class.

PRENATAL INJURY

Since the safe and efficient operation is premised on the need to protect the fetus, tort law relating to prenatal injuries is pertinent. The potential tort liability bears on the necessity for the exclusion. The law of Texas will be reviewed in regard to prenatal injuries. Texas was selected because of its large petrochemical industry.

The parents of a child suffering prenatal injuries resulting in its death have cause of action under the Texas wrongful death statute, provided the child was born alive and was viable at the time the injury was inflicted. In so ruling, the court stated that the statutory requirement of the Texas wrongful death statute, that the deceased has suffered an injury for which he could have recovered damages had he survived, was met. This holding of necessity implied that the Texas Supreme Court recognized a cause of action for a surviving child who is born alive with a birth defect caused by prenatal injuries. For a child born with birth defects, the cause of action exists for prenatal injuries at any time during pregnancy.

The Texas courts apparently have not yet decided whether parents have a cause of action under the wrongful death statute in cases where a child is stillborn due to prenatal injuries. The inquiry in such a case would revolve around the issue of whether a fetus is a person within the meaning of the wrongful death statute. Other state courts interpreting their wrongful death statutes have split on the issue.

Assuming that liability is established, Texas courts allow surviving parents to recover damages under the wrongful death act to compensate them for the pecuniary value of the child's service that would have been rendered during minority, less the cost and expense of the child's support, education, and maintenance, as well as economic benefits reasonably expected to have been contributed after reaching majority.

While it is generally held that some evidence of pecuniary loss is necessary to support a wrongful death judgment, the Texas courts have recognized that such proof cannot be supplied with any certainty or accuracy in cases involving young infants. Therefore, they leave the damages question largely to the discretion of the jury. Of course, a prenatally injured infant who manages to survive would be able to sue for his own personal injuries, including pain and suffering, loss of earning capacity, and any other damages, if applicable. Recognizing the "deep pocket syndrome," employers have a reasonable basis for being concerned about large tort recoveries.

The female employee's willing and informed consent to the assumption of the risk is not binding to the unborn child. Hence, obtaining a waiver from the female employee is an act with no legal significance other than documenting the employer's awareness of the unavoidably unsafe condition of the workplace for the fetus for use against the employer in tort litigation.

The employer should not be required to assume the risk of significant tort liability which could threaten the very existence of the enterprise, depending on the financial assets of the employer and the severity of injuries. Courts have required employers in discrimination cases to assume additional expense to achieve compliance with Title VII (costs of validation studies, loss of customer patronage, and training costs), but it is submitted that the magnitude of the risks of exposure to prenatal injuries and reproduction hazards should result in a different decision. The financial impact on the employer is important but certainly not the most important factor. A lifetime of suffering by future generations is worthy of societal concern. The Civil Rights Act does not exist in a vacuum.

Whether the purpose of the restriction is sufficiently compelling to override the adverse impact on women and is necessary to accomplish the employer's business purpose of ensuring a safe workplace without reproductive hazards will be decided by the scientific and medical data relating to the severity of the health hazard of the particular substance.

LESS RESTRICTIVE ALTERNATIVES

Under the business necessity principles of *Robinson v. Lorillard*, the employer must demonstrate the absence of "less restrictive alternatives" before relying on the affirmative defense. The Guidelines indicate that four factors should be considered. These are: whether the employer is complying with applicable occupational federal, state, and local safety and health laws; respirators or other protective devices are used to minimize or eliminate the hazard; product substitution is used; and affected employees are transferred without loss of pay or other benefits to areas of the plant where the reproductive hazard is minimal or nonexistent.

The employer's obligation to comply with its safety obligations under the Occupational Safety and Health Act is eminently reasonable, provided that it is recognized that the employer's obligation under OSHA only requires the use of technologically and economically feasible engineering and administrative controls. If engineering and administrative controls are not feasible, the employer must protect his employees by the use of personal protective devices. It is fair and reasonable to require an employer to satisfy his legal obligations under safety and health laws before excluding females from the workplace.

To suggest, however, that the employers change their products or provide rate retention for employees restricted from hazardous exposure is extreme and without legislative support. If Congress had intended to require substitution of products and rate retention for employees under Title VII, it would have done so explicitly. When, as here, these matters are at best tangentially related to nondiscrimination, Title VII is silent on the subject, and wages and rates of pay and seniority of workers transferred to jobs other than their usual jobs are mandatory subjects of collective bargaining, then a reasonable interpretation of the legislation is that Title VII does not impose this obligation of management.

If an employer intends to sustain his business necessity defense, there must be evidence that the employer has explored the feasible alternatives to imposing restrictions on the employment of fertile females. One alternative which must be considered is a system for individual screening and evaluation with restrictions imposed on the female only if she becomes pregnant. Serious medical questions are posed by this alternative. Indeed, for some teratogenic substances the first weeks of pregnancy are the most critical. During this period, a woman may not know that she is pregnant, and sophisticated tests may not reveal the pregnancy. The administration of such a program might raise serious personnel problems since female employees might object to continuous monitoring to determine whether they are pregnant.

CONCLUSION

The decade of the 1970s was the era of the testing cases under Title VII. The decade of the 1980s will be the era of large class actions involving the exclusion of fertile females from exposure to reproductive hazards.

On the extreme of one side will be those arguing that Title VII rejects these protections as Victorian, romantic paternalism which deprives the individual woman of the power to decide whether the economic benefits justify the risks. On the other extreme, some employers will argue that any possible risk of harm to the female's offspring require her exclusion.

An informed judiciary should consider not only the economic interests of the female employee and the employer but the societal concern for the quality and happiness of future generations as well. The Supreme Court in *Roe v. Wade* recognized that a state may properly assert important interests in protecting potential life. After evaluating the level, duration, and manner of exposure in the specific employer's workplace, if there is reputable scientific evidence of a recognized reproductive hazard, either from a mutagen with significantly greater risk for female workers or a teratogen, the employer should be allowed to exclude females from that workplace if the business necessity criteria are satisfied. The employer should have the right and, indeed, the duty and obligation to operate his facility with due concern for the safety and health of future generations.

POSTSCRIPT

Should Women Have the Same Right to Work as Men?

The *Johnson Controls* decision holds that excluding women from workplaces, except on the genuine inability of a woman to do the job, is illegal. The fetal protection policy, designed to protect the fetus and not the woman, is therefore illegal. But is it wrong? The answer to this question turns on a commitment of values: values concerning equality, especially equality between the sexes; values concerning the family and reproduction; and, significantly, values concerning the bottom line and the conditions of labor. The problem at Johnson Controls, Inc., was that there was lead in the atmosphere, which is why the company had adopted the contested policy. Some argue that there was a simpler way out—that all gender issues, fetal protection issues, Occupational Safety and Health Administration (OSHA) issues, and others would be solved if the employers, Johnson Controls, had just eliminated the lead problem.

The issue of tort liability dominated the *Johnson Controls* case. Management argued, unsuccessfully, that leaving women in the workplace was a sure invitation to horrendous lawsuits. The Court found instead that the mother's right to compensation, should her fetus be damaged by the lead, was waived because she was covered by workman's compensation. But, considering that the fetus was not covered by workman's compensation and had waived no rights whatsoever, do you agree with this argument?

SUGGESTED READINGS

"Comparable Worth in Industrialized Countries," *Monthly Labor Review* (November 1992).

Julia Flynn, "Julia Stasch Raises the Roof for Feminism," *Business Week* (January 25, 1993).

Val Hammond, "Opportunity 2000: A Culture Change Approach to Equal Opportunity," *Women in Management Review* (1992).

Harry A. Jessell, "Court Overturns FCC Gender Preference," *Broadcasting* (February 24, 1992).

Joanne D. Leck and David M. Saunders, "Hiring Women: The Effects of Canada's Employment Equity Act," *Canadian Public Policy* (June 1992).

Peter Lurie, "The Law as They Found It: Disentangling Gender-Based Affirmative Action Programs from Croson," *University of Chicago Law Review* (Fall 1992).

Charlene Marmer Solomon, "Are White Males Being Left Out?" *Personnel Journal* (November 1991).

John Southerst, "Public Policy: What Price Fairness?" *Canadian Business* (December 1991).

ISSUE 10

Does Blowing the Whistle Violate Company Loyalty?

YES: Sissela Bok, from "Whistleblowing and Professional Responsibility," *New York University Education Quarterly* (Summer 1980)

NO: Robert A. Larmer, from "Whistleblowing and Employee Loyalty," *Journal of Business Ethics* (vol. 11, 1992)

ISSUE SUMMARY

YES: Philosopher Sissela Bok asserts that although blowing the whistle is often justified, it does involve dissent, accusation, and a breach of loyalty to the employer.

NO: Robert A. Larmer, an associate professor of philosophy, argues that attempting to stop illegal or unethical company activities may be the highest type of company loyalty an employee can display.

Whistle-blowing occurs when an employee discovers a wrong at his or her place of employment and exposes it, thereby saving lives or a great deal of money, but almost always at great expense to him- or herself. Since the readings that follow are theoretical, some specific cases might be useful. In "The Whistle Blowers' Morning After," *The New York Times* (November 9, 1986), N. R. Kleinfeld portrays five of the early whistle-blowers, some of whom have become famous as case studies in business schools across the country. Each one has an interesting story to tell; each claims that if he had it to do over again he would, for he likes living with a clear conscience. But each has also paid a price: great stress, sometimes ill health, career loss, financial ruin, and/or loss of friends and family.

Charles Atchinson blew the whistle on the Comanche Park nuclear plant in Glen Rose, Texas, a power station that was unsafe. It cost him his job, plunged him into debt, and left emotional scars on his family. Kermit Vandivier, who blew the whistle on the B. F. Goodrich Aircraft Brakes scandal, also lost his job. He has since begun a new career as a journalist. James Pope claimed that the Federal Aviation Administration (FAA) found in 1975 an effective device, known as an airborne collision avoidance system, that would prevent mid-air crashes; but it chose instead to pursue an inferior device it had had a hand in developing. Mr. Pope was "retired" early by the FAA. The most famous whistle-blower of all may be A. Ernest Fitzgerald, the U.S. Air Force cost analyst who found huge cost overruns on Lockheed cargo planes that were being developed for the Air Force. After his revelations, he was discharged from the Air Force. He fought for 13 years to be reinstated, which he was, at full rank, in 1982. For some first-hand accounts by Fitzgerald, see *Pentagonists: An Insider's View of Waste, Mismanagement, and Fraud in Defense Spending* (Houghton Mifflin, 1989) and *The High Priests of Waste* (W. W. Norton, 1972). The common thread of these stories is that when someone detected a wrong and properly reported it, he was demoted, labeled a troublemaker, and disciplined or fired, even when the evidence was very much in his favor. All of them, incidentally, initially believed in their organizations, and not only were all of them sure that they were acting in an ethical manner, but they also believed that they would be thanked for their efforts and diligence.

Professors Myron Peretz Glazer and Penina Migdal Glazer, in *The Whistle Blowers: Exposing Corruption in Government and Industry* (Basic Books, 1989), tell the story of 55 whistle-blowers—why they did what they did, and what the consequences were for themselves and their families. The Glazers found that the dominant trait in these whistle-blowers was a strong belief in individual responsibility. As one of the spouses of a whistle-blower stated, "A corrupt system can happen only if the individuals who make up that system are corrupt. You are either going to be part of the corruption or part of the forces working against it. There isn't a third choice. Someone, someday, has to take a stand; if you don't, maybe no one will. And that is wrong."

The Glazers write that the strong belief in individual responsibility that drove these ethical resisters was often supported by professional ethics, religious values, or allegiance to a community. But the personal costs of public disclosure were high, and the results were less than satisfactory. In some cases the accused corporations made no changes. The whistle-blowers, however, had to recreate careers, relocate, and settle for less money in new jobs. For most resisters, the worst part was the devastating months or even years of dislocation, unemployment, and temporary jobs. In response to a question posed by the Glazers, 21 of the whistle-blowers advised other potential whistle-blowers to "forget it" or to "leak the information without your name attached." If blowing the whistle is unavoidable, however, then "be prepared to be ostracized, have your career come to a screeching halt, and perhaps even be driven into bankruptcy."

As you read the following selections by Sissela Bok and Robert A Larmer, think about these cases and others you may have heard about. Consider the motivations involved in whistle-blowing and whether they reflect loyalty or disloyalty to the company. How would you view an instance of whistle-blowing if you or your company were the target? Who deserves the greatest consideration in potential whistle-blowing situations: the individual, the company, or the public?

YES
Sissela Bok

WHISTLEBLOWING AND PROFESSIONAL RESPONSIBILITY

"Whistleblowing" is a new label generated by our increased awareness of the ethical conflicts encountered at work. Whistleblowers sound an alarm from within the very organization in which they work, aiming to spotlight neglect or abuses that threaten the public interest.

The stakes in whistleblowing are high. Take the nurse who alleges that physicians enrich themselves in her hospital through unnecessary surgery; the engineer who discloses safety defects in the braking systems of a fleet of new rapid-transit vehicles; the Defense Department official who alerts Congress to military graft and overspending: all know that they pose a threat to those whom they denounce and that their own careers may be at risk.

MORAL CONFLICTS

Moral conflicts on several levels confront anyone who is wondering whether to speak out about abuses or risks or serious neglect. In the first place, he must try to decide whether, other things being equal, speaking out is in fact in the public interest. This choice is often made more complicated by factual uncertainties: Who is responsible for the abuse or neglect? How great is the threat? And how likely is it that speaking out will precipitate changes for the better?

In the second place, a would-be whistleblower must weigh his responsibility to serve the public interest against the responsibility he owes to his colleagues and the institution in which he works. While the professional ethic requires collegial loyalty, the codes of ethics often stress responsibility to the public over and above duties to colleagues and clients. Thus the United States Code of Ethics for Government Servants asks them to "expose corruption wherever uncovered" and to "put loyalty to the highest moral principles and to country above loyalty to persons, party, or government."[1] Similarly, the largest professional engineering association requires members to speak out against abuses threatening the safety, health, and welfare of the public.[2]

From Sissela Bok, "Whistleblowing and Professional Responsibility," *New York University Education Quarterly*, vol. 11 (Summer 1980), pp. 2–7. Copyright © 1980 by Sissela Bok. Reprinted by permission.

A third conflict for would-be whistle-blowers is personal in nature and cuts across the first two: even in cases where they have concluded that the facts warrant speaking out, and that their duty to do so overrides loyalties to colleagues and institutions, they often have reason to fear the results of carrying out such a duty. However strong this duty may seem in theory, they know that, in practice, retaliation is likely. As a result, their careers and their ability to support themselves and their families may be unjustly impaired.[3] A government handbook issued during the Nixon era recommends reassigning "undesirables" to places so remote that they would prefer to resign. Whistleblowers may also be downgraded or given work without responsibility or work for which they are not qualified; or else they may be given many more tasks than they can possibly perform. Another risk is that an outspoken civil servant may be ordered to undergo a psychiatric fitness-for-duty examination,[4] declared unfit for service, and "separated" as well as discredited from the point of view of any allegations he may be making. Outright firing, finally, is the most direct institutional response to whistleblowers.

Add to the conflicts confronting individual whistleblowers the claim to self-policing that many professions make, and professional responsibility is at issue in still another way. For an appeal to the public goes against everything that "self-policing" stands for. The question for the different professions, then, is how to resolve, insofar as it is possible, the conflict between professional loyalty and professional responsibility toward the outside world. The same conflicts arise to some extent in all groups, but professional groups often have special cohesion and claim special dignity and privileges.

The plight of whistleblowers has come to be documented by the press and described in a number of books. Evidence of the hardships imposed on those who chose to act in the public interest has combined with a heightened awareness of professional malfeasance and corruption to produce a shift toward greater public support of whistleblowers. Public service law firms and consumer groups have taken up their cause; institutional reforms and legislation have been proposed to combat illegitimate reprisals.[5]

Given the indispensable services performed by so many whistleblowers, strong public support is often merited. But the new climate of acceptance makes it easy to overlook the dangers of whistle-blowing: of uses in error or in malice; of work and reputations unjustly lost for those falsely accused; of privacy invaded and trust undermined. There comes a level of internal prying and mutual suspicion at which no institution can function. And it is a fact that the disappointed, the incompetent, the malicious, and the paranoid all too often leap to accusations in public. Worst of all, ideological persecution throughout the world traditionally relies on insiders willing to inform on their colleagues or even on their family members, often through staged public denunciations or press campaigns.

No society can count itself immune from such dangers. But neither can it risk silencing those with a legitimate reason to blow the whistle. How then can we distinguish between different instances of whistleblowing? A society that fails to protect the right to speak out even on the part of those whose warnings turn out to be spurious obviously opens the door to political repression. But from the moral point of view there are important differences between the aims, messages, and methods of dissenters from within.

NATURE OF WHISTLEBLOWING

Three elements, each jarring, and triply jarring when conjoined, lend acts of whistleblowing special urgency and bitterness: dissent, breach of loyalty, and accusation.

Like all dissent, whistleblowing makes public a disagreement with an authority or a majority view. But whereas dissent can concern all forms of disagreement with, for instance, religious dogma or government policy or court decisions, whistleblowing has the narrower aim of shedding light on negligence or abuse, or alerting to a risk, and of assigning responsibility for this risk.

Would-be whistleblowers confront the conflict inherent in all dissent: between conforming and sticking their necks out. The more repressive the authority they challenge, the greater the personal risk they take in speaking out. At exceptional times, as in times of war, even ordinarily tolerant authorities may come to regard dissent as unacceptable and even disloyal.[6]

Furthermore, the whistleblower hopes to stop the game; but since he is neither referee nor coach, and since he blows the whistle on his own team, his act is seen as a violation of loyalty. In holding his position, he has assumed certain obligations to his colleagues and clients. He may even have subscribed to a loyalty oath or a promise of confidentiality. Loyalty to colleagues and to clients comes to be pitted against loyalty to the public interest, to those who may be injured unless the revelation is made.

Not only is loyalty violated in whistleblowing, hierarchy as well is often opposed, since the whistleblower is not only a colleague but a subordinate. Though aware of the risks inherent in such disobedience, he often hopes to keep his job.[7] At times, however, he plans his alarm to coincide with leaving the institution. If he is highly placed, or joined by others, resigning in protest may effectively direct public attention to the wrongdoing at issue.[8] Still another alternative, often chosen by those who wish to be safe from retaliation, is to leave the institution quietly, to secure another post, and then to blow the whistle. In this way, it is possible to speak with the authority and knowledge of an insider without having the vulnerability of that position.

It is the element of accusation, of calling a "foul," that arouses the strongest reactions on the part of the hierarchy. The accusation may be of neglect, of willfully concealed dangers, or of outright abuse on the part of colleagues or superiors. It singles out specific persons or groups as responsible for threats to the public interest. If no one could be held responsible—as in the case of an impending avalanche—the warning would not constitute whistleblowing.

The accusation of the whistleblower, moreover, concerns a present or an imminent threat. Past errors or misdeeds occasion such an alarm only if they still affect current practices. And risks far in the future lack the immediacy needed to make the alarm a compelling one, as well as the close connection to particular individuals that would justify actual accusations. Thus an alarm can be sounded about safety defects in a rapid-transit system that threaten or will shortly threaten passengers, but the revelation of safety defects in a system no longer in use, while of historical interest, would not constitute whistleblowing. Nor would the revelation of potential problems in a system not yet fully designed and far from implemented.[9]

Not only immediacy, but also specificity, is needed for there to be an alarm capable of pinpointing responsibility. A concrete risk must be at issue rather than a vague foreboding or a somber prediction. The act of whistleblowing differs in this respect from the lamentation or the dire prophecy. An immediate and specific threat would normally be acted upon by those at risk. The whistleblower assumes that his message will alert listeners to something they do not know, or whose significance they have not grasped because it has been kept secret.

The desire for openness inheres in the temptation to reveal any secret, sometimes joined to an urge for self-aggrandizement and publicity and the hope for revenge for past slights or injustices. There can be pleasure, too—righteous or malicious—in laying bare the secrets of co-workers and in setting the record straight at last. Colleagues of the whistleblower often suspect his motives: they may regard him as a crank, as publicity-hungry, wrong about the facts, eager for scandal and discord, and driven to indiscretion by his personal biases and shortcomings.

For whistleblowing to be effective, it must arouse its audience. Inarticulate whistleblowers are likely to fail from the outset. When they are greeted by apathy, their message dissipates. When they are greeted by disbelief, they elicit no response at all. And when the audience is not free to receive or to act on the information—when censorship or fear of retribution stifles response—then the message rebounds to injure the whistle-blower. Whistleblowing also requires the possibility of concerted public response: the idea of whistleblowing in an anarchy is therefore merely quixotic.

Such characteristics of whistleblowing and strategic considerations for achieving an impact are common to the noblest warnings, the most vicious personal attacks, and the delusions of the paranoid. How can one distinguish the many acts of sounding an alarm that are genuinely in the public interest from all the petty, biased, or lurid revelations that pervade our querulous and gossip-ridden society? Can we draw distinctions between different whistleblowers, different messages, different methods?

We clearly can, in a number of cases. Whistleblowing may be starkly inappropriate when in malice or error, or when it lays bare legitimately private matters having to do, for instance, with political belief or sexual life. It can, just as clearly, be the only way to shed light on an ongoing unjust practice such as drugging political prisoners or subjecting them to electroshock treatment. It can be the last resort for alerting the public to an impending disaster. Taking such clear-cut cases as benchmarks, and reflecting on what it is about them that weighs so heavily for or against speaking out, we can work our way toward the admittedly more complex cases in which whistleblowing is not so clearly the right or wrong choice, or where different points of view exist regarding its legitimacy—cases where there are moral reasons both for concealment and for disclosure and where judgments conflict....

INDIVIDUAL MORAL CHOICE

What questions might those who consider sounding an alarm in public ask themselves? How might they articulate the problem they see and weigh its injustice before deciding whether or not to reveal it? How can they best try to make sure their choice is the right one? In thinking about these questions it helps to keep in mind the three elements mentioned earlier: dissent, breach of loyalty, and accusation. They impose certain requirements—of accuracy and judgment in dissent; of exploring alternative ways to cope with improprieties that minimize the breach of loyalty; and of fairness in accusation. For each, careful articulation and testing of arguments are needed to limit error and bias.

Dissent by whistleblowers, first of all, is expressly claimed to be intended to benefit the public. It carries with it, as a result, an obligation to consider the nature of this benefit and to consider also the possible harm that may come from speaking out: harm to persons or institutions and, ultimately, to the public interest itself. Whistleblowers must, therefore, begin by making every effort to consider the effects of speaking out versus those of remaining silent. They must assure themselves of the accuracy of their reports, checking and rechecking the facts before speaking out; specify the degree to which there is genuine impropriety; consider how imminent is the threat they see, how serious, and how closely linked to those accused of neglect and abuse.

If the facts warrant whistleblowing, how can the second element—breach of loyalty—be minimized? The most important question here is whether the existing avenues for change within the organization have been explored. It is a waste of time for the public as well as harmful to the institution to sound the loudest alarm first. Whistleblowing has to remain a last alternative because of its destructive side effects: it must be chosen only when other alternatives have been considered and rejected. They may be rejected if they simply do not apply to the problem at hand, or when there is not time to go through routine channels or when the institution is so corrupt or coercive that steps will be taken to silence the whistleblower should he try the regular channels first.

What weight should an oath or a promise of silence have in the conflict of loyalties? One sworn to silence is doubtless under a stronger obligation because of the oath he has taken. He has bound himself, assumed specific obligations beyond those assumed in merely taking a new position. But even such promises can be overridden when the public interest at issue is strong enough. They can be overridden if they were obtained under duress or through deceit. They can be overridden, too, if they promise something that is in itself wrong or unlawful. The fact that one has promised silence is no excuse for complicity in covering up a crime or a violation of the public's trust.

The third element in whistleblowing—accusation—raises equally serious ethical concerns. They are concerns of fairness to the persons accused of impropriety. Is the message one to which the public is entitled in the first place? Or does it infringe on personal and private matters that one has no right to invade? Here, the very notion of what is in the public's best "interest" is at issue: "accusations" regarding an official's unusual sexual or religious experiences may well appeal to the public's interest without being information relevant to "the public interest."

Great conflicts arise here. We have witnessed excessive claims to executive privilege and to secrecy by government officials during the Watergate scandal in order to cover up for abuses the public had every right to discover. Conversely, those hoping to profit from prying into private matters have become adept at invoking "the public's right to know." Some even regard such private matters as threats to the public: they voice their own religious and political prejudices in the language of accusation. Such a danger is never stronger than when the accusation is delivered surreptitiously. The anonymous accusations made during the McCarthy period regarding political beliefs and associations often injured persons who did not even know their accusers or the exact nature of the accusations.

From the public's point of view, accusations that are openly made by identifiable individuals are more likely to be taken seriously. And in fairness to those criticized, openly accepted responsibility for blowing the whistle should be preferred to the denunciation or the leaked rumor. What is openly stated can more easily be checked, its source's motives challenged, and the underlying information examined. Those under attack may otherwise be hard put to defend themselves against nameless adversaries. Often they do not even know that they are threatened until it is too late to respond. The anonymous denunciation, moreover, common to so many regimes, places the burden of investigation on government agencies that may thereby gain the power of a secret police.

From the point of view of the whistleblower, on the other hand, the anonymous message is safer in situations where retaliation is likely. But it is also often less likely to be taken seriously. Unless the message is accompanied by indications of how the evidence can be checked, its anonymity, however safe for the source, speaks against it.

During the process of weighing the legitimacy of speaking out, the method used, and the degree of fairness needed, whistleblowers must try to compensate for the strong possibility of bias on their part. They should be scrupulously aware of any motive that might skew their message: a desire for self-defense in a difficult bureaucratic situation, perhaps, or the urge to seek revenge, or inflated expectations regarding the effect their message will have on the situation. (Needless to say, bias affects the silent as well as the outspoken. The motive for holding back important information about abuses and injustice ought to give similar cause for soul-searching.)

Likewise, the possibility of personal gain from sounding the alarm ought to give pause. Once again there is then greater risk of a biased message. Even if the whistleblower regards himself as incorruptible, his profiting from revelations of neglect or abuse will lead others to question his motives and to put less credence in his charges. If, for example, a government employee stands to make large profits from a book exposing the inequities in his agency, there is danger that he will, perhaps even unconsciously, slant his report in order to cause more of a sensation.

A special problem arises when there is a high risk that the civil servant who speaks out will have to go through costly litigation. Might he not justifiably try to make enough money on his public revelations—say, through books or public speaking—to offset his losses? In so doing he will not strictly speaking have *profited* from his revelations: he merely avoids being financially crushed by their sequels. He will nevertheless still be suspected at the time of revelation, and his message will therefore seem more questionable.

Reducing bias and error in moral choice often requires consultation, even open debate[10]: methods that force articulation of the moral arguments at stake and challenge privately held assumptions. But acts of whistleblowing present special problems when it comes to open consultation. On the one hand, once the whistleblower sounds his alarm publicly, his arguments will be subjected to open scrutiny; he will have to articulate his reasons for speaking out and substantiate his charges. On the other hand, it will then be too late to retract the alarm or to combat its harmful effects, should his choice to speak out have been ill-advised.

For this reason, the whistleblower owes it to all involved to make sure of two things: that he has sought as much and as objective advice regarding his choice as he can *before* going public; and that he is aware of the arguments for and against the practice of whistleblowing in general, so that he can see his own choice against as richly detailed and coherently structured a background as possible. Satisfying these two requirements once again has special problems because of the very nature of whistleblowing: the more corrupt the circumstances, the more dangerous it may be to seek consultation before speaking out. And yet, since the whistleblower himself may have a biased view of the state of affairs, he may choose not to consult others when in fact it would be not only safe but advantageous to do so; he may see corruption and conspiracy where none exists.

NOTES

1. Code of Ethics for Government Service passed by the U.S. House of Representatives in the 85th Congress (1958) and applying to all government employees and office holders.

2. Code of Ethics of the Institute of Electrical and Electronics Engineers, Article IV.

3. For case histories and descriptions of what befalls whistleblowers, see Rosemary Chalk and Frank von Hippel, "Due Process for Dissenting Whistle-Blowers," *Technology Review* 81 (June-July 1979); 48–55; Alan S. Westin and Stephen Salisbury, eds., *Individual Rights in the Corporation* (New York: Pantheon, 1980); Helen Dudar, "The Price of Blowing the Whistle," *New York Times Magazine*, 30 October 1979, pp. 41–54; John Edsall, *Scientific Freedom and Responsibility* (Washington, D.C.: American Association for the Advancement of Science, 1975), p. 5; David Ewing, *Freedom Inside the Organization* (New York: Dutton, 1977); Ralph Nader, Peter Petkas, and Kate Blackwell, *Whistle Blowing* (New York: Grossman, 1972); Charles Peter and Taylor Branch, *Blowing the Whistle* (New York: Praeger, 1972).

4. Congressional hearings uncovered a growing resort to mandatory psychiatric examinations.

5. For an account of strategies and proposals to support government whistleblowers, see Government Accountability Project, *A Whistleblower's Guide to the Federal Bureaucracy* (Washington, D.C.: Institute for Policy Studies, 1977).

6. See, e.g., Samuel Eliot Morison, Frederick Merk, and Frank Friedel, *Dissent in Three American Wars* (Cambridge: Harvard University Press, 1970).

7. In the scheme worked out by Albert Hirschman in *Exit, Voice and Loyalty* (Cambridge: Harvard University Press, 1970), whistleblowing represents "voice" accompanied by a preference not to "exit," though forced "exit" is clearly a possibility and "voice" after or during "exit" may be chosen for strategic reasons.

8. Edward Weisband and Thomas N. Franck, *Resignation in Protest* (New York: Grossman, 1975).

9. Future developments can, however, be the cause for whistleblowing if they are seen as resulting from steps being taken or about to be taken that render them inevitable.

10. I discuss these questions of consultation and publicity with respect to moral choice in chapter 7 of Sissela Bok, *Lying* (New York: Pantheon, 1978); and in *Secrets* (New York: Pantheon Books, 1982), Ch. IX and XV.

NO

Robert A. Larmer

WHISTLEBLOWING AND EMPLOYEE LOYALTY

Whistleblowing by an employee is the act of complaining, either within the corporation or publicly, about a corporation's unethical practices. Such an act raises important questions concerning the loyalties and duties of employees. Traditionally, the employee has been viewed as an agent who acts on behalf of a principal, i.e., the employer, and as possessing duties of loyalty and confidentiality. Whistleblowing, at least at first blush, seems a violation of these duties and it is scarcely surprising that in many instances employers and fellow employees argue that it is an act of disloyalty and hence morally wrong.[1]

It is this issue of the relation between whistleblowing and employee loyalty that I want to address. What I will call the standard view is that employees possess *prima facie* duties of loyalty and confidentiality to their employers and that whistleblowing cannot be justified except on the basis of a higher duty to the public good. Against this standard view, Ronald Duska has recently argued that employees do not have even a *prima facie* duty of loyalty to their employers and that whistleblowing needs, therefore, no moral justification.[2] I am going to criticize both views. My suggestion is that both misunderstand the relation between loyalty and whistleblowing. In their place I will propose a third more adequate view.

Duska's view is more radical in that it suggests that there can be no issue of whistleblowing and employee loyalty, since the employee has no duty to be loyal to his employer. His reason for suggesting that the employee owes the employer, at least the corporate employer, no loyalty is that companies are not the kinds of things which are proper objects of loyalty. His argument in support of this rests upon two key claims. The first is that loyalty, properly understood, implies a reciprocal relationship and is only appropriate in the

From Robert A. Larmer, "Whistleblowing and Employee Loyalty," *Journal of Business Ethics*, vol. 11 (1992), pp. 125–128. Copyright © 1992 by D. Reidel Publishing Co., Dordrecht, Holland, and Boston, U.S.A. Reprinted by permission of Kluwer Academic Publishers.

context of a mutual surrendering of self-interest. He writes,

> It is important to recognize that in any relationship which demands loyalty the relationship works both ways and involves mutual enrichment. Loyalty is incompatible with self-interest, because it is something that necessarily requires we go beyond self-interest. My loyalty to my friend, for example, requires I put aside my interests some of the time.... Loyalty depends on ties that demand self-sacrifice with no expectation of reward, e.g., the ties of loyalty that bind a family together.[3]

The second is that the relation between a company and an employee does not involve any surrender of self-interest on the part of the company, since its primary goal is to maximize profit. Indeed, although it is convenient, it is misleading to talk of a company having interests. As Duska comments,

> A company is not a person. A company is an instrument, and an instrument with a specific purpose, the making of profit. To treat an instrument as an end in itself, like a person, may not be as bad as treating an end as an instrument, but it does give the instrument a moral status it does not deserve...[4]

Since, then, the relation between a company and an employee does not fulfill the minimal requirement of being a relation between two individuals, much less two reciprocally self-sacrificing individuals, Duska feels it is a mistake to suggest the employee has any duties of loyalty to the company.

This view does not seem adequate, however. First, it is not true that loyalty must be quite so reciprocal as Duska demands. Ideally, of course, one expects that if one is loyal to another person that person will reciprocate in kind. There are, however, many cases where loyalty is not entirely reciprocated, but where we do not feel that it is misplaced. A parent, for example, may remain loyal to an erring teenager, even though the teenager demonstrates no loyalty to the parent. Indeed, part of being a proper parent is to demonstrate loyalty to your children whether or not that loyalty is reciprocated. This is not to suggest any kind of analogy between parents and employees, but rather that it is not nonsense to suppose that loyalty may be appropriate even though it is not reciprocated. Inasmuch as he ignores this possibility, Duska's account of loyalty is flawed.

Second, even if Duska is correct in holding that loyalty is only appropriate between moral agents and that a company is not genuinely a moral agent, the question may still be raised whether an employee owes loyalty to fellow employees or the shareholders of the company. Granted that reference to a company as an individual involves reification and should not be taken too literally, it may nevertheless constitute a legitimate shorthand way of describing relations between genuine moral agents.

Third, it seems wrong to suggest that simply because the primary motive of the employer is economic, considerations of loyalty are irrelevant. An employee's primary motive in working for an employer is generally economic, but no one on that account would argue that it is impossible for her to demonstrate loyalty to the employer, even if it turns out to be misplaced. All that is required is that her primary economic motive be in some degree qualified by considerations of the employer's welfare. Similarly, the fact that an employer's primary motive is economic does not imply that it is not qualified by considerations of the employee's welfare. Given the possibility of mutual qualification of admittedly primary economic motives, it is fallacious to argue that employee loyalty is never appropriate.

In contrast to Duska, the standard view is that loyalty to one's employer is appropriate. According to it, one has an obligation to be loyal to one's employer and, consequently, a *prima facie* duty to protect the employer's interests. Whistleblowing constitutes, therefore, a violation of duty to one's employer and needs strong justification if it is to be appropriate. Sissela Bok summarizes this view very well when she writes

> the whistleblower hopes to stop the game; but since he is neither referee nor coach, and since he blows the whistle on his own team, his act is seen as a violation of loyalty. In holding his position, he has assumed certain obligations to his colleagues and clients. He may even have subscribed to a loyalty oath or a promise of confidentiality. Loyalty to colleagues and to clients comes to be pitted against loyalty to the public interest, to those who may be injured unless the revelation is made.[5]

The strength of this view is that it recognizes that loyalty is due one's employer. Its weakness is that it tends to conceive of whistleblowing as involving a tragic moral choice, since blowing the whistle is seen not so much as a positive action, but rather the lesser of two evils. Bok again puts the essence of this view very clearly when she writes that "a would-be whistleblower must weigh his responsibility to serve the public interest *against* the responsibility he owes to his colleagues and the institution in which he works" and "that [when]

their duty [to whistleblow]... *so overrides loyalties to colleagues and institutions,* they [whistleblowers] often have reason to fear the results of carrying out such a duty."[6] The employee, according to this understanding of whistleblowing, must choose between two acts of betrayal, either her employer or the public interest, each in itself reprehensible.

Behind this view lies the assumption that to be loyal to someone is to act in a way that accords with what that person believes to be in her best interests. To be loyal to an employer, therefore, is to act in a way which the employer deems to be in his or her best interests. Since employers very rarely approve of whistleblowing and generally feel that it is not in their best interests, it follows that whistleblowing is an act of betrayal on the part of the employee, albeit a betrayal made in the interests of the public good.

Plausible though it initially seems, I think this view of whistleblowing is mistaken and that it embodies a mistaken conception of what constitutes employee loyalty. It ignores the fact that

> the great majority of corporate whistle-blowers... [consider] themselves to be very loyal employees who... [try] to use 'direct voice' (internal whistleblowing),... [are] rebuffed and punished for this, and then... [use] 'indirect voice' (external whistleblowing). They... [believe] initially that they... [are] behaving in a loyal manner, helping their employers by calling top management's attention to practices that could eventually get the firm in trouble.[7]

By ignoring the possibility that blowing the whistle may demonstrate greater loyalty than not blowing the whistle, it fails to do justice to the many instances where loyalty to someone constrains us to act in defiance of what that person believes to be in her best interests. I am not, for example, being disloyal to a friend if I refuse to loan her money for an investment I am sure will bring her financial ruin; even if she bitterly reproaches me for denying her what is so obviously a golden opportunity to make a fortune.

A more adequate definition of being loyal to someone is that loyalty involves acting in accordance with what one has good reason to believe to be in that person's best interests. A key question, of course, is what constitutes a good reason to think that something is in a person's best interests. Very often, but by no means invariably, we accept that a person thinking that something is in her best interests is a sufficiently good reason to think that it actually is. Other times, especially when we feel that she is being rash, foolish, or misinformed we are prepared, precisely by virtue of being loyal, to act contrary to the person's wishes. It is beyond the scope of this paper to investigate such cases in detail, but three general points can be made.

First, to the degree that an action is genuinely immoral, it is impossible that it is in the agent's best interests. We would not, for example, say that someone who sells child pornography was acting in his own best interests, even if he vigorously protested that there was nothing wrong with such activity. Loyalty does not imply that we have a duty to refrain from reporting the immoral actions of those to whom we are loyal. An employer who is acting immorally is not acting in her own best interests and an employee is not acting disloyally in blowing the whistle.[8] Indeed, the argument can be made that the employee who blows the whistle may be demonstrating greater loyalty than the employee who simply ignores the immoral conduct, inasmuch as she is attempting to prevent her employer from engaging in self-destructive behaviour.

Second, loyalty requires that, whenever possible, in trying to resolve a problem we deal directly with the person to whom we are loyal. If, for example, I am loyal to a friend I do not immediately involve a third party when I try to dissuade my friend from involvement in immoral actions. Rather, I approach my friend directly, listen to his perspective on the events in question, and provide an opportunity for him to address the problem in a morally satisfactory way. This implies that, whenever possible, a loyal employee blows the whistle internally. This provides the employer with the opportunity to either demonstrate to the employee that, contrary to first appearances, no genuine wrongdoing had occurred, or, if there is a genuine moral problem, the opportunity to resolve it.

This principle of dealing directly with the person to whom loyalty is due needs to be qualified, however. Loyalty to a person requires that one acts in that person's best interests. Generally, this cannot be done without directly involving the person to whom one is loyal in the decision-making process, but there may arise cases where acting in a person's best interests requires that one act independently and perhaps even against the wishes of the person to whom one is loyal. Such cases will be especially apt to arise when the person to whom one is loyal is either immoral or ignoring the moral consequences of his actions. Thus, for example, loyalty to a friend who deals in hard narcotics would not imply that I speak first to my friend about my decision to inform the police of his activities, if the only effect of my doing so would be to make him more careful in his criminal dealings. Similarly, a loyal employee is under no obligation to speak first to an employer about the employer's immoral actions, if the only response of the employer will be to take care to cover up wrongdoing.

Neither is a loyal employee under obligation to speak first to an employer if it is clear that by doing so she placed herself in jeopardy from an employer who will retaliate if given the opportunity. Loyalty amounts to acting in another's best interests and that may mean qualifying what seems to be in one's own interests, but it cannot imply that one take no steps to protect oneself from the immorality of those to whom one is loyal. The reason it cannot is that, as has already been argued, acting immorally can never really be in a person's best interests. It follows, therefore, that one is not acting in a person's best interests if one allows oneself to be treated immorally by that person. Thus, for example, a father might be loyal to a child even though the child is guilty of stealing from him, but this would not mean that the father should let the child continue to steal. Similarly, an employee may be loyal to an employer even though she takes steps to protect herself against unfair retaliation by the employer, e.g., by blowing the whistle externally.

Third, loyalty requires that one is concerned with more than considerations of justice. I have been arguing that loyalty cannot require one to ignore immoral or unjust behaviour on the part of those to whom one is loyal, since loyalty amounts to acting in a person's best interests and it can never be in a person's best interests to be allowed to act immorally. Loyalty, however, goes beyond considerations of justice in that, while it is possible to be disinterested and

just, it is not possible to be disinterested and loyal. Loyalty implies a desire that the person to whom one is loyal take no moral stumbles, but that if moral stumbles have occurred that the person be restored and not simply punished. A loyal friend is not only someone who sticks by you in times of trouble, but someone who tries to help you avoid trouble. This suggests that a loyal employee will have a desire to point out problems and potential problems long before the drastic measures associated with whistleblowing become necessary, but that if whistleblowing does become necessary there remains a desire to help the employer.

In conclusion, although much more could be said on the subject of loyalty, our brief discussion has enabled us to clarify considerably the relation between whistleblowing and employee loyalty. It permits us to steer a course between the Scylla of Duska's view that, since the primary link between employer and employee is economic, the ideal of employee loyalty is an oxymoron, and the Charybdis of the standard view that, since it forces an employee to weigh conflicting duties, whistleblowing inevitably involves some degree of moral tragedy. The solution lies in realizing that to whistleblow for reasons of morality is to act in one's employer's best interests and involves, therefore, no disloyalty.

NOTES

1. The definition I have proposed applies most directly to the relation between privately owned companies aiming to realize a profit and their employees. Obviously, issues of whistleblowing arise in other contexts, e.g., governmental organizations or charitable agencies, and deserve careful thought. I do not propose, in this paper, to discuss whistleblowing in these other contexts, but I think my development of the concept of whistleblowing as pos-

itive demonstration of loyalty can easily be applied and will prove useful.

2. Duska, R.: 1985, 'Whistleblowing and Employee Loyalty', in J. R. Desjardins and J. J. McCall, eds., *Contemporary Issues in Business Ethics* (Wadsworth, Belmont, California), pp. 295–300.

3. Duska, p. 297.

4. Duska, p. 298.

5. Bok, S.: 1983, 'Whistleblowing and Professional Responsibility', in T. L. Beauchamp and N. E. Bowie, eds., *Ethical Theory and Business*, 2nd ed. (Prentice-Hall Inc., Englewood Cliffs, New Jersey), pp. 261–269, p. 263.

6. Bok, pp. 261–2, emphasis added.

7. Near, J. P. and P. Miceli: 1985, 'Organizational Dissidence: The Case of Whistle-Blowing', *Journal of Business Ethics* 4, pp. 1–16, p. 10.

8. As Near and Miceli note 'The whistle-blower may provide valuable information helpful in improving organizational effectiveness... the prevalence of illegal activity in organizations is associated with declining organizational performance' (p. 1).

The general point is that the structure of the world is such that it is not in a company's long-term interests to act immorally. Sooner or later a company which flouts morality and legality will suffer.

POSTSCRIPT

Does Blowing the Whistle Violate Company Loyalty?

Whistle-blowing is a difficult choice. What would you do when faced with such a choice? The corporation is not the only setting for whistle-blowers. Would you report a friend for drug abuse, cheating on exams, or stealing? How do you weigh the possibility of damage being done to the community against the security of your own career (some damage done to many people versus much damage done to a few people)? If you see only painful consequences if you blow the whistle, does that settle the problem—or does simple justice and fidelity to law have a claim of its own?

Should we, as a society, protect the whistle-blower with legislation designed to discourage corporate retaliation? Richard T. DeGeorge and Alan F. Westin, two of the earliest business ethics writers to take whistle-blowing seriously, agree that companies should adopt policies that preclude the need for employees to blow the whistle. "The need for moral heroes," DeGeorge concludes in *Business Ethics*, 2d ed. (Macmillan, 1986), "shows a defective society and defective corporations. It is more important to change the legal and corporate structures that make whistle blowing necessary than to convince people to be moral heroes." In *Whistle Blowing: Loyalty and Dissent in the Corporation* (McGraw-Hill, 1981), Westin writes, "The single most important element in creating a meaningful internal system to deal with whistle blowing is to have top leadership accept this as a management priority. This means that the chief operating officer and his senior colleagues have to believe that a policy which encourages discussion and dissent, and deals fairly with whistle-blowing claims, is a good and important thing for their company to adopt.... They have to see it, in their own terms, as a moral duty of good private enterprise."

SUGGESTED READINGS

Tim Barnett, Ken Bass, and Gene Brown, "Religiosity, Ethical Ideology, and Intentions to Report a Peer's Wrongdoing," *Journal of Business Ethics* (November 1996), pp. 1161–1174.

Terry Morehead Dworkin and Janet P. Near, "A Better Statutory Approach to Whistle-Blowing," *Journal of the Society for Business Ethics* (January 1997), pp. 1–16.

Kenneth Kernaghan, "Whistle-Blowing in Canadian Governments: Ethical, Political and Managerial Considerations," *Optimum* (1991–1992).

ISSUE 11

Should Concern for Drug Abuse Overrule Concerns for Employee Privacy?

YES: Michael A. Verespej, from "Drug Users—Not Testing—Anger Workers," *Industry Week* (February 17, 1992)

NO: Jennifer Moore, from "Drug Testing and Corporate Responsibility: The 'Ought Implies Can' Argument," *Journal of Business Ethics* (vol. 8, 1989)

ISSUE SUMMARY

YES: Michael A. Verespej, a writer for *Industry Week,* argues that workers are the hardest hit when their coworkers use drugs, and he suggests that, for this reason, a majority of employees are tolerant of drug testing.

NO: Jennifer Moore, a researcher of business ethics and business law, asserts that a right is a right and that any utilitarian concerns that employers can cite to justify drug testing should not override the right of the employee to dignity and privacy on the job.

In 1928 U.S. Supreme Court justice Louis Brandeis defined the right of privacy as "the right to be let alone, the most comprehensive of rights and the right most valued by civilized men." The constitutional origins of that right are hazy, found variously in the Fourth Amendment (prohibiting illegal searches and seizures), the Fifth Amendment (prohibiting compulsory testimony), and parts of the Ninth Amendment. But the U.S. Constitution only limits *government* action, and worried Americans increasingly find that their employers can be a more dangerous threat to their privacy.

What right does an employee have to be "let alone" by his or her employer? Historically, none at all. Dictatorial employers had no qualms about making and enforcing rules governing not only job performance but dress and personal behavior on the job as well. Many also had rules for off-the-job behavior. School boards, for example, routinely enforced rules that required teachers to abstain from smoking and drinking, to attend church regularly, and to limit courting to one day a week. But with the advent of organized labor, the freedom of the employer to dictate the employee's lifestyle off the job almost disappeared. On-the-job requirements also ceased to be absolute. Although certain obvious safety rules could be enforced (such as prohibiting alcohol on the job and requiring that safety equipment be worn), the presumption was that rules should not be extended beyond necessity. Until very recently, we had seemed to be approaching an understanding that the employee's choices of amusements and associations off the job were sacrosanct and that his or her personal style of dress and grooming on the job could be regulated only to the extent that such appearances were reasonably job-related.

Then came drugs. Unlike alcohol, drugs can be easily concealed in one's clothing and cannot be detected on a person's breath after they are consumed. Seasoned foremen who would have no trouble spotting the slurred speech and wobbly walk caused by alcohol may not be able to detect drug use in their employees. The effect of drug use on judgment and behavior, especially for such people as pilots, bus drivers, and military personnel, can and does cause deaths.

While many may agree that this fact alone justifies testing for on-the-job drug use, there are many factors that complicate the issue. First, the only tests currently available to determine drug use are seriously invasive (unlike the Breathalyzer test for alcohol, for instance). In practice, the tester must take a blood sample from the worker or require the worker to give up a urine sample. The blood test requires a needle stick that some find painful and terrifying, and the urination must be observed to ensure that the test is valid—at an imaginable cost in embarrassment to the worker and to the observer. Second, the tests cannot distinguish between drug-use behavior on the job and off the job. Marijuana smoked on a Friday night may show up in urine that is expelled on the following Tuesday. So the worker subjected to testing at random may find his off-the-job activities severely restricted by the tests. To be sure, no one is interested in condoning off-the-job drug use, but the move from on-the-job regulation to 24-hour regulation is an unintended consequence that raises further legal and ethical issues.

Third, the tests are not always accurate. Most employers have a policy that if an employee fails one drug test, he or she can take another in order to ensure accuracy. If the employee fails twice, he or she is out. But the tests are only 90 to 95 percent accurate, at best. That means that 1 out of 10, or at best 1 out of 20, will yield a false positive (the employee will appear to have drugs in his or her system). One out of 100, or at best 1 out of 400, will yield a false positive upon retest of a false positive. But some firms have thousands of workers. Is it fair to impose a testing routine that commits gross injustice once in 100 cases—or even only once in 400 cases?

As you read the following selections by Michael A. Verespej and Jennifer Moore, ask yourself how society ought to balance the conflicting demands of privacy for the worker and safety for society. Given the doubts surrounding the practice, is routine randomized drug testing justified? On the other hand, given the terrible dangers that attend drug use on the job, can society afford to do without it?

YES

Michael A. Verespej

DRUG USERS—NOT TESTING— ANGER WORKERS

Drug testing by companies still elicits an emotional response from employees. But it's a far different one from four years ago.

Back then, readers responding to an IW [*Industry Week*] survey angrily protested workplace drug testing as an invasion of privacy and argued that drug testing should be reserved for occasions in which there was suspicion of drug use or in an accident investigation.

Today's prevailing view, based on a recent IW survey covering essentially the same questions, stands as a stark contrast. Not only do fewer employees see drug testing as an invasion of privacy, but a significantly higher percentage think that companies should extend the scope of drug testing to improve safety and productivity in the workplace.

Why aren't employees as leery of workplace drug testing as they were four years ago?

First, both the numbers and the comments suggest that employees and managers are less worried that inaccurate drug tests will brand them as drug users. Just 19.3% of those surveyed say that they consider drug testing an invasion of privacy, compared with 30% in the earlier survey.

Second, the tight job market appears to have made non-drug-users resent the presence of drug users in the workplace. Third, in contrast to four years ago, employees and managers are more concerned about the potential safety problems that drug users cause them than whatever invasion of privacy might result from a drug test. The net result: Unlike four years ago, employee thinking is now in sync with the viewpoints held for some time by top corporate management. "Job safety and performance are more important than the slight invasion of privacy caused by drug testing," asserts Lee Taylor, plant manager at U.S. Gypsum Co.'s Siguard, Utah, facility. "Freedom and privacy end when others are likely to be injured," adds the president of a high-tech business in Fort Collins, Colo.

G. A. Holland, chief estimator for a Bloomfield, Conn., construction firm, agrees: "Drug testing may be an invasion of privacy, but, because drug use puts others in danger, [drug testing] is an acceptable practice. The safety of employees overrides the right to privacy of another." Adds D. S. McRoberts, manager of a Green Giant food-processing plant in Buhl, Idaho: "The risks employees put themselves and their peers under when they use drugs justify testing."

Perhaps the most blunt response comes from Louis Krivanek, a consulting engineer with Omega Induction Services, Warren, Mich.: "I certainly wouldn't ride with a drinking alcoholic. Why should I work with a drug addict not under control?"

And the anti-drug-user attitude is not just a safety issue, either. "Drug users are also a financial risk to the employer," declares John Larkin, president of Overland Computer, Omaha, Nebr. "It's time to begin thinking about the health and welfare of the company," says William Pence, vice president and general manager of Kantronics Inc., Lawrence, Kans. "Drug testing is simply a preventive measure to ensure the future stability of a company."

The competitive factor also appears to be influencing workers' viewpoints. "A drug-free environment must exist if the quality of product and process is to be continuously improved," writes one employee.

"Productivity and company survival are too important to trust to an employee with a drug problem," says Jack Ver-Meulen, director of quality assurance at C-Line Products, Des Plaines, Ill. "Employees are a company's most valuable assets, and those assets must perform at the peak of their ability. Test them." One could argue that workers—and managers—have simply become conditioned to drug testing in the workplace because it is no longer the exception, but the rule. After all, 56% of the managers responding to the survey—twice as many

as four years ago—say their companies have drug-testing programs in place.

But the real reason for the change in opinion appears to be that four years of day-in, day-out experience with workplace drug problems have made managers and employees less tolerant of users. The attitude appears to be: Drug users are criminals and shouldn't be protected by the absence of a drug-testing program.

"Users are, by definition, criminals," declares Nick Benson, senior automation engineer at Babcock & Wilcox, Lynchburg, Va. "Drug users are breaking the law," states Naomi Walter, a data-processing specialist at Gemini Marketing Associates, Carthage, Mo. "So why let them get an advantage?"

Layoffs and plant and store closings are also behind the new lack of tolerance for the drug user. "I believe that if a company is paying a person to work for them," says one IW reader, "that person should be drug-free. A job is a privilege, not a right."

* * *

That lack of tolerance is reflected in significantly changed ideas of who in the workplace should be tested for drug use. A significantly higher percentage of respondents think that more workers should be tested at random or that *all* employees should be tested.

More than 45% of IW readers—compared with 29.6% four years ago—say that drug tests should be conducted at random. And 70.5% think all employees should be required to take drug tests. Only 60% felt that way in the last IW drug-testing survey. Not surprisingly, then, the percentage of readers who would take a drug test and who think that employers should be able to test employees for drug use is now 93%; it was 88% four years ago.

But several attitudes haven't changed. Workers and managers still think that when companies use drug testing, they should be required to offer rehabilitation through employee-assistance programs, that management should be tested as well as employees, and that alcohol problems are equally troublesome. "Employers should be prepared to help—not just fire someone if the drug or alcohol abuse is exposed," says H. A. Dellicker, programming manager at Siemens Nixdorf, Burlington, Mass. "You need a properly monitored rehabilitation program."

Readers are just as adamant that if the majority of employees is to be tested, then everyone should be included—all the way up to the CEO. "Drug testing should be conducted on all employees, from top management down to the lowest position," asserts Sharon Hyitt, a drafting technician at Varco Pruden Buildings, Van Wert, Ohio. And IW readers contend that any drug-testing program should test for alcohol abuse as well. "Drug testing stops short," argues a reader in Muncie, Ind. "Alcoholism is more widespread in our workplace and just as destructive."

A plant superintendent in Ohio agrees and laments, "Alcohol is the most abused drug in our workplace, but it is not covered under our testing program. While the 'heavy' drugs get the spotlight because of the violence associated with their distribution, alcohol does the most damage in the workplace."

A product-testing engineer agrees, "Alcohol should be included in the tests and then perhaps lunch-time drinking would decrease. Why is it O.K. for those who have three-martini lunches to come back to work and try to function?"

NO   Jennifer Moore

DRUG TESTING AND CORPORATE RESPONSIBILITY: THE "OUGHT IMPLIES CAN" ARGUMENT

In the past few years, testing for drug use in the workplace has become an important and controversial trend. Approximately 30% of Fortune 500 companies now engage in some sort of drug testing or screening, as do many smaller firms. The Reagan administration has called for mandatory testing of all federal employees. Several states have already passed drug testing laws; others will probably consider them in the future. While the Supreme Court has announced its intention to rule on the testing of federal employees within the next few months, its decision will not settle the permissibility of testing private employees. Discussion of the issue is likely to remain lively and heated for some time.

Most of the debate about drug testing in the workplace has focused on the issue of privacy rights. Three key questions have been: Do employees have privacy rights? If so, how far do these extend? What kinds of considerations outweigh these rights? I believe there are good reasons for supposing that employees do have moral privacy rights,[1] and that drug testing usually (though not always) violates these, but privacy is not my main concern in this paper. I wish to examine a different kind of argument, the claim that because corporations are responsible for harms committed by employees while under the influence of drugs, they are entitled to test for drug use.

This argument is rarely stated formally in the literature, but it can be found informally quite often.[2] One of its chief advantages is that it seems, at least at first glance, to bypass the issue of privacy rights altogether. There seems to be no need to determine the extent or weight of employees' privacy rights to make the argument work. It turns on a different set of principles altogether, that is, on the meaning and conditions of responsibility. This is an important asset, since arguments about rights are notoriously difficult to settle. Rights claims frequently function in ethical discourse as conversation-stoppers or non-negotiable demands.[3] Although it is widely recognized that rights are not absolute, there is little consensus on how far they extend, what kinds of considerations should be allowed to override them, or even how to go

From Jennifer Moore, "Drug Testing and Corporate Responsibility: The 'Ought Implies Can' Argument," *Journal of Business Ethics*, vol. 8 (1989), pp. 279–287. Copyright © 1989 by D. Reidel Publishing Co., Dordrecht, Holland, and Boston, U.S.A. Reprinted by permission of Kluwer Academic Publishers.

about settling these questions. But it is precisely these thorny problems that proponents of drug testing must tackle if they wish to address the issue on privacy grounds. Faced with the claim that drug testing violates the moral right to privacy of employees, proponents of testing must either (1) argue that drug testing does not really violate the privacy rights of employees;[4] (2) acknowledge that drug testing violates privacy rights, but argue that there are considerations that override those rights, such as public safety; or (3) argue that employees have no moral right to privacy at all.[5] It is not surprising that an argument that seems to move the debate out of the arena of privacy rights entirely appears attractive.

In spite of its initial appeal, however, I will maintain that the argument does not succeed in circumventing the claims of privacy rights. Even responsibility for the actions of others, I will argue, does not entitle us to do absolutely anything to control their behavior. We must look to rights, among other things, to determine what sorts of controls are morally permissible. Once this is acknowledged, the argument loses much of its force. In addition, it requires unjustified assumptions about the connection between drug testing and the prevention of drug-related harm.

AN "OUGHT IMPLIES CAN" ARGUMENT

Before we can assess the argument, it must be set out more fully. It seems to turn on the deep-rooted philosophical connection between responsibility and control. Generally, we believe that agents are not responsible[6] for acts or events that they could not have prevented. People are responsible for their actions only

if, it is often said, they "could have done otherwise". Responsibility implies some measure of control, freedom, or autonomy. It is for this reason that we do not hold the insane responsible for their actions. Showing that a person lacked the capacity to do otherwise blocks the normal moves of praise or blame and absolves the agent of responsibility for a given act.

For similar reasons, we believe that persons cannot be obligated to do things that they are incapable of doing, and that if they fail to do such things, no blame attaches to them. Obligation is empty, even senseless, without capability. If a person is obligated to perform an action, it must be within his or her power. This principle is sometimes summed up by the phrase "ought implies can". Kant used it as part of a metaphysical argument for free will, claiming that if persons are to have obligations at all, they must be autonomous, capable of acting freely.[7] The argument we examine here is narrower in scope, but similar in principle. If corporations are responsible for harms caused by employees under the influence of drugs, they must have the ability to prevent these harms. They must, therefore, have the freedom to test for drug use.

But the argument is still quite vague. What exactly does it mean to say that corporations are "responsible" for harms caused by employees? There are several possible meanings of "responsible". Not all of these are attributable to corporations, and not all of them exemplify the principle that "ought implies can". The question of how or whether corporations are "responsible" is highly complex, and we cannot begin to answer it in this paper.[8] There are, however, four distinct senses of "responsible" that appear with some regularity in the argument. They can be characterized, roughly, as follows: (a) legally liable; (b) culpable or guilty; (c) answerable or accountable; (d) bound by an obligation. The first is purely legal; the last three have a moral dimension.

Legal Liability

We do hold corporations legally liable for the negligent acts of employees under the doctrine of *respondeat superior* ("let the master respond"). If an employee harms a third party in the course of performing his or her duties for the firm, it is the corporation which must compensate the third party. *Respondeat superior* is an example of what is frequently called "vicarious liability". Since the employee was acting on behalf of the firm, and the firm was acting through the employee when the harmful act was committed, liability is said to "transfer" from the employee to the firm. But it is not clear that such liability on the part of the employer implies a capacity to have prevented the harm. Corporations are held liable for accidents caused by an employee's negligent driving, for example, even if they could not have foreseen or prevented the injury. While some employee accidents can be traced to corporate negligence,[9] there need be no fault on the part of the corporation for the doctrine of *respondeat superior* to apply. The doctrine of *respondeat superior* is grounded not in fault, but in concerns of public policy and utility. It is one of several applications of the notion of liability without fault in legal use today.

Because it does not imply fault, and its attendant ability to have done otherwise, legal liability or responsibility **a** cannot be used successfully as part of an "ought implies can" argument. Holding corporations legally liable for harms committed by intoxicated employees while at the same time forbidding drug-testing is not inconsistent. It could simply be viewed as yet another instance of liability without fault. Of course, one could argue that the notion of liability without fault is itself morally unacceptable, and that liability ought not to be detached from moral notions of punishment and blame. This is surely an extremely important claim, but it is beyond the scope of this paper. The main point to be made here is that we must be able to attribute more than legal liability to corporations if we are to invoke the principle of "ought implies can". Corporations must be responsible in sense **b**, **c**, or **d**—that is, *morally* responsible—if the argument is to work.

Moral Responsibility

Are corporations morally responsible for harms committed by intoxicated employees? Perhaps the most frequently used notion of moral responsibility is sense **b**, what I have called "guilt" or "culpability".[10] I have in mind here the strongest notion of moral responsibility, the sense that is prevalent in criminal law. An agent is responsible for an act in this sense if the act can be imputed to him or her. An essential condition of imputability is the presence in the agent of an intention to commit the act, or *mens rea*.[11] But does an employer whose workers use drugs satisfy the *mens rea* requirement? The requirement probably would be satisfied if it could be shown that the firm intended the resulting harms, ordered its employees to work under the influence of drugs, or even, perhaps (though this is less clear) turned a blind eye to blatant drug abuse in the workplace.[12] But these are all quite farfetched possibilities.

It is reasonable to assume that most corporations do not intend the harms caused by their employees, and that they do not order employees to use drugs on the job. Drug use is quite likely to be prohibited by company policy. If corporations are morally responsible for drug-related harms committed [by] employees, then, it is not in sense **b.**

Corporations might, however, be morally responsible for harms committed by employees in another sense. An organization acts through its employees. It empowers its employees to act in ways in which they otherwise would not act by providing them with money, power, equipment, and authority. Through a series of agreements, the corporation delegates its employees to act on its behalf. For these reasons, one could argue that corporations are responsible, in the sense of "answerable" or "accountable" (responsibility **c**), for the harmful acts of their employees. Indeed, it could be argued that if corporations are not morally responsible for these acts, they are not morally responsible for any acts at all, since corporations can only act through their employees.[13] To say that corporations are responsible for the harms of their employees in sense **c** is to say more than just that a corporation must "pay up" if an employee causes harm. It is to assign fault to the corporation by virtue of the ways in which organizational policies and structures facilitate and direct employees' actions.[14]

Moreover, corporations presumably have the same obligations as other agents to avoid harm in the conduct of their business. Since they conduct their business through their employees, it could plausibly be argued that corporations have an obligation to anticipate and prevent harms that employees might cause

in the course of their employment. If this reasoning is correct, corporations are morally responsible for the drug-related harms of employees in sense **d**—that is, they are under an obligation to prevent those harms. The "ought implies can" argument, then, may be formulated as follows:

1. If corporations have obligations, they must be capable of carrying them out, on the principle of "ought implies can".
2. Corporations have an obligation to prevent harm from occurring in the course of conducting their business.
3. Drug use by employees is likely to lead to harm.
4. Corporations must be able to take steps to eliminate (or at least reduce) drug use by employees.
5. Drug testing is an effective way to eliminate/reduce employee drug use.
6. Therefore corporations must be permitted to test for drugs.[15]

THE LIMITS OF CORPORATE AUTONOMY

This is surely an important argument, one that deserves to be taken seriously. The premise that corporations have an obligation to prevent harm from occurring in the conduct of their business seems unexceptionable and consistent with the actual moral beliefs of society. There is not much question that drug use by employees, especially regular drug use or drug use on the job, leads to harms of various kinds. Some of these are less serious than others, but some are very serious indeed: physical injury to consumers, the public, and fellow employees—and sometimes even death.[16]

Moreover, our convictions about the connections between responsibility or obligation and capability seem unassailable. Like other agents, if corporations are to have obligations, they must have the ability to carry them out. The argument seems to tell us that corporations are only able to carry out their obligations to prevent harm if they can free themselves of drugs. To prevent corporations from drug testing, it implies, is to prevent them from discharging their obligations. It is to cripple corporate autonomy just as we would cripple the autonomy of an individual worker if we refused to allow him to "kick the habit" that prevented him from giving satisfactory job performance.

But this analogy between corporate and individual autonomy reveals the initial defect in the argument. Unlike human beings, corporations are never fully autonomous selves. On the contrary, their actions are always dependent upon individual selves who are autonomous. Human autonomy means self-determination, self-governance, self-control. Corporate autonomy, at least as it is understood here, means control over others. Corporate autonomy is essentially derivative. But this means that corporate acts are not the simple sorts of acts generated by individual persons. They are complex. Most importantly, the members of a corporation are frequently not the agents, but the objects, of "corporate" action. A good deal of corporate action, that is, necessitates doing something not only *through* corporate employees, but *to* those employees.[17] The act of eliminating drugs from the workplace is an act of this sort. A corporation's ridding itself of drugs is not like an individual person's "kicking the habit". Rather, it is one group of persons making another group of persons give up drug use.

This fact has important implications for the "ought implies can" argument. The argument is persuasive in situations in which carrying out one's obligations requires only *self*-control, and does not involve controlling the behavior of others. Presumably there are no restrictions on what one may do to oneself in order to carry out an obligation.[18] But a corporation is not a genuine "self", and there *are* moral limits on what one person may do to another. Because this is so, we cannot automatically assume that the obligation to prevent harm justifies employee drug testing. Of course this does not necessarily mean that drug testing is *unjustified*. But it does mean that before we can determine whether it is justified, we must ask what is permissible for one person or group of persons to do to another to prevent a harm for which they are responsible.

Are there any analogies available that might help to resolve this question? It is becoming increasingly common to hold a hostess responsible (both legally and morally) for harm caused by a drunken guest on the way home from her party. In part, this is because she contributes to the harm by serving her guest alcohol. It is also because she knows that drunk driving is risky, and has a general obligation to prevent harm. What must she be allowed to do to prevent harms of this kind? Persuade the guest to spend the night on the couch? Surely. Take her car keys away from her? Perhaps. Knock her out and lock her in the bathroom until morning? Surely not.

Universities are occasionally held legally and morally responsible for harms committed by members of fraternities —destruction of property, gang rapes, and injuries or death caused by hazing. What may they do to prevent such harms? They may certainly withdraw institutional recognition and support from the fraternity, refusing to let it operate on the campus. But may they expel students who live together off-campus in fraternity-like arrangements? Have university security guards police these houses, covertly or by force? These questions are more difficult to answer.

We sometimes hold landlords morally (though not legally) responsible for tenants who are slovenly, play loud music, or otherwise make nuisances of themselves. Landlords are surely permitted to cancel the leases of such tenants, and they are justified in asking for references from previous landlords to prevent future problems of this kind. But it is not clear that a landlord may delve into a tenant's private life, search his room, or tap his telephone in order to anticipate trouble before it begins.

Each of these situations is one in which one person or group of persons is responsible, to a greater or a lesser degree, for the prevention of harm by others, and needs some measure of control in order to carry out this responsibility.[19] In each case, there is a fairly wide range of actions which we would be willing to allow the first party, but there are some actions which we would rule out. Having an obligation to prevent the harms of others seems to permit us some forms of control, but not all. At least one important consideration in deciding what kinds of actions are permissible is the *rights* of the controlled parties.[20] If these claims are correct, we must examine the rights of employees in order to determine whether drug testing is justified. The relevant right in the case of drug testing is the right to privacy. The "ought implies can" argument, then, does not circumvent the claims of privacy rights as it originally seemed to do.

THE AGENCY ARGUMENT

A proponent of drug testing might argue, however, that the relation between employers and employees is significantly different from the relation between hosts and guests, universities and members of fraternities, or landlords and tenants. Employees have a special relation with the firm that employs them. They are *agents*, hired and empowered to act on behalf of the employer. While they act on the business of the firm, it might be argued, they "are" the corporation. The restrictions that apply to what one independent agent may do to another thus do not apply here.

But surely this argument is incorrect, for a number of reasons. First, if it were correct, it would justify anything a corporation might do to control the behavior of an employee—not merely drug testing, but polygraph testing, tapping of telephones, deception, psychological manipulation, whips and chains, etc.[21] There are undoubtedly some people who would argue that some of these procedures are permissible, but few would argue that all of them are. The fact that even some of them appear not to be suggests that we believe there are limits to what corporations may do to control employees, and that one consideration in determining these limits is the employees' rights.

Secondly, the argument implies that employees give up their own autonomy completely when they sign on as agents, and become an organ or piece of the corporation. But this cannot be true. Agency is a moral and contractual relationship of the kind that can only obtain between two independent, autonomous parties. This relationship could not be sustained if the employee ceased to be autonomous upon signing the contract. Employees are not slaves, but autonomous agents capable of upholding a contract. Moreover, we expect a certain amount of discretion in employees in the course of their agency. Employees are not expected to follow illegal or immoral commands of their employers, and we find them morally and legally blameworthy when they do so. That we expect such independent judgment of them suggests that they do not lose their autonomy entirely.[22]

Finally, if the employment contract were one in which employees gave up all right to be treated as autonomous human beings, then it would not be a legitimate or morally valid contract. Some rights are considered "inalienable"—people are forbidden from negotiating them away even if it seems advantageous to them to do so. The law grants recognition to this fact through anti-discrimination statutes, minimum wage legislation, workplace health and safety standards, etc. Even if I would like to, I may not trade away, for example, my right not to be sexually harassed or my right to know about workplace hazards.

Again, these arguments do not show that drug testing is unjustified. They do show, however, that *if* drug testing is justified, it is not because the "ought implies can" argument bypasses the issue of employee rights, but because drug testing does not impermissibly violate those rights.[23] To think that obligation, or responsibility for the acts of others, can circumvent rights claims is to misunderstand the import of the "ought implies can" principle. The principle tells us that there is a close connection between obligation or responsibility and capability.

But it does not license us to disregard the rights of others any more than it guarantees us the physical conditions that make carrying out our obligations possible. It may well prove that employees' right to privacy, assuming they have such a right, is secondary to some more weighty consideration. I take up this question briefly below. What has been shown here is that the issue of the permissibility of drug testing will not and cannot be settled *without* a close scrutiny of privacy rights. If we are to decide the issue, we must eventually determine whether employees have privacy rights, how far they extend, and what considerations outweigh them—precisely the difficult questions the "ought implies can" argument sought to avoid.

IS DRUG TESTING NECESSARY?

The "ought implies can" argument also has another serious flaw. The argument turns on the claim that forbidding drug testing prevents corporations from carrying out their obligation to prevent harm. But this is only true if drug testing is *necessary* for preventing drug-related harm. If it is merely one option among many, the forbidding drug testing still leaves a corporation free to prevent harm in other ways. For the argument to be sound, in other words, premise 5 would have to be altered to read, "drug testing is a necessary element in any plan to rid the workplace of drugs."

But it is not at all clear that drug testing *is* necessary to reduce drug use in the workplace. Its necessity has been challenged repeatedly. In a recent article in the *Harvard Business Review*, for example, James Wrich draws on his experience in dealing with alcoholism in the workplace and suggests the use of broadbrush educational and rehabilitative programs as alternatives to testing. Corporations using such programs to combat alcohol problems, Wrich reports, have achieved tremendous reductions in absenteeism, sick leave, and on-the-job accidents.[24] Others have argued that impaired performance likely to result in harm could be easily detected by various sorts of performance-oriented tests—mental and physical dexterity tests, alertness tests, flight simulation tests, and so on. These sorts of procedures have the advantage of not being controversial from a rights perspective.[25]

Indeed, many thinkers have argued that drug testing is not only unnecessary, but is not even an effective way to attack drug use in the workplace. The commonly used and affordable urinalysis tests are notoriously unreliable. They have a very high rate both of false negatives and of false positives. At best the tests reveal, not impaired performance or even the presence of a particular drug, but the presence of metabolites of various drugs that can remain in the system long after any effects of the drug have worn off.[26] Because they do not measure impairment, such tests do not seem well-tailored to the purpose of preventing harm—which, after all, is the ultimate goal. As Lewis Maltby, vice president of a small instrumentation company and an opponent of drug testing, puts it,

> ... [T]he fundamental flaw with drug testing is that it tests for the wrong thing. A realistic program to detect workers whose condition put the company or other people at risk would test for the condition that actually creates the danger.[27]

If these claims are true, there is no real connection between the obligation to prevent harm and the practice of drug testing, and the "ought implies can" argument provides no justification for drug testing at all.[28]

CONCLUSION

I have made no attempt here to determine whether drug testing does indeed violate employees' privacy rights. The analysis... above suggests that we have reason to believe that employees have some rights. Once we accept the notion of employee rights in general, it seems likely that a right to privacy would be among them, since it is an important civil right and central for the protection of individual autonomy. There are also reasons, I believe, to think that most drug testing violates the right to privacy. These claims need much more defense than they can be given here, and even if they are true, this does not necessarily mean that drug testing is unjustified. It does, however, create a *prima facie* case against drug testing. If drug testing violates the privacy rights of employees, it will be justified only under very strict conditions, if it is justified at all. It is worth taking a moment to see why this is so.

It is generally accepted in both the ethical and legal spheres that rights are not absolute. But we allow basic rights to be overridden only in special cases in which some urgent and fundamental good is at stake. In legal discourse, such goods are called "compelling interests".[29] While there is room for some debate about what counts as a "compelling interest", it is almost always understood to be more than a merely private interest, however weighty. Public safety might well fall into this category, but private monetary loss probably would not. While more needs to be done to determine what kinds of interests justify drug testing, it seems clear that if testing does violate the basic rights of employees, it is only justified in extreme cases— far less often than it is presently used. Moreover, we believe that overriding a right is to be avoided wherever possible, and is only justified when doing so is *necessary* to serve the "compelling interest" in question. If it violates rights, then drug testing is only permissible if it is necessary for the protection of an interest such as public safety and if there is no other, morally preferable, way of accomplishing the same goal. As we have seen above, however, it is by no means clear that drug testing meets these conditions. There may be better, less controversial ways to prevent the harm caused by drug use; if so, these must be used in preference to drug testing, and testing is unjustified. And if the attacks on the effectiveness of drug testing are correct, testing is not only unnecessary for the protection of public safety, but does not serve any "compelling interest" at all.

What do these conclusions tell us about the responsibility of employers for preventing harms caused by employees? If it is decided that drug testing is morally impermissible, then there can be no duty to use it to anticipate and prevent harms. Corporations who fail to use it cannot be blamed for doing so. They cannot have a moral obligation to do something morally impermissible. Moreover, if it turns out that there is no other effective way to prevent the harms caused by drug use, then it seems to me we may not hold employers morally responsible for those harms. This seems to me unlikely to be the case—there probably are other effective measures to control drug abuse in the workplace. But corporations can be held responsible only to the extent that they are permitted to act. It would not be inconsistent, however, to hold corporations legally liable for the harms caused by intoxicated employees under the doctrine of *respondeat superior*, even if drug testing is forbidden, for this kind of liability does not imply an ability to have done otherwise.

NOTES

1. Employees do not, of course, have legal privacy rights, although the courts seem to be moving slowly in this direction. Opponents of testing usually claim that employees have *moral* rights to privacy, even if these have not been given legal recognition. See, for example, Joseph Des Jardins and Ronald Duska, "Drug Testing in Employment", in *Business Ethics: Readings and Cases in Corporate Morality*, 2nd edition, ed. W. M. Hoffman and J. M. Moore (McGraw-Hill, forthcoming).

2. See, for example, "Work-Place Privacy Issues and Employer Screening Policies," Richard Lehr and David Middlebrooks, *Employee Relations Law Journal* 11, 407. Lehr and Middlebrooks cite the argument as one of the chief justifications for drug testing used by employers. I have also encountered the argument frequently in discussion with students, colleagues, and managers.

3. Ronald Dworkin has referred to rights as moral "trumps". This kind of language tends to suggest that rights overwhelm all other considerations, so that when they are flourished, all that opponents can do is subside in silence. Rights are frequently asserted this way in everyday discourse, and in this sense rights claims tend to close, rather than open, the door to fruitful ethical dialogue.

4. In his article "Privacy, Polygraphs, and Work," *Business and Professional Ethics Journal* 1, Fall, 1981, 19, George Brenkert has developed the idea that my privacy is violated when some one acquires information about me that they are not entitled, by virtue of their relationship to me, to have. My mortgage company, for example, is entitled to know my credit history; a prospective sexual partner is entitled to know if I have any sexually transmitted diseases. Thus their knowledge of this information does not violate my privacy. One could argue that employers are similarly entitled to the information obtained by drug tests, and that drug testing does not violate privacy for this reason. A somewhat different move would be to argue that testing does not violate privacy because employees

give their "consent" to... drug testing as part of the employment contract. For a sustained attack on these and other Type 1 arguments, see Joseph Des Jardins and Ronald Duska, "Drug Testing in Employment".

5. One might defend this position on the ground that the employer "owns" the job and is therefore entitled to place any conditions he wishes on obtaining or keeping it. The problem with this argument is that it seems to rule out *all* employee rights, including such basic ones as the right to organize and bargain collectively, or the right not to be discriminated against, which have solid legal as well as ethical grounding. It also implies that ownership overrides all other considerations, and it is not at all clear that this is true. One might take the position that by accepting a job, an employee has agreed to give up all his rights save those actually specified in the employment contract. But this makes the employment contract look like an agreement in which employees sell themselves and accept the status of things without rights. And it overlooks the fact that we believe there are some things ("inalienable" rights) that persons ought not to be permitted to bargain away. Alex Michalos has discussed some of the limitations of the employment contract in "The Loyal Agent's Argument", in *Ethical Theory and Business*, 2nd edition, ed. Tom L. Beauchamp and Norman E. Bowie (Englewood Cliffs, NJ: Prentice-Hall, 1983), p. 247.

6. The term "responsibility" is deliberately left ambiguous here. Several different meanings of it are examined below.

7. See Immanuel Kant, *Critique of Practical Reason*, trans. Lewis White Beck (Indianapolis: Bobbs-Merril, 1956), p. 30.

8. In this paper I have tried to avoid getting embroiled in the question of whether or not corporations are themselves "moral agents", which has been the question to dominate the corporate responsibility debate. The argument I offer here does, I believe, have important implications for the problem of corporate agency, but does not require me to take a stand on it here. I am content to have those who reject the notion of corporations as moral agents read my references to corporate responsibility as shorthand for some complex form of individual or group responsibility.

9. One example would be negligent hiring, which is an increasingly frequent cause of action against an employer. Employers can also be held negligent if they give orders that lead to harms that they ought to have foreseen. Domino's Pizza is now under suit because it encouraged its drivers to deliver pizzas as fast as possible, a policy that accident victims claim should have been expected to cause accidents.

10. This understanding of moral responsibility often seems to overshadow other notions. In an article on corporate responsibility, for example, Manuel Velasquez concludes that because corporations are not responsible in this sense, they are "not responsible for anything they do". "Why Corporations Are Not Responsible For Anything They Do", *Business and Professional Ethics Journal* 2, Spring, 1983, 1.

11. There is also an *actus reus* requirement for this type of responsibility—that is, the act must be traceable to the voluntary bodily movements of the agent. Obviously, corporations do not have bodies, but the people who work for them do. The question, then, has become when may we call an act by one member of the corporation a "corporate act". If it is possible to do so at all, the decisive feature is probably the presence of some sort of corporate "intention." This is why I focus on intention here, and why intention has been central to the discussion of corporate responsibility.

12. There are some, like Velasquez, who hold that a corporation can never satisfy the *mens rea* requirement because this would require a collective mind. If this were true, the argument would collapse at the outset. Others believe that a *mens rea* can be attributed to corporations metaphorically, if it can be shown that company policy includes an "intention" to harm, and it is this model I follow here.

13. There are, of course, those who take precisely this position. See Velasquez, "Why Corporations Are Not Responsible For Anything They Do".

14. See, for example, Peter French, *Collective and Corporate Responsibility* (New York: Columbia University Press, 1984).

15. It is tempting to conclude from this argument that drug testing is not only permissible, but obligatory, but this is not the case. The reason why it is not provides a clue to one of the major weaknesses of the argument. Drug testing would be obligatory only if it were *necessary* for the prevention of harm due to drug use, but it is not clear that this is so. But [it] also means that it is not clear that corporations are deflected from their duty to prevent harm by a prohibition against drug testing. See below for a fuller discussion of this problem.

16. For example, it has been claimed that employees who use drugs cause four times as many work-related accidents as do other employees. The highly publicized Conrail crash in 1987 was determined to be drug-related. Of course there are harms to the company itself as well, in the form of higher absenteeism, lowered productivity, higher insurance costs, etc. But since these types of harm raise the question of what a company may do to preserve its self-interest, rather than what it may do to prevent harms to others for which they are responsible, I focus here on harm to employees, consumers, and the public.

17. In our eagerness to assign "corporate responsibility", this fact has frequently been overlooked. This in turn has led, I believe, to an oversimplified view of corporate action. I discuss this problem more fully in a paper in progress entitled "The Paradox of Corporate Autonomy".

18. It is an interesting question whether there are limitations on what individuals can do to themselves to control their own behavior. What about individuals who undergo hypnosis, or who have their jaws wired shut in order to lose weight? Are they violating their own rights? Undermining their own autonomy? It could be argued plausibly that these kinds of things are not permissible, on the Kantian ground that we have a duty not to treat ourselves as merely as means to an end. Of course, if there are such restrictions, it makes the "ought implies can" argument as applied to corporations even weaker.

19. None of these analogies is perfect. In the case of the hostess and guest, for example, the guest is clearly intoxicated. This is rarely true of employees who are tested for drugs; if the employee were visibly intoxicated, there would be no need to test. Moreover, in the hostess/guest case the hostess contributes directly to the intoxication. There are important parallels, however. In each case one party is held morally (and in two of the cases, legally) responsible for harms caused by others. Moreover, the first parties are responsible in close to the same way that employers are responsible for the acts of their employees: they in some sense "facilitate" the harmful acts, they have some capacity to prevent those acts, and they are thus viewed as having an obligation to prevent them. One main difference, of course, is that employees are "agents" of their employers....

20. There are other, utility-related considerations, as well—for example, harm to employees who are unjustly dismissed, a demoralized workforce, the costs of testing, etc. I concentrate here on rights because they have been the primary focal point in the drug testing debate.

21. The assumption here is that persons are entitled to do whatever they wish to themselves. See Note 18.

22. See Michalos, "The Loyal Agent's Argument".

23. Some violations of right, of course, are permissible....

24. James T. Wrich, "Beyond Testing: Coping with Drugs at Work", *Harvard Business Review* Jan.–Feb. 1988, 120.

25. See Des Jardins and Duska, "Drug Testing in Employment", and Lewis Maltby, "Why Drug Testing is a Bad Idea", *Inc.* June 1987. While other sorts of tests also have the potential to be abused, they are at least a direct measurement of something that an employer is entitled to know—performance capability. Des Jardins and Duska offer an extended defense of this sort of test.

26. See Edward J. Imwinkelreid, "False Positive", *The Sciences*, Sept.–Oct. 1987, 22. Also David Bearman, "The Medical Case Against Drug Testing", *Harvard Business Review* Jan.–Feb. 1988, 123.

27. Maltby, "Why Drug Testing is a Bad Idea", pp. 152–153.

28. It could still be argued that drug testing *deters* drug use, and thus has a connection with preventing harm, even though it doesn't directly provide any information that enables companies to prevent harm. This is an important point, but it is still subject to the restrictions discussed in the previous section. Not everything that has a deterrent value is permissible. It is possible that a penalty of capital punishment would provide a deterrent for rapists, or having one's hand removed deter shoplifting, but there are very few advocates for these penalties. Effectiveness is not the only issue here; rights and justice are also relevant.

29. The principle that fundamental rights may not be overridden by the state unless doing so is necessary to serve a "compelling state interest" is a principle of constitutional law, but it also reflects our moral intuitions about when it is appropriate to override rights. The legal principle would not apply to all cases of drug testing in the workplace because many of these involve private, rather than state, employees. But the principle does provide us with useful guidelines in the ethical sphere. Interestingly, Federal District Judge George Revercomb recently issued an injunction blocking the random drug testing of Justice Department employees on the ground that it did not serve a compelling state interest. Since there was no evidence of a drug problem among the Department's employees, the Judge concluded, there is no threat that would give rise to a compelling interest. See "Judge Blocks Drug Testing of Justice Department Employees", *New York Times* July 30, 1988, 7.

POSTSCRIPT

Should Concern for Drug Abuse Overrule Concerns for Employee Privacy?

In the controversy over drug testing, the two sides seem to be reasoning from different moral principles and to different consequences. The proponents of randomized drug testing cite the principle of Least Harm: left to themselves to take drugs, the workforce is likely to turn out terribly harmful results—damaged products, derailed trains, and the pervasive negligence that makes products unsafe and the workplace dangerous.

At least some professions—such as firefighter, peace officer, and airplane pilot—are not only incompatible with drug use but are also so important to the public's safety and vulnerable to public distrust that the public deserves assurances that such employees are demonstrably drug free. For the sake of those assurances alone there should be a policy of random drug testing for those occupations. Meanwhile, the threat of being tested should deter those workers from using drugs; this deterrence provides a separate consequentialist argument for the testing.

The opponents of drug testing, however, find more harm than good resulting from drug testing. Given the potential for error, good employees will be not only fired but stigmatized; the morale of the workforce will suffer as the invasions of privacy threaten the dignity and self-esteem of the worker; and the atmosphere of suspicion built up by the testing policy will result in worker resentment.

Both sides also cite nonconsequentialist arguments to their conclusions. Those in favor of drug testing cite the importance of subordinating individual freedom to community interest in times of emergency, and they find worker resentment of drug testing not only suspicious (what are they trying to hide?) but also antisocial and obstructionist. Those against drug testing cite the importance of individual privacy and dignity—especially against the kind of invasion that drug testing entails—and further cite the importance of maintaining trust between employer and employee, which is violated by drug testing policies.

Troubling for both sides is the scope of the principle. After all, why stop with drugs? Once the employer has a license to regulate personal habits for the greater good of the customer, the company, and society, why not put that license to work in other areas? Can the employer tell the employees not to smoke tobacco, on or off the job? It would be to an employer's advantage since health insurance costs are reduced for companies with smoke-free environments. What about alcohol? Alcohol is at least as dangerous as other recreational drugs, with far-reaching effects on areas as diverse as family happiness, general health, and safety on the roads. Can employers regulate dating habits among their employees similar to the old school boards' practices? And what about AIDS? What role, if any, should testing for HIV infection play in the workplace?

Finally, once testing for these dangers has begun, who will keep the records of those who fail, and who will have access to those records? Publicly revealing negative results of any test could constitute defamation of character. How could the confidentiality of employee records be ensured?

It is difficult to predict the future of drug testing in the workplace. If it is to be allowed—and, according to the surveys reported by Verespej, it should—more reliable tests are needed on the front line. There is now a very expensive test for which 99.9 percent accuracy is claimed, which is often used as a backup if an employee fails a drug test once. But generally, it is not used to screen candidates for employment, so there is still the risk of excluding good employees because of false positives or ruining credibility with too many false negatives. Primarily, drugs are not a company problem or an affliction of American business or capitalism. They are proliferating in the society at large, and until drugs are removed from the street, there is little hope of getting them out of the workplace. Under these circumstances, it seems that the certainty of invasion outweighs the possibility of preventing drug use. On the other hand, the corporations may be the perfect place to begin to confront drug abuse.

SUGGESTED READINGS

Rob Brookler, "Industry Standards in Workplace Drug Testing," *Personnel Journal* (April 1992).

Bruce A. Campbell, "Alcohol and Drug Abuse in the Workplace: Major Problem or Myth?" *R. F. Goodell Business Quarterly* (Autumn 1990).

Michael Janofsky, "Drug Use and Workers' Rights," *The New York Times* (December 28, 1993).

Laura Lally, "Privacy Versus Accessibility: The Impact of Situationally Conditioned Belief," *Journal of Business Ethics* (November 1996).

Rita C. Manning, "Liberal and Communitarian Defenses of Workplace Privacy," *Journal of Business Ethics* (June 1997).

Charles L. Redel and Augustus Abbey, "The Arbitration of Drug Use and Testing in the Workplace," *Arbitration Journal* (March 1993).

J. K. Ross III and B. J. Middlebrook, "AIDS Policy in the Work Place, Will You Be Ready?" *Advanced Management Journal* (Winter 1990).

Barbara Steinburg, "Foolproofing Drug Tests Results," *Business and Health* (December 1990).

Kimberly A. Weber and Robin E. Shea, "Drug Testing: The Necessary Evil," *Bobbin* (August 1991).

On the Internet . . .

http://www.dushkin.com

Business Cycle Indicators

This site leads to the 256 data series known as the U.S. Business Cycle Indicators, which are used to track and predict U.S. business activity. The subjects of the data groups are clearly listed.
http://www.globalexposure.com/bci.html

Voice of the Shuttle: Postindustrial Business Theory Page

This site links to a variety of resources on many subjects related to business theory, including restructuring, reengineering, downsizing, flattening, the team concept, outsourcing, business and globalism, human resources management, labor relations, statistics, and history, as well as information and resources on job searches, careers, working from home, and business start-ups.
http://humanitas.ucsb.edu/shuttle/commerce.html

PART 4

Moving the Product: Marketing and Consumer Dilemmas

What right does a consumer have to expect that the product he or she buys will cause no harm? At the start of the twentieth century, the buyer tended to be stuck with a purchase, however reached, and responsible for her or his own safety in using the product. This is no longer the rule governing product liability. In this section, we look at five cases: advertising, in and of itself; the marketing of a product that is essentially harmful (tobacco); the moral obligations of multinational corporations; the effects of the North American Free Trade Agreement; and the function of sweatshops in less developed countries. Questions of intent and effect are inextricably linked in all five cases.

■ Is Advertising Fundamentally Deceptive?

■ Should Tobacco Advertising Be Banned?

■ Are Multinational Corporations Free from Moral Obligations?

■ Does NAFTA Make Life Better for Americans?

■ Are Sweatshops Necessarily Evil?

ISSUE 12

Is Advertising Fundamentally Deceptive?

YES: Roger Crisp, from "Persuasive Advertising, Autonomy, and the Creation of Desire," *Journal of Business Ethics* (vol. 6, 1987)

NO: John O'Toole, from *The Trouble With Advertising* (Chelsea House, 1981)

ISSUE SUMMARY

YES: Philosopher Roger Crisp argues that persuasive advertising removes the possibility of real decision making by manipulating consumers without their knowledge, for no good reason, and thus destroys personal autonomy.

NO: John O'Toole, president of the American Association of Advertising Agencies, argues that advertising is only salesmanship functioning in the paid space and time of mass media and that it is no more coercive than an ordinary salesperson.

Advertisers do one thing—they persuade us to buy products that otherwise we would not buy. If we would buy the products anyway, there would be no point in producers spending the money to purchase magazine space or television time to display ads. That advertising seems necessary in today's market and is used to sell everything from cars to movies raises the question of whether the art of promotion aids the consumer or cons consumers into throwing money away on products they neither need nor desire.

Where, in pure capitalism, is there room for salesmanship? According to Scottish economist Adam Smith (1723–1790), the decision to buy is based solely on need, price, and (perceived) quality. The customer desires the exchange and wants to maximize the value obtained by it. But human psychology does not necessarily work as Smith's theory postulates. When some people shop, they are often tired and in a hurry, and they will buy the first thing they see that satisfies a need and that falls within an acceptable range of price and quality. As a matter of fact, they may buy the first thing that grabs their attention and looks attractive—and therein is the sales pitch. Attention and attractiveness are the keys to sales, and the customer's hypothesized needs, plans, and comparisons may have very little to do with the actual decision to buy.

Salesmanship, then, works in defiance of and at variance with the rational satisfaction of need in the free market. The salesman will not succeed in inducing people to buy things they never thought of or conceived a use for because he does not have the time to plant the idea of some new need and help it to grow. But when a willing buyer wanders into the market, the aggressive salesman can certainly accelerate the decision to buy and influence the buyer to choose one vendor rather than another.

If the salesman has more time, however, can he produce new needs? Suppose the national widget maker makes twice too many widgets one year, and there is no real need for the excess. Could he hire a salesman to persuade people that widgets make fine lawn ornaments (a use no one had thought of), that lawn ornaments are essential to the good life (also unthought), and that, therefore, they truly need his widgets? According to Smith's theory, consumers should see through such a ploy, and no sale would ever take place. But here is where advertising enters the consumer's life as a picture or a fantasy of a life more valuable than his or her own. By associating this beautiful life with a product, not really an object of need but beginning to seem so, the advertiser can build up an inclination to buy, well away from the point of sale, and predispose a consumer first to pay attention to, and then to *need*, the manufacturer's product. Sales, in that case, are not need driven, proceeding from the customer's life and needs, but are product driven, proceeding from the producer's desire to sell and the advertiser's skill.

In the following selections, Roger Crisp is primarily interested in the effect of advertising on the individual and the problems of preserving any notion of autonomy in a world overrun with persuasive messages. John O'Toole does not try to present advertising as an objective exercise in consumer education. But, he argues, if salesmanship in the marketplace is acceptable, and it surely seems to be, then what possible objection can there be to extending salesmanship to the print and broadcast media?

As you read these selections, ask yourself how *you* react to advertising. Do you think about it? Talk back to it? Absorb it? Can you think of an advertisement that really changed your idea of what was good and valuable and worth buying? Should there be limits on pitches beyond the federal prohibition of outright deception? Why? Is advertising just clean fun that fools no one, entertains us, and in a thoroughly harmless way persuades us to try something we might like?

YES

Roger Crisp

PERSUASIVE ADVERTISING, AUTONOMY, AND THE CREATION OF DESIRE

In this paper, I shall argue that all forms of a certain common type of advertising are morally wrong, on the ground that they override the autonomy of consumers.

One effect of an advertisement might be the creation of a desire for the advertised product. How such desires are caused is highly relevant as to whether we would describe the case as one in which the autonomy of the subject has been overridden. If I read an advertisement for a sale of clothes, I may rush down to my local clothes store and purchase a jacket I like. Here, my desire for the jacket has arisen partly out of my reading the advertisement. Yet, in an ordinary sense, it is based on or answers to certain properties of the jacket —its colour, style, material. Although I could not explain to you why my tastes are as they are, we still describe such cases as examples of autonomous action, in that all the decisions are being made by me: What kind of jacket do I like? Can I afford one? And so on. In certain other cases, however, the causal history of a desire may be different. Desires can be caused, for instance, by subliminal suggestion. In New Jersey, a cinema flashed sub-threshold advertisements for ice cream onto the screen during movies, and reported a dramatic increase in sales during intermissions. In such cases, choice is being deliberately ruled out by the method of advertising in question. These customers for ice cream were acting 'automatonously', rather than autonomously. They did not buy the ice cream because they happened to like it and decided they would buy some, but rather because they had been subjected to subliminal suggestion. Subliminal suggestion is the most extreme form of what I shall call, adhering to a popular dichotomy, persuasive, as opposed to informative, advertising. Other techniques include puffery, which involves the linking of the product, through suggestive language and images, with the unconscious desires of consumers for power, wealth, status, sex, and so on; and repetition, which is self-explanatory, the name of the product being 'drummed into' the mind of the consumer.

The obvious objection to persuasive advertising is that it somehow violates the autonomy of consumers. I believe that this objection is correct, and that, if one adopts certain common-sensical standards for autonomy, non-persuasive forms of advertising are not open to such an objection. Very high standards for autonomy are set by Kant, who requires that an agent be entirely external to the causal nexus found in the ordinary empirical world, if his or her actions are to be autonomous. These standards are too high, in that it is doubtful whether they allow *any* autonomous action. Standards for autonomy more congenial to common sense will allow that my buying the jacket is autonomous, although continuing to deny that the people in New Jersey were acting autonomously. In the former case, we have what has come to be known in recent discussions of freedom of the will as *both* free will *and* free action. I both decide what to do, and am not obstructed in carrying through my decision into action. In the latter case, there is free action, but not free will. No one prevents the customers buying their ice cream, but they have not themselves made any genuine decision whether or not to do so. In a very real sense, decisions are made for consumers by persuasive advertisers, who occupy the motivational territory properly belonging to the agent. If what we mean by autonomy, in the ordinary sense, is to be present, the possibility of decision must exist alongside.

Arrington (1981) discusses, in a challenging paper, the techniques of persuasive advertising I have mentioned, and argues that such advertising does not override the autonomy of consumers. He examines four notions central to autonomous action, and claims that, on each count, persuasive advertising is exonerated on the charge we have made against it. I shall now follow in the footsteps of Arrington, but argue that he sets the standards for autonomy too low for them to

be acceptable to common sense, and that the charge therefore still sticks.

(a) *Autonomous desire:* Arrington argues that an autonomous desire is a first-order desire (a desire for some object, say, Pongo Peach cosmetics) accepted by the agent because it fulfils a second-order desire (a desire about a desire, say, a desire that my first-order desire for Pongo Peach be fulfilled), and that most of the first-order desires engendered in us by advertising are desires that we do accept. His example is an advertisement for Grecian Formula 16, which engenders in him a desire to be younger. He desires that both his desire to be younger and his desire for Grecian Formula 16 be fulfilled.

Unfortunately, this example is not obviously one of persuasive advertising. It may be the case that he just has this desire to look young again rather as I had certain sartorial tastes before I saw the ad about the clothes sale, and then decides to buy Grecian Formula 16 on the basis of these tastes. Imagine this form of advertisement: a person is depicted using Grecian Formula 16, and is then shown in a position of authority, surrounded by admiring members of the opposite sex. This would be a case of puffery. The advertisement implies that having hair coloured by the product will lead to positions of power, and to one's becoming more attractive to the opposite sex. It links, by suggestion, the product with my unconscious desires for power and sex. I may still claim that I am buying the product because I want to look young again. But the real reasons for my purchase are my unconscious desires for power and sex, and the link made between the product and the fulfillment of those desires by the advertisement. These reasons are not reasons I could avow to myself as good reasons for buying the product, and, again, the possibility of decision is absent.

Arrington's claim is that an autonomous desire is a first-order desire which we accept. Even if we allow that it is possible for the agent to consider whether to accept or to repudiate first-order desires induced by persuasive advertising, it seems that all first-order desires induced purely by persuasive advertising will be non-autonomous in Arrington's sense. Many of us have a strong second-order desire not to be manipulated by others without our knowledge, and for no good reason. Often, we are manipulated by others without our knowledge, but for a good reason, and one that we can accept. Take an accomplished actor: much of the skill of an actor is to be found in unconscious body-language. This manipulation we see as essential to our being entertained, and thus acquiesce in it. What is important about this case is that there seems to be no diminution of autonomy. We can still judge the quality of the acting, in that the manipulation is part of its quality. In other cases, however, manipulation ought not to be present, and these are cases where the ability to decide is importantly diminished by the manipulation. Decision is central to the theory of the market-process: I should be able to decide whether to buy product A or product B, by judging them on their merits. Any manipulation here I shall repudiate as being for no good reason. This is not to say, incidentally, that once the fact that my desires are being manipulated by others has been made transparent to me, my desire will lapse. The people in New Jersey would have been unlikely to cease their craving for ice cream, if we had told them that their desire had been subliminally induced. But they would no longer have voiced acceptance of this desire, and, one assumes, would have resented the manipulation of their desires by the management of the cinema.

Pace Arrington, it is no evidence for the claim that most of our desires are autonomous in this sense that we often return to purchase the same product over and over again. For this might well show that persuasive advertising has been supremely efficient in inducing non-autonomous desires in us, which we are unable even to attempt not to act on, being unaware of their origin. Nor is it an argument in Arrington's favour that certain members of our society will claim not to have the second-order desire we have postulated. For it may be that this is a desire which we can see is one that human beings *ought* to have, a desire which it would be in their interests to have, and the lack of which is itself evidence of profound manipulation.

(b) *Rational desire and choice:* One might argue that the desires induced by advertising are often irrational, in the sense that they are not present in an agent in full possession of the facts about the product. This argument fails, says Arrington, because if we require *all* the facts about a thing before we can desire that thing, then all our desires will be irrational; and if we require only the *relevant* information, then prior desires determine the relevance of information. Advertising may be said to enable us to fulfil these prior desires, through the transfer of information, and the supplying of means to ends is surely a paradigm example of rationality.

But, what about persuasive, as opposed to informative, advertising? Take puffery. Is it not true that a person may buy Pongo Peach cosmetics, hoping for an adventure in paradise, and that the product will not fulfil these hopes? Are they really in possession of even the relevant facts? Yes, says Arrington. We wish to purchase *subjective* effects, and these are genuine enough. When I use Pongo Peach, I will experience a genuine feeling of adventure.

Once again, however, our analysis can help us to see the strength of the objection. For a desire to be rational, in any plausible sense, that desire must at least not be induced by the interference of other persons with my system of tastes, against my will and without my knowledge. Can we imagine a person, asked for a reason justifying their purchase of Pongo Peach, replying: "I have an unconscious desire to experience adventure, and the product has been linked with this desire through advertising'? If a desire is to be rational, it is not necessary that all the facts about the object be known to the agent, but one of the facts about that desire must be that it has not been induced in the agent through techniques which the agent cannot accept. Thus, applying the schema of Arrington's earlier argument, such a desire will be repudiated by the agent as non-autonomous and irrational.

Arrington's claim concerning the subjective effects of the products we purchase fails to deflect the charge of overriding autonomy we have made against persuasive advertising. Of course, very often the subjective effects will be lacking. If I use Grecian Formula 16, I am unlikely to find myself being promoted at work, or surrounded by admiring members of the opposite sex. This is just straight deception. But even when the effects do manifest themselves, such advertisements have still overridden my autonomy. They have activated desires which lie beyond my awareness, and over behaviour flowing from which I therefore have no control. If these claims appear doubtful, consider whether this advertisement is likely to be successful: 'Do you have a feeling of adventure? Then use this brand of cosmetics'. Such an advertisement will fail, in that it appeals to a *conscious* desire, either which we do not have, or which we realise will not be fulfilled by purchasing a certain brand of cosmetics. If the advertisement were for a course in mountain-climbing, it might meet with more success. Our conscious self is not so easily duped by advertising, and this is why advertisers make such frequent use of the techniques of persuasive advertising.

(c) *Free choice:* One might object to persuasive advertising that it creates desires so covert that an agent cannot resist them, and that acting on them is therefore neither free nor voluntary. Arrington claims that a person acts or chooses *freely* if they can adduce considerations which justify their act in their mind; and *voluntarily* if, had they been aware of a reason for acting otherwise, they could have done so. Only occasionally, he says, does advertising prevent us making free and voluntary choices.

Regarding free action, it is sufficient to note that, according to Arrington, if I were to be converted into a human robot, activated by an Evil Genius who has implanted electrodes in my brain, my actions would be free as long as I could cook up some justification for my behaviour. I want to dance this jig because I enjoy dancing. (Compare: I want to buy this ice cream because I like ice cream.) If my argument is right, we are placed in an analogous position by persuasive advertising. If we no longer mean by freedom of action the mere non-obstruction of behaviour, are we still ready to accept that we are engaged in free action? As for whether the actions of consumers subjected to persuasive advertising are voluntary in Arrington's sense, I am less optimistic than he is. It is likely, as we have suggested, that the purchasers of ice cream or Pongo Peach would have gone ahead with their purchase even if they had been made aware that their desires had been induced in them by persuasive advertising. But they would now claim that they themselves had not made the decision, that they were acting on a desire engendered in them which they did not accept, and that there was, therefore, a good reason for them not to make the purchase. The unconscious is not obedient to the commands of the conscious, although it may be forced to listen.

In fact, it is odd to suggest that persuasive advertising does give consumers a choice. A choice is usually taken to require the weighing-up of reasons. What persuasive advertising does is to remove the very conditions of choice.

(d) *Control or manipulation:* Arrington offers the following criteria for control:

A person C controls the behaviour of another person P if (1) C intends P to act in a certain way A, (2) C's intention is causally effective in bringing about A, and (3) C intends to ensure that all of the necessary conditions of A are satisfied. He argues that advertisements tend to induce a desire for X, given a more basic desire for Y. Given my desire for adventure, I desire Pongo Peach cosmetics. Thus, advertisers do not control consumers, since they do not intend to produce all of the necessary conditions for our purchases.

Arrington's analysis appears to lead to some highly counter-intuitive consequences. Consider, again, my position as

human robot. Imagine that the Evil Genius relies on the fact that I have certain basic unconscious desires in order to effect his plan. Thus, when he wants me to dance a jig, it is necessary that I have a more basic desire, say, ironically, for power. What the electrodes do is to jumble up my practical reasoning processes, so that I believe that I am dancing the jig because I like dancing, while, in reality, the desire to dance stems from a link between the dance and the fulfilment of my desire for power, forged by the electrodes. Are we still happy to say that I am not controlled? And does not persuasive advertising bring about a similar jumbling-up of the practical reasoning processes of consumers? When I buy Pongo Peach, I may be unable to offer a reason for my purchase, or I may claim that I want to look good. In reality, I buy it owing to the link made by persuasive advertising between my unconscious desire for adventure and the cosmetic in question.

A more convincing account of behaviour control would be to claim that it occurs when a person causes another person to act for reasons which the other person could not accept as good or justifiable reasons for the action. This is how brainwashing is to be distinguished from liberal education, rather than on Arrington's ground that the brainwasher arranges all the necessary conditions for belief. The student can both accept that she has the beliefs she has because of her education and continue to hold those beliefs as true, whereas the victim of brainwashing could not accept the explanation of the origin of her beliefs, while continuing to hold those beliefs. It is worth recalling the two cases we mentioned at the beginning of this paper. I can accept my tastes in dress, and do not think that the fact that their origin is unknown to me detracts from my autonomy, when I choose to buy the jacket. The desire for ice cream, however, will be repudiated, in that it is the result of manipulation by others, without good reason.

It seems, then, that persuasive advertising does override the autonomy of consumers, and that, if the overriding of autonomy, other things being equal, is immoral, then persuasive advertising is immoral.

An argument has recently surfaced which suggests that, in fact, other things are not equal, and that persuasive advertising, although it overrides autonomy, is morally acceptable. This argument was first developed by Nelson (1978), and claims that persuasive advertising is a form of informative advertising, albeit an indirect form. The argument runs at two levels: first, the consumer can judge from the mere fact that a product is heavily advertised, regardless of the form or content of the advertisements, that that product is likely to be a market-winner. The reason for this is that it would not pay to advertise market-losers. Second, even if the consumer is taken in by the content of the advertisement, and buys the product for that reason, he is not being irrational. For he would have bought the product *anyway*, since the very fact that it is advertised means that it is a good product. As Nelson says:

> It does not pay consumers to make very thoughtful decisions about advertising. They can respond to advertising for the most ridiculous, explicit reasons and still do what they would have done if they had made the most careful judgements about their behaviour. 'Irrationality' is rational if it is cost-free.

Our conclusions concerning the mode of operation of persuasive advertising, however, suggest that Nelson's argument cannot succeed. For the first level to work, it would have to be true that a purchaser of a product can evaluate that product on its own merits, and then decide whether to purchase it again. But, as we have seen, consumers induced to purchase products by persuasive advertising are not buying those products on the basis of a decision founded upon any merit the products happen to have. Thus, if the product turns out to be less good than less heavily advertised alternatives, they will not be disappointed, and will continue to purchase, if subjected to the heavy advertising which induced them to buy in the first place. For this reason, heavy persuasive advertising is not a sign of quality, and the fact that a product is advertised does not suggest that it is good. In fact, if the advertising has little or no informative content, it might suggest just the opposite. If the product has genuine merits, it should be possible to mention them. Persuasive advertising, as the executives on Madison Avenue know, can be used to sell anything, regardless of its nature or quality.

For the second level of Nelson's argument to succeed, and for it to be in the consumer's interest to react even unthinkingly to persuasive advertising, it must be true that the first level is valid. As the first level fails, there is not even a *prima facie* reason for the belief that it is in the interest of the consumer to be subjected to persuasive advertising. In fact, there are two weighty reasons for doubting this belief. The first has already been hinted at: products promoted through persuasive advertising may well not be being sold on their merits, and may, therefore, be bad products, or products that the consumer would not desire on being confronted with unembellished facts about the product. The second is that this form of 'rational irrationality' is anything but cost-free. We consider it a great cost to lose our autonomy. If I were to demonstrate to you conclusively that if I were to take over your life, and make your decisions for you, you would have a life containing far more of whatever you think makes life worth living, apart from autonomy, than if you were to retain control, you would not surrender your autonomy to me even for these great gains in other values. As we mentioned above in our discussion of autonomous desire, we have a strong second-order desire not to act on first-order desires induced in us unawares by others, for no good reason, and now we can see that that desire applies even to cases in which we would *appear* to be better off in acting on such first-order desires.

Thus, we may conclude that Nelson's argument in favour of persuasive advertising is not convincing. I should note, perhaps, that my conclusion concerning persuasive advertising echoes that of Santilli (1983). My argument differs from his, however, in centering upon the notions of autonomy and causes of desires acceptable to the agent, rather than upon the distinction between needs and desires. Santilli claims that the arousal of a desire is not a rational process, unless it is preceded by a knowledge of actual needs. This, I believe, is too strong. I may well have no need of a new tennis-racket, but my desire for one, aroused by informative advertisements in the newspaper, seems rational enough. I would prefer to claim that a desire is autonomous and at least *prima facie* rational if it is not induced in the agent without his knowledge and for no good reason, and allows

ordinary processes of decisionmaking to occur.

Finally, I should point out that, in arguing against all persuasive advertising, unlike Santilli, I am not to be interpreted as bestowing moral respectability upon all informative advertising. Advertisers of any variety ought to consider whether the ideological objections often made to their conduct have any weight. Are they, for instance, imposing a distorted system of values upon consumers, in which the goal of our lives is to consume, and in which success is measured by one's level of consumption? Or are they entrenching attitudes which prolong the position of certain groups subject to discrimination, such as women or homosexuals? Advertisers should also carefully consider whether their product will be of genuine value to any consumers, and, if so, attempt to restrict their campaigns to the groups in society which will benefit (see Durham, 1984). I would claim, for instance, that all advertising of tobacco-based products, even of the informative variety, is wrong, and that some advertisements for alcohol are wrong, in that they are directed at the wrong audience. Imagine, for instance, a liquor-store manager erecting an informative bill-board opposite an alcoholics' rehabilitation centre. But these are secondary questions for prospective advertisers. The primary questions must be whether they are intending to employ the techniques of persuasive advertising, and, if so, how those techniques can be avoided.

ACKNOWLEDGEMENT

I should like to thank Dr. James Griffin for helpful discussion of an earlier draft of this paper.

REFERENCES

Arrington, R.: 1982, 'Advertising and Behaviour Control,' *Journal of Business Ethics* I, 1

Durham, T.: 1984, 'Information, Persuasion, and Control in Moral Appraisal of Advertising Strategy,' *Journal of Business Ethics* III, 3

Nelson, P.: 1978, 'Advertising and Ethics,' in *Ethics, Free Enterprise, and Public Policy,* (eds.) R. De George and J. Pichler, New York: Oxford University Press

Santilli, P.: 1983, 'The Informative and Persuasive Functions of Advertising: A Moral Appraisal,' *Journal of Business Ethics* II, 1.

NO

John O'Toole

THE TROUBLE WITH ADVERTISING

Advertising is an inescapable part of almost everyone's life in America. Thus, almost everyone has an attitude about the subject. And the attitudes, as expressed, seem extremely negative, in terms of both the product and those who produce it.

Back in 1975, Dr. Margaret Mead was quoted in one of our too-numerous trade journals as saying. "The only reason many people are in advertising is because no other business would pay them so much money." She added, "Most advertising people don't believe in the products they advertise or the words they are writing about their clients' products." In *The Lonely Crowd*, sociologist David Riesman writes, "Why, I ask, isn't it possible that advertising as a whole is a fantastic fraud, presenting an image of America taken seriously by no one, least of all by the advertising men who create it?"

According to a survey done in 1978 by Market Facts, Inc. for *Advertising Age* magazine, 43 percent of respondents not involved in advertising chose my craft as the one with "the lowest ethical standards." In 1977, a Gallup poll revealed the relative ranking of 20 occupational groups in terms of honesty and ethical standards. The public rated advertising practitioners 19th, just after labor union leaders and state officeholders. We did, however, beat car salesmen. The same year, a Harris survey asked respondents how much confidence they had in the people who ran various institutions. Ad agencies ranked last. Humorist Kin Hubbard once characterized us this way: "It used to be that a fellow went on the police force when all else failed, but today he goes into the advertising game."

Now, I am no more insensitive to boors, scam artists, dolts and loudmouths than the next person. And over something more than a quarter of a century in advertising, though I've encountered a few of each, I've not noticed a disproportionate representation in my craft—certainly no more than among the lawyers, doctors, journalists, accountants, academicians, clergymen, clerks, civil servants and businessmen I've met.

* * *

Why do people feel that way about us? Was it something we said? Where do these staunchly held and mainly negative impressions come from? Well, a book entitled *The Hucksters* made a mighty contribution. It was published in 1946 by Frederick Wakeman, who, I'm grieved to admit, worked for the same agency I work for now (but so did Alan Jay Lerner, whose lyrics for *Camelot* provided a cheerier type of fantasy).

The Hucksters depicted ad people as fast-talking, double-dealing, hard-drinking scoundrels who yielded every ethical point to unscrupulous clients. It would probably have faded away on the remainder shelves had it not been made into a movie starring Clark Gable. The film was a hit and reappears to this day, like a spirit that cannot find eternal rest, on late-night television. Subsequent movies developed the stereotype into a character as morally impoverished as those in *The Hucksters* but far less acute. The adman became an exploitable hustler who was usually played by Jack Lemmon. With a few refinements, this persona surfaced as second banana in the television series *Bewitched*, in which Dick York added the further dimension of ineptitude.

Then, of course, self-destructive and self-serving advertising people contributed their share to what they perceived as an increasingly popular myth. Autobiographical books detailing the zany goings-on inside advertising agencies "where anything can happen and usually does" began to proliferate. Most bore the same relationship to advertising as *Dr. Doolittle* does to zoology, but the public loved them because they amused and didn't challenge the mind by questioning the stereotype. Foremost among these was *From Those Wonderful Folks Who Brought You Pearl Harbor* by Jerry della Femina. Jerry works hard at being an enfant terrible and masking the fact that he's a serious advertising practitioner. He succeeded at both in his book.

All of this has shaped the impressions people have of those of us in advertising. But it's not the whole story. There have been novels and TV programs and films aplenty about corrupt congressmen, venal businessmen and crooked lawyers, yet members of those occupations can attend cocktail parties relatively unassailed. The reason is that their activities affect most people indirectly or through third parties. At least the products of their efforts are less proximate, less numerous and less ubiquitous than is advertising.

Attitudes about advertising, which color attitudes about those who practice it, are obviously a concern to me. Because of the importance of advertising to a system that produces a lot of good living and good jobs for a lot of good people, it's worth looking into what those attitudes are, what has caused them, who is at fault, and what can be done about it.

In the first instance, it's important to separate public attitudes—those measured by polling a sample of citizens representing all of us—from the attitudes of specialized publics: educators, journalists, consumer advocates and government. Each of the latter influence public opinion to some extent and should be looked at in terms of how and how much.

Whatever the influences, public attitudes toward advertising do not bring cheer to the heart of one who makes his living at it. A 1980 study by Yankelovich, Skelly & White reported that 70 percent of the American population was concerned with truth, distortion and exaggeration in advertising. A 1979 Louis Harris poll showed 81 percent feeling that "the claims for most products advertised on TV are exaggerated," and 52 percent saying that most or all TV advertising is "seriously misleading."

A survey conducted by my own company in 1977 found 36 percent of the national sample objecting to most TV advertising; the adjectives chosen most frequently were "dumb" and "juvenile." A 1974 study done by our industry association indicated that 59 percent of the respondents believed "most advertising insults the intelligence of the average consumer." It's interesting to note, however, that in the same study 88 percent said that advertising is essential and 57 percent that advertising results in better products.

The professional critics come at us from a somewhat different direction. Since there are few more professional or critical than John Kenneth Galbraith, let us begin with him. In *The New Industrial State*, Galbraith says, "In everyday parlance, this great machine, and the demanding and varied talents that it employs are said to be engaged in selling goods. In less ambiguous language, it means that it is engaged in the management of those who buy goods." Similarly, in his book *The Sponsor: Notes on a Modern Potentate*, Columbia University professor Erik Barnouw defines television advertising as "selling the unnecessary."

Philip Slater writes, in *The Pursuit of Loneliness*, "If we define pornography as any message from any communication medium that is intended to arouse sexual excitement, then it is clear that most advertisements are covertly pornographic." Novelist Mary McCarthy attacks us thusly in *On the Contrary*: "The thing, however, that repels us in these advertisements is their naive falsity to life. Who are these advertising men kidding? ... Between the tired, sad, gentle faces of the subway riders and the grin-ning Holy Families of the Ad-Mass, there exists no possibility of even a wishful identification." I could go on and on were it not for a narrow threshold for self-inflicted pain. I'll conclude with a definition of advertising by Fred Allen: "85 percent confusion and 15 percent commission."

The criticisms leveled against advertising by the general public are clearly of a different nature from those of the specialized groups. The people are faulting advertising on what it's doing wrong or what it's not doing well enough or what it's doing too much of. The specialists are criticizing advertising on the basis of a totally different set of standards. The distinction is important because it explains why the advertising industry often responds so ineptly to its professional critics. It's hard to come up with answers when you not only don't understand the question but can't conceive why anyone would ask it.

The fact is that academicians, journalists, consumer advocates and government regulators criticize—and dislike—advertising because it isn't something else.

It accomplishes little to carry on about automobiles because they weren't made to fly or to reproach dogs because they don't climb trees. It is not in the nature of dogs to do what cats do, nor were the evolutionary forces that produced them guided by any imperative to develop that capacity. By the same token, it accomplishes little to condemn advertising because it isn't journalism or education or entertainment. It is fruitless to hold that advertising should be hidden, since it is not advertising if it's not seen. And it is witless to excoriate advertising for having arcane powers to brainwash or to make people act against their will when it clearly wouldn't and couldn't function as advertising if it did.

Yet such charges form the case made against advertising by many professional critics. Before I answer them, it's important for all of us to understand what advertising actually *is*. Only then can we put aside criticism based on what it isn't and get down to the positive challenge of making it better.

Archeologists have discovered evidence of some kind of advertising among the artifacts of every civilization that communicated by writing. The moment one man began growing or raising more than he needed and saw the opportunity to have what someone else was producing, the concept of bartering was born. Now, the only way to extend bartering beyond the chance encounter of two individuals with corresponding needs and surpluses was for each to post what he had and what he wanted in a public place where many could learn about it. The introduction of currency simplified the process by allowing people to post only what they were offering.

This "poster" concept dominated advertising for millennia. Its elements were the item or service offered, the name and location of the offerer, and sometimes the price. Often the most gifted artists of the era were employed to visualize for the prospect what he would receive for his money. Toulouse-Lautrec was one, and the graphics he created to lure customers into the Moulin Rouge now hang in the great art museums of the world.

Such embellishments brought a new dimension of creativity to the simple exposition of product, seller and price but did not change the basic approach; the poster remained the principal form of advertising until relatively recent years. As newspapers and magazines appeared,

the poster concept was transferred to paid space in their pages. Early advertising agencies did little to advance the craft and develop its potential, for they had been formed essentially as brokers of space. They bought advertising space in quantity from newspapers and magazines at a 15 percent discount, then sold it to advertisers at full price. To justify this "commission," they counseled their clients on what to put in that space. But such advice was a relatively simple sideline to the space-brokering function since the poster concept more or less limited the information to product, seller and price.

In fact, in the early 1900s, the generally accepted definition of advertising was the one coined by the leading agency of the time (still in business today), N. W. Ayer. Ayer said advertising was "keeping your name before the public." But all that was to change with the new century. As a result of two men meeting in Chicago, the real energy of advertising was unlocked, its enormous potential tapped, and its true nature revealed.

One spring afternoon in 1904, in an office building at Wabash and Randolph Streets that was eventually replaced by Marshall Field's department store, two men were chatting. One was Ambrose Thomas, one of the founders of the Lord & Thomas advertising agency. The other was a bright young man named Albert Lasker, who, it was already apparent, would soon be running the agency.

Following a polite knock, an office boy came in with a note and handed it to Thomas. Upon reading it, Thomas snorted and gave it to Lasker. The note said: "I am downstairs in the saloon, and I can tell you what advertising is. I know that you don't know. It will mean much to me to have you know what it is and it will mean much to you. If you wish to know what advertising is, send the word 'yes' down by messenger." It was signed by a John E. Kennedy.

Thomas asked Lasker if he had ever heard of the man, and when Lasker said he hadn't, Thomas decided Kennedy was probably mad and wasn't worth wasting time on. But Lasker, who was dissatisfied with the concept of "keeping your name before the public," was willing to take a chance. He sent down for Kennedy, and the two spent an hour in Lasker's office. Then they headed for the saloon downstairs, not to emerge until midnight.

Kennedy was a former Royal Canadian Mounted Policeman, a dashing, mustachioed chap who in 1904 was employed as a copywriter for an elixir known as Dr. Shoop's Restorative. What he said to Lasker that day resulted in his being hired on the spot for the unheard-of salary of $28,000 a year. Within 24 months, he was making $75,000.

What did he say to Lasker? Simply this: "Advertising is salesmanship in print."

It seems so simple and obvious today. But what this definition did in 1904 was to change the course of advertising completely and make possible the enormous role it now plays in our economy. For, by equating the function of an advertisement with the function of a salesman who calls on a prospect personally, it revealed the true nature of advertising.

For the first time, the concept of persuasion, which is the prime role of a salesman, was applied to the creation of advertising. Information was considered in a new light, since information is what a salesman must be equipped with and what he uses to persuade. An ad was seen as a means of conveying the personality of the advertiser, just as a good salesman reflects the standards of his company. Reason and logic became part of advertising planning. And so, for the first time, did the consumer.

With its possibilities revealed, advertising exploded. Now it could be refined, made more effective and applied to new tasks. Agencies proliferated, and those that understood the new definition flourished. None flourished more than Lord & Thomas, the birthplace of the revolution. Under Albert Lasker's leadership it became the biggest, most successful agency of its time.

* * *

Advertising, then, is salesmanship functioning in the paid space and time of mass media. To criticize it for being that, for being true to its nature, is to question whether it should be permitted—a position taken by only the most rabid, none of whom have come up with a reasonable substitute for its role in the economy. And to criticize it for not being something else—something it might resemble but by definition can never be—is equally fruitless. Yet much of the professional criticism I spoke of has its feet planted solidly on those two pieces of shaky ground.

As a format of conveying information, advertising shares certain characteristics with journalism, education, entertainment and other modes of communication. But it cannot be judged by the same standards because it is essentially something else. This point is missed by many in government, both the regulators and the elected representatives who oversee the regulators.

The Federal Trade Commission was pushing not too long ago for one of those quasi-laws they call a Trade Regulation Ruling (when they were empowered to write the law of the land, I don't know; but that's another argument). This particular TRR would have required an ad or commercial for any product claiming to be nutritious to list all its nutritive elements. For two reasons advertising cannot comply with such a requirement and still end up as advertising.

One, advertising is salesmanship, and good salesmanship does not countenance boring the prospect into glassy-eyed semiconsciousness. Yet I am sure—and consumers on whom sample ads and commercials were tested agreed—that a lengthy litany of niacin, riboflavin, ascorbic acid and so on is as interesting as watching paint dry.

Less subjective is the fact that such a listing can't be given for many good, wholesome products within the confines of a 30-second commercial. Since that's the standard length today, the end result of the proposed TRR would have been to ban those products from television advertising. The FTC staff did not consider that advertising necessarily functions in the paid space and time of mass media. Adding 20 or more seconds of Latin makes that impossible.

This example illustrates the problems that can arise when regulators try to dictate what must go into advertising. An FTC attorney named Donald F. Turner was quoted by Professor Raymond Bauer in a piece for the *Harvard Business Review* as saying, "There are three steps to informed choice. (1) The consumer must know the product exists. (2) The consumer must know how the product performs. (3) He must know how it performs compared to other products. If advertising only performs step one and appeals on other than a performance basis, informed choice cannot be made."

This is probably true in an ad for a new floor wax from S. C. Johnson or an antiperspirant from Bristol-Myers. But what about a new fragrance from Max Factor? How do you describe how Halston performs compared with other products? Is it important for anyone to know? Is it salesmanship to make the attempt? Or suppose you're advertising Coca-Cola. There can't be many people left in the world who don't know Coke exists or how it performs. Granted, there may be a few monks or aborigines who don't know how it performs in relation to other products, but you can't reach them through advertising. So why waste the time or space?

The reason Coca-Cola advertises is to maintain or increase a level of awareness about itself among people who know full well it exists and what it tastes like, people whom other beverage makers are contacting with similar messages about their products. Simple information about its existence and its popularity—information that triggers residual knowledge in the recipient about its taste and other characteristics—is legitimate and sufficient. It does what a salesman would do.

On the other hand, advertising for a big-ticket item—an automobile, for instance—would seemingly have to include a lot of information in order to achieve its end. But the advertising is not attempting to sell the car. It is an advance salesman trying to persuade the prospect to visit a showroom. Only there can the principal salesman do the complete job. Turner's definition is neither pertinent nor possible in the case of automobiles. In such cases mass communications media cannot convey the kind of information one needs in order to "know how the product performs" or to "know how it performs compared to other products." You have to see it, kick the tires, ask the salesman questions about it, let the kids try out the windshield wipers. And surely you have to drive it.

In the paid space and time of mass media, the purpose of automobile advertising is to select the prospect for a particular car and, on the basis of its appeal to his income, life-style or basic attitudes, to persuade him he's the person the designers and engineers had in mind when they created this model. If the information is properly chosen and skillfully presented, it will point out the relevance of the car to his needs and self-image sufficiently to get him into the showroom. Then it's up to the salesman to sell him the car—but with a different package of information, including the tactile and experiential, than could be provided in the ad.

From time to time some government regulator will suggest that advertising information should be limited to price and function. But consider how paleolithic that kind of thinking is. Restricting advertising to a discussion of price and function would eliminate, among other things, an equally essential piece of information: what kind of people make and market this product or provide this service.

The reputation, quality standards, taste and responsibility of the people who put out a product is information that's not only important to the consumer but is increasingly demanded by the consumer. It's information that can often outweigh price and function as these differences narrow among products within the same category. It's information that is critical to the advertising my agency prepares for clients like Johnson's Wax, Sunkist Growers, Hallmark, Sears and many others. Advertising would not be salesmanship without it. Put it this way: if surgeons advertised and you had

a hot appendix, would you want the ads to be limited to price and function information?

The government regulators, and the consumer advocates dedicated to influencing them, do not understand what advertising is and how it is perceived by the consumer. And their overwhelming fear that one is always trying to deceive the other leads them to demand from advertising the kind of product information that characterizes *Consumer Reports*. They expect advertising to be journalism, and they evaluate it by journalistic standards. Since it is not, advertising, like the ugly duckling, is found wanting.

* * *

It is not in the nature of advertising to be journalistic, to present both sides, to include information that shows the product negatively in comparison with other entries in the category (unless, of course, the exclusion of such information would make the ad misleading or product usage hazardous). For example, advertising for Sunkist lemons, which might point out the flavor advantages of fresh lemons over bottled juice, should not be expected to remind people that fresh lemons can't be kept as long as a bottle of concentrate. Information is selected for journalism—or should be— to provide the recipient with as complete and objective an account as possible. Information is selected for advertising to persuade the recipient to go to a showroom or make a mental pledge to find the product on a store shelf.

Advertising, like the personal salesman, unabashedly presents products in their most favorable light. I doubt that there's a consumer around who doesn't understand that. For instance, would you, in a classified ad offering your house for sale, mention the toilet on the second floor that doesn't flush? I doubt that even a conscience as rigorous as Ralph Nader's would insist, in an ad to sell his own used car, on information about that worn fan belt or leaky gasket. No reader would expect it. Nor does anyone expect it from our clients.

Information, as far as advertising is concerned, is anything that helps a genuine prospect to perceive the applicability of a product to his or her individual life, to understand how the product will solve a problem, make life easier or better, or in some way provide a benefit. When the knowledge can't safely be assumed, it also explains how to get the product. In other words, it's salesmanship.

It is not witchcraft, another craft government regulators and otherwise responsible writers are forever confusing with mine. For the same reasons people like to believe that someone is poisoning our water supply or, as in the Joseph McCarthy era, that pinkos proliferate in our government and are trying to bring it down, someone is always rejuvenating the idea of subliminal advertising.

Subliminal advertising is defined as advertising that employs stimuli operating below the threshold of consciousness. It is supposed to influence the recipient's behavior without his being aware of any communication taking place. The most frequently cited example, never fully verified, involved a movie theater where the words "Drink Coke" were flashed on the screen so briefly that while the mind recorded the message, it was not conscious of receiving it. The result was said to be greatly increased sales of Coca-Cola at the vending counter.

I don't like to destroy cherished illusions, but I must state unequivocally that there is no such thing as subliminal advertising. I have never seen an example of it, nor have I ever heard it seriously discussed as a technique by advertising people. Salesmanship is persuasion involving rational and emotional tools that must be employed on a conscious level in order to effect a conscious decision in favor of one product over its competitive counterparts, and in order to have that decision remembered and acted upon at a later time. Furthermore, it's demeaning to assume that the human mind is so easily controlled that anyone can be made to act against his will or better judgment by peremptory commands he doesn't realize are present.

Even more absurd is the theory proposed by Wilson Bryan Key in a sleazy book entitled *Subliminal Seduction*. From whatever dark motivations, Key finds sexual symbolism in every ad and commercial. He points it out to his readers with no little relish, explaining how, after reducing the prospect to a pliant mass of sexual arousal, advertising can get him to buy anything. There are some who might envy Mr. Key his ability to get turned on by a photograph of a Sunkist orange.

Most professional critics are much less bizarre in their condemnations. Uninformed about the real nature of advertising, perhaps, but not mad. For instance, they often ascribe recondite powers to advertising—powers that it does not have and that they cannot adequately define—because it is not solely verbal. Being for the most part lawyers and academics, they are uncomfortable with information conveyed by means other than words. They want things spelled out, even in television commercials, despite the fact that television is primarily a visual medium. They do not trust graphic and musical information because they aren't sure that the meaning they receive is the same one the consumer is receiving. And since they consider the consumer much more gullible and much less astute than they, they sound the alarm and then charge to the rescue. Sorcery is afoot.

Well, from time immemorial, graphics and music have been with us. I suspect each has been part of the salesman's tool kit for as long as they have been salesmen. The songs of medieval street vendors and Toulouse-Lautrec's Jane Avril attest.

A mouth-watering cake presented photographically as the end benefit of Betty Crocker Cake Mix is just as legitimate as and more effective than a verbal description. The mysteriously exuberant musical communication "I Love New York" honestly conveys the variety of experiences offered by New York State; it is not witchcraft. It is not to be feared unless you fear yourself. But perhaps that is the cradle that spawns consumer advocates and government regulators. There is something murky in that psyche, some kink in the mentality of those who feel others are incapable of making mundane decisions for themselves, something Kafka-like in the need to take over the personal lives of Americans in order to protect them from themselves.

I read with growing disquiet a document put out by the Federal Trade Commission in 1979 entitled *Consumer Information Remedies*. In discussing how to evaluate consumer information, they wrote, "The Task Force members struggled long and hard to come up with a universally satisfactory definition of the *value* of consumer information. Should the Commission consider a mandatory disclosure to be a valuable piece of information, for instance, if it were later shown that although consumers understood the information, they did not use it when making purchase decisions? Is there a value in improving the *quality* of market decisions through the provision of relevant information, or is it necessary for the information to change behavior to have value?" The ensuing "remedies" make it clear that the staff really judges the value of a mandatory disclaimer by the degree to which it changes consumer behavior in the direction they are seeking.

But wait a minute. I'm a consumer, too. Who are they to be wondering what to do with me next if I understand but choose to ignore some dumb disclaimer they've forced an advertiser to put in his ad? It's my God-given right to ignore any information any salesman presents me with—and an ad, remember, is a salesman. And what's this about changing behavior? Well, mine is going to change if the employees of a government I'm paying for start talking like that out loud. It's going to get violent.

Later in the same document, the staff addresses "Sub-Optional Purchases." While I have no quarrel with their intent, I find my hackles rising as they define the problem in terms of people "misallocating resources," consumers wasting their dollars on "products that do not best satisfy their needs." Listen, fellows, those are *my* resources you're talking about. Those are *my* dollars, what there is of them after you guys in Washington have had your way with my paycheck. I'm going to allocate them as I damn well please. And if I want to waste a few on products that do not best satisfy my needs—an unnutritious but thoroughly delicious hot dog at the ball park, for example—try to stop me.

Perhaps I, in return, am seeking evidence of conspiracy. Perhaps I'm looking under beds. But I think I understand the true nature of government bureaucrats. They, on the other hand, do not understand that of advertising. They and other professional critics—the journalists, consumerists, academicians—don't understand that it's not journalism or education and cannot be judged on the basis of objectivity and exhaustive, in-depth treatment. Thorough knowledge of a subject cannot be derived from an advertisement but only from a synthesis of all relevant sources: the advertising of competitors, the opinions of others, the more impartial reports in newspapers, magazines and, increasingly, television.

The critics also don't understand that advertising isn't witchcraft, that it cannot wash the brain or coerce someone to buy what he doesn't want. It shouldn't be castigated for what it cannot and does not purport to do. And it isn't entertainment, either. A commercial should offer some reward to the viewer in return for his time, but that reward need not always take the form of entertainment. Sometimes the tone should be serious, even about seemingly frivolous subjects. Hemorrhoids are not funny to those who have them.

Advertising sometimes resembles other fields, just as an elephant resembles a snake to the blind man who feels its trunk, and a tree to another who feels its leg. But advertising is really salesmanship functioning in the paid space and time of mass media.

POSTSCRIPT

Is Advertising Fundamentally Deceptive?

The issue in advertising comes down to social expectation. If advertising is a gentle put-on that is expected and appreciated by all, a way of displaying a product for sale that might persuade a customer to try it once, and no more than that, then surely it is a harmless addition to the pages and airwaves of our experience. Advertising can be uplifting, appealing, funny, and even beautiful. If advertising remains only in the inessential margins of our lives, it can do no real harm. The manufacturer of the advertised product obtains value from having people try his product just once, and from that value comes the justification to hire the advertising firm and to place the messages in print or on the air. This placement in turn funds the magazines and the entertainment of radio and television, and it therefore brings otherwise unobtainable value to our lives. There seems to be no moral percentage in insisting on the strict theoretical line, that if advertising in any way influences you to spend a penny on anything that you would not have bought if not for the advertising, then it is manipulative and wrong.

But what if it is *not* at the margins of our lives? Those who take advertising more seriously hold that the practice is wrong because it distorts our perception of what is socially valuable and of what is personally redeeming.

The first line of attack on the advertising industry was developed originally by economist John Kenneth Galbraith in *The Affluent Society*. Galbraith was interested not so much in the decision to buy one good rather than another in the market but the decision to allot funds to the private rather than to the public sector. The decision to vote for or against taxes to buy public goods, after all, is an economic decision. Galbraith argued that since only private firms purchase advertising space and time, advertising distorts the normal decision-making process of a society in favor of the purchase of private goods (cars, swimming pools, and video games, for example) and against the selection of public goods (such as clean air, better roads, and pleasant parks), thus systematically starving the public sector in favor of the private. For Galbraith, then, advertising is not only a nuisance but a seriously unethical strategy to funnel the national wealth into the hands of the industrialists and away from public needs.

The second line of reasoning notes the psychological targets of typical advertising. People are weak, vulnerable, and plagued, on occasion, by feelings of inadequacy and social inferiority. These feelings are not at all marginal but go to the core of the social creatures that we are. They are painful, and we are grateful for relief. Advertising learns to ask questions that expose our vulnerabilities and then answers the questions with products that explicitly promise to strengthen us at those weak points. The deception of advertising is not in the lies that the advertisers tell but in the implication that there are products that can remedy the fear and imperfections of the human condition itself. As such, advertising is doubly harmful: it leads us to believe falsehoods about what will and will not make us smarter, more popular, thinner, more attractive to the opposite sex, and in all other ways the better social person many of us would like to be. More important, it portrays the weakness of human nature only as a deplorable and shameful condition, not to be acknowledged or faced in company with others who share it but to be quickly remedied before others notice. Fortunately, the advertising says, the remedy for human inadequacies, in the form of the advertised product, is at hand. If you cannot or do not purchase it, you have only yourself to blame for your continuing social failures.

In this manner, critics argue, humans are stripped of the real means to help them cope with their weaknesses—the support of other humans with similar weaknesses. Instead, they are isolated in their feelings of inadequacy and left with a false remedy that can never do what it so glowingly promises to do. When the false remedy is only a perfume that promises to make you fantastically attractive, one may still argue that no *real* harm is done and that you really do enjoy the fantasy. But when the false remedy is a cigarette that purports to turn you into a strong and self-sufficient cowboy, then the purveyance of images and the law and practices that condone it begin to appear harmful.

Is advertising a fraud and a deception, the more fraudulent advertising being the more successful, or is advertising a harmless practice of American business, helping the economy by keeping goods, especially new goods, flowing?

SUGGESTED READINGS

Robert L. Arrington, "Advertising and Behavior Control," *Journal of Business Ethics* (1981).

Sissela Bok, *Lying: Moral Choice in Public and Private Life* (Pantheon Books, 1978).

William A. Cook, "Truth, in the Eye of the Beholder?" *Journal of Advertising Research* (December 1991).

John Fraedrich, O. C. Ferrell, and William Pride, "An Empirical Examination of Three Machiavellian Concepts: Advertisers vs. The General Public," *Journal of Business Ethics* (September 1989).

John Kenneth Galbraith, *The Affluent Society*, 3rd ed. (Houghton Mifflin, 1976).

Jonathan Karl, "Lotto Baloney," *The New Republic* (March 4, 1991).

Barbara J. Phillips, "In Defense of Advertising: A Social Perspective," *Journal of Business Ethics* (February 1997).

ISSUE 13

Should Tobacco Advertising Be Banned?

YES: Mark Green, from "Luring Kids to Light Up," *Business and Society Review* (Spring 1990)

NO: John C. Luik, from "Tobacco Advertising Bans and the Dark Face of Government Paternalism," *International Journal of Advertising* (vol. 12, 1993)

ISSUE SUMMARY

YES: Mark Green, commissioner of Consumer Affairs in New York City, attacks a popular cigarette advertising campaign that seems to be aimed directly at children and claims that such unconscionable methods of advertising should be prevented.

NO: Professor of philosophy John C. Luik argues that restricting the freedom of commercial speech cannot be justified unless it is shown to be absolutely necessary to avoid certain harm, which has not been done in the case of tobacco advertising.

The quarrel here is specifically about tobacco advertising. Some background on the product is necessary to understand the problem with marketing it.

First, there is a good amount of evidence that smoking tobacco is hazardous to one's health. Wherever tobacco is consumed, mortality and morbidity rates go up in direct proportion to the amount of tobacco consumed, especially when the tobacco is smoked. Smoking cigarettes is the most common form of tobacco use.

Second, curbing the tobacco industry is, economically, very serious business. It is a multibillion-dollar industry that employs tens of thousands. It builds and finances schools, churches, state governments, and regional economies. It was America's first export product, and it remains one of the best. The market for tobacco is still growing all over the world, and the export of tobacco might be one of the most hopeful ways to reduce the U.S. trade deficit.

Third, there is no compulsion to smoke cigarettes and lots of encouragement not to smoke them. Yet, people do choose to smoke all the same. Setting aside the claim that just being in the same room with a smoker can harm nonsmokers, people should have a right to make decisions about their own health. The issue, as John C. Luik sees it, is that banning tobacco advertising would represent an erosion of citizen autonomy, or the basic freedom of American people to make their own choices with respect to their own lives.

The dilemma here begins before the first ad hits the page: There is reason to believe that certain sorts of behavior are harmful to those who engage in them. In the normal exercise of the police power of the state, we could try to make sure that people do not indulge in that behavior, either by educating the people to avoid it, by quietly abolishing the purveyors of the means to engage in it, or both. But some people will not abstain, and the tobacco industry is too big and economically important to be shut down without a very clear consensus that it should be done.

In this situation, the proposal to ban the advertising of tobacco from all media (it has already been banned from radio and television) has certain attractions. First, to underscore Mark Green's point, it would end the exposure of young people to the traditional images of sophistication and worldliness that go with smoking. This would strengthen the claims of the tobacco industry that they are not trying to lure new smokers into the habit but are only trying to communicate product information to those who are already smokers. Since the major function of advertising is to persuade a nonuser to try the product once, there is no reason to advertise tobacco. If smokers wish to receive product information, they can sign up to receive it. It is not clear, however, that there is any sense in which smokers need such information.

On the positive side, banning advertising would leave the industry alone to make money abroad. There are signs that it will continue to do this well. At present, American cigarettes are being sold and promoted abroad; America is encouraging farmers in the less developed countries to grow tobacco and sending agronomists to teach them how to do it. There seems to be no problem with receptivity in these countries: Farmers enjoy growing a high-income crop; governments enjoy the taxes collected both on cigarette sales and on the income from the tobacco crops; and the tobacco customers of the developing countries, a large and growing population, enjoy having available to them products of a higher quality than their indigenous industry could provide. Whether or not Americans have a right to take advantage of that receptivity for their own profit is another question—one that is closely related to the question of whether or not they have the right to take advantage of that receptivity at home.

As you read the following selections by Green and Luik, ask yourself what weight should be given to human freedom and what weight should be given to human welfare. In general, what is the responsibility of business in this dilemma? To serve customers what they want until the law tells it not to? Or to take a proactive stance and arrange business dealings so as to do the least harm and promote the most good for those affected by such dealings?

YES

Mark Green

LURING KIDS TO LIGHT UP

Earlier this year, Mark Green, the New York City Commissioner of Consumer Affairs, wrote the following letter to Louis V. Gerstner, Jr., the chairman and chief executive officer of RJR Nabisco. The letter appeals to the tobacco manufacturer to end its current Camel cigarette advertising campaign, which Green views as a thinly veiled attempt to lure children to start smoking.

As the father of two young children and the new Commissioner of Consumer Affairs, I am appalled at your "Smooth Character" Camel advertising campaign which risks addicting children to cigarettes.

I first noticed the prevalence and pitch of your ads in mid-January. On one day, I saw a Smooth Character poster when I bought a paper in the morning at the 86th Street and York Avenue newsstand, then another on the crosstown bus ("Un Tipo Suave," it read in Spanish), and yet another on the Lexington Avenue subway en route to work. Finally, later that day, I came across your huge, pull-out poster "suitable for framing" in *Rolling Stone*, along with language urging readers to send away for any of eight colorful posters. The posters involve cartoon characters such as your "Old Joe" camel and comely women, along with symbols one needn't be Freud to understand.

WHERE THERE'S SMOKE

However, it wasn't until I spotted the perforated fold at the bottom of the *Rolling Stone* poster, which allows readers to delete the congressionally mandated warning label, that I decided to write you to ask this question: Isn't this ad campaign an obvious attempt to lure children into smoking in violation of the tobacco industry's own 1964 code against advertising directed at children?

True, the *Rolling Stone* ad does say in extremely small print that a person sending in a coupon for posters is supposed to "certify that I am a smoker 21 years of age or older." On the other hand:

• Who puts posters up on their walls—kids or adults?

- Who watches and talks about cartoon characters—kids or adults?
- Who is impressionable enough to associate smoking with success and sex —kids or adults?
- Why do these advertisements run in magazines such as *Rolling Stone, National Lampoon,* and *Movies, U.S.A.,* which have so many teenage readers? (*Movies, U.S.A.* says its target is "a captive audience of one million moviegoers" who are, in its words, "youthful and image-conscious.")
- Was *Advertising Age* correct when it said on July 11, 1988, that "R. J. Reynolds is updating its Camel and Salem advertising to lure younger voters away from Marlboro country?"
- Why don't any of the posters one can order by mail have warning labels on them?

You know the adage that if something walks like a duck and quacks like a duck... it's a duck. Based on the most obvious circumstantial evidence, RJR's campaign is not a duck but a camel aimed directly at the health of our children. It was just such concerns that prompted the authors of *Barbarians at the Gate* to write of Theodore Forstmann, one of RJR's suitors, "Debating future demand in the teen market made him feel like a drug pusher."

Already, children in 1990 America live under multiple threats: One in five lives in poverty, the worst rate in the industrial West; more than a third in our city schools drop out before senior year; the United States has the highest rate of teenage pregnancy and one of the lowest investments in primary education among industrial nations; one-parent and no-parent families are on the rise, especially in minority areas. For those and other reasons, New York City Mayor David Dinkins made the welfare of children his top priority in his Inaugural Address last month. And today, at my swearing-in, I followed suit and pledged to focus on children as consumers.

UNCONSCIONABLE CAMEL?

At the same time, tobacco is not just another product. It is the number-one preventable cause of death and disease in America and the only product that causes disease and death in its normal use. The Surgeon General estimates that smoking causes nearly 400,000 premature deaths annually—or fifty times more than those who die from drug abuse; the Federal Office on Smoking and Health concluded in 1987 that smoking contributed to 16 percent of all deaths (heart disease, lung cancer, emphysema, etc.), including more than 2,500 deaths of infants attributed to smoking by the mother. And, of course, smoking is a very powerful addiction, as much so as alcohol and drugs. Indeed, even after undergoing heart and lung surgery, half of all smokers still continue their habit.

Consequently, the goal of public officials concerned with already imperiled children must be to discourage them from smoking in the first place. Some 80 percent of all adults who smoke began before or during their teen years; 50 percent of all smokers first lit up by age 13, and 25 percent by 11. Smoking can also be a "gateway" to illegal drugs: "Virtually all children involved in hard drug use," concluded Sen. Edward Kennedy (D-Mass.), "began with cigarettes." So if we can keep our teenagers tobacco-free, they will live longer, healthier lives.

Which brings me back to your Smooth Character advertising campaign. I am writing you as my first official act because there are few if any marketplace abuses worse than inducing children to smoke, and RJR's ads appear to be inherently misleading, if not unconscionable.

They're potentially misleading because their images convey that smoking a Camel leads to social success and happiness, not to disease and death. And in our MTV era, many kids get more information from images than words. It is very hard to square your ads with the *Tobacco Industry's Principles Covering Cigarette Advertising and Sampling*'s provision that "Cigarette advertising shall not suggest that smoking is essential to social prominence, distinction, success, or sexual attraction."

The ads are potentially unconscionable because they appear to be targeted to unsophisticated minors who feel immortal and are uniquely subject to peer pressure—and who may, as a result, get addicted for life, a shortened life at that. For example, 35 percent of high school seniors don't think that smoking a pack a day causes serious harm. And while 95 percent of high school smokers believe they will later stop smoking, eight years later only 25 percent of them have.

INDUSTRY ARGUMENTS

In reviewing the literature in your industry, I find that tobacco spokespeople make at least four arguments to frustrate government actions designed to reduce these health hazards—namely, paternalism, censorship, preemption, and advertising.

Legislation to restrict or even ban cigarette advertising, for example, is attacked as "paternalism" and "censorship." Of course, the Latin origin of paternalism is "pater," meaning like a fa-

ther. But what's wrong with acting like a parent when government tries to protect children from harm?

As for censorship, there is no First Amendment right to sell or advertise a dangerous product, as four Supreme Court decisions over a half century make clear. Unlike political speech, commercial speech can be regulated, which is precisely what our consumer protection law does when it forbids false or misleading advertising. In any event, the worst censorship of all is a product that censors life itself.

Periodically, when local officials such as myself attempt to reduce this health hazard, industry holds up federal law as a bar. But the preemption clause that is cited applies to local attempts to add to the Federal Trade Commission's warning label, not to actions against, for example, misleading ads or unconscionable trade practices. Also, it's getting harder to maintain the fiction that warning labels on cigarette packs are sufficient disclosure when the FTC has twice described (in 1969 and 1981) the warning's "futility," when it doesn't even use provable words like "addiction," or "death," and when it is all but invisible on billboards, including your famous one in Times Square. Or, as satirist Calvin Trillin has written, "Anyone who wants to see that warning would have to have the sort of long-range vision usually associated with the pilot of an F-14."

Last, industry leaders argue that the $2.6–billion-plus spent on cigarette ads and other promotions—or $9 for every man, woman and child—doesn't persuade anyone to smoke. At best, it is said, these ads only influence a small percentage of existing smokers to switch among brands. Whether you personally believe this thesis or not, surely Madison Avenue doesn't.

Advertising experts agree that market expansion, especially for an industry that loses over 2 million consumers a year who die or quit, is an important objective of nearly all advertising. Emerson Foote, former chairman of McCann-Erickson, one of the world's largest advertising agencies, once remarked that "I am always amused by the suggestion that advertising, a function that has been shown to increase consumption of virtually every other product, somehow miraculously fails to work for tobacco products." Foote's view is seconded by advertising executive Charles Sharp, a former vice president of Ogilvy & Mather: "By depicting a product as an integral part of a highly desirable life-style and personal image, in addition to current users, an advertiser can attract individuals who do not currently use that product but who want to emulate that life-style [and] want to be like the people in the ads."

SIX QUESTIONS

Your industry finds itself in the ironic position of killing off your own consumers. A thousand times a day, or forty times an hour, there's a funeral and grieving because someone was addicted to smoking. If the public were told that a new product society could live without had killed forty people a year, there would be outrage and probably a legislative prohibition. Companies talking about their First Amendment right to sell such a product would be laughed out of court or Congress. Yet cigarettes kill not forty people a year but an hour.

A group of tobacco executives who have previously told us that smoking is not dangerous now tells us that

---

AD INDUSTRY FIDDLES WHILE AMERICA BURNS

There are nearly a dozen bills before Congress to restrict print advertising for tobacco products. As the pols in the smoke-free backrooms of Washington contemplate such legislation, not only the cigarette industry is worried.

The Leadership Council on Advertising, an advertising industry lobbying group, estimates that more than 4,000 jobs would be lost and 165 periodicals would fold if tobacco advertising were banned. This study, as reported in *Publishing News*, is "designed to diffuse some of the anti-tobacco din around the halls of Congress."

Of course, 4,000 jobs are about 1 percent of the number of people who die prematurely each year from diseases caused by smoking. And the study apparently does not account for the potential success of the legislation's goal: to reduce the number of smokers. If an ad ban were to work, people might live longer and, thus, buy and read more magazines. Up to 400,000 people is one heck of an untapped market.

$2.6 billion in advertising and promotion doesn't increase smoking and that cartoon posters that appeal to children weren't intended for children. Frankly, that insults our intelligence and injures the most vulnerable among us. And it makes my job as a parent that much harder.

Consequently, I'd like to solicit your responses to six questions, while preserving my options for possible future action. For if RJR now acts with the responsibility of, say, Johnson & Johnson during the Tylenol tragedy, it could yet find some common ground with concerned parents and avoid an outright ban on all advertising:

1. Since data proves that "the vast majority of new [smoking] recruits are children and teenagers," according to a health coalition including the American Cancer Society, do you still maintain that these Camel ads aren't intended for this very audience?

2. Isn't it inherently misleading to associate a disease-causing product such as smoking with attractive, healthy women?

3. Would you agree to immediately stop marketing all Smooth Character posters, especially since they lack federal warnings?

4. Would you agree to stop all Smooth Character ads on billboards within three months since viewers include children and since the warning label is essentially unreadable?

5. Would you agree to cease and desist your entire Smooth Character ad campaign by 1991, or before the 500th anniversary of Columbus' discovery of America *and* tobacco?

6. Would you consider supporting: (a) Rep. Henry Waxman's legislation allowing only informational cigarette ads without pictures (like securities ads); and (b) Sen. Edward Kennedy's bill, which encourages federally funded counteradvertising for undereducated cigarette consumers?

Mr. Gerstner, beyond any legal requirements, I am appealing to your demonstrated sense of civic obligation to avoid unnecessary disease and death. For prior to becoming chairman and CEO, you did serve on the National Cancer Advisory Board on Cancer Prevention and Early Detection, a body which urged America to evolve into a "tobacco-free" society by the year 2000. Given your personal sensitivity to this urgent topic, I hope RJR might now aspire to be a good corporate citizen and consider cooperative efforts to reduce the incidence of teenage smoking.

For kids' sake, I look forward to your prompt and favorable response.

NO

John C. Luik

TOBACCO ADVERTISING BANS AND THE DARK FACE OF GOVERNMENT PATERNALISM

The question is whether the State has the right through the elimination of all competing messages, to impose on its citizens its view and only its view of what is right in an attempt to mould their thoughts and behaviour?

—Justice Chabot

Liberty in a free and democratic society does not require the State to approve the personal decisions made by its citizens; it does, however, require the State to respect them.

—Justice Wilson

It is by now *de rigueur* amongst the right thinking to dismiss both the tobacco industry and its patrons as, at best moral myopics and at worst moral outlaws unworthy of consideration in civilized society. Thus the first reaction of many who read Canadian Judge Jean-Jude Chabot's decision affirming the right of tobacco companies to advertise their products will be to dismiss it as an idiosyncratic piece of dry legal argument emanating from a purely provincial court that completely fails to grasp the real dimension of the tobacco problem in contemporary society. However, to read Justice Chabot's judgement in such a fashion is to be profoundly unfair, for the decision deals with such crucial and central issues as the nature and value of freedom of expression, of autonomy, respect and rational public policy in a democratic society that go far beyond the question of the legitimacy of tobacco advertising bans. Though the Chabot decision is about such bans, it is equally about the State's right, both covertly and directly, to legislate not just a style of living but also a style of thinking.

The Chabot decision is admittedly complex and deals in part with issues that are relevant only to Canada. But the central part of the decision centres on two interrelated issues which, because they lie at the heart of what a democratic government and a democratic society are fundamentally about, are of significance far beyond Canada. The first of these issues is the question of the legitimacy of government paternalism, of the State's attempts to suppress particular styles of living through legislating the 'truth'. The second issue is the question of the legitimacy of government restriction of fundamental rights such as freedom of expression, individual autonomy and respect, when such restrictions are undertaken without compelling evidence that they will produce a significant good that outweighs the harm arising from the restriction. We will examine each of these questions in turn.

If posed in a slightly different fashion, the answer to the question of what is wrong with bans on tobacco advertising is that such bans offend our democratic sensibilities in two respects. First, they are based on values fundamentally at odds with individual autonomy and respect; and second, they are based on shoddy, biased and unreliable evidence.

PATERNALISM AND HEALTH PATERNALISM

In order to understand how banning tobacco advertising constitutes an unacceptable instance of government paternalism, we need to understand first the general nature of paternalism; second, what paternalism means in the specific context of health and health-related measures undertaken by the government; and third, how such paternalism is fundamentally opposed to the two basic values of democratic society, personal autonomy, particularly freedom of expression and respect.

Paternalism comes in at least two varieties: a weaker version and a stronger version. What is common to both versions is a series of assumptions about reason, autonomy and the nature of persons that include the following: (1) Autonomy is not the foundational democratic value inasmuch as considerations of happiness and welfare frequently take precedence over it; (2) Individuals are frequently irrational in that they a) often do not understand their interests, and b) even if they do understand their interests, they do not know the means best suited for the realization of those interests; (3) Individuals need the State's help in a) discovering and realizing their 'true' interests, and b) avoiding irrational courses of action that entail unhappy consequences, e.g., the permanent alienation of their capacity for voluntary action. What is common to both versions is the belief that the State is justified in protecting competent adult persons from the harmful consequences of their actions through restricting their autonomy by forcing them to act or not to act in certain ways. The weaker and less offensive version of paternalism argues that the State can protect persons from the harmful consequences of their actions by forcing them to act in certain ways when a person's actions are neither fully informed nor fully 'his own'. The stronger version of paternalism asserts that the State can protect persons from the harmful consequences of their actions by forcing them to act or not to act in certain ways, even when a person's actions are fully voluntary and informed. In this instance the State asserts that it has the right to substitute its values and judgements about risks and rewards, its philosophy of an acceptable course of action and its determination of what constitutes a good life for those of the individual. In effect, strong paternalism justifies the State's action to prevent a possible harm that a reasonable person understands but chooses to ignore, for instance, smoking.

We can understand the nature and scope of both versions of paternalism by examining them within the context of a specific and restricted type of paternalist claim: health paternalism. Health paternalism is the claim that: (1) Health is the pre-eminent value which outweights, in most instances, all other values such that a rational person would not normally put his health at risk in the interests of some other value; (2) There is but one healthy/rational way to live one's life and such a way does not include activities that carry with them significant risks to well-being or longevity; (3) Individuals have a moral obligation to order their lives in this healthy-rational way; and (4) The State is justified, indeed the State has a moral obligation, to ensure that its citizens conform to this healthy-rational paradigm, even if they wish not to or are unable to through their own efforts. Health paternalism is thus a subtle shift away from the rarely contested right of individuals to good health to the right of the State to manipulate and coerce its citizens into conforming to a socially sanctioned definition of good health. And one justifiable instance of such coercion is the suppression of any inducement to unhealthy living, e.g. tobacco advertising.

Despite its highly problematic character, health paternalism has been to some degree immune from the sorts of objections that are routinely brought against other forms of paternalism. For instance, arguments fashioned along similar lines that called for the State to protect individuals against themselves by establishing and enforcing a 'correct' political, religious or artistic lifestyle would be quickly denounced as totalitarian. Health paternalism's immunity from criticism stems in part from two factors. First, the practice of medicine has a long tradition, preached by physicians and usually casually accepted by patients, of turning one's health over to the experts. Second, health paternalism's policy recommendations—for instance, banning tobacco advertisements—are perceived as being based either on fact and thus being entirely objective and unquestionable, or on 'indubitable' values.

HEALTH PATERNALISM AND TOBACCO

The structure and substance of many of the arguments deployed against the use and promotion of tobacco products is based on paternalism in general and health paternalism in particular. For instance, weak paternalist opponents to the tobacco industry argue that inasmuch as the use of tobacco products is addictive, individuals who use them have not made genuinely voluntary and informed decisions and the State is thus justified in intervening in the lives of these persons to save them from themselves. Or, to take another example, the strong paternalist opponent of the tobacco industry frequently argues that even though the individual who uses tobacco products uses them voluntarily and in full knowledge of their possible consequences, his decision is none the less irrational and deserves to be altered by the State. Again, the health paternalist argues that those who use tobacco products fail to understand the meaning of such scientifically unquestionable concepts as health, rational and risk, or if they understand the meaning of these concepts they are unable or unwilling to accept their moral obligation to act upon them. From the health paternalist's perspective, those who use tobacco are either doing so because they cannot help themselves or because, despite everything they know, they choose to do so. In the former instance they are weak and in the latter instance they are foolish and immoral. In both instances they are unhealthy and in need of salvation. As for those who promote tobacco products, they are, from the perspective of health paternalism, either intellectually dishonest and morally despicable or intellectually ignorant and morally naïve. In either instance they deserve to be suppressed.

Put in this fashion the health paternalist appears to have all of the trump cards, whether moral, logical or scientific, in the debate about tobacco advertising and use. We wish to argue, however, that: (1) Health paternalism a) rests on an unexamined and dubious assumption about the value of health and the relationship between health and rationality, and b) it restricts individual autonomy and demeans the dignity and worth of individuals in ways that are inappropriate in a democratic society; and (2) Without the support of such an unacceptable health paternalism there is no place for tobacco advertising bans in the democratic tradition.

THE VIABILITY OF HEALTH PATERNALISM: THE PRIMACY OF HEALTH

Let us begin with the assumptions of the health paternalist. Health paternalism, as was noted above, appears to be intellectually compelling because it argues from what seems to be the high ground of scientific objectivity and finality. 'Health'—i.e. sound body and mind, the proper functioning of the organism—is apparently something about which we can in-

disputably be certain. But even assuming that we can arrive at a scientifically precise and unquestionable definition of what being healthy is, this fails to provide health paternalism with a scientific status for the reason that health paternalism gives a highly ideological, value-laden characterization to the concept of being healthy and the place of health in an individual's life. Being healthy for the health paternalist is the prime moral value and individuals have a duty to themselves and others to order their lives around this obligation and governments have the obligation to compel them to do so if they choose not to follow this path. The health paternalist builds into his model of a rational/good/ideal/normal person the primary value assumption that reducing health risks and increasing longevity is an unquestionable value and that all rational/moral people will do so. From this he concludes that departures and inducements to depart (e.g. tobacco advertisements) from this model are wrong.

But is this in fact the case? Is it self-evident that a rational/good person will order his life so as to maximize his health? Is it obvious that to trade off an increased health risk or shortened life span for some other value is wrong, and not simply wrong but so grossly wrong that it is justifiably suppressed by the State? Do we not make such trade-offs routinely? 'Consider an individual who wishes to travel to another town. The person could travel by car or by train. The risk of accident and injury is far less by train but the individual decides to go by car because of the increased convenience. Is the individual irrational?' ... Is ... a healthy, long and comparatively unexciting life to be preferred to a risky, short and exciting one?

As Joel Feinberg reminds us:

> Imprudence may not pay off in the long run, and impulsive adventurers and gamblers may be losers in the end, but they do not always or necessarily have regrets. Hangovers are painful and set back one's efforts, but careful niggling prudence is dull and unappealing. Better the life of spontaneity, impulse, excitement, and risk, even if it be short, and even if the future self must bear the costs. We all know that there are people who have such attitudes and have them authentically.

> ... In short, health paternalism is flawed in the first instance because it mistakenly describes the place of health and longevity in the value schemes of many individuals by failing to allow for the trade-offs between health and other values that are routinely made and that we do not characterize as either irrational or immoral. An individual's life plan might include quite idiosyncratic readings of such things as health, risk, fulfilment and happiness, as well as quite idiosyncratic determinations of how to make trade-offs between them, and not, simply in virtue of its idiosyncratic character, be irrational.

In response to this line of argument the health paternalist can claim that while it is true that certain individuals may not acknowledge the primacy of health and may prefer the alleged rewards of risk-taking to either well-being or longevity, they should not act this way, and the State is justified, *for their own good*, in preventing them from adopting this course of action. Thus the health paternalist inevitably finds himself in the position of advocating as a matter of public policy significant restrictions on individual autonomy.

It is this belief in the moral necessity of protecting individuals from themselves that provides the foundation for restrictions on both the use and promotion of tobacco products. Since the smoker... refuses to accept the 'fact' that health is the pre-eminent value, that there is one healthy/rational way to order his life, and that he has a moral obligation to live this way, then he opens himself up to the fourth claim, namely, that the State is justified, indeed has a moral obligation, to ensure that he conforms to the healthy/rational paradigm. Put in another fashion, since we cannot accept the values or the rationality of the smoker or the potential smoker we must protect these individuals from their wrong choices by eliminating the possibility of those wrong choices. And advertising bans are one extremely effective way of eliminating the possibility of wrong choices about smoking....

THE VIABILITY OF HEALTH PATERNALISM: TOBACCO ADVERTISING BANS AND THE PRIMACY OF AUTONOMY

Tobacco advertising bans infringe the right to individual autonomy in at least three senses. In the first sense they suppress the right to free expression in that they deprive not only speakers of their right to say certain things but also listeners of their right to hear certain things. As Justice Chabot observes:

> The Act deprives a third of the adult population of Canada, consumers of the product, of information regarding existing products, new trademarks or products, changes to products in terms of tar, nicotine and CO, in short information which will allow them to make informed economic choices. As previously noted

by the Court, freedom of commercial expression protects both the speaker and the listener and plays a significant role in allowing individuals to make informed choices, which represents an important aspect of self-fulfillment and personal autonomy.

... Indeed, in an even more specific sense the process of advertising is founded on the same sorts of freedom—freedom to enquire, create and advocate —that are to be found in political, religious and cultural life. As the political philosopher John Gray has argued,

> Freedom of expression in the arts and freedom of expression in advertising are not two categorically different things, subject to different standards and having different justifications; they are the same freedom, exercised in different contexts, with the same justification.

The second problem with such a line of argument is that it could be urged against other forms of speech as well, forms that are considered legitimate. Political and religious speech, for instance, is rarely devoid of appeals to our emotions as well as to our intellects. Are we then through parity of reasoning to conclude that the 'manipulative' emotionalism of the fundamentalist preacher who seeks to 'control' our religious choices is speech that should be suppressed? Or what of the illogical rantings of the populist politician? The difficulty with much speech is that it is, when viewed from a certain perspective manipulative and uninformed, but when judged from another perspective persuasive and legitimate. In order to judge conclusively what kind of speech it is, we must secure some 'objective' vantage point from which the 'truth' of the matter becomes clear. When the argument is cast in this form, it becomes

obvious that advocates of restrictions on speech must of necessity justify those restrictions by claiming that the speech they wish to suppress is somehow in error and that they—the advocates of suppressing such speech—possess the truth about the matter in question. Suppressing speech is thus a form of legislating the truth.

Such a position is, however, open to at least two quite decisive objections. The first is that such restrictions on speech and such officially determined readings of truth are inherently undesirable because they necessarily destroy personal autonomy through fudging the environment in which individuals discover for themselves what is true and false and through imposing a state-enforced doctrine of what to think and how to live.

Indeed, this is precisely why the connection between freedom of speech, individual autonomy and democracy is so necessarily intimate and why government paternalism, however benign, is such a menace to the democratic ethos. Without freedom of speech and the intellectual, cultural, economic and political diversity that it represents, genuine individual autonomy becomes impossible, and without genuine individual autonomy the democratic process is in turn impossible. When the government, for whatever reasons, seeks to control freedom of speech, it inevitably attempts, generally in the most covert and hence most reprehensible fashion, to restrict individual autonomy. And in restricting individual autonomy it undermines democracy itself.

The second objection is that even if such restrictions on speech were desirable, they are in most instances impossible in practice given that they require that those who are suppressing a certain type of speech be indisputably in possession of the truth of the matter. But where is one to find such a vantage point of truth and objectivity and how are we to judge whether those who claim to have found it have really done so? Who, for instance, is really in possession of the truth: the fundamentalist preacher or his agnostic critic? Freedom of speech is considered valuable largely because of the assumption that no individual or group is likely to have the entire truth about anything, and truth is more likely to emerge through the vigorous clash of opposing points of view than through the incontestable edicts of some authority.

Given this crucial connection between commercial expression and individual autonomy, the Supreme Court of Canada, as Judge Chabot notes, rejected the argument that commercial expression is unworthy of constitutional protection.

> The Supreme Court of Canada unanimously rejected this argument. It held to the contrary, that commercial speech not only has intrinsic social value as a means of expression, but, in addition, that it constitutes an important aspect of individual self-fulfillment and personal autonomy....
>
> *Over and above its intrinsic value as expression, commercial expression which, as has been pointed out, protects listeners as well as speakers plays a significant role in enabling individuals to make informed economic choices, an important aspect of individual self-fulfillment and personal autonomy. The Court accordingly rejects the view that commercial expression serves no individual or societal value in a free and democratic society and for this reason is undeserving of any constitutional protection.* (Emphasis J. Chabot)

... Tobacco advertising bans... infringe the right to autonomy in a second and indeed far more serious sense in that they indirectly attempt to manipulate the social environment in such a fashion as to control the thoughts and choices of citizens. And such attempts to manipulate the thoughts and choices of citizens through suppressing competing points of view, in effect through eliminating certain kinds of information, have no place in a democratic society. As US Supreme Court Justice Blackmun observed with respect to attempts by the State to restrict information about a product, such attempts can never be justified since they represent a 'covert attempt by the State to manipulate the choices of its citizens, not by persuasion or direct regulation but by depriving the public of the information needed to make a free choice'. Indeed, as Justice Dickson... notes, 'coercion includes indirect forms of control which determine or limit alternative courses of conduct available to others'.

The State's purpose in banning speech about tobacco products is clearly to effect such an 'indirect form of control' in order to restrict both one's awareness of and beliefs about certain sorts of behaviours and lifestyles. It is not just that the State attempts to control what its citizens believe about a particular choice, but also that it attempts to eliminate the realization that the choice exists. This form of manipulation is in the end no less coercive than the 'direct commands to act or refrain from action on pain of sanction' cited by Justice Dickson since its purpose is to 'determine or limit alternative courses of conduct'....

CONCLUSION

The Chabot decision thus shows that the case for tobacco advertising bans is irremediably flawed in that upon close inspection it turns out to be both theoretically and empirically bankrupt. What it promises is the worst of all possible exchanges—a significant impairment of our democratic health through the erosion of the core values of autonomy and respect in return for no demonstrable improvement in our collective physical health.

'The spirit of the age', writes Lewis Lapham,

> favors the moralist and the busybody, and the instinct to censor and suppress shows itself not only in the protests for and against abortion or multiculturalism but also in the prohibitions against tobacco and pet birds. It seems that everybody is forever looking out for everybody else's spiritual or physical salvation. Doomsday is at hand, and the community of the blessed ... can be all too easily corrupted by the wrong diet, the wrong combination of chemicals, the wrong word.

The spirit of our age may well find its clearest voice in the neo-puritanism of a health paternalism that urges us to suppress, censor and ultimately manage the lives of others for their own good. But the values of autonomy and respect still remind us how deeply such urges trespass on the most crucial of democracy's rights: the right, for better or for worse, to be ourselves.

POSTSCRIPT

Should Tobacco Advertising Be Banned?

Green and Luik seem to argue past each other. In the name of autonomy, Luik wants to ensure a no-censorship policy for rational adults; in the name of harm prevention, Green wants to ensure protection of vulnerable adolescents from harmful messages. But since there is no practicable way of sending one set of messages to rational adults and another set to vulnerable adolescents, the question of advertising must remain as one question, and we may have to choose which of the two values is more important in this case.

When we cannot agree on the moral status of the endpoint or product of an inquiry—when we cannot decide which value is more important—we may simply have to agree that there is no just outcome and that each side has an equal right to prevail. But we may be able to agree on a just procedure, a way of reaching a decision that all can trust, and agree to accept whatever result the procedure yields, despite what our preference may have been to begin with. One just procedure would be to submit the proposal to ban advertising to the appropriate legislature and accept the results of the debate, the vote, and the acquiescence of the executive branch and the courts.

SUGGESTED READINGS

Michele Barry, "The Influence of the U.S. Tobacco Industry on the Health, Economy, and Environment of Developing Countries," *The New England Journal of Medicine* (March 28, 1991).

Rae Corelli, "Smokers Go to War," *Macleans* (January 17, 1991).

Kathleen Deveny, "With Help of Teens, Snuff Sales Revive," *The Wall Street Journal* (May 3, 1990).

Joseph R. DiFranza and John W. Richards, Jr., "RJR Nabisco's Cartoon Camel Promotes Camel Cigarettes to Children," *Journal of the American Medical Association* (December 11, 1991).

Michael McCarthy, "Tobacco Critics See a Subtle Sell to Kids," *The Wall Street Journal* (May 3, 1990).

Morton Mintz, "The Nicotine Pushers: Marketing Tobacco to Children," *The Nation* (May 6, 1991).

Elise Truly Sautter and Nancy A. Oretskin, "Tobacco Targeting: The Ethical Complexity of Marketing to Minorities," *Journal of Business Ethics* (July 1997).

Kenman L. Wong, "Tobacco Advertising and Children: The Limits of First Amendment Protection," *Journal of Business Ethics* (October 1996).

ISSUE 14

Are Multinational Corporations Free from Moral Obligations?

YES: Manuel Velasquez, from "International Business, Morality and the Common Good," *Business Ethics Quarterly* (January 1992)

NO: John E. Fleming, from "Alternative Approaches and Assumptions: Comments on Manuel Velasquez," *Business Ethics Quarterly* (January 1992)

ISSUE SUMMARY

YES: Professor of business ethics Manuel Velasquez doubts that, in the absence of accepted enforcement agencies, any multinational corporation will suffer for violating rules that restrict business for the sake of the common good. He argues that since any business that tried to conform to moral rules in the absence of enforcement would cease to be competitive, moral strictures cannot be binding on such companies.

NO: Professor emeritus John E. Fleming asserts that multinational corporations tend to deal with long-term customers and suppliers in the goldfish bowl of international media and must therefore adhere to moral standards or lose business.

This issue is a complex one with many gray areas.

In the first selection, for example, Manuel Velasquez perceives the issue to be between the Hobbesian realists (those who adhere to the philosophies of Thomas Hobbes), who value the bottom line above all else, and those who believe that high moral thoughts influence world affairs. Velasquez concludes that a Hobbesian realist, knowing the worst about human nature, must acknowledge that moral obligations simply do not apply in the absence of moral community. John E. Fleming does not counter Velasquez's argument in the tone of lofty idealism but in that of a practitioner who has to keep an enterprise afloat from day to day. He concludes that the only way to serve the bottom line is through moral behavior.

Second, Velasquez perceives right action to be on trial. He asks, Can morality justify itself with regard to profit? Can we show that acting for the common good will not damage the profit picture or detract from the increase in shareholder wealth? If not, Velasquez suggests, then we will have to forgo morality. Fleming seems to say that right action is compatible with (in fact, necessary for) the health of the bottom line and the corporate enterprise in general. If Fleming is right, then the major premise of Hobbesian capitalism—that the sole social responsibility of business is to increase its profits—may be unworkable. Any activity that might be expected to follow from the injunction to serve the bottom line and increase profits, activity in total disregard of the moral persuasions of all others in society, may result in lost business, leaving shareholders with valueless promises.

Third, according to both Velasquez and Fleming, the dispute is over human behavior in business situations—both about the way humans *will* behave and the way they *should* behave. Both authors condition their predictions and advice on the nature of the international business community. Fleming claims that the international business scene is not at all how Velasquez portrays it—strangers interacting in strange lands on a one-time basis only—but is a place of custom, regular habits, and familiar people, where memories are long, word gets around, and tolerance for being taken advantage of is very low.

As you read the following selections, consider how international dealings differ from domestic dealings. Aren't folks abroad rather like folks at home, with just a few differences in manners? What are the real controls on human behavior—enforcement of laws or the simple social expectations of peers and colleagues?

YES

Manuel Velasquez

INTERNATIONAL BUSINESS, MORALITY AND THE COMMON GOOD

During the last few years an increasing number of voices have urged that we pay more attention to ethics in international business, on the grounds that not only are all large corporations now internationally structured and thus engaging in international transactions, but that even the smallest domestic firm is increasingly buffeted by the pressures of international competition....

Can we say that businesses operating in a competitive international environment have any moral obligations to contribute to the international common good, particularly in light of realist objections? Unfortunately, my answer to this question will be in the negative....

INTERNATIONAL BUSINESS

... When speaking of international business, I have in mind a particular kind of organization: the multinational corporation. Multinational corporations have a number of well known features, but let me briefly summarize a few of them. First, multinational corporations are businesses and as such they are organized primarily to increase their profits within a competitive environment. Virtually all of the activities of a multinational corporation can be explained as more or less rational attempts to achieve this dominant end. Secondly, multinational corporations are bureaucratic organizations. The implication of this is that the identity, the fundamental structure, and the dominant objectives of the corporation endure while the many individual human beings who fill the various offices and positions within the corporation come and go. As a consequence, the particular values and aspirations of individual members of the corporation have a relatively minimal and transitory impact on the organization as a whole. Thirdly, and most characteristically, multinational corporations operate in several nations. This has several implications. First, because the multinational is not confined to a single nation, it can easily escape the reach of the laws of any particular nation by simply moving its resources or operations out of one nation and transferring them to another nation. Second, because the multinational is not confined to a single nation,

From Manuel Velasquez, "International Business, Morality and the Common Good," *Business Ethics Quarterly* (January 1992). Copyright © 1992 by The Society for Business Ethics. Reprinted by permission. Notes omitted.

its interests are not aligned with the interests of any single nation. The ability of the multinational to achieve its profit objectives does not depend upon the ability of any particular nation to achieve its own domestic objectives....

THE TRADITIONAL REALIST OBJECTION IN HOBBES

The realist objection, of course, is the standard objection to the view that agents —whether corporations, governments, or individuals—have moral obligations on the international level. Generally, the realist holds that it is a mistake to apply moral concepts to international activities: morality has no place in international affairs. The classical statement of this view, which I am calling the "traditional" version of realism, is generally attributed to Thomas Hobbes....

In its Hobbsian form, as traditionally interpreted, the realist objection holds that moral concepts have no meaning in the absence of an agency powerful enough to guarantee that other agents generally adhere to the tenets of morality. Hobbes held, first, that in the absence of a sovereign power capable of forcing men to behave civilly with each other, men are in "the state of nature," a state he characterizes as a "war... of every man, against every man." Secondly, Hobbes claimed, in such a state of war, moral concepts have no meaning:

> To this war of every man against every man, this also is consequent; that nothing can be unjust. The notions of right and wrong, justice and injustice have there no place. Where there is no common power, there is no law: where no law, no injustice.

Moral concepts are meaningless, then, when applied to state of nature situations. And, Hobbes held, the international arena is a state of nature, since there is no international sovereign that can force agents to adhere to the tenets of morality.

The Hobbsian objection to talking about morality in international affairs, then, is based on two premises: (1) an ethical premise about the applicability of moral terms and (2) an apparently empirical premise about how agents behave under certain conditions. The ethical premise, at least in its Hobbsian form, holds that there is a connection between the meaningfulness of moral terms and the extent to which agents adhere to the tenets of morality: If in a given situation agents do not adhere to the tenets of morality, then in that situation moral terms have no meaning. The apparently empirical premise holds that in the absence of a sovereign, agents will not adhere to the tenets of morality: they will be in a state of war. This appears to be an empirical generalization about the extent to which agents adhere to the tenets of morality in the absence of a third-party enforcer. Taken together, the two premises imply that in situations that lack a sovereign authority, such as one finds in many international exchanges, moral terms have no meaning and so moral obligations are nonexistent....

REVISING THE REALIST OBJECTION: THE FIRST PREMISE

... The neo-Hobbsian or realist... might want to propose this premise: When one is in a situation in which others do not adhere to certain tenets of morality, and when adhering to those tenets of morality will put one at a significant competitive disadvantage, then it is not immoral for one to like-wise fail to adhere to them. The realist might want to argue for this claim, first, by pointing out that in a world in which all are competing to secure significant benefits and avoid significant costs, and in which others do not adhere to the ordinary tenets of morality, one risks significant harm to one's interests if one continues to adhere to those tenets of morality. But no one can be morally required to take on major risks of harm to oneself. Consequently, in a competitive world in which others disregard moral constraints and take any means to advance their self-interests, no one can be morally required to take on major risks of injury by adopting the restraints of ordinary morality.

A second argument the realist might want to advance would go as follows. When one is in a situation in which others do not adhere to the ordinary tenets of morality, one is under heavy competitive pressures to do the same. And, when one is under such pressures, one cannot be blamed—i.e., one is excused—for also failing to adhere to the ordinary tenets of morality. One is excused because heavy pressures take away one's ability to control oneself, and thereby diminish one's moral culpability.

Yet a third argument advanced by the realist might go as follows. When one is in a situation in which others do not adhere to the ordinary tenets of morality it is not fair to require one to continue to adhere to those tenets, especially if doing so puts one at a significant competitive disadvantage. It is not fair because then one is laying a burden on one party that the other parties refuse to carry.

Thus, there are a number of arguments that can be given in defense of the revised Hobbsian ethical premise that when others do not adhere to the tenets of morality, it is not immoral for one to do likewise....

REVISING THE REALIST OBJECTION: THE SECOND PREMISE

Let us turn, to the other premise in the Hobbsian argument, the assertion that in the absence of a sovereign, agents will be in a state of war. As I mentioned, this is an apparently empirical claim about the extent to which agents will adhere to the tenets of morality in the absence of a third-party enforcer.

Hobbes gives a little bit of empirical evidence for this claim. He cites several examples of situations in which there is no third party to enforce civility and where, as a result, individuals are in a "state of war." Generalizing from these few examples, he reaches the conclusion that in the absence of a third-party enforcer, agents will always be in a "condition of war."...

Recently, the Hobbsian claim... has been defended on the basis of some of the theoretical claims of game theory, particularly of the prisoner's dilemma. Hobbes' state of nature, the defense goes, is an instance of a prisoner's dilemma, and *rational* agents in a Prisoner's Dilemma necessarily would choose not to adhere to a set of moral norms....

A Prisoner's Dilemma is a situation involving at least two individuals. Each individual is faced with two choices: he can cooperate with the other individual or he can choose not to cooperate. If he cooperates and the other individual also cooperates, then he gets a certain payoff. If, however, he chooses not to cooperate, while the other individual trustingly cooperates, the noncooperator gets a larger payoff while the cooperator suffers a loss. And if both choose not to cooperate, then both get nothing.

It is a commonplace now that in a Prisoner's Dilemma situation, the most rational strategy for a participant is to choose not to cooperate. For the other party will either cooperate or not cooperate. If the other party cooperates, then it is better for one not to cooperate and thereby get the larger payoff. On the other hand, if the other party does not cooperate, then it is also better for one not to cooperate and thereby avoid a loss. In either case, it is better for one to not cooperate.

... In Hobbes' state of nature each individual must choose either to cooperate with others by adhering to the rules of morality (like the rule against theft), or to not cooperate by disregarding the rules of morality and attempting to take advantage of those who are adhering to the rules (e.g., by stealing from them). In such a situation it is more rational . . . to choose not to cooperate. For the other party will either cooperate or not cooperate. If the other party does not cooperate, then one puts oneself at a competitive disadvantage if one adheres to morality while the other party does not. On the other hand, if the other party chooses to cooperate, then one can take advantage of the other party by breaking the rules of morality at his expense. In either case, it is moral rational to not cooperate.

Thus, the realist can argue that in a state of nature, where there is no one to enforce compliance with the rules of morality, it is more rational from the individual's point of view to choose not to comply with morality than to choose to comply. Assuming—and this is obviously a critical assumption—that agents behave rationally, then we can conclude that agents in a state of nature

will choose not to comply with the tenets of ordinary morality....

Can we claim that it is clear that multinationals have a moral obligation to pursue the global common good in spite of the objections of the realist?

I do not believe that this claim can be made. We can conclude from the discussion of the realist objection that the Hobbsian claim about the pervasiveness of amorality in the international sphere is false when (1) interactions among international agents are repetitive in such a way that agents can retaliate against those who fail to cooperate, and (2) agents can determine the trustworthiness of other international agents.

But unfortunately, multinational activities often take place in a highly competitive arena in which these two conditions do not obtain. Moreover, these conditions are noticeably absent in the arena of activities that concern the global common good.

First, as I have noted, the common good consists of goods that are indivisible and accessible to all. This means that such goods are susceptible to the free rider problems. Everyone has access to such goods whether or not they do their part in maintaining such goods, so everyone is tempted to free ride on the generosity of others. Now governments can force domestic companies to do their part to maintain the national common good. Indeed, it is one of the functions of government to solve the free rider problem by forcing all to contribute to the domestic common good to which all have access. Moreover, all companies have to interact repeatedly with their host governments, and this leads them to adopt a cooperative stance toward their host government's objective of achieving the domestic common good.

But it is not clear that governments can or will do anything effective to force multinationals to do their part to maintain the global common good. For the governments of individual nations can themselves be free riders, and can join forces with willing multinationals seeking competitive advantages over others. Let me suggest an example. It is clear that a livable global environment is part of the global common good, and it is clear that the manufacture and use of chlorofluorocarbons is destroying that good. Some nations have responded by requiring their domestic companies to cease manufacturing or using chlorofluorocarbons. But other nations have refused to do the same, since they will share in any benefits that accrue from the restraint others practice, and they can also reap the benefits of continuing to manufacture and use chlorofluorocarbons. Less developed nations, in particular, have advanced the position that since their development depends heavily on exploiting the industrial benefits of chlorofluorocarbons, they cannot afford to curtail their use of these substances. Given this situation, it is open to multinationals to shift their operations to those countries that continue to allow the manufacture and use of chlorofluorocarbons. For multinationals, too, will reason that they will share in any benefits that accrue from the restraint others practice, and that they can meanwhile reap the profits of continuing to manufacture and use chlorofluorocarbons in a world where other companies are forced to use more expensive technologies. Moreover, those nations that practice restraint cannot force all such multinationals to discontinue the manufacture or use of chlorofluorocarbons because many multinationals can escape the reach of their laws. An exactly parallel, but perhaps even more compelling, set of considerations can be advanced to show that at least some multinationals will join forces with some developing countries to circumvent any global efforts made to control the global warming trends (the so-called "greenhouse effect") caused by the heavy use of fossil fuels.

The realist will conclude, of course, that in such situations, at least some multinationals will seek to gain competitive advantages by failing to contribute to the global common good (such as the good of a hospitable global environment). For multinationals and rational agents, i.e., agents bureaucratically structured to take rational means toward achieving their dominant end of increasing their profits. And in a competitive environment, contributing to the common good while others do not, will fail to achieve this dominant end. Joining this conclusion to the ethical premise that when others do not adhere to the requirements of morality it is not immoral for one to do likewise, the realist can conclude that multinationals are not morally obligated to contribute to such global common goods (such as environmental goods).

Moreover, global common goods often create interactions that are not iterated. This is particularly the case where the global environment is concerned. As I have already noted, preservation of a favorable global climate is clearly part of the global common good. Now the failure of the global climate will be a one-time affair. The breakdown of the ozone layer, for example, will happen once, with catastrophic consequences for us all; and the heating up of the global climate as a result of the infusion of carbon dioxide will happen once, with catastrophic consequences for us all. Because these environmental disasters are a one-time affair, they represent a non-iterated prisoner's dilemma for multinationals. It is irrational from an individual point of view for a multinational to choose to refrain from polluting the environment in such cases. Either others will refrain, and then one can enjoy the benefits of their refraining; or others will not refrain, and then it will be better to have also not refrained since refraining would have made little difference and would have entailed heavy losses.

Finally, we must also note that although natural persons may signal their reliability to other natural persons, it is not at all obvious that multination-als can do the same. As noted above, multinationals are bureaucratic organizations whose members are continually changing and shifting. The natural persons who make up an organization can signal their reliability to others, but such persons are soon replaced by others, and they in turn are replaced by others. What endures is each organization's single-minded pursuit of increasing its profits in a competitive environment. And an enduring commitment to the pursuit of profit in a competitive environment is not a signal of an enduring commitment to morality.

NO

John E. Fleming

ALTERNATIVE APPROACHES AND ASSUMPTIONS: COMMENTS ON MANUEL VELASQUEZ

INTRODUCTION

I feel that Professor Velasquez has written a very interesting and thought-provoking paper on an important topic. His initial identification with a "strong notion of the common good" raises the level of analysis to a high but very complex plane. The author introduces the interesting and, from my view, unusual *realist objection* in the Hobbsian form. After a rigorous analysis of this concept Professor Velasquez reaches what I find to be a disturbing conclusion: "It is not obvious that we can say that multinationals have an obligation to contribute to the global common good...." He then finishes the paper with a strong plea for the establishment of "an international authority capable of forcing everyone to contribute toward the global good."

It would be presumptuous of me to question the fine ethical reasoning that appears in the paper. I am impressed with its elegance. However, in a topic of this complexity I would like to think that there might be alternative approaches and assumptions that would lead us to a different conclusion. The presentation of such alternatives will be the path that I will take, examining the conceptual and empirical underpinnings of the argument from a management viewpoint.

THE MODEL OF A MULTINATIONAL CORPORATION

The profit-maximizing, rational model of a multinational corporation presented in the paper is consistent with traditional economics and serves as a useful approximation of the firm from a theoretical viewpoint. But it falls somewhat short in less than purely competitive environments and was never intended to describe the decision processes of actual managers. Empirical studies of firms can lead to a profit-sacrificing, bounded rational model. The importance of profit is still there, but the stockholder does not get all the benefits. Other stakeholders are considered and rewarded. Out of all this can come the important concept of corporate social responsibility, which can include such topics as concerns for the environment and for host country governments.

I also find the faceless and interchangeable bureaucrat a poor model for business executives, particularly the chief executive officers of large corporations. Many of these individuals have a personal impact on the organization, including such areas as business ethics and corporate responsibility. There are also important behavioral aspects of management, such as pride in the firm and corporate culture, that are fertile soil for the nurture of ethics.

Most large American multinational corporations have codes of ethics and some have well-developed programs concerned with ethical behavior worldwide. A number of these firms emphasize that their one code of conduct applies everywhere that they do business. At the GTE Corporation its vision and values statements have been translated into nine different languages and distributed to all its employees to ensure this worldwide understanding of how it conducts its business. This is a far cry from the situational ethics described in the model used by Professor Velasquez.

MODEL OF THE INTERNATIONAL BUSINESS CLIMATE

The planning and decision environment of the managers conducting international business is different from that described in the paper. There is the very real problem of a lack of an overarching global government and enforceable laws for the international arena. Nevertheless, there are other very strong restraining forces on companies that prevent the "state of nature" (or law of the jungle) described in the paper. For example, the national governments that do exist influence the ethical behavior of companies acting within their boundaries and beyond. The Foreign Corrupt Practices Act of the United States has set a new standard of behavior in the area of bribery that dictates how American companies will behave world-wide. The financial practices of large banks and securities markets have added major constraints to global corporate behavior. There are also a number of regional and functional organizations in the areas of trade and monetary issues that provide limitations to managerial decision making.

The decisions of multinational executives are also constrained by such factors as public opinion and the pressures of special interest groups. In this area the media also plays a strong role. Examples of these forces are the actions of interest groups that forced marketing changes on infant formula manufacturers and the strong "green" movement that is affecting business decisions throughout many parts of the world. My own view is that considerable progress has been made in the area of limiting the manufacture and release of chlorofluorocarbons. This is a very complex issue involving tremendous social and economic changes that are far more critical, widespread and controlling than the profits of the producing companies. Even with the existence of an enforcing government there is no guarantee that the problem would be solved speedily. An example in point is the acid rain problem of the United States.

MODEL OF THE PRISONER'S DILEMMA

From the standpoint of managerial decision making the Prisoner's Dilemma model does not simulate a situation that is frequently found in international business. An executive generally would not be negotiating or making mutually beneficial decisions with competitors. I would see the greatest amount of effort of multinational decision makers devoted to the development of repeat customers. Such an accomplishment comes about through solving customer problems with better product/service at a lower cost. An emphasis on efficiency and excellence is a far more effective use of executive time than questionable negotiations with a competitor. I believe that the weakness Professor Velasquez identifies in the Prisoner's Dilemma model as a one-time event with competitors applies even more to negotiations with customers.

The author also points out a major weakness of the model in the signaling of intent that goes on between individuals. He then states that this same signaling is not found to any great extent between companies. I would disagree with this thought. An important part of corporate strategic planning is analyzing market signals. United States antitrust forbids direct contact between competitors on issues relating to the market. But there is no limitation on independent analysis of competitive actions and the interpretation of actions by competitors. When Kodak introduced its instant camera, both Kodak and Polaroid watched the other's actions to determine whether it signaled detente or fight.

CONCLUSION

For the reasons enumerated above I tend to question the models and assumptions that Professor Velasquez has used in his ethical analysis. And, with these underpinnings in jeopardy, I also tend to question the tentative conclusion of his moral reasoning as it relates to the managerial aspects of international business. I feel that multinationals *do* have a strong obligation to contribute to the global common good.

POSTSCRIPT

Are Multinational Corporations Free from Moral Obligations?

As we write, international business has sunk into a sea of troubles: the once-booming Asian economies seem to be self-destructing, prominent public figures such as movie stars and athletes are being accused of exploitation and owning sweatshops, and trade in securities has gone global and is running wild. What are the possibilities for the comprehensive set of international laws, guidelines, and the committees to enforce them, as suggested by Velasquez?

Is national sovereignty an idea whose time has come, gone, and gone south? While national boundaries between peoples are in violent dispute worldwide, and while the economy goes global with blinding speed, does the concept of national boundaries make any sense at all? How else would we know what each central government controls? What is the reason for the centrality of national sovereignty?

SUGGESTED READINGS

Corporate Ethics: A Prime Business Asset, Report of the Business Roundtable (1988).

Ashay B. Desai and Terri Rittenburg, "Global Ethics: An Integrative Framework for MNEs," *Journal of Business Ethics* (June 1997), pp. 791–800.

Thomas Donaldson, *The Ethics of International Business* (Oxford University Press, 1989).

W. Michael Hoffman, Ann E. Lange, and David A. Fedo, eds., *Ethics and the Multinational Enterprise* (University Press of America, 1986).

Kevin T. Jackson, "Globalizing Corporate Ethics Programs: Perils and Prospects," *Journal of Business Ethics* (September 1997), pp. 1227–1235.

ISSUE 15

Does NAFTA Make Life Better for Americans?

YES: Catherine Houghton, from "American Firms Are Doing Well in Canada Under NAFTA: Small Companies Land Canadian Government Contracts," *Business America* (April 1997)

NO: Dan McGraw, from "Happily Ever NAFTA?" *U.S. News and World Report* (October 28, 1996)

ISSUE SUMMARY

YES: Catherine Houghton, an officer of the U.S. Commerical Service, states that the North American Free Trade Agreement (NAFTA) has been good for small American companies, especially in high-tech areas.

NO: Dan McGraw, senior editor of *U.S. News and World Report*, surveys a few of the companies impacted most by NAFTA and finds that where Mexico and the United States make similar products, Mexican products can sell for significantly less in the market because of lower labor costs. He predicts that tariffs may be needed to save small manufacturing in the United States.

The Scottish economist Adam Smith argued vociferously for the theory of free trade in the eighteenth century: If every manufacturer in the world will make his goods as efficiently as he can, and if every merchant will purchase goods as cheaply as he can (for any level of quality) and sell as dearly as he can, and if every consumer will make the best possible purchases for himself in the marketplace, the competition will inevitably favor the most efficient, and goods of higher and higher quality will be available to all at lower prices. Smith believed that the less efficient manufacturers or merchants would inevitably go out of business, freeing up resources (land, labor, etc.) for use by the more efficient manufacturers to expand their operations. According to Smith, as long as competition is open and trade is free, the world comes out the winner.

The government is often tempted to bail out inefficient industries with tariffs and subsidies and the like. Ailing companies claim that all they need is a hand up to be competitive again. But let this kind of subsidy get established, Smith argued, and we will all be the losers. He warned that subsidized companies become lazy and inefficient and that the quality of their product slides even as the costs rise, while the more efficient producers are forced out of the market. Everyone loses.

The U.S. government has long been in the business of saving jobs in U.S. industries. The usual kind of protection makes specific reference to the borders of the country: goods made abroad are taxed as they are brought into the country to prevent the importer from selling them at a profit without raising the price to the point where American-made goods can compete. This tax is called a "tariff," and nations use tariffs to protect their industries, enabling companies to employ more people and make a bigger profit, so they will not be put out of business by the more efficient foreign competition. Before it was approved, the debate over the North American Free Trade Agreement (NAFTA) was whether it was better for the United States to protect jobs, taxes, and communities by keeping its industries profitable even when there was more efficient foreign competition, or whether it was better to protect consumers, importers, and multinationals by throwing open U.S. borders to trade.

By the time President Bill Clinton signed NAFTA into law on December 8, 1993, the debate over the impact it would have on U.S. trade and employment had raged for a full presidential election year. Third-party candidate Ross Perot predicted that whole industries would move out of the country. "That 'great sucking sound' you hear," he told his audiences, "is Mexico pulling all our good jobs down below the border." He was not entirely wrong. In the summer of 1997, for instance, Fruit of the Loom laid off thousands of workers in Kentucky specifically to move operations to Mexico, Central America, and the Caribbean—moves that would not have been profitable before NAFTA. In all, Fruit of the Loom has eliminated 6,000 jobs in the last two years, and its managers are quick to fix the blame on NAFTA.

Some cite political and ethical problems with NAFTA. The victims of free trade—those whose jobs are moved overseas and whose businesses cannot compete with low-wage foreign industry—become very important on the political scene because of their power to vote. The main beneficiaries—the consumers, who pay lower prices at the store for better goods—are not likely to notice that NAFTA is responsible and will tend to sympathize with the displaced workers rather than be grateful for the cheaper products.

The ethical problem may be the human cost of the free trade relocations. The reason why operations are so much more profitable in Mexican factories than in U.S. factories is that wages are just above subsistence level in Mexico. By legislation and by agreement with the labor unions, wages in the United States are relatively very high. So without the tariff barrier to make up the difference, U.S. industry must bring goods to market at a higher cost than foreign goods. Economic laws dictate the move to foreign goods.

As you read the following selections by Catherine Houghton and Dan McGraw, ask yourself what it is we are trying to preserve when we talk about protecting the American dream, or the American way of life. Is it worth fighting for, even at the cost of global economic efficiency? Is protectionism still an option for American foreign policy?

YES

Catherine Houghton

AMERICAN FIRMS ARE DOING WELL IN CANADA UNDER NAFTA

When the NAFTA agreement went into effect over two years ago, its advocates promised it would bring gains for U.S. exporters and the U.S. economy. With many now asking if this has happened, the U.S. Commercial Service in Canada recently took a look at one area of trade that can be tracked—Canadian Government procurement—to see how U.S. firms have done. This is what they found: American companies, particularly small- to medium-sized enterprises, are doing very well and landing contracts in a wide range of product and service areas. Most of the contracts are below US$100,000, and many are in high-tech sectors. The companies winning these contracts come from 42 states and the District of Columbia. If the first two years are any indication, NAFTA is good for U.S. exports to Canada and should continue to draw new companies to this market.

CS Ottawa looked at Canadian Government purchasing decisions since late 1994 to size up U.S. companies' success in obtaining contracts under the new, more liberal North American Free Trade Agreement (NAFTA) rules. Concern had been expressed in some quarters that NAFTA had not delivered the benefits to U.S. companies that had been widely expected when the agreement was signed more than two years earlier. In at least one area of trade—Canadian Federal Government procurement—CS Ottawa found this concern to be unwarranted.

Since NAFTA, U.S. companies have captured a steady share of the procurement business across a broad range of produce and service areas. They have done this, in fact, during a period of drastic spending cuts by the Canadian Government. Many of the winners have been small- to medium-sized American firms, new to the Canadian market, whose specific technology and expertise are just what the Canadian Government is seeking.

WHAT EXACTLY DID NAFTA DO?

NAFTA took the more liberal rules offered by the earlier U.S.-Canada Free Trade Agreement (the FTA) and extended them to cover services as well as

From Catherine Houghton, "American Firms Are Doing Well in Canada Under NAFTA: Small Companies Land Canadian Government Contracts," *Business America* (April 1997). *Business America* is a publication of the U.S. Department of Commerce.

goods. It also enlarged the scope of the agreement to cover more of Canada's federal entities, and the Crown Corporations (parastatals), too. The FTA had already opened much wider government procurement markets to American firms by significantly lowering the minimum dollar amount of contracts accessible to them, by laying out fair and transparent bidding procedures, and by offering national treatment to all companies competing for a contract award. NAFTA preserved the FTA's lower minimum contract amounts, and it offered new ones to U.S. firms in Canada.

SMEs SEIZE MARKET SHARE

The data on contracts awarded to U.S. companies by the Canadian Government over the last two years show a surge of new activity by small- to medium-sized U.S. firms (SMEs) at year-end 1994. This was just nine months after the implementation of the NAFTA agreement. Activity by U.S. SMEs continued strong in the first half of 1995 and thereafter, with continuing successes. This successful bidding activity occurred despite an up-and-down pattern of public procurement, overall, during the period.

The yo-yo pattern in Canada's public procurement started with a dramatic drop in contracting activity in the latter half of 1995—probably the lag effect of Canada's deficit reduction initiative ushered in by the Liberal Party the year before. Under this belt-tightening, there were fewer new government tenders, and existing tenders were implemented much more slowly by down-sized staffs of civil servants. In the first quarter of 1996, the number of contracts awarded rose again sharply, reflecting strong spending at the end of Canada's fiscal year (March 31).

But the recovery was only partial, and it was short-lived: contracts awarded and total dollars did not return to the levels of the first six months of 1995. In the second and third quarters of 1996, they fell off sharply again.

Against these radical swings in procurement activity, however, U.S. companies continued to do well, and NAFTA continued to figure importantly in their participation in this market. The one constant in the statistics is the percentage of contracts awarded to U.S. firms which can be attributed to NAFTA provisions. These "NAFTA contracts" represented 15 percent of all the contracts awarded to U.S. firms in the last quarter of 1994. That was the quarter which saw the first big surge after NAFTA implementation. This percentage stayed at 15 to 16 percent of the total throughout 1995 and 1996. Moreover, new-to-market American firms drawn to Canada for the first time by the NAFTA regime appeared to be also going after non-NAFTA-related procurement opportunities. For example, the NAFTA rules do not apply to provincial government procurement in Canada, yet U.S. participation in those opportunities has been growing.

DIVERSITY OF AWARDS, NOT SIZE

One of the most interesting features of the U.S. presence in this procurement market is the modest size of the deals. The lion's share of contracts awarded to U.S. firms has been overwhelmingly in the US$500,000-and-below range. During some of the period covered, contracts below US$50,000 were the most numerous. This supports other evidence of increased SME contracting activity in Canada since NAFTA. In the two years for which data exist, there were no awards over US$50

Table 1

Totals for contracts awarded to U.S. firms by the Canadian Government

	1st Qtr. 1994	1st-4th Qtr. 1995	1st-3rd Qtr. 1996
Total contracts to U.S. firms	210	744	204
NAFTA contracts to U.S. firms	32	111	32
	(15%)	(15%)	(16%)
US$ amount of total contracts to U.S.	$25.3M	$64M	$10M
US$ amount of NAFTA contracts to U.S.	$3.8M	$9.6M	$1.6M

million, and those over US$1 million were infrequent.

The breakdown of contracts for the United States by industry sector brings no surprises. More contracts were awarded to U.S. bidders for computer hardware and software than for any other sector in 1995. Contracts for telecommunications equipment were in second place, and overtook computer contracts in 1996. Instrumentation had a slight lead over both at the end of 1994, and ran a close third or fourth in 1995 and 1996. Other leading sectors were aviation and aerospace equipment, electrical and electronic equipment, defense-related procurement, engineering and professional consultancy services, engines, turbines, and related equipment, fabricated materials, transportation equipment, R&D, education and training, medical equipment, environmental technology, and energy-related equipment. Contracts were also awarded for chemicals, industrial equipment, construction materials, supply of publications and paper, security and firefighting equipment, marine equipment, office equipment and supplies, machinery and tools, textiles, air conditioning and refrigerating equipment, quality control and testing services, natural resources services, agro equipment, and furniture and home products. In short, American firms winning contracts in Canada have reflected the diversity and strength of U.S. industry at home.

The geographical reach of NAFTA extends from the Pacific to the Atlantic. California consistently leads the states in success at landing Canadian contracts. Massachusetts, the District of Columbia, New York, New Jersey, and Virginia vie with each other for runner-up. Washington state rose high on the list in mid-1995, reflecting the lead position that Microsoft Corporation has assumed in number of contracts won. Other states very active in Canadian public procurement are Ohio, Michigan, Minnesota, Illinois, Maryland, Florida, Pennsylvania, Texas, and Arizona. In addition, companies from Georgia, Missouri, Colorado, Connecticut, Kansas, Tennessee, Alabama, Oklahoma, New Hampshire, Indiana, Idaho, Vermont, Arkansas, Utah, North Carolina, South Carolina, Oregon, Kentucky, Nevada, Wyoming, Iowa, Hawaii, Wisconsin, Maine, Delaware, and Rhode Island have won contracts.

THE NAFTA WELCOME MAT TO THE NORTH

Most of the successful U.S. firms in NAFTA-related government procurement are small- to medium-sized: there are relatively few *Fortune 500* firms on the list. This reflects the kinds of products that a Canadian Government operating under a tight budget is buying to keep running. But it also reflects growing export activity by the SMEs in the United States. Another year of two of data will almost certainly reinforce the picture of a procurement market, wide open under NAFTA, that welcomes U.S. companies of any size who offer the range of products and services that the Canadian Government needs to stay in business during an era of shrinking public resources.

NO

Dan McGraw

HAPPILY EVER NAFTA?

Jorge Trevino runs a broom factory in Cadereyta, a small, dusty town in rural northern Mexico with narrow brick streets and whitewashed stucco buildings. Every month, Trevino's workers churn out about 300,000 corn brooms made from the natural straw grown nearby. About three fourths are exported, most to the United States, where they are sold at stores like Kmart.

About 1,200 miles away in rural Illinois, Bill Libman runs his own broom-making operation, which has been in his family for nearly a century. He imports the same straw from Mexico that Trevino uses, and his workers produce about the same number of brooms each month as their Mexican counterparts. Most of Libman's brooms are sold in the United States.

If these two companies seem similar, it is because they are, save for one important distinction. Trevino's broom makers earn an average of about $2.30 an hour; Libman's workers can make up to four or five times that, and because labor constitutes about 25 percent of the cost of a broom, his products cost $2 more than those made in Mexico. Before the North American Free Trade Agreement was enacted nearly three years ago, the U.S. government slapped a 32 percent tariff on Mexican brooms to make up the difference in labor costs. Under NAFTA, the tariffs have been eliminated, and Trevino has seen his exports double. Meanwhile, sales for American broom makers, which employ about 600 people in small factories scattered throughout the Midwest and Southeast, have dropped by about 25 percent each year since NAFTA was signed.

While the U.S. broom industry is a relative speck of dust in the $7 trillion U.S. economy, the effects of NAFTA on the manufacturing of this common household item raise key questions about the trade pact: Do the benefits to the consumer—in this case, cheap brooms—outweigh the loss of jobs? The short answer is that it is still too soon to tell. Indeed, as NAFTA begins its fourth year of existence in a few months, there are more questions left unanswered than answered about the treaty. The anecdotal evidence cuts both ways. But as more of the treaty's provisions are implemented in the coming months and years, NAFTA's impact should become easier to discern.

From Dan McGraw, "Happily Ever NAFTA?" *U.S. News and World Report* (October 28, 1996). Copyright © 1996 by *U.S. News and World Report*. Reprinted by permission.

At least this much is clear: During the first year, trade increased between both countries, and the United States ran a small ($1.3 billion) trade surplus with Mexico. But in 1995, with the meltdown of the Mexican economy from the peso devaluation, the U.S. trade deficit with Mexico ballooned to $15.4 billion, as Mexican consumers had no money to buy American products and goods produced in Mexico were cheaper than ever. This year, as the Mexican economy improves, the trade imbalance is still running at more than $1 billion a month.

Keep on trucking. Wary of losing blue-collar voters in key Midwest industrial states, President Bill Clinton and Republican challenger Bob Dole—both NAFTA supporters—have barely mentioned the treaty during this year's campaign. But the Clinton administration's recent actions speak volumes, and it has been retreating on several fronts. It delayed allowing Mexican trucks to operate in border states—officially because of questions of safety and drug trafficking, but more likely a concession to the powerful Teamsters Union. And last week, the administration appeased vegetable growers in Florida by pressuring Mexico to stop the shipment of $800 million of low-price tomatoes into the United States. As the White House noted, Florida has 25 electoral votes; Mexico has none.

Such are the realities of trade issues during an election year. But the truth about NAFTA—at least so far—is that it is neither the economic boon proponents had predicted nor the "giant sucking sound" of jobs going south that Reform Party presidential candidate Ross Perot feared. Three years ago, both sides oversold their argument in the heat of political debate; this year, NAFTA is being avoided by both Clinton and Dole for the same reasons.

But if the experts are right—and that's a big "if"—NAFTA may be harder to avoid in the future. According to a report by the trade consulting analyst Dean International Inc. in Dallas, bilateral U.S.-Mexico trade will jump more than 100 percent, to $200 billion a year, within five years. The impact of trade on the economy—both positive and negative—will rise accordingly, the report states.

This forecast is based on the assumed benefits of free trade: When trade barriers are removed, the theory goes, each nation does what it does best and consumers in both countries benefit. In the case of NAFTA, such specialization has already become apparent in the corridor between San Antonio, Texas, and Monterrey, Mexico. Monterrey is the industrial heart of Mexico and the origin of 60 percent of all manufactured goods coming into the United States from Mexico.

North of the border, San Antonio is poised to become a top distribution center and provider of American services to manufacturers in Monterrey. Top law firms and accounting firms are opening offices in San Antonio with eyes on the Mexican market, while Kelly Air Force Base, which closed last year, is being turned into a huge distribution center.

Throughout Monterrey, factories and assembly plants combine American capital goods and high-tech know-how with Mexican manufacturing skill and cheap labor. At Lamina Desplegada, a company that makes wire mesh used in everything from satellite dishes to the grates that separate prisoners from the cops in police cars, the computers in the office are made by Hewlett-Packard, the phone system is AT&T, and the huge machines that stamp the rolled steel are from Alliance, Ohio.

The truck trailers out in the parking lot waiting to head north bear the name of J. B. Hunt.

Robert Wheeler, Lamina's export manager and an American who has lived in Mexico for eight years, predicts that the full implementation of NAFTA will have a huge impact. "American consumers and businesses will get far cheaper products," says Wheeler. "And we in turn will be buying more capital equipment and computers from American companies."

It is this dynamic, say free traders, that will offset any temporary job displacement caused by NAFTA. Exports of industrial machinery, computer equipment and transportation equipment from Texas alone accounted for $9.6 billion in sales to Mexican companies in 1995, and the rebounding trade to Mexico has helped lower the unemployment rate in Texas to 5.6 percent—the lowest in 12 years. "Manufacturing of most products in Mexico is still uncompetitive," says Ignacio Urabazzo, president of IBC Commerce Bank in Laredo. "But as we raise their standards of manufacturing through our technology, we'll increase their ability to buy our consumer goods, and we'll grow our own economy at an even greater rate."

There is no doubt that NAFTA has increased trade and will continue to do so. The central question that remains unanswered and will remain so for many years is the effect of cheap Mexican labor on U.S. jobs. Because of high unemployment caused by the peso devaluation, and the fact that nearly 40 percent of the Mexican population is under the age of 18, most economists think that the new economic growth in Mexico will take the form of more jobs rather than higher wages. The average starting wage at an assembly plant in Nuevo Laredo is 69 cents an hour, and few economists expect that to rise to U.S. minimum-wage levels soon.

But as more American technology goes to Mexico—such as decent phone service and better banking and transportation systems—NAFTA opponents fear that even high-tech jobs will soon head south. "You think that high tech is somehow sacred?" asks Reform Party vice presidential candidate Pat Choate, one of the few economists who oppose NAFTA. "Almost anything we can make here can be replicated down there, including computer chips. What will happen is that we will be eliminating the middle class from our society."

Most economists think Choate and Perot are just blowing hot air. "NAFTA is a net benefit, but its impact will be minuscule as long as the Mexican economy is as small as it is," says Bernard Weinstein, an economist at the University of North Texas. The official numbers thus far bear economists like Weinstein out. The U.S. trade office estimates that NAFTA has cost only about 44,000 jobs. Even if the real number is much higher than that, it is still a drop in the bucket for an economy with 120 million jobs in all.

So has NAFTA worked? It depends on whom you ask. For Mexican broommaker Trevino, the benefits of free trade are clear: "We are more competitive because we can get our product to the consumer for $2 less than our competitors," he says. Likewise, U.S. broom maker Libman sees the downside of less protection: "We're not a bunch of crybabies," he says, "but we need basic manufacturing jobs in this country because not everyone can be a computer engineer."

But in the future, job displacement and job growth could be significantly higher as tariffs continue to come down and trade grows. Then the question of whether America benefits enough from cheaper goods to make up for lost jobs will assume greater urgency. The U.S. broom industry thinks it already knows the answer to that one: no. And in July, the U.S. International Trade Commission seemed to agree, recommending that a 32 percent tariff be restored on imported brooms to save the industry. Not coincidentally, President Clinton will not have to decide whether to invoke the new tariffs until after the election.

In the next few years, with trade increasing and politics moving to the background, some clear patterns will no doubt emerge. And more than likely, neither side will be totally vindicated or vilified. Instead, NAFTA will produce some winners and some losers, with most likely to find themselves somewhere in between.

POSTSCRIPT

Does NAFTA Make Life Better for Americans?

As McGraw states, the jury is still out on the ultimate impact of NAFTA. Not every job went south, and some that did came back. If we tear our eyes away from Mexico and look to Canada, the United States seems to be competing well. This is encouraging to many.

However, Americans are not sufficiently encouraged to repeat the experiment. Late in 1997, when President Bill Clinton asked Congress for the authority to negotiate further trade pacts without congressional power to amend them (so-called fast track authority), he was turned down—with many of his own party, who had supported him on NAFTA, voting against him. Four years was enough to hear from all the displaced workers. The question may be whether or not *all* affected parties have been heard from—prospering consumers as well as laid-off workers. Would the benefit of NAFTA and potential benefit of fast track authority then outweigh the costs? It may be too soon to tell.

SUGGESTED READINGS

Donald K. Belch, "Free Trade: Patient Needs Resuscitating," *American Metal Market* (November 25, 1996), p. 114.

Leslie Crawford, "Hazardous Trades Bring Pollution and Health Fears Down Mexico Way," *The Financial Times* (June 6, 1997), p. 6.

Federal Reserve Bank of Chicago, "A Dynamic Macroeconomic Analysis of NAFTA," *Economic Perspectives* (January/February 1997), pp. 14–35.

Bryan W. Husted and Jeanne M. Logsdon, "The Impact of NAFTA on Mexico's Environmental Policy," *Growth and Change* (Winter 1997), pp. 24–25.

"Lopsided NAFTA," *Industry Week* (January 20, 1997), p. 80.

David E. Rosenbaum, "Sour Taste of NAFTA: Old Friends Become Foes," *The New York Times* (November 7, 1997), p. A10.

ISSUE 16

Are Sweatshops Necessarily Evil?

YES: Susan S. Black, from "Ante Up," *Bobbin* (September 19, 1996)

NO: Allen R. Myerson, from "In Principle, a Case for More 'Sweatshops,'" *The New York Times* (June 22, 1997)

ISSUE SUMMARY

YES: Susan S. Black, publisher of *Bobbin*, argues that customers will not tolerate goods made by slave labor, children, or women working in inhumane conditions. She maintains that customers are willing to pay more to make sure that the goods they buy were not made in sweatshops.

NO: Allen R. Myerson, a writer for the *New York Times*, looks at the economies of less developed countries and finds that allowing their citizens to work in sweatshops may be the only option these nations have to accumulate capital.

The Scottish economist Adam Smith's recommendation regarding government regulation of the terms of commercial contracts was to let every player in the market make his or her own best bargain, and in the end everyone would be better off.

Consider the conditions for the "voluntary exchange": there must be no fraud or misrepresentation on either side—both parties must know what they are getting into—and there must be no coercion. Simply put, this means that there must be no gun held to the head of either party. Less obviously, there must be no economic coercion: one party may not be under absolute economic coercion to sign. For example, if someone takes a job for the money to buy a new car, that decision seems to be perfectly free. But if the person needs the job immediately just to feed his or her family, it could be argued that the individual is not "free" to turn it down—the offer of a job is impossible to refuse. When one party has enormous economic power, and the other has none, there cannot be a free or voluntary agreement—there must be a certain degree of economic equality between the contracting parties, not absolute but not nonexistent, or there is no voluntariness.

Smith probably never imagined that this situation could arise. In a society with many employers in competition with each other for labor and other resources, not one of which is large enough to dominate the market, the laborer can simply withhold his or her services until he or she finds the employer that is willing to pay the most. There was a time when independent craftspeople made their contracts with individual buyers and when many small farmers needed help at harvest time. Then perhaps the economic power of the contracting parties was approximately equal and all exchanges were voluntary. But in the day of the huge factory that dominates the town and of the replaceable unskilled worker, one side seems to hold all the chips, and the other side holds none.

It could be argued that sweatshops—huge mass-production facilities where hundreds work in barbaric conditions for subsistence wages—built the United States. Workers rendered vulnerable by their immigrant status, disorientation in unfamiliar urban settings, and irremediable poverty were forced to take whatever jobs were available; entrepreneurs with access to capital threw up factories, and so the sweatshop was born. The union movement in the United States is all about the abolition of the sweatshop and the development of the modern factory—clean, safe, pleasant, and paying its workers adequate wages and benefits.

Clean, safe, pleasant, and losing money, modern entrepreneurs might say. In many industries, like the garment industry, the major cost of manufacture is labor. As long as there is no alternative, consumers seem willing to pay whatever they have to for their merchandise. But as soon as less expensive products become available—and with the growth of Asian competition, they certainly have become available—consumers buy them instead. Some say that only by continuing to manufacture offshore, in the sweatshops of Asia, can America remain competitive.

Meanwhile, the nations in which America is building these sweatshops do not seem to be complaining. On the contrary, they complain when U.S. multinational corporations shut down the sweatshops in response to American protests against them. Because so many of these nations' people can obtain jobs in American sweatshops, these shops are considered by some to be the only way the nations can grow.

As you read the following selections by Susan S. Black and Allen R. Myerson, ask yourself whether or not the outrage over sweatshop conditions in the developing world is justified. Are we importing standards appropriate to the late-twentieth-century United States rather than putting these manufactures against a backdrop of the lives lived by the workers before the factory came? Should a country be allowed to oppress or exploit its people in an effort to get its economy started?

YES

Susan S. Black

ANTE UP

Another chapter in the U.S. Labor Department's self-proclaimed war on apparel industry sweatshops was played out in mid-July when Secretary of Labor Robert Reich hosted a group of some 300, including *Bobbin*, to discuss what could be done about the problem.

The "Fashion Industry Forum," held at Marymount University just outside of Washington, D.C., drew manufacturers and retailers, union leaders, industry association representatives and such celebrity endorsers at Kathie Lee Gifford and Cheryl Tiegs, many of whom participated in panel presentations.

While Reich said he didn't expect "major headlines" to result from the forum, he did say that he hoped it would be a "turning point" and that he expected it to foster a "renewed commitment" to battle sweatshops and child labor. Of course, the fact that such major players as Wal-mart Stores, Kmart Corp., Nordstrom, Liz Claiborne, Patagonia Inc. and Levi Strauss & Co. participated in the forum is evidence in itself that Reich has managed to focus industry's attention on the subject of sweatshops. And whether one agrees with Reich's tactics or not—I don't—it seems almost certain that his momentum-gaining antisweatshop campaign is going to result in changes for our industry, namely that both retailers and manufacturers are going to have to incur additional expenses to prove to consumers that their goods are made under fair and legal labor conditions.

Among the options put on the table at the forum were "no-sweat" labeling programs, independent third-party monitoring of factories and increasing the duties of quality assurance personnel to encompass monitoring responsibilities—each of which undoubtedly comes with a price tag and such possible complex concerns as, "Who monitors the monitors?" If additional monitoring and labeling programs do come to fruition, the key question is who will pay the price. Opinions on the level of cost and who should bear responsibility for that cost varied at the forum, but my bet is that ultimately it will be the entire soft goods chain—and the consumer—that pays.

"The customer can't have its cake and eat it too," said Tiegs, who first licensed her name for an apparel line in the 1980s. "They must pay the price."

John Ermatinger, senior vice president of operations and sourcing for Levi Strauss North America, said it's time to stop placing blame and time to start finding solutions. "I would like to spend more time working on this issue and less time talking about it," he said. "It's unfair to focus on the retailer. It's a supply chain challenge and we will have to find flexible, non-mandated solutions. It's not a one-size-fits-all solution."

Levi's success in producing no-sweat goods (it first established standards for monitoring contractors in 1991) is a result of making monitoring an integral part of the business. "This is how we do business," Ermatinger said. "It's part of how we measure performance."

As part of its reengineering, Levi's also has cut its supplier base by 50 percent, said Ermatinger, "enabling us to focus more efficiently on our remaining base."

Roberta Karp, vice president of corporate affairs and general counsel for Liz Claiborne, agreed that there is no "recipe to follow" when it comes to monitoring. She said Claiborne has its own internal monitoring program, but might consider expanding it. "We must reach out to partnerships [in monitoring]," she said.

Warren Flick, president of merchandising for Kmart, said for its part, the merchant is "rebuilding" its entire buying organization. He said Kmart will have fewer vendors, and longer-term relationships with those vendors.

Flick also said Kmart has created a new executive position, based in Hong Kong, to oversee Kmart's global monitoring efforts. "Our eyes and ears are wide open," he added. "We know what products and regions where our focus needs to be."

Gale Cottle, executive vice president for Nordstrom who said that Nordstrom will not tolerate vendors who use illegal practices, also pointed to some of the challenges a retailer has in monitoring the conditions under which its goods are made. For starters, she said Nordstrom has 13,000 U.S. vendors, and 870 decentralized buyers who buy on a customized level according to changing fashion needs. She said: "A buyer cannot identify cost in a showroom... and even the right price doesn't guarantee the right conditions."

Also bringing a practical slant to the forum was Tracy Mullin, president of the National Retail Federation (NRF), who observed that while retailers cannot afford to jeopardize their reputations and want to take "aggressive steps forward," there are a myriad of considerations in handling sweatshop accusations. Noting that the problem of sweatshops often involves organized crime and immigration violations, she recommended coordinated efforts among the Internal Revenue Service, the Immigration and Naturalization Service and the Justice Department.

The granddaddy retailer of them all, Wal-Mart—around which much media attention has been generated after it was discovered that Kathie Lee Gifford apparel was being produced in a New York, NY, sweatshop—said at the forum that it never had inspected U.S. factories with whom it does business, but is doing so now. It also will be recertifying the overseas factories with whom it does business, and has studied an independent monitoring program used by The Gap, said Lee Scott, executive vice president of merchandise and sales for Wal-Mart.

Still, Scott cautioned that there could be a tendency to migrate toward using only large, well-established vendors, which would "keep out the young, innovative companies."

If the Fashion Industry Forum means that some companies will adopt more careful monitoring practices with their contractors and subcontractors, there's no question the results will be positive. After all, good manufacturing practices logically should result in better quality and higher profits. But it's important to note that behind the publicly spoken words at the forum were many forces at play, several with distinctly different motives. Government, unions, retailers, manufacturers, contractors—each has its own self-interests.

Let's just hope that as many of the already law-abiding businesses in our industry commit themselves to more thorough documentation of how their goods are made, the illicit businesses and sweatshops will fall by the wayside in greater numbers. Because the last thing this industry needs is more bad publicity based on the actions of a few.

One last thought. Did you know that the members of the American Apparel Manufacturers Association (AAMA)—which represent about two-thirds of the garments made in the United States—manufacture 85 percent of their goods in their own plants? And that the average U.S. apparel worker makes double the minimum wage, plus another 30 percent in benefits?

Those statistics came from AAMA president Larry Martin at the forum. I think they're worth remembering—and repeating.

NO

Allen R. Myerson

IN PRINCIPLE, A CASE FOR MORE "SWEATSHOPS"

CAMBRIDGE, Mass.

For more than a century, accounts of sweatshops have provoked outrage. From the works of Charles Dickens and Lincoln Steffens to today's television reports, the image of workers hunched over their machines for meager rewards has been a banner of reform.

Last year, companies like Nike and Wal-Mart and celebrities like Kathie Lee Gifford struggled to defend themselves after reports of the torturous hours and low pay of the workers who produce their upscale footwear or downmarket fashions. Anxious corporate spokesmen sought to explain the plants as a step up for workers in poor countries. A weeping Mrs. Gifford denied knowing about the conditions.

Now some of the nation's leading economists, with solid liberal and academic credentials, are offering a much broader, more principled rationale. Economists like Jeffrey D. Sachs of Harvard and Paul Krugman of the Massachusetts Institute of Technology say that low-wage plants making clothing and shoes for foreign markets are an essential first step toward modern prosperity in developing countries.

Mr. Sachs, a leading adviser and shock therapist to nations like Bolivia, Russia and Poland, is now working on the toughest cases of all, the economies of sub-Saharan Africa. He is just back from Malawi, where malaria afflicts almost all its 13 million people and AIDS affects 1 in 10; the lake that provided much of the country's nourishment is fished out.

When asked during a recent Harvard panel discussion whether there were too many sweatshops in such places, Mr. Sachs answered facetiously, "My concern is not that there are too many sweatshops but that there are too few," he said.

Mr. Sachs, who has visited low-wage factories around the world, is opposed to child or prisoner labor and other outright abuses. But many nations, he says, have no better hope than plants paying mere subsistence wages. "Those are precisely the jobs that were the steppingstone for Singapore and Hong

Kong," he said, "and those are the jobs that have to come to Africa to get them out of their backbreaking rural poverty."

Rising Stakes

The stakes in the battle over sweatshops are high and rising. Clinton Administration officials say commerce with the major developing nations like China, Indonesia and Mexico is crucial for America's own continued prosperity. Corporate America's manufacturing investments in developing nations more than tripled in 15 years to $56 billion in 1995—not including the vast numbers of plants there that contract with American companies.

In matters of trade and commerce, economists like Mr. Sachs, who has also worked with several Government agencies, are influential. A consensus among economists helped persuade President Clinton, who had campaigned against President Bush's plan of lowered restrictions, to ram global and North American trade pacts through Congress.

Paradoxically, economists' support of sweatshops represents a sort of optimism. Until the mid-1980's, few thought that third world nations could graduate to first world status in a lifetime, if ever. "When I went to graduate school in the early to mid-1970's," Mr. Krugman said, "it looked like being a developed country was really a closed club." Only Japan had made a convincing jump within the past century.

Those economists who believed that developing nations could advance often prescribed self-reliance and socialism, warning against foreign investment as a form of imperialism. Advanced nations invested in the developing world largely to extract oil, coffee, bananas and other resources but created few new jobs or industries. Developing nations, trying to lessen their reliance on manufactured imports, tried to bolster domestic industries for the home market. But these protected businesses were often inefficient and the local markets to small to sustain them.

From Wigs to Cars

Then the Four Tigers—Hong Kong, Singapore, South Korea and Taiwan —began to roar. They made apparel, toys, shoes and, at least in South Korea's case, wigs and false teeth, mostly for export. Within a generation, their national incomes climbed from about 10 percent to 40 percent of American incomes. Singapore welcomed foreign plant owners while South Korea shunned them, building industrial conglomerates of its own. But the first stage of development had one constant. "It's always sweatshops," Mr. Krugman said.

These same nations now export cars and computers, and the economists have revised their views of sweatshops. "The overwhelming mainstream view among economists is that the growth of this kind of employment is tremendous good news for the world's poor," Mr. Krugman said.

Unlike the corporate apologists, economists make no attempt to prettify the sweatshop picture. Mr. Krugman, who writes a column for Slate magazine called "The Dismal Scientist," describes sweatshop owners as "soulless multinationals and rapacious local entrepreneurs, whose only concern was to take advantage of the profit opportunities offered by cheap labor." But even in a nation as corrupt as Indonesia, he says, industrialization has reduced the portion of malnourished children from more than half in 1975 to a third today.

In judging the issue of child labor also, Mr. Krugman is a pragmatist, asking what else is available. It often isn't education. In India, for example, destitute parents sometimes sell their children to Persian Gulf begging syndicates whose bosses mutilate them for a higher take, he says. "If that is the alternative, it is not so easy to say that children should not be working in factories," Mr. Krugman said.

Not that most economists argue for sweatshops at home. The Untied States, they say, can afford to set much higher labor standards than poor countries—though Europe's are so high, some say, that high unemployment results.

Labor leaders and politicians who challenge sweatshops abroad say that they harm American workers as well, stealing jobs and lowering wages—a point that some economists dispute. "It is especially galling when American workers lose jobs to places where workers are really being exploited," said Mark Levinson, chief economist at the Union of Needletrades, Industrial and Textile Employees, who argues for trade sanctions to enforce global labor rules.

Yet when corporations voluntarily cut their ties to sweatshops, the victims can be the very same people sweatshop opponents say they want to help. In Honduras, where the legal working age is 14, girls toiled 75 hours a week for the 31-cent hourly minimum to make the Kathie Lee Gifford clothing line for Wal-Mart. When Wal-Mart canceled its contract, the girls lost their jobs and blamed Mrs. Gifford.

No Jobs in Practice

Mr. Krugman blames American self-righteousness or guilt over Indonesian women and children sewing sneakers at 60 cents an hour. "A policy of good jobs in principle, but no jobs in practice, might assuage our consciences," he said, "but it is no favor to its alleged beneficiaries."

POSTSCRIPT

Are Sweatshops Necessarily Evil?

As the troubles now afflicting Asia remind us, no economic powerhouse is forever. Before the current crumbling of Asian economies, Americans had watched in fascination while the once-invulnerable Japan went through a "miniature U.S. history": workers clamoring for better conditions, people spending more on consumer goods and saving less, and wages rising steadily. Then, of course, manufacture shifted to Thailand and other places where labor was very inexpensive.

SUGGESTED READINGS

David R. Henderson, "The Case for Sweatshops," *Fortune* (October 28, 1996), pp. 48–52.

Mark Henricks, "Labor Says No Sweat," *Apparel Industry Magazine* (January 1996), pp. 68–70.

James Mamarella, "Decent Labor Standards Should Be the Standard," *Discount Store News* (April 1, 1996), p. 2.

Jack A. Raisner, "Using the 'Ethical Environment' Paradigm to Teach Business Ethics: The Case of the Maquiladoras," *Journal of Business Ethics* (September 1997), pp. 1331–1346.

"Watching the Sweatshops," *The New York Times* (August 20, 1997).

On the Internet . . .

FAQs About Free-Market Environmentalism

Sponsored by the Thoreau Institute, this site answers frequently asked questions about free-market environmentalism. It is the institute's position that a free-market system can solve many environmental problems better than more government regulation can.
http://www.racc.org/~rot/faqs.html

Pennsylvania Department of Environmental Protection Home Page

This site, maintained by the Pennsylvania Department of Environmental Protection, monitors environmental responsibility.
http://www.dep.state.pa.us/

Working Assets

This site has been developed to provide information for businesses to establish humane and environmentally sustainable practices. *http://www.wald.com/*

PART 5

Environmental Policy and Corporate Responsibility

Mankind's attempts to protect the environment have involved many conflicts over fundamental values. We know that the environment must be protected, but the natural environment cannot participate in our political processes as an interest group nor can it buy itself protection on the open market. So we have to put aside the fundamental model of human action as rule-governed competition; nature cannot compete. In this section, we consider debates on property rights and the environment, the industrial use of chlorine, and strategies for preventing the destruction of the tropical rain forests.

■ Should Property Rights Prevail Over Environmental Protection?

■ Should the Industrial Use of Chlorine Be Phased Out?

■ Can Green Marketing Save Tropical Rain Forests?

ISSUE 17

Should Property Rights Prevail Over Environmental Protection?

YES: Richard Epstein, from "Property Rights and Environmental Protection," *Cato Policy Report* (May/June 1992)

NO: John Echeverria, from "Property Rights and Environmental Protection," *Cato Policy Report* (May/June 1992)

ISSUE SUMMARY

YES: Professor of law Richard Epstein notes that if the government takes a person's private property, it must pay that person the market value, or at least "fair compensation," for it. Epstein argues that if a law is passed that robs an individual's property of all value, that amounts to the same thing, and he or she should therefore be compensated.

NO: John Echeverria, a legal counsel to the National Audubon Society, argues that property rights have never included a right to do public harm and that environmental regulations, like other laws, do not violate a right to one's property.

The United States has always held the belief of liberty under law. However, the truth is that every law limits liberty in some way. Even though all American citizens have a right to liberty, every law infringes some possible rights, and every new law infringes some existing right. This is how it must be, for conditions change, needs evolve, and, above all, our knowledge base expands. It could be argued that all the major changes that have evolved in society during the twentieth century have come about because of the growth of knowledge. One of the largest areas of change-producing knowledge is the workings of the natural environment and environmental health.

As recently as two centuries ago, after 10,000 years of settled agricultural living, the connection between waterborne microorganisms and disease was not understood, the connection between airborne particulates and lung dysfunction was not understood, and the connection between sanitation in living habits—from latrine use to cleanliness of food and utensils—and general public health was a complete mystery. Infant and child mortality was extremely high in the most civilized societies as well as in the least, and epidemics raged through the cities periodically. People's lives were changed dramatically by knowledge (empirically grounded, if not scientifically grounded at the time) of connections between disease and unsanitary conditions and by government action following swiftly upon that knowledge. The government action inevitably limited liberty: the liberty to dispose of wastes indiscriminately as in the past, to use wells without controls as in the past, and to raise animals for food under the same unsanitary conditions as generations of farmers had in the past. The result of all that legislation is that we are currently alive in greater numbers and are far healthier than humans have been at any other time in history.

Knowledge continues to advance, including knowledge of the workings of the natural environment. On the downside, the success of the first wave of public health legislation has allowed a greater number of people than anticipated to occupy the fragile ecosystems of our salt- and fresh-water borders. The area under contention in *Lucas v. South Carolina Coastal Council*, the case that launches the debate that follows, would never have been inhabited by human beings a century or two ago; the mosquitoes from the swamps would have ensured that periodic epidemics of yellow fever and malaria swept the beaches clean of human inhabitants. Now we have the knowledge to protect ourselves from disease and other natural foes, and, consequently, nature cannot stop us from building on the barrier beaches and wetlands of our coasts.

As we have gained the technology to build on these fragile ecosystems, we have also learned why we should not: the marshes and the dunes should be left alone—unfilled, undug, undumped in—if we wish to preserve the larger life of the sea and the inland coastal areas. So where nature used to exercise its own rough zoning prerogatives through periodic disease and hurricanes, legislation now steps in to ensure public health and safety in the long run.

The debate that follows turns on two points: First, is there any wisdom in creating the environmental protection legislation under question? Or are the agencies of government, the legislature and the regulatory agency, carrying the desire for ecosystem preservation too far, into what Richard Epstein calls "institutional overclaiming"? Second, whatever the wisdom of the legislation, does it constitute a "taking" under the Constitution, requiring compensation for the property owner whose property falls under the regulations? After all, there may be excellent, even compelling, reasons for a superhighway, but if you knock down my house in order to build it, you have to pay me for my house.

As you read the following selections by Epstein and John Echeverria, ask yourself what is really meant by the right of private property. Is property an exclusive "right" held *against* the commonwealth? Or is it primarily a "stewardship" held *within* the commonwealth, utilized by private parties for public good as well as private?

YES

Richard Epstein

PROPERTY RIGHTS AND ENVIRONMENTAL PROTECTION

In December 1986 David H. Lucas purchased two undeveloped waterfront lots, which were zoned for single-family homes, on the Isle of Palms, South Carolina. Lucas's intention was to build one home to sell and a second as his own residence. In 1988, after Hurricane Hugo, South Carolina passed the Beachfront Management Act [BMA], which prohibited all new construction beyond certain setback lines and thereby rendered Lucas's property essentially useless for the purposes he had intended. The trial court found that the BMA constituted a "taking" and awarded Lucas compensation. The South Carolina Supreme Court reversed that decision, and Lucas appealed to the U.S. Supreme Court, which will soon decide whether government must compensate property owners under the Fifth Amendment's takings clause when it forbids them to develop their land. . . .

If you understand exactly what a comprehensive system of property rights entails, not only do you say that there is no opposition between property rights and environmentalism but you also say that property rights and environmental claims are mutually supportive when correctly understood.

Even though we recognize zones of autonomy, there have to be some limitations on what property owners can do with their own. It is in those limitations, I think, that one finds the effective reconciliation of property rights and environmental concerns.

The common law of nuisance, which developed over time to police disputes between property owners, is best understood as a mechanism designed to arbitrate and to reconcile disputes so as to maximize the value of each person's respective property holdings. The moment one starts to deviate from that understanding, there will be excesses in one direction or the other. If landowners, for example, are entitled to pollute more or less at will, then activities that are relatively small in value will be allowed to continue even though they cause enormous harms to other individuals. And if a system

From Richard Epstein, "Property Rights and Environmental Protection," *Cato Policy Report* (May/June 1992). Copyright © 1992 by The Cato Institute, Washington, DC. Reprinted by permission.

of land-use restrictions is imposed as a matter of positive law when there are no such externalities, relatively trivial gains will be exacted at the cost of enormous private losses. The system must maximize the value of inconsistent claims under general rules.

The eminent domain clause of the Fifth Amendment says, "Nor shall private property be taken for public use without just compensation." It says nothing of the justifications for governments' assuming control of property without compensating the owners—an activity that goes under the heading of police power. Therefore, to understand *Lucas* [*v. South Carolina Coastal Council*], we must first ask what kinds of activities engaged in by government *do* constitute a taking, that is, do move into the sphere of protected liberties. Then we must ask whether we can find some kind of public justification for the restrictions thus imposed.

On the first issue, it is quite clear that the common law did not draw a distinction that the constitutional lawyers insist on drawing: the modern claim that there is a vast distance between physical occupation by government and a mere regulation or restriction of use. That contemporary distinction is designed to say that we don't have to look closely at anything government does if it leaves a person in bare possession of his property.

In effect, the position of the environmentalists on this issue is, "We will allow you to keep the rind of the orange as long as we can suck out all of its juice for our own particular benefit." But exclusive possession of property is not an end in itself. The reason you want exclusive possession is to make some use of your property and if you can't make good use of it, you'd like to be able to sell or trade it to somebody else. The modern law essentially says that all those use and disposition decisions are subject to public veto.

What's wrong with that? Chiefly, it encourages a massive amount of irresponsible behavior on the part of government in its treatment of private endeavors. Essentially, a government now knows that it can attain 90 percent of its objectives and pay nothing. Why, then, would it ever bother to assume the enormous burden of occupying land for which it would then have to pay full market value? Thus, we see government regulations pushing further and further, regardless of private losses, which will never be reflected on the public ledgers —precisely the situation we find in *Lucas*.

We have in *Lucas* a change in value brought about, not because people don't want to live on the beach anymore, but because they are prohibited from using their land in the ordinary fashion. And the simplest question to ask is, what kinds of public benefits could justify that private loss?

Nobody on the Isle of Palms or anywhere else along the Carolina coast regards the restrictions in question as having been enacted for his benefit. We know that because before the regulation was imposed, land values were very high and appreciating rapidly; after the regulation was imposed, everybody who was subject to it was wiped out. When we see such a huge wipeout, we have to look for the explanation of the statute that caused it, not in the protection of the local community, but in external third-party interests who will gain something, although far less than the landowners have lost.

In the usual case, when we take property for public use, we want to make sure that there's no disproportionate burden on the affected parties, but that consideration is rightly discarded when we can say to a particular fellow that we're concentrating losses on him because he has done something of great danger to the public at large. So we now have to think about Mr. Lucas's one-family house sitting on the beach front and find in it the kind of terror that might be associated with heavy explosives or ongoing, menacing pollution.

Can we do it? I think the question almost answers itself. There is no way that we can get within a thousand miles of a common law nuisance on the facts of this particular case. There is no immediate threat of erosion. We're told we're really worried about the infliction of serious external harms. Can we get an injunction on the grounds that the roof might blow off a particular building and land in the hapless fields of a neighbor? The question again more or less answers itself.

The original statute made very little if any reference whatsoever to the problem of safety. It referred instead to promoting leisure among South Carolina citizens, promoting tourism, and promoting a general form of retreat. The moment we see safety introduced during litigation, we have to wonder whether it's a pretext for some other cause.

Another difficulty involves the breadth of the restriction. If the concern is hurricane damage, the appropriate solution is, not to limit the statute in question to just beach-front owners, but to pass a general order that says: after Hurricane Hugo, nobody is entitled to rebuild in South Carolina—in Charleston or anywhere else.

There's also the question of the relationship between means and ends. If there was $10 billion worth of damage attributable to the hurricane, at least $100 of that damage must have been attributable to flying debris and falling houses. That is a trivial problem, and even if it were serious, there are surely better ways of dealing with it. We might say, for example, that anybody whose house could be found littering the beach had to remove all debris.

We hear over and over again that the government's environmental programs will shrink in size if compensation is required in *Lucas*. Those programs *should* shrink, because when government is allowed to take without compensation, it claims too much for environmental causes relative to other kinds of causes that command equal attention. Unless we introduce a system that requires the government to take and pay when it restricts private use not associated with the prevention of harms, we'll face an institutional overclaiming problem. The expansion of government will become the major issue. The just compensation clause is designed to work a perfectly sensible and moderate accommodation, to force the government to make responsible choices.

... According to Mr. Echeverria, it would be within the state's power to order everybody who has a home on those islands to dismantle it immediately so that there would be no flying roofs to hurt anybody else. The state could order the demolition of old construction as well as enjoin new construction.

Moreover, the beach front is not the only area peculiarly exposed to the environmental and hurricane risks that we're talking about. What about Charleston? It's also exposed to those risks. Do we say, in effect, that in the name of environmental protection we must raze the entire city without compensation because somebody's house might fall on somebody else's?

This is not a question of environmental interaction. We now have a set of restrictions that promises to cause billions in private losses, and we've heard it said that we can stop houses from being knocked down by ordering them to be razed.

There is no sense of proportion or balance in Echeverria's position. An ounce of environmental angst is sufficient to allow draconian measures that forbid the very activities that enable people to use the environment constructively. This is a classic case of overclaiming, which occurs because the environmental lobby can go to the state legislature and say, "Let us have our way. You're not going to have to pay for this." And environmentalists can prove that the benefit is greater than the political cost. But that's the wrong test. From a social point of view, the *right* test is whether the benefit is greater than the cost inflicted on the property holders.

NO

John Echeverria

PROPERTY RIGHTS AND ENVIRONMENTAL PROTECTION

As everybody in this room knows, our national politics is driven by sound bites. The same is true in a judicial context. The hard facts of a particular case can make bad law, and the sound bite in this case is that David Lucas purchased a piece of property for about $1 million and two years later the South Carolina legislature passed a law that left him with nothing. But that's the sound bite, and the sound bite obscures the entirely genuine and legitimate goals that the South Carolina legislature had in mind—to prevent harms to the public, which are not trivial concerns.

My goal in this debate is to convince you that once you get past the sound bite of the impact on Lucas, you'll understand that the Supreme Court should and will conclude that there was no taking in this case. Before I get into it though, . . . I want to try to correct the sound bite by reciting to you the facts of a case the Supreme Court dealt with in 1987. That case involved a similar kind of regulation and raised the same fundamental issues of principle but leads to quite a different sound bite. I am referring to *First English Evangelical Lutheran Church v. County of Los Angeles.* The church had set up a camp for handicapped children in a flood plain, and a fire occurred in the watershed upstream from the camp. The county recognized immediately that there was enormous danger, since the vegetation had been removed, that flood waters could come down the river and wipe out the camp. In fact, a storm did occur, a flood did occur and the camp was completely wiped out. In response, the county put in place an interim ordinance that said there could be no inhabitable structures, which could be wiped out once again, within the flood plain. When the Supreme Court got the case it did not resolve it on the merits. Instead, it used that case to reach the conclusion that a temporary taking is compensable under the Fifth Amendment. But in the dissenting opinion, several of the justices said there was no question that the ordinance was a valid public health and safety regulation and there was no taking. And Chief Justice Rehnquist said that the Court didn't have to touch that issue and would leave it to the lower courts to find out whether there had been a taking. The case was sent back to the lower courts. No taking was found, and

From John Echeverria, "Property Rights and Environmental Protection," *Cato Policy Report* (May/June 1992). Copyright © 1992 by The Cato Institute, Washington, DC. Reprinted by permission.

when the case went up for review, the Supreme Court, which probably has some understanding of sound bites itself, declined to review it.

Lucas, as it was actually presented to the trial court, is actually a fairly easy case, in my view. The Supreme Court should conclude that Lucas did not establish a taking because he presented his claim based on the completely preposterous theory that if he suffered economic harm, that alone, regardless of any other consideration, entitled him to compensation under the Fifth Amendment. The fact of the matter is that the Supreme Court has never held, and I predict will never hold, that economic injury, standing alone, is sufficient grounds for a Fifth Amendment claim. The Court has consistently rejected that way of thinking for several reasons. First, the Court has recognized that every piece of property held in the United States is subject to the condition that it can't be used to harm others. That goes back to common law. Property rights are not absolute. They're conditional upon a responsibility to the community in which one resides.

The Department of Justice recommended initially that the United States in its brief take the position that economic harm, standing alone, constitutes a taking. Happily, wiser heads prevailed, and the solicitor general filed a brief that specifically repudiated that theory.

Richard Epstein, in his amicus brief, admits that a complete wipeout does not, by itself, make out a taking. We disagree about the range of activities in which the government can engage to prevent public harm without providing compensation. But we agree that within that range of activities, the government can act to prevent harm and no compensation is due regardless of the impact. I think it's on that issue that this case will basically turn.

Epstein's point, at least as I understand it from his brief, is that the burden of proof is on the government to show the legitimacy of the regulation, to show that it is in fact a public harm–prevention measure. But again, one doesn't have a property interest in harming others, and if the government is trying to prevent a landowner from harming others, then there's simply no taking.

I think that Epstein and I agree that there is a line between private property and the ability of people to impose external harms on others and to harm the general public by the use of property. The question is, where is that line drawn and on what side of the line does this particular regulation fall?

I submit that the harm the South Carolina legislature was trying to deal with here was both very real and very substantial. Barrier islands are not like other real estate. They literally migrate; they move. They're unconsolidated sandy sediments that migrate laterally up and down the shore and landward in response to the action of waves and winds. They are unstable areas that are very hazardous for construction. Barrier islands in the natural state provide the most important defense for coastal areas against the effects of storms, high winds, and storm surges associated with hurricanes. Building on the beach dune system, which destroys the dune, or trying to stabilize the dune fundamentally undermines the integrity of the system. Sand naturally moves from a dune down to the beach area, replenishing the beach and allowing it to serve as a barrier to storms. If the beach dune system is stabilized, its natural function is destroyed.

It is not simply a question of harm to somebody who builds on such an unstable area, although I think there are some reasons to support paternalism in some circumstances. It is also a question of harm to others. Landward properties depend on the defense provided by the beach dune system. If that system is destroyed, those properties are exposed to storm damage. Epstein belittled what the coastal geologists refer to as projectile damage, but it's a very real phenomenon. Buildings that are on the ocean shore in front of or on top of the dunes are particularly exposed to the effects of wind and storms. After Hurricane Hugo in South Carolina, the primary adverse effects on landward structures were found to be due precisely to exposed properties that were hurled landward. All of those risks also have to be considered in light of global warming and a consequent sea level rise—again, exacerbating the hazardous nature of construction on the ocean shore and the dangers to other property owners posed by such construction.

The South Carolina Beachfront Management Act is an entirely rational, thoughtful, well-tailored response to a public hazard. The first purpose of the act, and clearly the primary purpose as recited in the act itself, is to protect the public. The act recites the fact that beaches are important recreational areas and identifies other public purposes that are served by the beaches. But what is most clear is that the regulation at issue here is specifically tailored to address a public-hazard problem.

My final point, and perhaps the most important, is that the statute specifically provided that Mr. Lucas, if he believed the line drawn pursuant to the legislative scheme was unfair, could present evidence to the coastal council and explain that the line on his property should be drawn at a different point. He never took advantage of that opportunity. He simply said, "I've been hurt and I am entitled to compensation." I believe the Supreme Court will disagree.

POSTSCRIPT

Should Property Rights Prevail Over Environmental Protection?

Political conservatives and liberals tend to divide along different lines at different points in history. In the early nineteenth century, the conservatives believed that the right of the community came before the right of the individual, while the liberals championed individual liberty over community control and democratic equality over the traditional hierarchy. With regard to the current debate, this earlier terminology has been abandoned largely because the focus of ethical debate has changed from the *political* to the *economic* questions—from questions of community governance to questions of resource management. In short, the United States has moved from an era of *political philosophy* to an era of *business management,* where the entire nation is seen as a collective resource to be managed by those with authority over it. However, if the more political terms are applied, the roles of Epstein and Echeverria may be seen in this way: Echeverria is the conservative businessman, conserving resources and letting nature take its course, while Epstein is the defender of the strategy of instant consumption.

If you were the judge who had to decide the *Lucas* case, how would you rule? Do you believe that Lucas is entitled to compensation, as argued by Epstein, or that there was no instance of compensable taking involved in the legislation, as argued by Echeverria? Does your response reflect the conservative or the liberal position?

SUGGESTED READINGS

Robert M. Andersen, "Technology, Pollution Control, and EPA Access to Commercial Property: A Constitutional and Policy Framework," *Boston College Environmental Affairs Law Review* (Fall 1989).

Rogene Buchholz, *Principles of Environmental Management: The Greening of Business* (Prentice Hall, 1993).

John Campbell and Leon N. Lindberg, "Property Rights and the Organization of Economic Activity by the State," *American Sociological Review* (October 1990), pp. 634–647.

Rachel Carson, *The Edge of the Sea* (Houghton Mifflin, 1955).

Arthur Chan, "The Changing View of Property Rights in Natural Resources Management," *American Journal of Economics and Sociology* (April 1989).

G. Tyler Miller, *Living in the Environment,* 7th ed. (Wadsworth, 1992).

David E. Mills, "Zoning Rights and Land Development Timing," *Land Economics* (August 1990).

ISSUE 18

Should the Industrial Use of Chlorine Be Phased Out?

YES: Joe Thornton, from "Chlorine: Can't Live With It, Can Live Without It," Speech Prepared for the Chlorine-Free Debate Held in Conjunction With the International Joint Commission Seventh Biennial Meeting, Windsor, Ontario, Canada (October 1993)

NO: Ivan Amato, from "The Crusade to Ban Chlorine," *Garbage: The Independent Environmental Quarterly* (Summer 1994)

ISSUE SUMMARY

YES: Greenpeace research coordinator Joe Thornton argues that a systematic phaseout of chlorinated organic compounds is the only effective means of protecting humans and animals from the toxic effects of these chemicals.

NO: Science writer Ivan Amato argues that only a few chlorinated compounds are proven health threats and that Greenpeace's claims that substitutes exist are misleading.

The campaign to ban the industrial uses of chlorine began with a 1991 initiative by Greenpeace, the largest international grassroots environmental organization in the United States. The basis for the initiative was the growing evidence that a wide variety of chlorinated compounds—such as dioxins, PCBs, chlorinated pesticides, vinyl chloride, and chloroform—are highly toxic or carcinogenic, and that chlorine-containing compounds, especially the chlorofluorocarbons, are destroying the earth's protective ozone layer.

The first chemicals to be regulated or banned by law were the clear and obvious threats to public health—the mercury- or arsenic-containing agricultural chemicals or radioactive isotopes. Following the publication of Rachel Carson's *Silent Spring* in 1962, which documented the unanticipated effects of DDT on the environment, there was a sharp increase in environmental consciousness—especially about the potential human health and ecological impacts of the enormous number of synthetic chemicals introduced into industrial use following World War II. Numerous laws that were passed to address these impacts were designed to reduce environmental pollution or public exposure to a rapidly growing list of proven, or suspected, hazardous substances. These laws attempt to limit air emissions, water contamination, land contamination, food contamination, and industrial exposure.

The established practice for developing legislation considers each suspected chemical individually. This conservative approach, assuming harmlessness until harm is shown, avoids needless panic, but is expensive and time-consuming; it has resulted in a growing backlog of untested industrial chemicals being introduced into processes or products that result in exposure to workers and consumers. Citizens groups concerned about hazardous chemicals have unsuccessfully lobbied for a policy of requiring proof of harmlessness before a new chemical is introduced into the market or the waste stream.

Given the historical success in maintaining the presumption of chemical innocence, the chemical industry was caught off guard by the rapidity with which the proposal to phase out nonessential uses of chlorine compounds led to endorsements and action. Chlorine gas has been eliminated as a bleach for pulp and paper in Europe. Norway has commissioned research on the policy effects of a total chlorine ban, and the International Joint Commission (IJC) on the Great Lakes has recommended a broad organochlorine phaseout. The UN Economic Commission for Europe is negotiating an agreement with 50 countries that would restrict the use of many persistent chlorinated compounds, including PCBs and DDT. The American Public Health Association issued a resolution in 1993 supporting a reduction in industrial uses of chlorine. Although the new drinking water and pesticide regulations adopted by the 104th Congress do not ban the use of chlorine or chlorinated compounds, they do require screening for the presence of those chlorine-containing chemicals that act as endocrine disrupters.

The chlorine industry promptly launched a counterattack. This industry initiative is multifaceted, with various articles aimed at the different claims of Greenpeace, the IJC, and other activist groups. The literature includes a solid defense of the role of chlorine in disinfecting drinking water (which Greenpeace does not deny) and measured rebuttals of claims that organochlorines are implicated in specific cancers or patterns of occurrence of cancer. Defenders of the industry point out further that chlorine is used in an enormous variety of beneficial products and employs tens of thousands of people, suggesting that bans or restrictions would drive industry offshore, increasing unemployment in the United States and raising prices of essential products. Other presentations take up some of the clear dangers of chlorine-associated production (the emission of dioxins into the waterways, for instance) and show how the industry itself has addressed the production problems that led to the danger and has reduced the emissions. In reply to the attacks a common argument is that against the benefits derived from the use of chlorine, the associated risks do not justify restriction or ban.

As you read the following selections by Joe Thornton and Ivan Amato, bear in mind that neither regulation nor the lack of regulation is cost-free; citizens will have to decide whether or not the current benefits of a thriving chlorine industry should be sacrificed for the possible long-term benefits of a chlorine-free environment.

YES

Joe Thornton

CHLORINE: CAN'T LIVE WITH IT,
CAN LIVE WITHOUT IT

In medicine, an ounce of prevention is worth a pound of cure. When it comes to the global environment, however, an ounce of prevention is priceless, for serious damage to the biosphere cannot be repaired before the health of millions of humans and other species has been affected. Already, toxic chlorine-based organic chemicals—called organochlorines—have contaminated the global environment and caused widespread damage to human health and the ecosystem; these chemicals cannot be removed from the tissues of the human population, the food chain or the general environment. It is time for society to adopt a precautionary strategy to prevent further damage by organochlorines.

My purpose here is three-fold: first, to show that organochlorines are a major hazard to health and the global environment; second, to show that for the purpose of environmental policy these thousands of related chemicals should be treated as a class, and that a planned phase-out of the industrial production and use of chlorine and organochlorines is necessary to prevent further injury to health and the environment; and third, to show that a phase-out of chlorine is technologically and economically feasible.

Already, numerous international institutions have called for a chlorine phase-out. For instance, the International Joint Commission on the Great Lakes (IJC)—a binational advisory body to the governments of the U.S. and Canada—concluded in 1992 and reiterated in 1994 that chlorine-based organic chemicals are a primary hazard to human health and the environment. On the IJC's list of the eleven pollutants requiring the most urgent action, eight are organochlorines; of the 362 on the "secondary track," more than half are chlorinated. The IJC argued that these chemicals should be treated as a class and subject to a policy of Zero Discharge, and recommended that the governments of the U.S. and Canada should, "in consultation with industry and other affected interests, develop timetables to sunset the use of chlorine and chlorine-containing compounds as industrial feedstocks."

Such diverse organizations as the Paris Commission on the Northeast Atlantic—a ministerial convention of 15 European governments—the

International Whaling Commission, the Arctic Wildlife Congress, and the 21-nation Barcelona Convention on the Mediterranean have all concluded that discharges of persistent, bioaccumulative substances—particularly organochlorines—should be eliminated entirely.

In late 1993, the American Public Health Association, the nation's premier organization of public health scientists and professionals, resolved that "chlorinated organic chemicals are found to pose public health risks involving the workplace, consumer products, and the general environment," and recognized that "elimination of chlorine and/or chlorinated organic compounds from certain manufacturing processes, products, and uses may be the most cost-effective and health protective way to reduce health and environmental exposures to chlorinated organic compounds." The APHA concluded that organochlorines should be treated as a class, presumed harmful unless shown otherwise, and phased-out, with exceptions made only if a given use or substance can be proven safe or essential.

And in early 1994, the Clinton White House announced as part of its proposal for the Clean Water Act that the Environmental Protection Agency (EPA) be authorized to conduct a study and develop a strategy to "substitute, reduce, or prohibit the use of chlorine and chlorine-containing compounds." The White House specifically sited growing evidence that links contamination of the environment by these persistent toxic substances "not only to cancer but also to neurological, reproductive, developmental, and immunological adverse effects."

WHAT ARE ORGANOCHLORINES?

Organochlorines are the products and by-products of industrial chlorine chemistry. In nature, chlorine exists almost solely in its stable ionic form, called chloride. Chloride ions circulate constantly through our bodies and the ecosystem, primarily in the familiar form of sea salt (sodium chloride, NaCl); these ions do not react or combine with the carbon-based organic matter that is the basis of living things.

The chemical industry takes this sea salt and subjects it to a powerful electric current, transforming ionic chloride into elemental chlorine gas (Cl_2), along with the co-product sodium hydroxide. The energy input in this "chlor-alkali process" fundamentally changes the chemical character of the chlorine atom. Unlike natural chloride, chlorine gas is a toxic, greenish gas that is highly unstable, combining quickly and randomly with organic matter to produce a new class of chemicals called organochlorines.

Since World War II, the chlorine industry has grown very rapidly, reaching production of 40 million tons of chlorine each year. Of this, about 80 percent is used within the chemical industry to manufacture 11,000 different organochlorine products, including plastics, pesticides, and solvents. The remainder is sold to other industries—most of it to the pulp and paper industry—for uses such as bleaching and disinfection. In addition to the many organochlorines produced on purpose, thousands more—including dioxin—are formed as accidental by-products in all uses of chlorine, and whenever organochlorines are used or disposed in reactive environments, such as incinerators.

Chlorine is useful in industry for the same reasons it is a hazard to health and the environment. Its reactivity makes it a powerful bleach and disinfectant—and an effective reactant in chemical synthesis—but this quality results in the formation of unintended by-products. Organochlorines tend to be very stable, resisting natural breakdown processes, so they are useful as plastics, refrigerants, di-electric fluids, pesticides, and other chemicals, but this same quality makes them long-lived in the environment and in the bodies of living organisms. Further, organochlorines tend to be oil-soluble, so they work well as degreasing solvents, but this causes them to concentrate in the tissues of living things. And organochlorines tend to be toxic, so they are powerful pesticides and drugs; the negative impacts of this characteristic are obvious.

In contrast to the now large-scale industrial production of these chemicals, organochlorines are largely foreign to living systems. Only one organochlorine is produced naturally in significant amounts—chloromethane, the simplest organochlorine, which serves in the natural regulation of the stratospheric ozone layer. Several hundred organochlorines are produced in trace amounts, primarily by lower organisms such as algae and fungi; none are known to occur naturally in the tissues of mammals or terrestrial vertebrates, and none circulate freely and ubiquitously throughout the general environment. Moreover, the organisms that produce organochlorines do so precisely because of their toxicity or other biological activity: organochlorines serve in nature not in the mainstream of biochemistry but as chemical defenses against predators and parasites, as pesticides, and as signalling molecules (i.e., pheromones). The limited role of organochlorines in nature confirms the view that this class of compounds is hazardous to complex living organisms.

GLOBAL CHLORINE POLLUTION

After only about fifty years of large-scale industrial chlorine production, the entire planet is now blanketed with a cocktail of hundreds or thousands of toxic, long-lived organochlorines. This is because of the huge quantities of these chemicals produced by the chemical industry, and because organochlorines tend to persist in the environment and build up in the food chain. Even those organochlorines that do break down almost always degrade into other organochlorines—which are often more toxic and/or persistent than the original substance—compounding the problem further.

In the Great Lakes, for instance, 168 organochlorines have been unequivocally identified in the water, sediments or food chain—making up about half of all the pollutants that have been found in that ecosystem. The list includes the most infamous organochlorines—PCBs, dioxins, and pesticides like DDT and aldrin—but it also contains scores of lesser known organochlorines. Great Lakes contaminants span the entire spectrum of the class of these substances—including simple chlorinated solvents and refrigerants, a host of chlorinated benzenes, phenols and toluenes, a selection of exotic chlorinated by-products, alcohols, acids, and the newer chlorinated pesticides like atrazine and alachlor.

The problem, of course, is not just in North America but is truly global. Because organochlorines tend to be so persistent in the environment, they can travel thousands of miles on currents of wind and water, resulting in a distribution that affects everyone on the planet. In the Arctic circle, for instance, far from any known sources of these compounds, some of the world's highest concentrations of organochlorines can be found in the tissues of polar bears, people, and other species.

And because many organochlorines are more soluble in fat than in water, they bioaccumulate, concentrating in the fatty tissues of living things and multiplying in concentration as they move up the food chain. Concentrations of these chemicals in the bodies of predator species may be millions of times greater than the levels found in the ambient environment. Thus, the bulk of the general population's exposure to many of these compounds occur through the food supply—particularly foods high in fat such as fish, meats, and dairy products.

Since humans are inextricably connected with our environment—though we often forget it—we too are contaminated. Because we are at the top of the foodchain, we bear some of the highest exposures of all. 177 organochlorines have been identified in the fat, blood, mother's milk, semen, and breath of the general population of the U.S. and Canada. These chemicals are in absolutely everyone's body, not just people living near pulp mills and chemical plants.... Organochlorines accumulated in the body are also passed from one generation to the next through the placenta and through mothers' milk.

Worst of all, these 177 organochlorines that have been identified are just the tip of the iceberg: they represent only a fraction of the thousands of contaminants that are known present in our bodies but have not yet been specifically identified....

HEALTH AND ENVIRONMENTAL IMPACTS

The health damage that organochlorines can cause has been well-established, though the existing data may only hint at the full-scale of the problem. Organochlorines are known to disrupt the body's hormones, to cause genetic mutations and metabolic changes, to cause or promote cancer, to reduce fertility, impair childhood development, cause neurological damage, and suppress the function of the immune system. The International Agency for Research on Cancer has identified 117 organochlorines or groups of organochlorines that are known or suspected carcinogens.

Some organochlorines are among the most potent poisons ever studied, though the potency and specific effects vary from one chemical to another. A recent study for the U.S. and Canadian pulp and paper industry admitted that adding chlorine to an organic chemical almost always increases its toxicity, persistence, and tendency to bioaccumulate.

As the America Public Health Association concluded, "virtually all organochlorines that have been studied exhibit at least one of a wide range of serious toxic effects..., often at extremely low doses, and many chlorinated organic compounds... are recognized as significant workplace hazards." A large body of scientific literature shows that people exposed in the workplace to a wide variety of organochlorines—pesticides, PCBs, dioxins, solvents, vinyl chloride, chemical intermediates, and so on—have elevated rates of cancer, infertility, hormonal abnormalities, nervous system damage, and other effects.

By itself, this information is enough to justify a phase-out of these chemicals.

Common sense tells us that we should not be exposing ourselves and other species to chemicals that can cause such a wide range of severe health effects. If they persist or bioaccumulate—making the impacts long-lived and virtually irreversible —the folly of dumping these compounds into the environment becomes even more obvious....

Because these chemicals are persistent and ubiquitous, we confront a threat to our health unlike most hazards associated with toxic chemicals: a global hazard to the health of the entire population, not simply a local set of exposures and health risks.... Although it is so difficult for epidemiologists and environmental scientists to catalogue long-term, large-scale damage and trace it back to its causes, a large body of scientific information that has emerged over the last few years indicates that organochlorines are causing a global epidemic of serious health effects among people and wildlife.

Some of the best information comes from the Great Lakes—one of the best-studied large ecosystems in the world. Here, scientists have documented severe chemically-induced epidemics among 14 species—virtually every predator species in the ecosystem, from bald eagles to salmon, mink to snapping turtles, herring gulls to humans. In each case, the consumption of Great Lakes fish contaminated with organochlorine mixtures appears to be the cause. These epidemics primarily affect reproduction and development, with effects including population declines, inability to reproduce, physical and behavioral feminization of males, birth defects, embryonic mortality, wasting syndrome and other developmental effects, behavioral changes and learning impairment, and immune system suppression. Most alarming, the ef-

fects are most severe not in the exposed generation but in its offspring, and they are often not apparent until the offspring reach adulthood.

The problem is not getting any better. Some of the pesticides and PCBs that were restricted in the 1970s declined somewhat by the mid-1980s, but those chemicals have now stabilized at levels that are still unsafe. Others, such as the chlorinated dibenzofurans, are actually increasing. This summer, four newborn eaglets were discovered with life-threatening birth defects, including crossed bills and clubbed feet, that are consistent with organochlorine exposure. Finding one deformed eagle in a single year would be cause for concern; finding four, especially in a population that is bearing few young anyway, is truly alarming.

Similar effects are occurring worldwide. Epidemics of infertility, reproductive problems, hormonal disruptions and population declines have been documented among seals, fish and birds in the Baltic, the North Sea, the Wadden Sea, the Mediterranean, and the Pacific coast of North America. And organochlorines have been implicated in the mass die-offs of dolphins in recent years, as immune suppression caused by these chemicals appears to have made the animals more susceptible to infectious diseases.

What does this evidence mean for humans? Because they tend to have shorter generation times and more consistent feeding habits than people, wildlife are canaries in the coal mine for effects that can be expected in humans....

In fact, the evidence suggests that the impacts on human health are starting to occur already. In Michigan, a series of studies has found that children born to mothers who had eaten just two to three meals per month of organochlorine-contaminated Great Lakes fish were born sooner, weighed less, and had smaller heads. As they developed, these children suffered an impaired ability to learn, with measurable impacts on short-term memory. These impacts lasted for years, and the severity correlated with the concentrations of organochlorines in the mother's blood. The results from Michigan are consistent with other studies from Wisconsin, North Carolina, Taiwan, and New York state that have found similar behavioral and neurological effects among the offspring of women and animals exposed to PCB, dioxin, or contaminated Great Lakes fish. Based on the severity of the effects and the low doses at which they occur, scientists have concluded that a substantial number of children from the general population may be suffering from this "diminished potential" due to chemical exposures.

Since World War II, average sperm density among men worldwide has declined by about half, and the proportion of men who are infertile has increased accordingly. Dioxin, PCBs, pesticides and other organochlorines that disrupt the body's hormones are known to cause male reproductive impairment, including low sperm counts, feminization, smaller gonad size, and reduced sex drive—even when only a tiny dose is fed to the mother on a single critical day of pregnancy. Several studies have found a relationship between low sperm count and high concentrations of certain organochlorines in a man's semen or blood. Recent articles in the scientific literature have argued that organochlorine exposure of the male fetus before birth may be an important factor in the worldwide decline in male fertility. This body of evidence also suggests that organochlorines may also be factors in testicular cancer and other defects of the male reproductive tracts, both of which can be caused by hormone-disruptors and have increased by 2- to 4-fold in recent decades.

Organochlorines have also been linked in a number of excellent studies to the worldwide epidemic of breast cancer that now strikes about one in nine women in most industrialized nations. Chlorinated solvents and the by-products of chlorination in drinking water have been linked to leukemia, bladder cancer, and colorectal cancer. And a recent large study by the New Jersey Department of Health links these same chemicals in drinking water to increased risk of spontaneous abortion, low birth weight, and a number of types of birth defects, particularly those —such as malformations of the cardiovascular system—that have been rising at an alarming rate among the general population.

In 1994, U.S. EPA released its long-awaited reassessment of the toxicity of dioxin. This three-year effort concluded that dioxin has severe effects upon a wide range of organ systems in humans and animals, that the evidence from studies of people suggests that dioxin has caused cancer, hormonal changes, and an array of biochemical effects in groups of people exposed to dioxin in the workplace or in their community, and that the most severe effects of dioxin are impairment of reproduction, development, and immune system function. Particularly sobering is EPA's conclusion that the current "background" body burden of dioxin and related chemicals in the tissues of the general U.S. population is already in the range at which these effects are known to occur in laboratory animals. There is no margin of safety remaining.

Finally, a few words about the impacts of the destruction of the stratospheric ozone layer, which has been caused primarily by chlorine-containing refrigerants and solvents. The United Nations Environment Programme has estimated that current ozone depletion trends will result in an additional 300,000 cases of skin cancer every year, plus at least 1.6 million cases of cataracts and an unknown but probably very large number of cases of immune suppression. Also expected are worldwide decreases in the productivity of agriculture and the marine foodchain, possibly leading to serious consequences for both humans and the global ecosystem.

... I will stop with these examples, and make two points about all the effects that have been linked to organochlorines. First, none were predicted before the chemicals went into commerce, and all required a lag time of decades before they were discovered. Once the evidence was in, the damage was irreversible. Second, in no study have scientists been able to pinpoint individual chemicals that are responsible for these health and ecological impacts, because it is the mixture of hundreds of organochlorines—along with other factors—that is causing the injury.

POLICY APPROACHES TO ORGANOCHLORINE POLLUTION

... The chemical industry would have us regulate organochlorines one by one. Risk assessments can be used, the industry argues, to determine exposure levels that are safe and environmental concentrations that do not exceed the ecosystem's "assimilative capacity." From these assessments, "acceptable discharges" can be calculated, and the industry proposes using pollution control and disposal devices—filters, incinerators, and the like—to keep releases within those limits.

But this is precisely the current regulatory system, which is primarily reactive: it attempts to control chemicals after they have been produced, and these actions are taken only after the chemicals have been shown to cause harm. The industry's suggestion represents no change from the status quo, really.... This may explain part of why the industry advocates it.

... We need a fundamental shift to a precautionary, public health-based approach. Such a policy seeks to *prevent* damage to our health and the environment before it happens; it accepts the irreversibility of harm and the limits of our scientific knowledge and technological control over toxic chemicals. This new approach is based upon three central ideas: the precautionary principle, zero discharge, and clean production processes.

First, the precautionary principle. Our current system is reactive: it takes action only after harm has already occurred. DDT, PCBs, and CFCs were phased-out, but only after overwhelming evidence linked them to severe impacts on health and the environment. The precautionary principle, which has already been adopted by the UN and other international fora, says that chemicals that *may* cause harm should not be discharged into the environment. In the face of scientific uncertainty, we should err on the side of caution. This idea is analogous to the first laws of medicine and public health practice: first do no harm, with prevention the goal.

Second, zero discharge. Approving "acceptable" discharges of persistent toxic chemicals is a recipe for disaster, because these chemicals—even when released in small amounts—build up in the environment over time, eventually reaching levels that cause health effects. The assumption that the environment has an "assimilable capacity" for pollution may be appropriate for conventional pollutants like oil and grease, which break down in the environment. But for persistent toxic substances, as the IJC has said, the ecosystem's assimilative capacity is zero....

Finally, clean production. We know that "back-end" solutions—pollution control and disposal measures that deal with chemicals and wastes after they are produced—have failed utterly to prevent toxic discharges, because they merely move chemicals from one environmental medium to another. Only front-end solutions—eliminating the production and use of toxic substances and feedstocks—truly prevent environmental contamination. As Barry Commoner has shown, the history of environmental regulations for the last two decades supports the view that pollution control has been marginally effective at best, while bans and phase-outs—on leaded gasoline, PCBs, and certain pesticides, for example—are responsible for all of our major success stories.

... [W]e need to eliminate the use of chlorine and chlorinated compounds by installing chlorine free alternative production processes. As discussed below, chlorine-free technologies are available for all major uses of chlorine—including plastics, pesticides, paper bleaching, solvents, and other chemical uses.

TREATING ORGANOCHLORINES AS A CLASS

The current system, which regulates each compound one-by-one, considers chemicals "innocent until proven guilty."

There are 80,000 chemicals in commerce —11,000 of them organochlorines—plus thousands more formed as accidental by-products. Only a handful have been subject to thorough hazard assessments, and many have not even been identified. Although virtually all organochlorines that have been tested have turned out to cause one or more adverse effects, we continue to presume that the untested ones are safe.

Chemicals do not have constitutional or human rights. The current system mistakenly grants chemicals the right to be considered innocent until proven guilty, while treating people as if we were guinea pigs who should be experimentally exposed to untested chemicals.... It is people who are innocent until proven guilty, and it is people who have the right not be exposed to chemicals that may harm their health.

... The precautionary principle tells us that synthetic chemicals—and the industrial processes that generate them —should be presumed harmful until demonstrated safe and compatible with the basic processes of the ecosystem....

Reversing the burden of proof also allows us to leave behind the cumbersome focus on individual organochlorines numbering in the thousands, and in the impossible bureaucracy that approach creates. Instead, we can target the far smaller set of processes and feedstocks that produce these diverse mixtures. For instance, dioxin and related compounds appear to be formed in virtually all uses of elemental chlorine (including the manufacture of a full range of organochlorine products, including pesticides, solvents, PVC feedstocks, and chemical intermediates), in many uses of organochlorines (especially those that take place in reactive or high-temperature environments) and whenever organochlorines are burned in incinerators, recycling facilities, or in accidental fires. Dioxin is even produced when chlorine gas is produced from salt. Even if our goal is simply to eliminate pollution by dioxin—the single most hazardous organochlorine known—we would have to restrict the use of chlorine in dozens of processes, along with the myriad of individual organochlorine products that are associated with dioxin at some point in their lifecycle.

We do know that all these organochlorines share a common root: the chlorine feedstock. That fact presents the opportunity for a clear and focused chemical policy: we should seek to replace chlorine-based processes with clean alternatives. With a single program, we can eliminate the largest and most hazardous group of toxic pollutants on the planet—a goal that the regulatory bureaucracy now in place has not even been able to consider.

IMPLEMENTING A CHLORINE PHASE-OUT

A chlorine phase-out does not mean that all chlorine-based processes are banned overnight. The process of conversion should be well-planned in order to set priorities, minimize costs, maximize benefits, and insure that both are equitably distributed. The program should begin with a reversal of the burden of proof: organochlorines and the processes that produce them will be presumed to be phased-out unless industry can provide convincing evidence of their safety.

Second, priorities should be set so that the largest, most polluting processes for which alternatives are available now are addressed first. PVC, pulp and paper, solvents, pesticides, other major chemical manufacturing processes, incineration of chlorine-containing waste, and in-plant water disinfection are logical priorities. Of course, products that serve a compelling social need for which alternatives are not yet available—such as certain pharmaceuticals, which account for well under one percent of all chlorine use —could be exempted.

Finally, a transition fund should be established to insure that workers and communities do not bear the economic burden of the transformation to a non-toxic economy. This fund, financed with revenues from a tax on chlorine and related products, should be used for two purposes. First, the fund should be used [for] local new investment and to create new jobs in clean production processes in the same communities in which dislocation is most likely, thus placing priority on keeping people employed. Second, workers whose jobs are eliminated should be offered meaningful assistance, protection, and new opportunities: one proposal is the GI Bill for Workers, advocated by the Oil, Chemical and Atomic Workers International Union, would provide full income, up to four years of higher education, and health care coverage to all workers whose jobs are lost because of phase-outs of industries that are incompatible with environmental concerns. Governance of the transition planning fund should include full participation by all interested parties— particularly workers and communities.

CHLORINE ALTERNATIVES AND ECONOMICS

The chemical industry has responded to the calls for a chlorine phase-out by arguing that such a program will result in exorbitant costs (about $100 billion per year) and massive job losses in the U.S. and Canada. The industry's scenario, however, is based upon invalid assumptions that drastically overestimate the costs and underestimate the benefits of a well-planned transition from chlorine-based process to clean production.

In fact, society can realize significant economic gains in this transition, provided that the process is guided by careful planning to use the best alternatives, set sensible priorities, minimize costs, maximize benefits, and insure that both are equitably distributed. Safe, effective alternatives are available now for all major uses of chlorine, preserving or even increasing employment. Further, a prevention-based approach would eliminate the gargantuan social costs and economic drag caused by expenditures on pollution control ($90–$150 billion per year in the U.S.) and contaminated site remediation (up to $750 billion to remediate the current legacy of toxic sites). Further, the International Joint Commission's Virtual Elimination Task Force has estimated that health care costs associated with the effects of persistent toxic substances range from $100 to $200 billion per year. The net contribution of polluting industries to our economy does not appear to be positive.

By prioritizing major chlorine use-sectors, the cost of the phase-out can be substantially reduced. The industry's alarming figures assume that the chlorine phase-out will be implemented all at once, without thought or prioritization and without any attempt to use the most effective and least expensive alternatives. Even based on the industry's own inflated estimates, 97 percent of all chlorine use could be phased out for just $22 billion per year—one-fifth of the assumed cost of a total phase-out and only a

fraction of the amount spent annually on toxics-related health care.

The industry has also drastically inflated its estimates of job loss by assuming that all jobs that involve chlorinated chemicals in some way will be lost when chlorine is restricted. But alternative processes will be used instead of chlorine, a chlorine phase-out does not mean that all productive economic activity once associated with chlorinated chemicals will stop.... In many cases, these alternatives create jobs because they are more labor-intensive than the current chemical-intensive processes.

For instance, traditional materials or chlorine-free plastics can substitute for all major uses of PVC plastic—the largest single chlorine use sector. There are dozens of communities, several hospitals and numerous manufacturers of autos, furniture, flooring, and packaged products—mostly in Europe—that have entirely or virtually eliminated the use of PVC. For instance, Tarkett AG—one of the world's largest flooring manufacturers—recently announced it will phase-out all PVC products from its line in favor of chlorine-free plastics and other materials. Tarkett workers will still be employed; they will simply use a different material to produce flooring.

Pulp and paper mills use chlorine to bleach wood pulp bright white, releasing huge quantities of organochlorine discharges in the process. But oxygen-based bleaching processes (using ozone, hydrogen peroxide, oxygen gas, enzymes, and improved control over production conditions) are capable of producing top-quality chlorine-free paper. Already, there are 55 mills around the world producing totally-chlorine-free (TCF) paper for the most demanding uses, including the large-circulation high-profile newsweeklies Der Spiegel and Stern in Germany. TCF production is rapidly coming to dominate paper production and consumption in Western Europe, and the North American industry risks being left behind in the global marketplace if it does not adopt these technologies. In fact, chlorine-free pulp production—following an initial investment—is less expensive than chlorine bleaching because of reduced costs for chemicals, pollution control and disposal, and energy consumption; by switching to chlorine-free bleaching, the North American industry could reduce its operating costs by over $500 million per year.

Chlorinated solvents—used primarily for cleaning and coating in manufacturing industries—are the next largest chlorine use sectors. But in the last 5 years, dozens of manufacturers of electronics, autos, and other types of equipment—including IBM and GE—have begun to eliminate chlorinated solvents in favor of process changes, such as aqueous or mechanical cleaning and coating. According to the U.S. Office of Technology Assessment, these changes result in net savings due to reduced costs for chemical procurement, waste disposal, and liability. For example, U.S. EPA concluded last year that clothing dry cleaners can replace chlorinated solvents with a water-based process that is just as effective but requires a 42 percent lower capital investment and provides a 78 percent better return on investment, a 5 percent increase in profits, a 21 percent increase in jobs and a 38 percent increase in total wages.

As for chlorinated pesticides, the U.S. National Academy of Sciences has found that farmers who eliminate their use of pesticides in favor of organic agriculture lower their costs and increase their yields. Farmers now spend close to $8 billion per year on synthetic pesticides, of which 99 percent are dispersed into the environment without ever reaching their target crop....

Wastewater treatment accounts for about 4 percent of chlorine use, while drinking water treatment uses less than 1 percent of the chlorine in the U.S. Alternatives are available in [this] sector, as well. Hundreds of wastewater treatment plants in the U.S. and Canada are already using ultraviolet light for disinfection prior to discharge, with operating costs lower than those associated with chlorine. Several hundred drinking water systems—mostly in Europe, including those in Berlin and Amsterdam—use UV, ozone, or modern filtration methods to provide safe, chlorine-free water to their communities.

There is no doubt that phasing out chlorine will require substantial technological conversion. Based on industry estimates, the investment in new technology would itself stimulate the creation of about 925,000 job-years of employment. But while we expect the net economic effect to be positive, there will be real disruption for some sectors—specifically those involved in the production of chlorine and chlorinated chemicals. Some chemical firms will have to establish a new production line or go out of business. There are already signs that the largest chemical manufacturers—including Dow, DuPont, Monsanto, and Bayer—are introducing chlorine-free products and seeking to eliminate chlorine from their own processes to anticipate the trend away from chlorine. But who is thinking about the chemical industry workers and communities whose jobs may be moved or lost in the transition? The transition planning fund described above can help preserve jobs, prevent dislocation, and provide meaningful protection for workers and communities, who should not bear the burden of the conversion to a non-toxic economy.

CONCLUSION

Chlorine pollution is not a fact of life. It is the result of decisions made by industry in the last five decades to produce and use toxic synthetic chemicals for convenience, efficiency, or profit. And it is our society that has decided to permit industry to make such choices. We as citizens have the right not to be contaminated by toxic chemicals. We have the right not to worry that our grandchildren will be denied the opportunity to live full and healthy lives because their world has been contaminated by long-lived poisons. We have the right to decide —based on current scientific evidence and our commitment to an ethical public policy on health and the environment— that chlorine chemistry should no longer play a role in our society's production processes.

NO

Ivan Amato

THE CRUSADE TO BAN CHLORINE

Only in the past year or two did the chemical industry realize a meteor was coming its way: a dead-serious proposal to eliminate or drastically curtail the industrial use of chlorine, skillfully brought to legislators and the public by Greenpeace and other environmentalists known for anti-technology positions. "This is the most significant threat to chemistry that has ever been posed," says Brad Lienhart, a longtime industry executive who heads the Chemical Manufacturers Association's new $5 million campaign to counter as much of that threat as possible, for as long as possible.

At issue is the industry's previously unquestioned right to use massive amounts of chlorine, number 17 on the Periodic Table of Elements. Since the end of World War II, chlorine, a pale green gas in its elemental form, has become central to the chemical industry, and thus to thousands of processes and consumer products. "It is the single most important ingredient in modern [industrial] chemistry," says W. Joseph Stearns, director of chlorine issues for Dow Chemical Company, one of the largest producers and users of chlorine.

"It is such a valuable and useful molecule because it does so many things and is involved in so many end products," remarks John Sesody, vice president and general manager of Elf Atochem North America's basic chemical business. Chemists and chemical engineers acknowledge that chlorine is dangerous to use and handle, but argue that industry can manage these dangers well enough for society to safely enjoy chlorine's many benefits.

In fact, many in the chemical industry are passionate about the overall good they say chlorine chemistry does for society (as passionate as the anti-chlorine forces are about its potential for damage). With uses ranging from making pesticides to commodity polymers to synthesizing pharmaceuticals and disinfecting 98% of the nation's water supply, say defenders, chlorine is a substance society cannot do without.

Detractors couldn't disagree more. Polarizing the issue perfectly, "There are no uses, of chlorine that we regard as safe," remarks Joe Thornton, a Greenpeace research analyst who in 1991 authored Greenpeace's case for a chlorine phaseout in a document titled "The Product is the Poison."

From Ivan Amato, "The Crusade to Ban Chlorine," *Garbage: The Independent Environmental Quarterly* (Summer 1994). Copyright © 1994 by *Garbage: The Independent Environmental Quarterly*, 2 Main St., Gloucester, MA 01930. Reprinted by permission.

Among the documented "criminal actions" of some chlorine-containing chemicals: contaminating riverbeds and lush aquatic habitats such as the Great Lakes water basin; accumulating in the tissue of birds and other wildlife, where they contribute to reproductive disorders and increased incidence of disease; and causing a rare form of liver cancer in some plastics workers who were exposed to high amounts of vinyl chloride monomer (the building block of polyvinylchloride [PVC]) during the 1960s, before the Occupational Safety and Health Administration imposed stringent exposure regulations.

Chlorinated organic molecules have been found in human tissues, and anti-chlorine advocates assert they may be responsible for some of the increase in breast-cancer rates over the past few decades. *No one can claim a causal link* between chlorine-containing chemicals and breast cancer, but the mere suggestion alarms the anti-chlorine camp enough for them to call for its phaseout. As alternatives are available for at least some chlorine-containing products and processes, activists conclude it's better to play it safe and simply banish the element from industry. For example, activists have claimed in all sincerity, we could return to metal piping instead of PVC.

SCIENCE ISN'T THE NAME OF THE PLAYING FIELD

When asked what they think of the call to eliminate industrial use of chlorine, most chemists throw back a "yeah, right" look. Then they denounce it. "The idea of banning chlorine is patently ridiculous and scientifically indefensible," says Steven Safe, a Texas A&M toxicologist who for 20 years has studied such chlorinated compounds as dioxins and PCBs [polychlorinated biphenyls]. Mario Molina, the atmospheric chemist now at M.I.T. who, with Sherwood Rowland, first identified the link between CFCs [chlorofluorocarbons] and ozone depletion, agrees. He told *Science* magazine last summer that banning chlorine "isn't taken seriously from a scientific point of view."

Industry may have been counting on science to throw out this challenge. Yet many participants and observers of the debate doubt that standard scientific study will play a decisive role in determining the fate of chlorine chemistry. Each side of the chlorine debate has corralled vast amounts of data (quite often the same data) to support their diametrically opposed arguments. But public perception can change much more quickly than science can unambiguously determine the real impact of chlorine on the environment and on human health.

That point hit industry in the solar plexus this past February when EPA [Environmental Protection Agency] Administrator Carol Browner was quoted in the *New York Times*, the *Washington Post*, and other national media as saying that the agency's proposals for reauthorizing the Clean Water Act would include a "national strategy for substituting, reducing, or prohibiting the use of chlorine and chlorinated compounds." Ms. Browner's bombshell drew 2,000 angry letters from citizens and elected officials, and an additional 300 letters from industry, says an EPA source who asked not to be identified. "We quickly answered the ones from Congress, and now we are getting into the boxes [of letters.]"

The EPA's reply, which its public-affairs office has been busy delivering to reporters, is more in line with what most scientists would suggest. The Agency's prepared statement says it "will study chlorine and chlorinated compounds to determine whether actions may be necessary to protect aquatic resources from discharges of these compounds, and it is premature to draw any conclusions about EPA's final actions before the study is completed." Even if the study becomes part of a reauthorized Clean Water Act, it is extremely unlikely that any action would be in the form of a blanket ban on chlorine, say EPA insiders.

Despite that clarification, the potential fact of industrial life without elemental chlorine, which the coverage of Ms. Browner's statements displayed in neon, puts raw fear into the heart of chlorine's defenders.

The chemical industry has never been known as a master of public relations. Greenpeace, on the other hand, the most aggressive member of the anti-chlorine consortium, could have written the book. With their "Chlorine Free" campaign, Greenpeace and allies have used every outlet to make their case.

Realizing the court of public relations will likely adjudicate the chlorine debate, the Chemical Manufacturer's Association established and bankrolled the Chlorine Coordinating Council (since renamed the Chlorine Chemistry Council [CCC]), with Brad Lienhart as its managing director. The group hopes to counter what it views as anti-chlorine prejudice fueled more by environmentalist hysteria than hard science and sober risk assessment. Chlorine compounds, they say, ought to be regulated like other compounds—based on determinations of their individual risks and benefits, not on the mere presence of chlorine atoms in their molecular anatomies.

As its first order of business, the CCC commissioned reports on chlorine which included a massive analysis—totaling 10 volumes and 4,000 pages—of the toxicological literature on chlorinated organic compounds. The Chlorine Institute, an older industry group devoted "to the safe production, handling, and use of chlorine," has even prepared packaged school lessons and a video that takes students on a tour of chlorine's role in everyday products. Big chemical companies including Dow have created new full-time positions such as Director of Chlorine Issues. The aim of this emerging infrastructure, says Lienhart, is to offer the public a different view of chlorine chemistry than the one anti-chlorine forces have been purveying unchallenged for years.

Industry remains the underdog. Last October 15, the anti-chlorine lobby got the likes of Bella Abzug, the fiery former New York congresswoman and a cancer survivor, to publicly endorse a Greenpeace document linking the rise of chlorine chemistry over the past few decades to rising rates of breast cancer. The Associated Press reported the event and sent the story over the wires. That sort of lachrymose (and toxicologically meaningless) coverage just isn't available to the CCC.

ELEMENTAL CHLORINE IS A CORNERSTONE OF INDUSTRIAL CHEMISTRY

To the community of manufacturers, chlorine remains a cornerstone of chemistry, playing a role in virtually every nook and cranny of modern society. By volume, chlorine is one of the largest chemical feedstocks, rivaling even petroleum. Global chlorine production now hovers around 38 million tons a year.

In the United States, the number is more like 11 million tons of chlorine.

The Chlorine Institute reports that about 28% of the chlorine supply goes into making plastics, mostly polyvinyl-chloride (PVC), from which thousands of products are derived, among them wall coverings, floor tiles, siding, pipes, shoe soles, electrical insulation, automobile components, and medical equipment. Saran Wrap is made from another major chlorine-containing polymer —polyvinylidene chloride. Just over one-third of the chlorine supply is used for synthesizing an estimated 11,000 commercial chemicals. Among the lengthy list of chlorine-dependent products are most herbicides and pesticides, dyes, chlorosilanes for making semiconductor materials, carbon tetrachloride for making nonstick cookware and refrigerants, dichlorophenyl sulfone for making computer components and power-tool housings, propylene chlorohydrin that is used first to make propylene oxide, which in turn is used to make a range of products including lubricants, coatings, brake fluids, cleaners, adhesives, pharmaceuticals, and soft-drink syrups.

Just under one-fifth of the chlorine supply is consumed by chlorinated solvents such as methylene chloride, a degreaser and paint stripper, although demand for such solvents is declining as manufacturers switch to water-based and otherwise less environmentally troublesome materials and methods. Approximately 14% of the chlorine supply is used for bleaching pulp and paper; the pulp and paper industry is likewise undergoing a transition toward bleaching processes that use less chlorine or no chlorine at all. The remaining few percent of the chlorine supply goes mostly into agents for purifying drinking and waste water, and for manufacturing pharmaceuticals.

Although undisputed estimates are hard to come by, in one way or another chlorine use amounts to at least tens of billions of dollars of commerce each year in the United States alone. It employs directly or indirectly at least hundreds of thousands of people. The highest estimates, from a widely cited and much disputed economic analysis conducted for the Chlorine Institute by the Charles River Associates consulting firm in Boston, contends that chlorine accounts for $91 billion of economic input in the U.S. and, directly and indirectly, over 1.3 million jobs.

THE SEEDS OF CONTROVERSY WERE PLANTED IN THE 1960s

The controversy began well before Greenpeace focused its worldwide campaign on chlorine chemistry in the mid-1980s, following the lead of Germany's Green Party. Never mind the once undisputed public-health successes of chlorine use in disinfecting water, controlling insect-borne diseases, and manufacturing pharmaceuticals. Such benefits to society can easily be forgotten once the anti-chlorine alliance unleashes its ordnance.

Consider DDT, an insecticide so effective against malaria that the World Health Organization once considered shortages as threats to public health. DDT, which stands for dichlorodiphenyl-trichloro-ethane and includes five chlorine atoms in its molecular structure, became the rallying point of the then-nascent environmental movement when Rachel Carson documented its unanticipated effects on the environment and wildlife in her 1962 book *Silent Spring*. (Although DDT has never been proved to be a significant human hazard, it was banned from use in the U.S. because it was known to bioaccumulate or be deposited in body fat at relatively low levels of exposure.)

Add the notoriety of chlorovillain PCBs, or polychlorinated biphenyls, a family of about 180 compounds that have anywhere from two to ten chlorine atoms in their molecular anatomies. PCBs' stability, low flammability; and insulating properties made them favorites for electrical and hydraulic equipment, but those same properties (along with their solubility in fat) likewise enabled them to accumulate to levels of concern in the cells and fat tissue of animals and people.

DDT and PCBs are not the only so-called organochlorine compounds that have a place among chemicals non grata. Even inorganic chlorine compounds that do not themselves persist in the environment, and presumably pose little long-term risk on their own, can break down into harmful molecules that do stick around. When the elemental chlorine used to bleach paper and the volatile chemicals used to make PVC plastic break down in the environment, they can spawn polychlorinated dibenzodioxins (PCDDs) and polychlorinated dibenzofurans (PCDFs). Both are suspected human carcinogens and both have documented adverse affects on wildlife in the Great Lakes region and elsewhere.

CFCs, or chlorofluorocarbons, whose nontoxicity, low cost, and physical and chemical properties had for decades made them just about perfect for large-scale cleaning and refrigeration uses, have become perhaps the best known and most vilified chlorinated compounds of all. CFCs' probable ozone-depleting properties, which never occurred to their originators in the 1930s, now overshadow all that's good about them. By the end of 1995, industry will halt the manufacture of CFCs in accordance with the international Montreal Protocol, a global response that anti-chlorine advocates view as an important precedent for their more ambitious goal of banning the industrial use of chlorine entirely.

The above-noted "chemical black list" represents a tiny fraction of the chlorinated compounds in use. Even so, activists in Germany's Green Party and then at Greenpeace began, as Brad Lienhart puts it, "connecting the dots" between those few notorious chlorovillains and all chlorine-containing compounds. Even though the majority of chlorinated compounds have never been studied for their toxicological effects, Greenpeace views them as a single class of chemicals that should be considered unfit for commercial use until proven safe—a virtual impossibility, both scientifically and economically.

If Greenpeace were alone in its fight against chlorine, the Dows, Monsantos, and Du Ponts of the world might not have much to worry about. But the chemical industry decided that the call for a ban was more than environmentalist bravado when a normally conservative United States/Canadian commission, the International Joint Commission [IJC], officially announced comprehensive anti-chlorine recommendations, to their respective governments in their biannual report of 1992.

The IJC's scientific panels and advisors convinced its six commissioners that chlorinated compounds are persistent enough in the Great Lakes region that a recommendation to phase them out is prudent. Although the Commission concedes that many of the synthetic chlorinated organic substances identified in the water, sediment, and biota of the region have not been identified as individually toxic, it concludes that many of these chemicals—because of their shared chemical characteristics—will be identified as persistent toxicants.

The IJC recommended in 1992 that the U.S. and Canada "develop timetables to sunset [phase out] the use of chlorine and chlorine-containing compounds as industrial feedstocks, and the means of reducing or eliminating other uses [such as water treatment and paper bleaching] be examined." Moreover, other treaty organizations that oversee the use of international waters have articulated similar antichlorine positions.

"The IJC lit up our lives," says Rick Hinds, legislative director of Greenpeace's toxics campaign.

Despite rigorous lobbying by the CCC to stop lumping the entire menagerie of chlorine-containing compounds into one huge regulatory class, the IJC is standing firm. Its 1994 biannual report, issued following its most recent gathering in Windsor, Ontario, redoubled calls for sunsetting chlorine. Brad Lienhart, who participated in the IJC meeting, thinks that some gains were made despite the anti-chlorine message. The IJC's Virtual Elimination Task Force, which develops strategies to eventually eliminate all toxic inputs to the Great Lakes, agreed there is a need for "a thorough and complete analysis of chlorine chemistry before any schedule for sunsetting chlorine is implemented," Mr. Lienhart says. He believes such an analysis will vindicate much of chlorine chemistry as a sensible, environmentally responsible choice for manufacturers.

Following that mild concession by the IJC, though, another voice joined the anti-chlorine chorus. In early November,

the American Public Health Association, which represents 50,000 public-health workers, registered some of the strongest anti-chlorine positions yet heard. A final draft of the APHA's position states "the only feasible and prudent approach to eliminating the release and discharge of chlorinated organic chemicals and consequent exposure is to avoid the use of chlorine and its compounds in manufacturing processes." The resolution concedes that not *all* uses of chlorine, especially such public-health uses as disinfecting drinking water and pharmaceutical production, have feasible alternatives—thereby implying that those uses of chlorine ought to be continued. But APHA calls for provisions to retrain workers displaced from a shrinking chlorine industry.

THE CASES FOR AND AGAINST MAY REST ON RISK OR BENEFIT TO SOCIETY

Like looking at clouds, both sides can see what they want in existing data, or commission hand-picked scientists to do studies that lend credence to their respective interpretations.

In lieu of objective scientific debate, methodological and philosophical issues are at the fore. One of the largest gulfs between the two camps centers on the unprecedented call to consider all chlorinated compounds in use as a single class subject to regulatory action. The case for banning all industrial uses of chlorine is easier to explain, which gives it a decided advantage over the more complicated argument of chlorine's defenders. The basic argument starts with reference to DDT, PCBS, dioxins, CFCs and a few other compounds that have documented effects. Next the argument points out that all of these compounds have one thing in common, namely, the presence of chlorine atoms in their molecular structures.

Finally, the argument takes an inferential step—and this is the precise point of contention. It concludes that, because of this commonality, all other chlorine compounds are suspected environmental and biological hazards. The concept of "reverse onus" would be applied to all chlorinated compounds: an assumption that they produce toxicity unless otherwise proved by the seller. Since chlorine detractors admit that most chlorine-dependent compounds have never been shown to have hazardous effects and have never even been studied, they refer to this conclusion as "the precautionary principle."

Another key component of the argument points to correlations between the presence of chlorinated organics in sediments, water basins, and tissues of animals and humans, on the one hand, and, on the other, incidences of wildlife population declines, reproductive and developmental anomalies in animals and people, and various diseases, including cancer. Theo Colborn, a Fellow at the World Wildlife Fund who chaired an often-cited gathering of toxicologists, ecologists, immunologists, and other scientists three years ago, said in an interview that "we have reached a point [of loading toxic synthetic chemicals in the environment and living tissue] that we ought to be concerned about releasing more."

The so-called "precautionary principle" is seductively simple. There are simply too many chlorinated compounds to study on a one-by-one basis to assess their safety. "There aren't enough rats in the world to assess individual compounds and what their combined effects might be," says Tufts University biologist Ana Soto, who is studying how compounds including PCBs can mimic the hormonal effects of estrogen.

Nevertheless, the pro-chlorine advocates assert that the only scientifically defensible way to ascertain chlorine's health and environmental effects is to do toxicological, epidemiological, and other studies of specific organochlorine chemicals. They point out that the scientific data simply does not exist to implicate any but a very few organochlorine compounds, such as DDT and PCBs—which have been studied for many years. Brad Lienhart tirelessly points out that the many thousands of organochlorine compounds in use cannot legitimately be thought of as a single class because they are chemically, physically, and biologically heterogeneous. Adds W. Joseph Stearns, Dow's director of chlorine issues: "The substantive part of this issue is that *some* organochlorines are persistent toxics, not that all organochlorines contain chlorine."

Indeed, many organochlorine compounds have short lifespans in the natural world. Mr. Stearns argues that to condemn any compound because it contains chlorine in its molecular structure will lead to a whole host of environmental regulations that the actual risks do not call for. And depriving society of thousands of useful, chlorine-based products without ascertaining if the risks are unacceptable, says the pro-chlorine camp, is a misguided formula that will greatly damage the nation's economic strength and standard of living.

GREENPEACE'S INSISTENCE THAT "SUBSTITUTES EXIST" IS MISLEADING

Chlorine's defenders can point out the importance of its use in modern industrial chemistry, and try to explain the complex toxicological reasons why tens of thousands of compounds having nothing in common but chlorine should not be treated as a single class of chemicals. But their strongest argument may be that, while substitutes for chlorine and chlorinated compounds may exist in many cases, the costs to switch are prohibitive and the substitutes not necessarily any less risky.

Susan Sieber, a toxicologist and Deputy Director of the Division of Cancer Etiology at the National Cancer Institute, warns that hasty blanket bans can have the unwanted effect of pushing alternatives that are worse. "You need to assess the risks and benefits," she says.

Attempts at sober assessment that would fall between the two camps have begun in earnest. One example is a 180-page report that the M.I.T. Program in Technology, Business and Environment prepared for the Norwegian government and European industry groups. The report begins the daunting task of assessing the economic, social, and environmental costs and gains of non-chlorine substitutes, focusing on several areas including cleaning solvents in the electronics industry, polyvinylchloride (PVC) plastic, chlorinated pesticides, and chlorine-based bleaching agents.

The report notes that a trend toward chlorine-free bleaching technologies in the paper industry shows that major categories of chlorine use are not absolutely necessary for the industries that have been heavy chlorine users. "This suggests that concerns over the unavailability of such alternatives in other cases of chlorine use may be overblown," concludes the summary of the report's findings.

Availability of substitutes, however, is only part of the story. Among the big caveats:

- Substitutes carry their own environmental and health effects. For example, water-based substitutes for CFCs in the electronics industry add a new source of water pollution. The return of hydrocarbon coolants and insulating fluids for electrical transformers has brought back the fire hazards that PCBs had virtually eliminated.

- Chlorine-based technologies themselves may have been less hazardous replacements for nastier technologies. A chlorine-dependent route to titanium dioxide, a widely used pigment in white paint, replaced the dangerous lead-based pigments that contributed to a public-health calamity. The chlorine-dependent process produces one-sixth the hazardous waste of an alternative process that relies on sulfuric acid.

- Affordable alternatives that can perform as well as the chlorine-dependent product may not exist. In these cases, technological innovation and development can take a long time, at great cost. The report cites the absence of any drop-in replacements for CFCs that automakers could use for air conditioning systems of cars after the CFC ban goes into effect.

FEW SEE THE WHOLE PICTURE, BUT LEGISLATORS AND USER GROUPS HAVE BEGUN TO REACT

Greenpeace believes it has industry on the run. "The writing is on the wall," says Jay Palter, Toronto director of the group's Chlorine Free campaign. "A chlorine phaseout is inevitable and industry is just stalling for time."

Industry representatives don't see it that way. "Greenpeace is not fundamentally changing the way we do business," says Michael W. Berezo, director of environmental strategy for Monsanto. At the moment, neither EPA nor its Canadian counterpart, Environment Canada, has accepted the notion that all chlorine compounds ought to be regulated or phased out as a class. Berezo does concede that the ascent of the chlorine issue is pushing Monsanto and other companies to look more aggressively at alternatives to chlorine-containing chemicals. But industry's dilemmas lack easy answers.

Specific user groups have begun to wrestle with the chlorine issue as it affects them. The Jan/Feb '94 issue of the newsletter *Environment Building News* ran a 10-page article titled "Should We Phase Out PVC?" The report makes a Herculean effort to integrate the available information on PVC's benefits and the dangers stemming from its manufacture into a picture that might guide its readers. After concluding that its account left more questions than answers, the article counseled the 1,200 builders and architects who subscribe to the newsletter to "seek out better, safer, and more environmentally responsible alternatives" to polyvinylchloride—without actually suggesting that readers completely avoid vinyl materials. PVC accounts for more than a quarter of worldwide chlorine use, so such recommendations can have far-reaching effects.

Perhaps the most newsworthy feature of the chlorine controversy is that it has progressed to the point where a ban is being taken seriously by governments and industry. And even if the meteor of a ban is deflected by pragmatic concerns, chlorine chemistry may be forever changed by an asteroid shower of legislation. In October, Rep. Bill Richardson (D-NM) delighted environmentalists by reintroducing a bill that would legislate chlorine out of the pulp and paper industry within five years. In October, the Clinton administration nearly issued an executive order that would have mandated government to buy paper made without chlorine. (The requirement didn't make it into the final order.)

Even a year ago, engineering professor David Marks, who is coordinating M.I.T.'s $1.8 million cross-disciplinary study of chlorine, thought the anti-chlorine movement couldn't box its way out of an unbleached paper bag. Now he wonders. "The chlorine industry could wake up one day and see many anti-chlorine bills on the table in Congress," he warns. "Things are moving so fast, it's hard to tell how it will end up."

Industry is well aware how quickly a few Bella Abzugs can alter public perception. Despite the difficulties in switching to chlorine-free production, progressive companies are eyeing such strategies as pollution prevention and substitution to preempt future, more costly adjustments. Truly farsighted companies aim to turn anti-chlorine sentiment into a market. Dow has created a new business entity called Advanced Cleaning Systems, which provides water-based cleaning technology and support services for green industrial niches. And Louisiana

Pacific, one of the country's largest paper manufacturers, is trumpeting its new chlorine-free bleaching process at a plant in Samoa, California.

Should there be a chlorine phaseout, it would probably occur in a piecemeal fashion, hopping from product category to product category. Both sides will continue to debate the data on what effects chlorinated compounds have on the environment and human health. But it seems quite possible that even without government-imposed limits, public perception and the market forces that follow from it will dictate the future of chlorine's role in industry and society.

POSTSCRIPT

Should the Industrial Use of Chlorine Be Phased Out?

Problems attend all efforts to find a scientifically valid, economically and politically feasible strategy for protecting the public and the ecosphere from the deleterious effects of hazardous substances. Among the factors that have plagued regulatory agencies are a lack of adequate data for valid risk assessments; an inability to do direct, controlled tests on human subjects; questions about the validity of deducing human health concerns from animal test data; the difficulty of interpreting the results of epidemiological studies; a lack of access to industrial data that is considered proprietary; and complications due to possible synergistic effects among different pollutants.

What makes a product "unsafe"? We know that chlorine compounds can kill: from the phosgene used in World War I to the pesticides we use now, lethal chlorine compounds have been chosen *because* they kill and because they kill more thoroughly and inexpensively than the alternatives. But chlorine is used more generally, of course, in the myriad plastic products that make our lives more convenient. How much would it cost to replace the chlorine in such products? What would it cost to do without the products altogether? Given the general uncertainty about health risk attached to the processes used to produce these products, where does our vote lie?

SUGGESTED READINGS

Nuna Alberts, "Is Your Drinking Water Safe?" *Self* (August 1997).

Chlorine Chemistry Council, *Chlorine Stewardship Breakthroughs*, World Wide Web site: http://www.c3.org./aol/newsroom/stewardship/stewardship.html.

John Hausoul, "Safe Water Delivered Safely," *Financial Times* (September 8, 1997), p. 1.

Terry F. Yosie, "The Changing Landscape of the Chlorine Debate," *Environmental Science and Technology* (November 1996).

ISSUE 19

Can Green Marketing Save Tropical Rain Forests?

YES: Thomas A. Carr, Heather L. Pedersen, and Sunder Ramaswamy, from "Rain Forest Entrepreneurs: Cashing in on Conservation," *Environment* (September 1993)

NO: Jon Entine, from "Let Them Eat Brazil Nuts: The 'Rainforest Harvest' and Other Myths of Green Marketing," *Dollars and Sense* (March/April 1996)

ISSUE SUMMARY

YES: Economics professors Thomas A. Carr and Sunder Ramaswamy and mathematics teacher Heather L. Pedersen describe three projects to promote sustainable use of rain forest products, which they argue help to preserve the forest and support the local economy.

NO: Investigative reporter Jon Entine asserts that most green marketing programs do nothing to slow forest destruction and, moreover, frequently result in the mistreatment of employees, vendors, and customers.

The tropical rain forests of the world, spread in rapidly decreasing pockets over South America (especially in Brazil's Amazon region), Africa, and Malaysia, are the home of most of the species in the world. Due to the favorable climate and stability over many centuries, the speciation of the dominant varieties of life has progressed to degrees only imaginable elsewhere. Some whole species of insect, for instance, live on *only one tree* in the Amazonian forest. Each species—or rather, the DNA of each species—is a parcel of information that may be irreplaceably valuable in the human scheme of things. (The rosy periwinkle of Madagascar, for instance, found nowhere else, is the source of methetrexate and vincristine, two very effective cancer therapies.) There is no way we could invent for ourselves the variety of effective chemicals that are supplied free of charge by the rain forest.

More than that, the tropical rain forest, a huge green canopy spread under the hottest sun, is the lungs of the world. Every leaf in the canopy carries on the endless task of absorbing carbon from the air (in the form of the most problematic "greenhouse gas," CO_2, or carbon dioxide) and releasing oxygen. That huge canopy supplies a significant amount of the oxygen for the world's air-breathers.

With all these functions for our good, how can it be that the rain forest would be destroyed? Tragically, the interests of a few people, in the absence of worldwide concerted action to protect it, conspire to cut down the trees of the rain forest. Tropical rain forests once covered 14 percent of the planet. Less than half remain, most of the loss occurring in the last 50 years; an area the size of Germany is lost every year.

Rapid regional decimation of tree cover is not a new phenomenon. By the end of the eighteenth century, France had cleared almost 85 percent of its forested land over a period of less than two centuries. Other contemporary industrialized countries, including the United States, have engaged in wholesale deforestation. Until recently, however, these practices have had relatively minor deleterious effects on human welfare.

As much as one-third of the annual contribution to the increase in atmospheric carbon dioxide, which contributes to global warming, comes from deforestation. The global warming connection comes from the fact that the cutting and combustion of trees release carbon dioxide that can only be balanced by an equal number of new trees removing that same amount of carbon dioxide as they grow. Not only do we lose the canopy that breathes for us, but we contribute to the greenhouse gases by allowing the forest to be cut. On the other hand, since global warming is an issue of concern to many, there is hope among environmentalists that it will serve to mobilize the enormous number of people needed to save the forests.

Tropical forests supply many useful commercial products and are the source of a wide variety of chemicals, including natural products that are used in the pharmaceutical industry. Among the serious consequences of rain forest destruction would be the loss of a principal source of organic chemicals used in medical research.

Designing and implementing appropriate and effective strategies for reducing or reversing rain forest decimation has produced heated controversy, both within the tropical nations where the destruction is occurring and in the international community. Among the proposals that have been advanced, along with the "debt for nature" swaps that would allow debtor nations to get rid of their national debt by promising to preserve forests, are many "green marketing" strategies whose goal is to enhance the economic worth of goods that can be produced from the forests in a sustainable manner. This is a means of motivating entrepreneurs to favor forest preservation over using forest land for profit.

In the following selections, Thomas A. Carr, Heather L. Pedersen, and Sunder Ramaswamy describe two projects involving the use of forest products and one ecotourism initiative, which they argue are the types of endeavors that "may be key to preserving the vital and fragile resources of the tropical rain forests." Jon Entine discusses green marketing "schemes," such as Ben and Jerry's promotion of Rainforest Crunch ice cream and Body Shop International's tropical skin and hair care products. He argues that, while encouraging consumers to "shop for a better world," these enterprises frequently mistreat employees, vendors, and customers, and do little or nothing to help preserve the forests or support the indigenous peoples.

YES

Thomas A. Carr, Heather L. Pedersen, and Sunder Ramaswamy

RAIN FOREST ENTREPRENEURS: CASHING IN ON CONSERVATION

Each year, nearly 17 million hectares of rain forest—an area roughly equal to that of Wisconsin—are lost world-wide as a result of deforestation. Because more than half of all species on the planet are found in rain forests, this destruction portends serious environmental consequences, including the decimation of biological diversity. Another threat lies in the fact that rain forests serve as an important sink for carbon dioxide, a greenhouse gas that contributes to global warming. The Amazon region alone stores at least 75 billion tons of carbon in its trees. Furthermore, when stripped of its trees, rain forest land soon becomes inhospitable and nonarable because the soil is nutrient-poor and ill-suited to agriculture. Under current practices, therefore, the forests are being destroyed permanently.

Economic forces result in exploitation of the rain forest to extract hardwood timber and fuel and in clearcutting the land for agriculture and cattle ranching, which are primary causes of the devastation. Mounting evidence shows that these conventional commercial and industrial uses of the rain forest (see Table 1) are not only ecologically devastating but also economically unsound. These findings have inspired an innovative approach to save the rain forest. Environmental groups are now targeting their efforts toward developing commercially viable and sustainable uses of the rain forest. Their strategy is to create economic incentives that encourage local inhabitants to practice efficient stewardship over the standing forests. These environmental entrepreneurs no longer view the market as their nemesis but as an instrument to bring about constructive social and environmental change. In theory, the strategy promotes win-win solutions: Environmentalists gain by preserving the rain forests, and local inhabitants gain from an improved standard of living that is generated by enlightened, sustainable development. In practice, the challenge lies in implementing such programs.

Three applications of environmental entrepreneurship in the rain forests have been particularly successful. Conservation International's "The Tagua Initiative," Shaman Pharmaceutical's search for useful drugs in the rain forest, and the management of ecotourism in Costa Rica are three projects that together provide an interesting cross section of the efforts under way to promote sustainable use of rain forest products. A number of common issues and challenges confront these environmental entrepreneurs.

RESPONDING TO DEFORESTATION

Although people everywhere may benefit from preserving the rain forest, the costs of preservation are borne mainly by the local inhabitants. Usually, the inhabitants' immediate financial needs far outweigh the long-term benefit gained by forgoing the traditional extractive methods of forestry or land conversion for agriculture. In many of these countries, high levels of poverty, rapid population growth, and unequal distribution of land encourage migration into the forest regions. Local inhabitants, confronted with the tasks of daily survival, cannot be expected to respond to appeals for altruistic self-sacrifice. Consequently, forests are cut and burned for short-term economic gains. This problem is often exacerbated by misguided government policies in many countries, such as government-sponsored timber concessions that promote inefficient harvest levels, tree selection, and reforestation levels. Governments may charge a royalty far below the true economic value of the standing forest. Such low royalties and special tax breaks raise the profits of logging companies, which thereby stimulate timber booms. In addition, some governments provide special land tenure rules or tax benefits to individuals who "improve" the land by clearing the forest. These rules encourage development in the rain forest region because they impel poor settlers

to seek land for agriculture and wealthy landowners to look for new investments.

Environmental entrepreneurs can create commercial alternatives to the traditional damaging uses of rain forest resources, but several factors must first be taken into consideration. For example, commercial development cannot be allowed to harm the ecological integrity of the ecosystem. This can be a difficult challenge as the scale of production increases for many projects. Also, if existing firms are profitable, new firms will be attracted into the industry, thus placing additional pressure on the fragile ecosystem. Of course, the product must also pass the test of the market; consumers must be willing to pay a price that covers the full cost of production. Some environmentally conscious consumers may be willing to pay a premium for sustainably harvested rain forest products. The size of this "green premium" would depend upon these consumers' willingness and ability to pay, as well as on the prices of other products competing with the rain forest products. To maintain the green premium over time, environmental entrepreneurs need to devise a strategy that differentiates their products from others through advertising and some type of institutionalized labeling system. These entrepreneurs must also anticipate the effect of expanding output on market prices. Previous studies have examined the market value of sustainable products from a single hectare. One study in the Amazonian rain forest in Peru found that sustainably harvested products such as fruit, nuts, rubber latex, and selectively logged timber yield more net value than do plantation forestry and cattle ranching. If harvests are expanded, however, market prices may be pushed down, and the profitability of the pro-

Table 1

Commercial and Industrial Products Derived from Tropical Rain Forests

Product	Value of imports by region (millions of U.S. dollars)	Marketshare of rain forest products (percent)	Region receiving imports	Year of estimate
Commercial products				
Fruit and vegetable juices	4,000	100	World	1988
Cut flowers	2,500	100	World	1985
Food additives	750	100	United States, European Community	1991
Spices	439	small	United States	1987
Nuts	216	100	World	1988
Food colorings	140	10	World	1987
Vitamins	67	small	United States	1990
Fiber	54	100	United States	1983/4
Industrial Products				
Fuel	60,000	< 1	United States	1984
Pesticides	16,000	1	World	1987
Natural rubber	666	100	United States	1978
Tannins	170	large	United States	1980
Construction material	12	1	United States	1984
Natural waxes	9.3	100	United States	1985

Note: James Duke, an economic botanist at the U.S. Department of Agriculture, has been compiling estimates of the economic value of hundreds of key commerical and industrial rain forest products. Some of the important estimates are summarized here. Although not all of the imported products are derived from tropical rain forest countries, Duke claims that they all have the potential to be sustainably harvested from these regions.

Source: James Duke, "Tropical Botanical Extractives" (Unpublished manuscript, U.S. Department of Agriculture, Washington, D.C., April 1989).

gram reduced. Another consideration is that entrepreneurs may be able to avoid the expense of developing extensive distribution networks and other marketing costs by forming alliances with established commercial firms. These firms typically have retail outlets and experienced business personnel that can assist the small entrepreneur.

Finally, the environmental entrepreneur must channel income back to the effective owners of the rain forests—the local indigenous people. This return raises the issue of rain forest property rights. The property rights over rain forest resources are not well defined or enforced. Rain forest land is often held collectively,

and government-owned land marked as a reserve is not always protected. Even private landowners have a difficult time preventing landless squatters from using their property. Without the enforcement of property rights, rain forests become an open-access resource that is over exploited. This result is not inevitable, however. History suggests that, when the benefits of establishing new property rights exceed the costs, societies often devise new ways to define property rights and improve the allocation of resources.

In addition to the question of physical property rights, there is the problem of defining intellectual property rights. Indigenous people possess a wealth of esoteric knowledge about local plants and animals and their usages. Conservation groups argue that the wisdom of the local inhabitants must be given an economic value or else that knowledge will disappear amidst the destruction of the forest. At the same time, scientists and entrepreneurs also contribute value to rain forest products by discovering useful medicinal compounds in the plants. If these interests are not protected, there will not be sufficient economic incentive to develop new products. During the Earth Summit in Rio de Janeiro [in June 1992], the Bush administration refused to sign an international treaty on biodiversity on the grounds that it would harm the interests of biotechnology firms. (The Clinton administration signed the biodiversity treaty on 4 June 1993.) A key challenge is to develop an institutional mechanism that recognizes the value of both the natives' knowledge and the scientists' and entrepreneurs's contributions, and therefore rewards both types of intellectual property rights in the development of rain forest products.

The Tagua Initiative

Conservation International is an environmental organization based in Washington, D.C., that works to conserve biodiversity by supporting local rain forest communities world-wide. Through a project entitled "The Tagua Initiative," Conservation International is attempting to synthesize "the approaches of business, community development, and applied science to promote conservation through the marketing of non-timber forest products." The tagua nut is an ivory-like seed that is harvested from tropical palm trees to make buttons, jewelry, chess pieces, carvings, and other arts and crafts. Conservation International links button manufacturers in the United States and other countries with rural tagua harvesters in the endangered rain forests of Esmeraldas in Ecuador. The organization works independently with participating companies to design unique marketing strategies tailored to those companies' individual images, product offerings, and marketing campaigns.

In 1990, Conservation International began expanding the market for tagua products and developing a local industry around tagua. Today, tagua buttons are being used by 24 clothing companies, including such major manufacturers as Smith & Hawken, Esprit, J. Crew, and L. L. Bean. The current distribution network links the Ecuadorian tagua producers to the clothing companies through four wholesale button manufacturers. Conservation International collects a royalty based on a percentage of sales to wholesale button manufacturers and uses the proceeds to support local conservation and community development programs in the rain forest. It has also focused its efforts on developing a viable local tagua industry that includes harvesting and manufacturing. A primary objective of The Tagua Initiative is to provide the 1,200 local harvesters with an attractive price for tagua so that they have an economic incentive to protect the standing forest. Recent figures indicate that the price paid to tagua collectors has risen 92 percent since the program began (a 32 percent real price increase after adjusting for the estimated inflation rate). To increase the flow of income to the native economy, Conservation International encourages the development of new tagua products that can be manufactured locally. Currently, the tagua production line has expanded to include eight manufacturers of jewelry, arts and crafts, and other items.

The Tagua Initiative provides a tremendously successful example, at least in the initial stages of development. Since February 1990, 850 tons of tagua have been delivered directly to factories, and the program has generated approximately $2 million in button sales to manufacturers in North America, Europe, and Japan. According to Robin Frank, tagua product manager at Conservation International, the organization is collaborating with about 50 companies worldwide, and many others have expressed interest. Moreover, The Tagua Initiative in Ecuador has become a role model for new projects in Colombia, Guatemala, Peru, the Philippines, and a number of other countries. In all of these cases, Conservative International is working with local organizations to identify and develop sustainable commercial products in a manner that protects sensitive ecosystems. These projects are expanding the rain forest product line to Brazil nuts and pecans from Peru, fibers for textiles, and waxes and oils for the personal health and hygiene market.

In addition to creating marketable rain forest products, Conservation International cooperates with conservation and community development programs, such as the Corporacion de Investigaciones para el Desarrollo Socio/Ambiental (CIDESA) in Ecuador. Ecologists, economic botanists, and conservation planners affiliated with Conservation International help CIDESA to identify critical rain forest sites and monitor harvesting practices to ensure their sustainability, among other things. The province of Esmeraldas in Ecuador is considered a critical "hot spot" because it contains some of the highest levels of bio-diversity in Latin America and harbors some of Ecuador's last remaining pristine tracts of western Andean rain forest. Coincidentally, it is one of Ecuador's poorest communities, with a meager annual average per-capita income of $600, about one-half of the national average. The community of Comuna Rio Santiago in Esmeraldas has a population of 70,000, which grows dramatically at an annual rate of 3.7 percent. Four out of every 10 children suffer from malnutrition, and the infant mortality rate is 60 per 1,000 births. There is a high level of alcoholism, and drug addiction is a growing problem. Life expectancy is just 50 years, and the illiteracy level is near 50 percent. All of these actualities indicate an urgent need to protect the natural resources found in this region, not only to maintain biodiversity but also to ensure the economic welfare of the local inhabitants. If these needs are addressed, the program will have the potential to change the current low standard of living in Ecuador by promoting both conservation and economic development.

Over the next 10 years, Conservation International plans to increase the use of numerous rain forest products, such as medicines, furniture, and baskets. These efforts can serve as a role model for firms in the industrial world that seek to create rain forest products and improve the well-being of rain forest inhabitants.

Shaman Pharmaceuticals

Shaman Pharmaceuticals, Inc., draws its name from rain forest *shamans*, traditional medicine men who possess a vast amount of knowledge about the use of plants for medicinal purposes. The shamans' ability to cure a variety of illnesses is founded on centuries of practice and an intimate association with, and dependence upon, indigenous plants. By tapping the knowledge of the shamans, scientists hope to reduce the research costs of identifying plants with beneficial medicinal properties. Furthermore, investigating plant species already known to possess healing characteristics yields a much higher chance of success in the screening process. This ethnobotanical approach—which combines the skills of anthropology and botany to study how native peoples utilize plants—is the basic premise by which Shaman Pharmaceuticals functions. By innovatively combining the disciplines of ethnobotany, isolation chemistry, and pharmacology with a keen market-driven strategy, the company hopes to create a more efficient drug-discovery program.

Shaman has formed strategic alliances with the pharmaceutical industry to enhance its prospects of turning a pharmaceutical discovery into a financial gain. "Shaman feels it is in a strong position to strike such alliances because the company is not only formed around a handful of products, but also around an efficient, ongoing process for generating compounds with a greater likelihood of being active in humans." The company has two main objectives in building these alliances: generating research funds through cooperative arrangements and gaining access to a larger marketing network. Three major pharmaceutical manufacturers have entered into agreements with Shaman: Inverni della Beffa, an Italian manufacturer of plant-derived pharmaceuticals, has signed licensing and marketing agreements and invested $500,000 in Shaman; Eli Lilly committed $4 million to Shaman and collaborates in developing drugs for fungal infections; and Merck & Company is working with Shaman on projects targeting analgesics and medicines for diabetes. (For more on this topic, see "Making Biodiversity Conservation Profitable: A Case Study of the Merck/INBio Agreement," by Elissa Blum, in the May 1993 issue of *Environment*.)

To address the question of intellectual property rights and needs of the indigenous population, Shaman Pharmaceuticals created a nonprofit conservation organization called "The Healing Forest Conservancy" to protect global plant biodiversity and promote sustainable development. The company initially donated 13,333 shares of its own stock to the conservancy and plans to channel future product profits into projects that benefit the people of the source country. The first conservancy project provided health care benefits for the indigenous peoples of Amazonian Ecuador, a region that supplies valuable medicinal plants to Shaman. In return for information about these plants, physician Charles Limbach extended his medical services to three communities and treated 30 children during a whooping cough epidemic. Additionally, the conservancy seeks to create sustainable harvesting techniques for plants with commercial medicinal value. These programs have the task of reconciling the ecological constraints on plant extraction with the economic realities of producing a marketable product. This strategy reflects Shaman's concern that both the physical and intellectual property rights of the indigenous population are protected and that the inhabitants benefit from the research on these products.

As a result of its research efforts over the past few years, Shaman Pharmaceuticals has a pipeline full of active plant leads. Two antiviral products are currently being tested in clinical trials and are expected to reach the market in 1996: Provir is an oral treatment for respiratory viral infections that are common in young children; Virend is a topical treatment for the herpes simplex virus. Both products use the ingredient known as SP-303, a compound that was derived from a medicinal plant that grows in South America and was isolated by the company's discovery process. Patents have been filed on both the pure compounds and the methods of use for these products, which have a target market greater than $1 billion worldwide. Another consequential find is an antifungal agent found in an African plant that is traditionally ingested to treat infections. Shaman is using this compound to make a product that treats thrush, a fungal infection of the mouth, esophagus, and gastrointestinal tract. Given this discovery, the company hopes to find new treatments for other types of fungal infection. Shaman has strategically targeted its product development to address problems for which few effective treatments exist, such as viral and fungal infections. Moreover, there is a growing demand to find treatment for herpes and thrush because the increasing population of immunocompromised patients (including AIDS, chemotherapy, and transplant patients) is particularly vulnerable to these ailments. A third promising line of product development is in the area of analgesics. Shaman has found two plants exhibiting special binding properties that raise the prospect of creating a nonaddictive pain-relief drug. The company is conducting laboratory tests to identify the pure compounds responsible for this analgesic activity and is expanding its screening process by collaborating with Merck.

The raw materials for the screening all come from plants that are either presently harvested or sustainably collected. This discovery process has been quite successful at identifying plants with potential medicinal properties. Based on thousands of field samples collected by ethnobotanical field researchers and on reviews by a scientific strategy team, the company has screened 262 plants and found 192 to be active—a "hit rate" of 73 percent in the discovery process. Future products will be developed from some of these "hits."

According to company president Lisa Conte, "Shaman's well-defined strategic focus and outstanding, dedicated scientists will create a successful business by uniquely combining the newest in technology with the oldest of tribal lore." As a leader in ethnobotanical investigations, Shaman hopes that its initial success will translate into the development of a market for plant-based drugs from rain forest countries. The goal here is to use the revenue generated by these medicines as an economic incentive to preserve the forests and the wisdom of the native healers.

Ecotourism in Costa Rica

Ecotourism has been defined as "purposeful travel that creates an understanding of cultural and natural history, while safeguarding the integrity of the ecosystem and producing economic benefits that encourage conservation." Successful ecotourism creates economic opportunities in terms of both employment and income for the local people. These benefits furnish the local community with a strong incentive to practice good stewardship over their natural resources.

In Costa Rica, ecotourism has become a large and growing industry. In 1986, tourism generated $132.7 million and ranked as Costa Rica's third largest source of foreign exchange. In 1989, more than 375,000 tourists visited Costa Rica, 36 percent of whom were motivated by ecotourism. Tourism to Costa Rica's parks increased 80 percent between 1987 and 1990 and surged another 25 percent in 1991. Costa Rica offers the ecotourist diverse rain forests, abundant biodiversity, and breathtaking scenery. To protect these valuable resources, a national park system was established in 1970, which now comprises 34 parks and covers 11 percent of the total Costa Rican land area. Some of the most popular sites for ecotourism in Costa Rica, such as the Monteverde Cloud Forest Reserve and the La Selva Biological Station, are also centers for important biological research. Recently, these areas have attracted thousands of visitors each year, primarily because of the rich flora (more than 2,000 plant species) and fauna (some 300 animal species).

During the mid 1980s, the Costa Rican government sought to reconcile conservation and development interests by pursuing a strategy of sustainable development. Ecotourism was viewed as a clean source of development that might facilitate the preservation of the natural resource base. The actual implementation of this strategy was left to the private sector. The early environmental entrepreneurs in Costa Rica's ecotourism industry included Costa Rica Expeditions, Tikal, Horizontes, and the Organization for Tropical Studies. The growth of the ecotourism industry has since put strains on the fragile resource base. For example, the large number of visitors at popular parks is causing such problems as erosion and water pollution. Given the attraction of tourist revenues and the danger of overcrowding, environmental entrepreneurs are finding it difficult

to create ecotourism programs that are consistent with the principles of sustainable development. Efforts to control ecotourism in Costa Rica are still in the early stages, and more research is needed soon if the industry is to serve its original purpose.

One firm that is striving to attain this balance is International Expeditions. This 11-year-old, Alabama-based company operates 30 travel programs on 6 continents. Company president Richard Ryel and Tom Grasse, the director of marketing and public relations, contend that the ecotourism industry needs to forgo short-run profits and adopt a four-part conservation ethic that includes increasing public awareness about the environment, maximizing economic benefits for local people, encouraging cultural sensitivity, and minimizing the negative impacts on the environment. International Expeditions applies these principles to business practices: For example, to create a flow of money into the local economy, the company uses the host country's airline when possible, employs local tour operators, and uses other services within the rain forest community. The company's tour of Costa Rica begins in San Jose and proceeds through the country's national parks. The tour organizers hire Costa Rican guides who are familiar with the local habitat, and both guides and tourists stay at accommodations close to the parks whenever possible. These steps are designed to prevent tourist revenue from leaking outside the local communities that live near the parks.

To minimize detrimental impacts on the ecosystem and to promote respect for the rain forests, International Expeditions arranges small, manageable groups, educates participants about the ecosystem, avoids fragile habitats, and minimizes disruptions to the wildlife. In keeping with its objective of promoting natural history and conservation education, International Expeditions has designed a series of workshops in Costa Rica. The workshops are led by some of the world's leading experts on life in the rain forest, including Alwyn Gentry of the Missouri Botanical Garden, Donald Wilson of the National Museum of Natural History, and James Duke of the U.S. Department of Agriculture. Participants join in small group sessions to engage in hands-on field experience, such as nature walks, boat trips, and bird watching, and visit such sites as the Monteverde Cloud Forest and Tortuguero National Park on the Caribbean coast. Various sites feature canopied walkways up to 125 feet off the forest floor, which allow participants to walk among the treetops and closely observe the flora and fauna. The local guides also educate tourists about the history, culture, and socioeconomic conditions of indigenous peoples.

During the 1992 season, the cost of the 10-day, general nature tour throughout Costa Rica was $1,998 per person, and the 8-day workshop cost $1,498 per person. Because roughly 50 percent of these expenditures go to Costa Rica, these trips create the dual benefits of educating the nature traveler and generating income for the local economy.

A KEY TO PRESERVATION

Clearly, sustainable development of rain forest products has the potential to bring about positive change, preserve biodiversity, and improve the welfare of local communities. Because deforestation is spiraling out of control, the efforts of organizations like Conservation International, Shaman Pharmaceuticals, Inc., and International Expeditions have become imperative. E. O. Wilson of the Museum of Comparative Zoology at Harvard University calculates that deforestation of the rain forest is responsible for the loss of 4,000 to 6,000 species a year —an extinction rate 10,000 times higher than the natural extinction rate before the emergence of humans on Earth. Furthermore, the unwritten knowledge of forest peoples is rapidly disappearing. Thomas Lovejoy, assistant secretary for external affairs at the Smithsonian Institution, asserts that the rain forest "is a library for life sciences, the world's greatest pharmaceutical laboratory, and a flywheel of climate. It's a matter of global destiny." The need to develop methods to deal with the issue is urgent, and environmental entrepreneurs may be key to preserving the vital and fragile resources of the tropical rain forests.

NO

Jon Entine

LET THEM EAT BRAZIL NUTS: THE "RAINFOREST HARVEST" AND OTHER MYTHS OF GREEN MARKETING

"Business is our new universal community," says the speaker, and there is an immediate murmur of agreement. With eyes closed, the scene echoes of a Rotary Club luncheon in a genial, Midwestern town. There is an air of optimism that everyone seems to share.

"Religion and government no longer work as forces for community and change. We are in the era of business, it defines our relationships and values, and it doesn't have to be driven by the bottom line." The burly, ruby-faced speaker is clearly taken by his own message. The all-white, well-heeled crowd is entranced. "We are the leaders who can turn business into a positive social force."

The audience rises from its seats and breaks into applause. Although the words ring of Des Moines, the audience is forty-something L.A. Aging baby boomers in khaki sportcoats and designer jeans mix with business executives in Ann Taylor power suits. One man with stylishly long hair, a black silk shirt, black pants and sunglasses whispers into a cellular phone. Judging by the cars in the parking lot, this crowd long since traded in its Beetles for BMWs and Broncos.

This was a June celebration to open the Los Angeles chapter of Business for Social Responsibility, a trade group that promotes itself as environmentally and socially progressive, and they have come to hear their hero. The slightly rumpled, three-time college dropout holds the audience spellbound with his prescription for 'saving the world through business.' Their affection, indeed the adulation, is tangible.

The object of their rapt attention is Ben Cohen, who, in the late 1970s, starting mixing batches of ice cream at an abandoned gas station in Burlington, Vermont, with his high school buddy Jerry Greenfield. Today, Ben & Jerry's Rainforest Crunch, Chunky Monkey, and Cherry Garcia are indulgences of choice for baby boomers. Although he no longer runs the company day-today, Cohen, 44, remains Chairman and eccentric corporate symbol of Ben & Jerry's Homemade, the 18-year-old, $160 million publicly traded company.

Ben & Jerry's is the best known of the "good guy" entrepreneurs with quixotic corporate personas and New Age social philosophies. Skin-and-hair-care franchiser The Body Shop International (BSI), eco-friendly apparel makers Patagonia and Esprit, Tom's of Maine natural toothpaste and personal-care wholesaler, and Reebok athletic shoes are a few of the companies which have sliced a sizable niche out of the retail pie by turning "green" issues—such as the rainforest, "natural" ingredients and an opposition to animal testing—into their points-of-difference in a fickle, ultra-competitive consumer market. Many of these companies started with non-existent advertising budgets but were run by executives with an intuitive understanding of how to play the media dominated by baby boomers like themselves. And no company has benefited more from friendly press coverage than Ben & Jerry's.

In Los Angeles, Cohen rails on about the greedy, soulless character of Corporate America, and then boasts about his special flavor of New Age business. "Rainforest Crunch," he says, "shows that harvesting Brazil nuts is a profitable alternative for Amazon natives who have seen their lands ravaged to create grazing areas or for mining." The crowd is on its feet.

Yet, Ben & Jerry's own annual report carries the not-so-socially responsible details of what some anthropologists now call the rainforest fiasco. Despite Cohen's rhetoric that buying Rainforest Crunch helps preserve the fragile Amazon environment and the aboriginals who live there—a theme repeated uncritically by most of the media—his Third World project offers a lesson in the dangers of paternalistic capitalism. In fact, many anthropologists believe the rainforest harvest has led to the worst possible scenario: an increase in clear-cutting and mining, and a greater dependence among Amazon natives on selling land for subsistence income.

GREEN MARKETING OR GREEN WASHING?

Cohen & Company preach an oxymoronic message: the generation that wanted to change the world now encourages consumers to "shop for a better world," the title of a best-selling "green" consumer guide. It's a two-for-one sale that rings up big profits: 'buy our not-tested-on-animals Brazil nut hair rinse or ice cream and get social justice for free.'

U.S. consumers spend upwards of $110 billion on products from companies they perceive as socially or environmentally progressive. According to a study last summer by the Social Investment Forum, $150 billion in teacher, union, church and other pension funds is held by investment managers using social screens; another $12 billion is invested in mutual funds which follow various "ethical" or "green" formulas. More than 45 funds in the U.S. alone screen out companies for manufacturing "sin" products such as cigarettes, while they include firms that promote social policies such as making "cruelty-free" products.

For years, The Body Shop was the favorite of the ethical investing community. Its founder, Anita Roddick, is the most visible and outspoken of the green marketing executives. Since opening a tiny shop in 1976 offering "one-stop ear piercing" and a range of natural-sounding lotions, Roddick has grown BSI into an $800 million multinational company with 1300 mostly-franchised stores in 45 countries. She has cultivated a reputation for promoting the latest politically-correct social campaign: saving the whales, recycling, animal rights, AIDS research, and most prominently, preserving the environment and indigenous cultures by sourcing ingredients from the Third World. Roddick dubbed these micro-projects "Trade Not Aid," popularizing the eco-liberal concept of using capitalism instead of aid projects to reduce Third World dependency.

Despite rhetoric of good intentions, BSI has had a string of fair trade fiascos. For instance, over a year ago in Ghana, The Body Shop bought $20,000 worth of shea-butter from 10 villages for use in its creams. According to a front-page article in the *Toronto Globe & Mail*, the creams didn't sell, and today, the project is abandoned and the local economy is in tatters. BSI made no follow-up orders and left villages with thousands of dollars of unsold butter and no buyers.

The Body Shop's fair trade program has been plagued with problems. Richard Adams, who has founded two fair trade organizations, remembers seeing leaflets at BSI's stores in 1987 promoting its first import, foot massagers made by orphan boys in India. As director of Traidcraft in the early 1980s, Adams had briefly carried wood carvings made by the same group of orphans, who lived in a home called The Boys' Town. "Joe Homan, its director, was sourcing carvings from child labor sweat shops," he recalls discovering after poor quality shipments prompted an investigation. Worse, the local community said boys were being molested. Adams immediately sent the Roddicks a letter. "I never heard back,"

he says. Homan, it turns out, had been kicked out of a Christian Brothers sect. Two alarmed members of the Jesuit order visited the Roddicks after getting wind of the project. Still, nothing was done.

"Gordon [Roddick] was aware of his reputation," says Anne Downer, former head BSI franchisee for much of Asia. Downer, who attended the christening of The Boys' Town with the Roddicks in 1987, remembers Gordon saying that he had heard the rumors but didn't believe them. "He didn't seem unduly concerned and didn't seem to take it seriously."

Over the next few years, as Homan went about stealing charity funds and molesting orphan boys, the Roddicks sent out glowing reports to their franchisees. "Joe's work in The Boys' Town is ceaseless, he cares for the boys and girls and they really appreciate what he is doing for them," gushed one account in 1989. The roof caved in the next year when the English and Indian press ran exposes of Homan's escapades. The Roddicks first tried to suppress the scandal and then attempted to turn it into a public relations advantage by claiming credit for exposing him. "This story has not hit the Canadian Press yet but could erupt at any time," read one memo. "It is important that you know your facts. Anita... blew the whistle on Joe." A similar bulletin went to all of its American franchisees.

Not one of the Body Shop's dozen "Trade Not Aid" projects has been accurately promoted. And by its own statistics, they represented just 0.165% of the company's business as recently as 1993, at the height of its self-promoting rhetoric. Yet, despite their tiny size and frequent problems, these projects have generated overwhelmingly favorable media coverage—including much of the 10,000 positive mentions the company says it averages each year.

RAINFOREST FIASCO

Over the past decade, the "rainforest harvest," as it has come to be called, has been the most publicized international fair trade program and a defining symbol of social activism. The marketing of the rainforest blends three cultural trends: the environmentalist struggle to protect the forest against clear-cutting, the movement to preserve indigenous peoples, and baby boom narcissism.

The rainforest movement gathered momentum after the annual Brazilian Peoples Conference in 1989. Roddick and various journalists, environmentalists and eco-celebrities, from Jane Fonda to Sting, gathered in Altamira for the event, which garnered headlines around the world. Not long after, BSI introduced rainforest bath beads made with babassu nut oil, and hair conditioner from nuts harvested and processed by two Kayapo villages in the eastern Amazon.

BSI attached a bright Trade Not Aid sticker to its rainforest bead display, although babassu nuts are not grown in the Amazon, and the beads were made mostly from super-refined oil sourced from the Croda Chemical company—tested on animals in 1986. The hair conditioner uses a tiny fraction of Brazil nut oil at what cosmetic experts say are ineffective levels. According to a study by UK-based Survival International, BSI pays the workers $1.33 per kilo of nuts collected—an average of $500 for a five month harvesting season. Yet in its public relations hand-outs, BSI has claimed that workers in its projects are paid "first world wages." Little money trickles down to the villages. The young Kayapo leaders ("socios") who run the project continue to sell off land rights to profiteers cutting down mahogany trees. The village has been nicknamed Kayapo, Inc. for cashing in their timber dollars for cars, Western-style homes and even an airplane.

HARVEST MOONSHINE

Ben & Jerry's rainforest project, which was more ambitious, has a serendipitous history. In 1988, at a party after a Grateful Dead rainforest fundraising concert, Ben Cohen casually mentioned that he was developing a new brittle for an ice cream using something more exotic than peanuts. According to those present, Jason Clay, an ambitious anthropologist with the Cambridge indigenous rights group Cultural Survival, lit up like a video game. He regaled Cohen with his pet project to market renewable non-timber rainforest products such as fruits, nuts and flowers. A few days after the concert, Cohen's new friend headed to Vermont carrying a 50-pound bag of rainforest nuts. "We mixed up the first batch of brazil nut crunch in Ben Cohen's kitchen and served it to the board of directors that night," recalled Clay, "and we were off."

Within months, Cohen founded and became half-owner of Community Products Inc. CPI was set up to source Brazil nuts from Cultural Survival (CS) and turn them into brittle for ice cream, and cosmetic products and candy made by other companies. His intentions were no doubt benevolent; CPI promised to pay harvesters a 5% "environmental premium" and give 60% of any profits to charity, a third of that to Cultural Survival.

Ben & Jerry's has long been a favorite of both green-oriented consumers and investors. It does set an impressive standard of ethical innovation: it has published state-of-the-art social audits, gives an astonishing 7.5% of pre-tax profits to charity and buys local dairy products to help preserve the family farm. But the company is most readily identified with its flagship Rainforest ice cream.

Ben & Jerry's launched Rainforest Crunch early in 1990. "Money from these nuts," read the label, "helps to show that rainforests are more profitable when cultivated for traditional harvest than when their trees are cut and burned for short-term gain." The Third World ice cream was an overwhelming, overnight success—for Ben & Jerry's, which reaped tens of millions of dollars in profits and free publicity. But the view from Amazonia was not nearly so sanguine.

Critics found little evidence to support the central premise of the harvest—that foraging for nuts could ever approximate the income natives collect by selling off land rights to miners and foresters. "Marketing the rainforest . . . perpetuates the process of leaving to the forest dwellers the resources of the least interest to the broader society," wrote anthropologist Michael Dove for the East-West Center in Honolulu, in a typical critique.

Outside of Cultural Survival, where founder David Maybury-Lewis and Jason Clay were positioned to reap fame and perhaps fortune as consultants if the harvest took off, anthropologists quietly urged a go-slow strategy on Ben & Jerry's and BSI, but were ignored.

The worst case scenario was soon realized. There was no established supply chain for Amazon nuts. Most natives such as the Kayapo, long since corrupted by Western interests and fighting a

losing battle to alcoholism, were not about to stop selling land rights to meet the expectations of social activists in London and Cambridge. Ben & Jerry's anticipated source for the nuts, the Xapuri cooperative (which had no native workers but was comprised of white rubber tappers, mostly of Portuguese ancestry) in western Brazil, never could meet the quality standards or quantity demands of the fad product.

To meet the sudden explosion in demand, market forces took hold and agribusinesses were drawn in to meet it. The harvest proved to be a windfall for landowners, who have long monopolized trade in this region. "That first year, we had to source all of our nuts from commercial suppliers," concedes Michelle McKinley, the former general manager of CS who left in November after reassembling the pieces of an organization nearly bankrupted by the ill-conceived harvest. Agri-barons elbowed out native suppliers and flooded the market. Nut prices, already soft, plummeted, cutting the incomes of tribes who did collect nuts. Amanakáa, a Brazilian peoples rights group, took Ben & Jerry's to task for sourcing directly from the Mutran family, a notorious Latin American agri-business convicted of killing labor organizers.

While the project was spinning out of control, harvest hype developed into a New Age business mantra. Sting set up the now-defunct Rainforest Foundation and began singing the praises of the free market. Usually-vigilant social critic Alexander Cockburn even became a convert; he attacked the UK-based indigenous rights organization Survival International after its director, Stephen Corry, published "Harvest Moonshine," a meticulously documented critique of the project which criticized Cockburn's friends at Cultural Survival.

Based in large measure on Roddick's self-promotion as a fair trade leader, Ralph Nader dubbed her "the most progressive business person I know," *Mother Jones* invited her onto its board, *USA Today* called her "The Mother Theresa of Capitalism," and the yuppie business magazine *Inc.* put Roddick on its cover with the headline, "This Woman Has Changed Business Forever."

The Brazilian and Bolivian governments took advantage of the harvest hype to justify cutting expensive, politically unpopular financial aid to native populations. A confidential report by the Alliance of Forest Peoples (a coalition including the Xapuri) attacked Cultural Survival for its "minimal" concrete support. "Their negative repercussions have been enormous," read the report. "We have not seen any return." Brazilian peoples groups, cowed at first by the Cohen-Roddick marketing barrage, gradually became more vocal. "A thriving market in forest products," said Julia Barbosa, president of the national Rubber Tappers Council which represented the Xapuri workers, "is no substitute for a political program that protects the forests and people who live in it."

To cover the economic shortfall, some native communities even sold off more land rights. In the end, the celebrated harvest has created a Brazil nut business dominated by some of Latin America's most notorious capitalists. Over the years, more than 95% of Ben & Jerry's Brazil nuts have been purchased on agri-business dominated markets; today, almost 100% are commercially sourced. According to Cultural Survival's McKinley, the so-called progressive retailers had been increasingly unwilling to pay the 5% environmental premium; last year only $22,000 was collected. "We rushed into this project recklessly," she now says. "We created a fad market overnight and the hard sell promotions have contributed to a lot of confusion. The harvest just didn't work."

In retrospect, early optimistic projections by rainforest capitalists seem almost ridiculous. Clay had estimated a $20–25 million market by 1996 with the benefits flowing to the rubber tappers and native communities. The business peaked in 1991 at $1.3 million, dropped to $250,000 in 1995, and has nearly sunk Cultural Survival. Clay was forced out. By the spring of '94, the Xapuri had cut off all supplies to CS. The project has run in the red for four years, generating no profits for Community Products and no charity.

NO WHALES HAVE BEEN KILLED BY MY COMPANY

Ironically, despite Ben Cohen's attempts to brush off the fiasco, his company did release an independent social audit documenting it. Paul Hawken, the environmentalist, author and businessman, published his analysis as part of Ben & Jerry's annual report released last summer. "It is a legitimate question," wrote Hawken, "whether representations made on Ben & Jerry's Rainforest Crunch package give an accurate impression to the customer." He quoted sharp criticism from Amazon rights groups, then concluded: "There have been undesirable consequences which some say were predictable and avoidable."

So, why have social activists, academics and journalists been caught off guard by the ethical contradictions of socially responsible business and New Age adventures such as the rainforest fiasco?

Does buying ice cream or hair rinse with Brazil nuts promote progressive social change or merely inure the public to the profligacy, and elitism, that has gradually coopted the green consumer movement?

The Sixties did inspire a new morality-based social philosophy that emphasizes the individual's responsibility to speak out against injustice and corruption. It drew its social vision from the civil rights movement, anti-Vietnam activism, environmental consciousness and feminism, and it continues to inspire social and environmental reforms. But there is an underside to the legacy of the counter-culture: narcissism, arrogance and self-indulgence.

Baby boomers—people born from the mid-1940s to 1960—are beginning to dominate the business and political landscape. Since 1990, their share of national leadership—Congress and governorships—has more than doubled from 21% to 45%, and will reach more than 70% within the decade. They are gradually becoming the American political and business establishment.

Yet, many conspicuous baby boom business leaders seem convinced of their socially responsible credentials, in large measure because they came of age in the Sixties. The visionaries at the vanguard of this movement—from Cohen and Roddick to Mo Siegel at Celestial Seasonings and Paul Fireman at Reebok—are loath to admit that "social responsibility" is in part a margin game. When profits are rolling in, as they were in the 1980s, progressive gestures are painless.

But facing growing pains and intense worldwide competition, many are firing workers, closing inner city stores, cutting back on charity projects, and making their products in overseas sweatshops.

Just last November, Reebok received reams of positive press when it gave a Human Rights Award, an annual event. Yet, it was curiously silent a few days later when reports surfaced that its workers in Thailand make 25 cents an hour for 18 hour days. Asked about the contradiction, Reebok's Paul Fireman told the UK newspaper *The Observer* that he will not "impose U.S. culture on other countries... 'when in Rome, do as the Romans.'" In other words, Reebok, BSI and other New Age entrepreneurs frequently act much like any business with bottom line challenges.

The not-so-pristine consequences of green consumerism have been largely absent from business reporting, since many journalists who have so slavishly profiled these successful entrepreneurs share with them common cultural pretensions. Many have convinced themselves that growing up protesting Vietnam and supporting Earth Day forever marks them as progressives, though today their closest brush with social responsibility may consist of little more than enjoying a Ben & Jerry's Peace Pop.

On close scrutiny, progressive business if often a land of alchemy where promises are easy to make, workers are frequently treated with indifference, and environmental reforms are superficially attempted. At best, the relatively small number of consumers with a high tolerance for high-priced goods—most of the products in question command a hefty premium over ordinary brands—play a modest role in raising awareness of social problems. (And even so, it's just a prosperous sliver of baby boomers affected.) At worse, cause-related marketing, as it is called, is little more than baby boom agitprop, masking serious ethical lapses. "Many socially responsible companies have noble corporate philosophies," observes Jon Lickerman, a social researcher with the Calvert Group of socially responsible mutual funds, "but mistreat their own employees, vendors, and customers."

They've also inspired a wave of green marketing by mainstream firms. Guardians of free speech and public health such as Philip Morris take out full-page ads decrying the sale of cigarettes to minors while railing against Big Government; Chevron brags that its sunken oil rigs are havens for Gulf fisheries; oil drillers, developers and natural gas companies band together to form the National Wetlands Coalition, complete with a logo featuring a duck flying over marshes, to front their attacks on environmental reform. Madison Avenue has embraced greenwashing with a vengeance, and the green business movement, with its facile posturing on complex issues, must bear some of the responsibility.

ICE CREAM POLITICS

"It's really a disingenuous marketing strategy to say if you spend $2.99, you'll help save the rainforest," warns Michelle McKinley, formerly of Cultural Survival, which no longer sources Brazil nuts for Ben & Jerry's. But her criticism hasn't dampened Ben Cohen's enthusiasm for hawking Rainforest Crunch. Today, Cohen and co-founder Jerry Greenfield spend little time running the company that has grown far beyond their man-agerial expertise. They can be found on a college ice cream tour. At the Wharton Business School in Philadelphia, Ben and Jerry sermonized on their usual topics: the crazy fun of starting a business, corporate ethics and of course Rainforest Crunch. "After the speech, I talked with both Ben and Jerry personally," wrote Ritu Kalra, an MBA graduate, in a recent e-mail discussion about the controversy. "Neither of them knew much about the harvest. When it came down to it, they didn't want to comment on it and didn't feel responsible at all for any misleading labeling or for telling half-truths to about 300 college students."

In the case of the rainforest, Cohen still seems oblivious to or afraid to admit the real impact of his now-collapsed pet project. "We have created demand for rainforest products," he boasted at the annual meeting of Business for Social Responsibility in San Francisco in November. There was no mention of the rapacious agri-businesses that supply most of his nuts.

The BSR members—many personal friends of Cohen and part of an informal intelligentsia of the "progressive" business community—were reluctant to press their wounded hero. They were far more eager to munch on Ben & Jerry's Rainforest Crunch donated for the event. "It's so inspiring," one BSR member was heard to say as she licked her spoon clean, "to know that business can make money and still do so much good."

POSTSCRIPT

Can Green Marketing Save Tropical Rain Forests?

It could be argued that this issue's antagonists, the professors and the journalist, are arguing past each other. On the one hand, optimistic innovation, both scientific and economic, will be required to cut through the political barriers protecting the destroyers of the rain forests, so Carr, Pedersen, and Ramaswamy should be encouraged to continue their work. On the other hand, hope does not justify hype, nor do good intentions justify false promises. The journalistic skepticism of Entine is helpful in sorting out the self-serving environmental promotion from solid efforts to use the tremendous potential of the free enterprise system to save a precious global resource.

The rain forest issue is not one of government (and the environmentalists) versus the market (the ranchers). The opinion of many is that the long-term economic opportunity in preserving and harvesting the rain forests easily surpasses any economic gain to be realized in cutting it down. It can be argued that the difficulty in preserving the forest arises because the political powers in place at this time would prefer to use the forest in nonproductive ways for the stabilization of their regimes (through homesteading of the urban poor) and the benefit of political cronies. For centuries, the only means of overwhelming personal political interests has been the higher force of personal economic interests. When we can convince the rulers of the forest that they have more to gain from joining the world in the preservation of the forest than from their present destructive course, optimism on the ultimate fate of the forests will be justified.

SUGGESTED READINGS

Erik Eckholm, "Secrets of the Rainforest," *The New York Times Magazine* (November 17, 1988), p. 20.

Sandra Hackman, "After Rio—Our Forests, Ourselves," *Technology Review* (October 1992).

Andrew Revkin, *The Burning Season* (Houghton Mifflin, 1990).

Alex Shoumatoff, *The World is Burning* (Little, Brown, 1990).

CONTRIBUTORS
TO THIS VOLUME

EDITORS

LISA H. NEWTON is a professor of philosophy and director of the Program in Applied Ethics at Fairfield University in Fairfield, Connecticut. She received a B.S. in philosophy, with honors, from Columbia University in 1962 and a Ph.D. from Columbia in 1967. She was an assistant professor of philosophy at Hofstra University in Hempstead, New York, from 1967 to 1969, and she began teaching at Fairfield University in 1969. Professor Newton's articles have appeared in *Ethics* and the *Journal of Business Ethics,* among other publications. She is a member of the American Philosophical Association, the Academy of Management, and the American Society of Law and Medicine. Professor Newton currently serves as president of the Society for Business Ethics.

MAUREEN M. FORD is an associate for the Program in Applied Ethics at Fairfield University in Fairfield, Connecticut. She received a B.S. in business management and applied ethics from Fairfield University. Active as a consultant to community agencies, Mrs. Ford is a former president of the YWCA in Bridgeport, Connecticut, and was for several years vice president–secretary for JHLF, Inc., a marketing and consulting firm in Westport, Connecticut.

AUTHORS

IVAN AMATO is an author who frequently writes about environmental issues. His work has been published in *Science* and *Garbage: The Independent Environmental Quarterly.*

GEORGE J. ANNAS is the Edward R. Utley Professor of Law and Medicine at Boston University's Schools of Medicine and Public Health in Boston, Massachusetts. He is also director of Boston University's Law, Medicine, and Ethics Program and chair of the Department of Health Law. His publications include *Judging Medicine* (Humana Press, 1988) and *Standard of Care: The Law of American Bioethics* (Oxford University Press, 1993).

SUSAN S. BLACK is an associate publisher and editor in chief of *Bobbin* magazine.

SISSELA BOK is a faculty member of the Center for Advanced Study in the Behavioral Sciences in Stanford, California, and a former associate professor of philosophy at Brandeis University in Waltham, Massachusetts. Her publications include *Lying: Moral Choice in Public and Private Life* (Random House, 1979), *Secrets: On the Ethics of Concealment and Revelation* (Vintage Books, 1983), and *A Strategy for Peace: Human Values and the Threat of War* (Pantheon Books, 1989).

THOMAS A. CARR is an assistant professor in the economics department at Middlebury College in Middlebury, Vermont.

CITIZENS' RESEARCH EDUCATION NETWORK is a nonprofit policy watch organization based in Hartford, Connecticut.

ROGER CRISP is editor of the interdisciplinary journal *Utilitas*. He received a B.A. and a B.Phil. from Oxford University in Oxford, England, and he has published several articles on practical ethics.

WILLIAM R. EADINGTON is a professor of economics and director of the Institute for the Study of Gambling and Commercial Gaming at the University of Nevada, Reno.

JOHN ECHEVERRIA is chief legal counsel to the National Audubon Society in New York City. A 1981 graduate of the Yale Law School and the Yale School of Forestry and Environmental Studies, he has also been a legal counsel and conservation director of American Rivers, Inc., and he has served as law clerk to U.S. district judge Gerhard A. Gesell.

FRIEDRICH ENGELS (1820–1895), a German socialist, was the closest collaborator of Karl Marx in the foundation of modern communism. The "official" Marxism of the Soviet Union relies heavily on Engels's contribution to Marxist theory. After the death of Marx in 1883, Engels served as the foremost authority on Marx and Marxism, and he edited volumes 2 and 3 of *Das Kapital* on the basis of Marx's incomplete manuscripts and notes. Two major works by Engels are *Anti-Duhring* and *Dialectics of Nature*.

JON ENTINE is a journalist specializing in business ethics, journalism ethics, sports, and society. His reporting over 20 years has earned him many awards, including two Emmys. He has served as adjunct professor of journalism at New York University, and he has lectured at Columbia University.

RICHARD EPSTEIN is the James Parker Hall Distinguished Service Professor of Law at the University of Chicago in Chicago, Illinois, where he has been teaching since 1972. He has been a member of the American Academy of Arts and Sciences since 1985 and a senior fellow of the Center for Clinical Medical Ethics at the University of Chicago Medical School since 1983. He has written numerous articles on a wide range of legal and interdisciplinary subjects, and he is the author of *Forbidden Grounds: The Case Against Employment Discrimination Laws* (Harvard University Press, 1992) and *Takings: Private Property and the Power of Eminent Domain* (Harvard University Press, 1985).

HUGH M. FINNERAN (d. 1985) was the senior labor counsel for PPG Industries, Inc., a *Fortune* 500 company based in Pittsburgh, Pennsylvania, that manufactures paints, glass, printing inks, paper coatings, varnishes, and adhesives, as well as many other products.

JOHN E. FLEMING is a professor emeritus at the University of Southern California, where he taught for 24 years and where he served as director of the doctoral program and chairman of the Department of Management. His research focuses on strategy and business ethics, and he has been published in the *Academy of Management Journal*, the *California Management Review,* and the *Journal of Business Ethics.*

MARK GREEN, former commissioner of Consumer Affairs for New York City, is currently the city's public advocate. He has published 14 books on government, business, and law, including *There He Goes Again: Ronald Reagan's Reign of Error* (Pantheon Books, 1983), coauthored with Gail MacColl.

LaRUE TONE HOSMER is a professor of corporate strategies in the Graduate School of Business Administration at the University of Michigan in Ann Arbor, Michigan.

CATHERINE HOUGHTON is a representative of the Canadian office of the Commercial Service of the U.S. Department of Commerce, which assists U.S. firms in exporting by providing counseling and advice, information on markets abroad, international contacts, and advocacy services.

ROBERT A. LARMER is an associate professor of philosophy at the University of New Brunswick in Fredericton, New Brunswick, Canada. His research interests focus on the philosophy of religion, the philosophy of the mind, and business ethics. He has written numerous articles in these fields, and he is the author of *Water into Wine: An Investigation of the Concept of Miracle* (McGill-Queens University Press, 1988). He received a Ph.D. from the University of Ottawa.

CHARLES G. LEATHERS is a professor of economics in the Department of Economics, Finance and Business Law at the University of Alabama in Tuscaloosa, Alabama.

JOHN C. LUIK is a senior associate in the corporate values and ethics programs of the Niagara Institute in Niagara-on-the-Lake, Ontario, Canada. He has also served as an ethics consultant to a number of government institutions, professional organizations, and corporations. He received degrees in politics and philosophy from Oxford University, and he has held academic appointments at the

University of Oxford, the University of Manitoba, and Brock University. In addition to the ethics of advertising, his research interests include business ethics, medical ethics, environmental ethics, political philosophy, and the philosophy of Immanuel Kant.

IAN MAITLAND is a professor of ethics and international business at the University of Minnesota, Twin Cities, and a senior fellow at the Center of the American Experiment.

KARL MARX (1818–1883) was the revolutionist, sociologist, and economist from whom the movement known as Marxism derives its name and many of its ideas. Together with Friedrich Engels he published *Manifest der Kommunistischen Partei* (1848), commonly known as *The Communist Manifesto*. His most important theoretical work is *Das Kapital*, an analysis of the economics of capitalism. He also became the leading spirit of the International Working Men's Association, later known as the First International. His works became the intellectual basis of European socialism in the late nineteenth century.

DAN McGRAW is a contributing journalist to *U.S. News and World Report*.

DAVID M. MESSICK is the Morris and Alice Kaplan Professor of Ethics and Decision in Management at the J. L. Kellogg Graduate School of Management at Northwestern University. He was an Eastern European Exchange Fellow of the National Academy of Science in 1990. A former editor of the *Journal of Experimental Social Psychology*, he is the author of more than 100 articles and chapters and has been published in many prominent academic journals. He is coeditor of a number of books, including *Codes*

of Conduct: Behavioral Research into Business Ethics, with Ann E. Tenbrunsel (Russell Sage Foundation, 1996), and *Negotiation as a Social Process*, with Roderick M. Kramer (Sage Publications, 1995).

TIMOTHY MIDDLETON is a contributing editor of *Nest Egg* and a regular contributor to *Individual Investor* and *Worth*. He also hosts a weekly business radio program on WCBS in New York City.

JENNIFER MOORE, a former assistant professor of philosophy at the University of Delaware in Newark, Delaware, has done teaching and research in business ethics and business law. She is coeditor, with W. Michael Hoffman, of *Business Ethics: Readings and Cases in Corporate Morality*, 2d ed. (McGraw-Hill, 1990).

ALLEN R. MYERSON is a contributing journalist for the *New York Times*.

JOHN O'TOOLE is president of the American Association of Advertising Agencies in New York City. He has had a long career in advertising, and he remained with the firm of Foote, Cone and Belding Communications, Inc., for 31 years, serving 5 of those years as chairman of the board.

HEATHER L. PEDERSEN is a mathematics teacher at the Colorado Springs School in Colorado.

PHARMACEUTICAL MANUFACTURERS ASSOCIATION, founded in 1958 and located in Washington, D.C., is an association of 93 manufacturers of pharmaceutical and biological products that are distributed under their own labels. It encourages high standards for quality control and good manufacturing practices, research toward the development of new and better medical products, and the enactment of uniform and reasonable drug legislation for the protection of public health.

J. PATRICK RAINES is an associate professor of economics, and he holds the F. Carlyle Tiller Chair in Business at the University of Richmond in Richmond, Virginia.

SUNDER RAMASWAMY is chairman of the economics department at Middlebury College in Middlebury, Vermont. He received his Ph.D. from Purdue University.

ARNOLD S. RELMAN is a professor of medicine and of social medicine at Harvard Medical School and a senior physician at Brigham and Women's Hospital in Boston. He was the editor in chief of the *New England Journal of Medicine* from 1977 to 1991.

BILL SHAW is the Woodson Centennial Professor of Legal and Ethical Studies in Business in the Graduate School of Business at the University of Texas. He is also editor of the *American Business Law Journal*.

ADAM SMITH (1723–1790) was a Scottish philosopher and economist and the author of *An Inquiry into the Nature and Causes of the Wealth of Nations*, 2 vols. (1776).

RICHARD A. SPINELLO is associate dean of faculties and an adjunct assistant professor of philosophy at Boston College in Chestnut Hill, Massachusetts. He has published numerous articles on business ethics and ethical theory and on the social implications of new information retrieval technologies. He is the author of a textbook on computer ethics entitled *Ethical Aspects of Information Technology* (Prentice Hall, 1994).

JOE THORNTON is research coordinator for the Greenpeace Toxics Campaign in New York City.

MANUEL VELASQUEZ is the Charles Dirksen Professor of Business Ethics at Santa Clara University, where he teaches courses in the legal, political, and social environment of the firm, in business strategy, and in business ethics. He has published numerous articles in journals such as the *Academy of Management Review*, the *Business Ethics Quarterly*, *Social Justice Research*, and the *Business and Professional Ethics Journal*, and he is the author of *Business Ethics: Concepts and Cases*, 4th ed. (Prentice Hall, 1998). He received his B.A. from Gonzaga University and his Ph.D. from the University of California at Berkeley.

MICHAEL A. VERESPEJ is a writer for *Industry Week*.

ANDREW C. WICKS is an assistant professor in the Department of Management and Organization at the University of Washington School of Business. He has a Ph.D. in religious studies, and his interests are in normative business ethics and the connections between medical ethics and business ethics. His articles have been published in such journals as *Soundings* and the *Journal of Business Ethics*.

INDEX

Abzug, Bella, 314, 320
acceptance, as social truth, 58
accusation, whistle-blowing and, 184–185
acid rain, 261
addiction: controversy over casino gambling and, 120–137; tobacco and, 239, 240, 241
advertising: controversy over, as deceptive, 216–233; controversy over tobacco, 238–250
Age Discrimination Act, 172
agency argument, for employee drug testing, 204–205
AIDS, 102–103
alachlor, 302
alcohol abuse, employee, 198, 205–206
aldrin, 302
all or nothings, 154
Alliance of Forest Peoples, 340
alternative medicines, 115
altruism, of health care workers, 91, 93, 96
Amato, Ivan, on industrial use of chlorine, 312–321
American Apparel Manufacturers Association, 280
American Cancer Society, 242
American Medical Association, 80, 84–85, 86, 91, 115, 116
American Pharmaceutical Association, 115
American Public Health Association, 301, 303, 317
Annas, George J., on workplace fetal protection policies, 162–167
antitrust law, medical profession and, 85–86
apparel industry: and controversy over sweatshops, 278–283; Tagua Initiative and, 329–330
apprentices, 12
Aquinas, St. Thomas, 65, 67
arbitrageurs, 148
Arctic Wildlife Congress, 301
Aristotle, 56, 64, 65, 66, 67, 68, 70, 71, 72, 74, 105, 108
Arrow, Kenneth, 33, 58
asset-based financial derivatives, 153
assimilable capacity, for pollution, 307
atrazine, 302
authenticity, principle of, in corporate codes of ethics, 29, 33
automobile advertising, 229–230
autonomy: limits of corporate, 202–204; personal, tobacco advertising and, 243–250; persuasive advertising and, 216–223
azidothymide, 102–103

back-end solutions, to pollution, 307
Barcelona Convention on the Mediterranean, 301

barrier islands, and controversy over property rights and environmental issues, 290–296
bartering, 227
Beachfront Management Act, and controversy over property rights and environmental issues, 290–296
Ben & Jerry's, Inc., and sustainable development of the rain forest, 335–342
Bentsen, Lloyd, 111–112
benzene, 302
bingo, 123, 132
biological diversity, decline in, and controversy over sustainable development of the rain forest, 326–342
black markets, 110
Black, Susan S., on sweatshops, 278–280
Blackmun, Harry, 163, 249
Body Shop International, and sustainable development of the rain forest, 335–342
Bok, Sissela, 189; on whistle-blowing, 180–186
bona fide occupational qualification, employment discrimination and, 163, 164, 171–172
bonds, convertible, 154
Borg-Warner Corporation, corporate code of ethics of, 27–28
bourgeois class, versus proletariat, 12–20
bribes, 71, 261
Brooks, Leonard, 29, 34
Browner, Carol, 313, 314
bucket shops, 143, 144–146, 149, 150
burghers, 13, 18
Burke, James, 25–28
Burroughs-Wellcome Company, 102–103
Bush, George, 86, 282, 329
Business for Social Responsibility, 335
business necessity, fetal protection policies and, 172, 173

Canada: advertising of tobacco products in, 243–250; North American Free Trade Agreement and, 266–269
cancer: organochlorines and, 303, 305, 306, 313, 316; smoking and, 239, 242
capitalism, 57, 94, 336; controversy over, 4–20
carbon tetrachloride, 315
Carr, Thomas A., on rain forest entrepreneurs, 326–334
cartels, 42
cartoons, use of, in tobacco advertising, 238–250
casino gambling, controversy over, 120–137
categorical imperative, Kant's, 67
cause-related marketing, 341
caveat emptor, 81, 90

censorship: corporate codes of ethics and, 24, 31; tobacco advertising and, 240
certificates of deposit, 146
Chabot, Jean-Jude, 243, 247–248, 249
charity, of health care workers, 91
chemical industry, and controversy over industrial use of chlorine, 300–321
Chicago Mercantile Exchange, 146, 148
child labor, sweatshops and, 282–283
chlorine, controversy over industrial use of, 300–321
chlorofluorocarbons (CFCs), 258, 261, 306, 313, 316, 317, 319
chloromethane, 302
cigarettes. See tobacco industry
circuses, 142
Citizens' Research Education Network, on casino gambling, 120–128
Civil Rights Act of 1964, 162, 163, 173
class struggle, capitalism and, 12–20
Clay, Jason, 338, 339, 340
Clayton Act, 145
Clean Water Act, 301, 313, 314
Clinton, Bill, 89, 113, 271, 273, 282, 301, 329
Cockburn, Alexander, 339, 340
codes of ethics, controversy over corporate, 24–36
Cohen, Ben. See Ben & Jerry's, Inc.
collateralized mortgage obligation (CMO), 152, 153, 155
collusion, 71
commercial speech, freedom of, 240
commodity futures, 143
Communist Manifesto, The (Marx and Engels), 12–20
Community Products Inc., 338
compelling interests, 206
compulsive gambling, controversy over legalized gaming and, 120–137
conflict of interest, in medicine, 90
Connecticut, casino gambling in Hartford, 120–128, 133
consequentialist versus deontological moral reasoning, 34
Conservation International, 329, 330, 334
conspiracy, 71
Consumer Information Remedies (Federal Trade Commission), 232
Consumer Price Index, 113
content, of corporate codes of ethics, 29
control, persuasive advertising and, 220–222
convertible bonds, 154
corporations, controversy over moral responsibility of multinational, 254–262
Corry, Stephen, 339–340
Costa Rica, ecotourism and, 332–333
crime, controversy over casino gambling and, 120–137
Crisp, Roger, on advertising, 216–223
culpability, moral responsibility and, 201

Cultural Survival, 334, 340, 342
currency contracts, 153

DDT, 302, 306, 315–316, 317, 318
deceptive, controversy over advertising as, 216–233
deforestation. See rain forests
della Femina, Jerry, 225
deontological versus consequentialist moral reasoning, 34
derivatives, controversy over financial, 142–155
desire, creation of, persuasive advertising and, 216–223
development and promulgation, of corporate codes of ethics, 29
diagnostic laboratories, for-profit, 84, 86–87
dichlorophenyl sulfone, 315
difference principle, Rawls's, 106
dioxin, 301, 305, 307, 308, 313, 317
discrimination, employment, and controversy over fetal protection policies, 162–175
disparate treatment, and controversy over fetal protection policies, 162–175
dissent, whistle-blowing and, 182, 184
distributive justice, 46
doctors. See medical profession
Doctor's Dilemma, The (Shaw), 82
Dothard v. Rawlinson, 171
downsizing, 25
drug testing, of employees, controversy over, 196–209
drug utilization reviews, 115
Duska, Ronald, 187, 188, 189, 191

Eadington, William R., on casino gambling, 129–137
Earth Day, 340
Earth Summit, 329
Easterbrook, Frank, 165–166
Echeverria, John, 292, 293; on property rights and environmental issues, 294–296
ecotourism, 327, 332–333
embezzlement, 123, 130
eminent domain clause, of the Fifth Amendment, and controversy over property rights and environmental issues, 290–296
emphysema, smoking and, 239
Engels, Friedrich, on capitalism, 12–20
Enlightenment, 56, 66, 67
Entine, Jon, on rain forest entrepreneurs, 335–342
entrepreneurs, and controversy over sustainable development of the rain forest, 326–342
environmental issues, 258; controversy over chlorine and, 300–321; controversy over property rights and, 290–296; and controversy over sustainable development of the rain forest, 326–342
Epstein, Richard, 295; on property rights and environmental issues, 290–293

Equal Employment Opportunity Commission (EEOC), 169
ethnobotany, 326–327, 330–334
Eurodollars, 146
exotic derivatives, 153–154
external whistle-blowing, 189

fairness, as market virtue, 62, 68, 73
family entertainment, casino gambling as, 124
Fannie Mae, 155
Fashion Industry Forum, 280
Federal Trade Commission, 85, 86, 228–229, 232, 240
fetal protection policies, controversy over, 162–175
feudalism, 12, 13, 14, 16, 20
Fifth Amendment, to the U.S. Constitution, and controversy over property rights and environmental issues, 290–296
financial derivative instruments, controversy over, 142–155
Finneran, Hugh M., on workplace fetal protection policies, 168–175
First Amendment, to the U.S. Constitution, 240, 241
First Axiom of Corporate Strategy, Freeman and Gilbert's, 31
First English Evangelical Lutheran Church v. County of Los Angeles, 294–296
Fleming, John E., on morality and international business, 260–262
Foreign Corrupt Practices Act of 1977, 30, 261
Fortune 500, 268
forward-based contracts, 153
Frank, Robert, 44, 45, 50–51, 61
Freddie Mac, 155
free trade, 14, and controversy over the North American Free Trade Agreement, 266–273
free will, Kant's theory of, 200
From Those Wonderful Folks Who Brought You Pearl Harbor (della Femina), 225

gambling, casino, controversy over, 120–137
Gap, The, 279
gateway drug, tobacco as, 239
Geldudig v. Aiello, 170
gender issues, and controversy over fetal protection policies, 162–175
General Electric Co. v. Gilbert, 170
Gerstner, Louis V., 238, 242
GI Bill for Workers, 308
Gifford, Kathie Lee, 278, 279, 281, 283
gifts, ethics of accepting, 24
global warming, 258
Goldfarb v. Virginia State Bar, 85–86
good, market and the, 64–66
Goodpaster, Kenneth, 104, 107
Green, Mark, on tobacco advertising, 238–242
green marketing, and controversy over sustainable development of the rain forest, 326–342

green premium, 327
Greenfield, Jerry. See Ben & Jerry's, Inc.
Greenpeace, 312, 314, 315, 316, 317, 319, 320
Griggs v. Duke Power Co., 170–171
guilds, medieval, 12, 13
guilt, moral responsibility and, 201
"Gyges Ring" illusion, 71

Hartford, Connecticut, casino gambling in, 120–128, 133
Healing Forest Conservancy, 331
health issues: and controversy over chlorine, 300–321; and controversy over fetal protection policies, 162–175; controversy over market values and, 80–98; and controversy over pharmaceutical price controls, 102–116; and controversy over tobacco advertising aimed at teens, 238–250
health maintenance organizations (HMOs), 91, 92, 115
heart disease, smoking and, 239
hedonism, 57
hierarchy, whistle-blowing and, 182
Himmelfarb, Gertrude, 57–58
Hippocratic oath, 80, 90
Hirsch, Fred, 58, 60
Hobbes, Thomas, 72, 255, 257, 260, 262
Hodgson v. Greyhound Lines, Inc., 171–172
Hoffman-LaRoche Corp., 107
home health care, 112, 113
Hosmer, LaRue Tone, 31, 32, 33; on corporate codes of ethics, 24–28
hospices, 113
hospitals, 112; voluntary, 84
Houghton, Catherine, on the North American Free Trade Agreement, 266–269
Hucksters, The (Wakeman), 225

immediacy, whistle-blowing and, 182–183
Immigration and Naturalization Service, 279
immune system, organochlorines and, 304, 305, 306
implementation, of corporate codes of ethics, 29
imports, foreign, 7–11
inalienable rights, 205
index arbitrage, 147
indigenous peoples, and controversy over sustainable development of the rain forest, 326–342
Industrial Revolution, 66
informative advertising, 216, 242
insider trading, 71
insurance, health, 116
intellectual property rights, of indigenous peoples, 328–329
interest rates futures. See financial derivative instruments
interest-rate swaps, 153
Internal Revenue Service, 125, 279

internal whistle-blowing, 189
International Brotherhood of Teamsters v. United States, 168
International Expeditions, 333–334
International Joint Commission on the Great Lakes (IJC), 300, 309, 316–317
International Union v. Johnson Controls, and controversy over workplace fetal protection policies, 162–175
International Whaling Commission, 301
Interstate Commerce Act, 145
inverse floaters, 154
Isle of Palms, South Carolina, and controversy over property rights and environmental issues, 290–296

Joe Camel, and controversy over tobacco advertising, 238–250
Johnson & Johnson, corporate code of ethics of, 25–28, 241
journeymen, 12
justice: distributive, 46; pricing policies and, 104–108; procedural, 47
Justice Department, 279

Kant, Immanuel, 64, 67, 105–106, 107, 200, 217
Kennedy, Edward, 239, 242
Kmart Corp., 278, 279
Krugman, Paul, 281, 282–283

labor, division of, 4–7, 13
laboratories, for-profit diagnostic, 84, 86–87
Larmer, Robert A., on whistle-blowing, 187–192
Lasker, Albert, 227–228
Leadership Council on Advertising, 241
Leathers, Charles G., on financial derivative instruments, 142–151
legal liability, employee drug testing and, 201
legalized gambling, controversy over, 120–137
Levi Strauss & Co., 278, 279
liability, vicarious, 201
liability-based derivatives, 153
Libman, Bill, 270, 272
librium, 107
Lickerman, Jon, 341–342
Lienhart, Brad, 312, 314, 316, 317, 318
living wills, 115
Liz Claiborne, 278–279
Lonely Crowd, The (Reisman), 224
lotteries, state, 123, 124, 130–131, 132
loyalty, employee, and controversy over whistle-blowing, 180–192
Lucas, David H., and controversy over property rights and environmental issues, 290–296
Luik, John C., on tobacco advertising, 243–250

MacIntyre, Alasdair, 57, 59, 70
magnetic resonance imaging, 84

Maitland, Ian, on the market as a teacher of virtue, 56–63; reaction to views of, 64–74
malaria, 315
management by objectives, 33
manipulation, persuasive advertising and, 220–222
market, controversy over, as a teacher of virtue, 56–74
Marx, Karl, on capitalism, 12–20
materialism, 57
McDonnell Douglas Corp. v. Green, 169
McGraw, Dan, on the North American Free Trade Agreement, 270–273
McKinley, Michelle, 339, 340, 342
Medicaid, 91, 112, 113, 115
medical profession, controversy over business ethics and, 80–98
Medicare, 86, 91, 112, 113
mens rea, 201
mercantilism, 64
Merck & Co., 93, 94–95, 96, 97, 329, 331
Messick, David M., on business ethics, 49–52
methylene chloride, 315
Mexico, North American Free Trade Agreement and, 270–273
Midanek, James I., 152, 154–155
Middle Ages, 12, 13, 14, 18
middle class, 14
Middleton, Timothy, on financial derivative instruments, 152–155
Mill, John Stuart, 67, 108
minimum wage, 205
Modern Industry, capitalism and, 12–20
money laundering, casino gambling and, 125, 127
monopoly, 10, 107
Monteverde Cloud Forest, Costa Rica, 333, 334
Montreal Protocol, 316
Moore, Jennifer, 30; on employee drug testing, 199–209
multinational corporations, controversy over morality and, 254–262
mutagens, fetal protection policies and, 162–175
mutual funds, 154–155
Myerson, Allen R., on sweatshops, 281–283

Nader, Ralph, 231, 340
Nashville Gas Co. v. Satty, 171
National Retail Federation, 279
Native Americans, casino gambling and, 127, 129, 131, 134, 136
neighborhoods, destruction of, in Hartford, Connecticut, due to casino gambling, 121–122
New York Stock Exchange, 148
Newton, Lisa H., on corporate codes of ethics, 29–36
Nichomachean Ethics (Aristotle), 108
Nike, 281
NIMBY (not in my backyard) syndrome, 42
Nixon, Richard, 111, 113, 181
Nordstrom, 278, 279

North American Free Trade Agreement (NAFTA), controversy over, 266–273
nursing homes, 112, 113

obligation, as social virtue, 58
Occupational Safety and Health Administration (OSHA), 164, 166, 174, 313
Office of Technology Assessment, 310
Oil, Chemical and Atomic Workers International Union, 308
On the Contrary (McCarthy), 226
operations, 153
optimism, toward business, 56, 59–60
organized crime, controversy over casino gambling and, 120–137
organochlorines. *See* chlorine
O'Toole, John, on advertising, 224–233
"ought implies can" argument, for employee drug testing, 199–209
ozone, depletion of atmospheric, 258, 302, 305–306, 313, 316

paper industry, use of chlorine in, 303, 308, 309–310, 315, 320–321
pari-mutuel wagering, 123, 130
Paris Commission on the Northeast Atlantic, 300–301
participation, principle of, in corporate codes of ethics, 29, 32
paternalism: green marketing and, 336; tobacco advertising and, 240, 243–250
patriarchy, 14, 17
patricians, 12, 64
Pedersen, Heather L., on rain forest entrepreneurs, 326–334
personhood, Kant's theory of, 105–106, 107
persuasive advertising, 216–223
pessimism, toward business, 56–57, 60, 65, 68
pesticides, use of chlorine in, 301, 303, 304, 307, 308, 310, 312, 315
pharmaceutical industry, 85, 93; chlorine use in, 312, 315; controversy over price controls of, 102–116; ethnobotany and, 326–329, 331–332
Pharmaceutical Manufacturers Association, on pharmaceutical price controls, 110–116
phase-out, of chlorine products, 307, 308, 313, 316
phenyl, 302
pheromones, 302
physicians. *See* medical profession
plastics, use of chlorine in, 301, 302, 309
Plato, 40, 41, 42, 44, 48
plebians, 12, 64
political corruption, controversy over casino gambling and, 120–137
polychlorinated biphenyls (PCBs), 302, 303, 304, 305, 306, 307, 313, 316, 317, 318
polygraph testing, 204
polyvinyl chloride (PVC), 307, 308, 309, 313, 315
pornography, 226

portfolio insurance, 147
poster concept, of advertising, 227
precautionary principle, organochlorines and, 306, 307
Preferred Provider Organizations, 115
pregnancy, and controversy over workplace fetal protection policies, 162–175
price fixing, 71
pricing, controversy over pharmaceutical industry and, 102–116
prisoner's dilemma, ethics of, 41–48, 70, 256–257, 259
privacy, right to, 165; and controversy over employee drug testing, 196–209
procedural justice, 47
program trading, 147
proletarian class, versus bourgeoisie, 12–20
property rights: controversy over environmental issues and, 290–296; rain forest, 328
Prospective Payment System, 112
Protestant work ethic, 57
puffery, as advertising technique, 216
Pursuit of Loneliness, The (Slater), 226
put options, 154

rain forest, controversy over sustainable development of, 326–342
Raines, J. Patrick, on financial derivative instruments, 142–151
Ramaswamy, Sunder, on rain forest entrepreneurs, 326–334
rate swaps, 153
rationing, of health care, 115
Rawls, John, 105–106
Reactionists, 14
Reagan, Ronald, 86, 199
realism, traditional, 254–259
Rehnquist, William, 164, 294
Relman, Arnold S., on compatibility of business and medicine, 80–88
repetition, as advertising technique, 216
reproductive health, and controversy over workplace fetal protection policies, 162–175; organochlorines and, 305, 313
Republic (Plato), 40, 41, 44
research and development, 111
resource-based scheduling, health care costs and, 112
respondeat superior, 201, 207
restraint, as social truth, 58
reverse onus, concept of, organochlorines and, 318–319
risk-benefit analysis, of organochlorine use, 317–318
river blindness, 94–95
riverboat gambling, 135–136
Robinson v. Lorillard, 173
Roddick, Anita. *See* Body Shop International
Roe v. Wade, 174–175

Ruoppolo Commission, 114

Sachs, Jeffrey D., 281–282
salesmanship, advertising as, 228–229
Securities and Exchange Commission, 72, 144, 145, 146, 149, 150
self-control, as market virtue, 61, 68, 71–72
self-interest model, of business, 94, 95
self-policing, whistle-blowing and, 181
serfs, 12, 13
Shaman Pharmaceuticals, 326–327, 330–334
Shaw, Bill, on the market as a teacher of virtue, 64–74
Shaw, George Bernard, 82
shea butter, 337
Sherman Antitrust Act, 85, 145
Siegel, Mo, 341
Sigler, Andy, 33
Silent Spring (Carson), 315
Slater, Philip, 226
slaves, 12
small- to medium-sized firms (SMEs), North American Free Trade Agreement and, 267, 269
Smith, Adam, 56, 57, 60, 65, 66, 68, 69, 70, 71, 72, 73, 94; on capitalism, 4–11
smoking. See tobacco industry
Social Limits to Growth (Hirsch), 58
Solerno, Anthony, 125
Solomon, Robert, 62
solvents, use of chlorine in, 301, 302, 303, 307, 308, 310, 315
Soto, Ana, 318
South Carolina, controversy over property rights and environmental issues and, 290–296
specificity, whistle-blowing and, 183
speech, freedom of, advertising and, 240
Spinello, Richard A., on pharmaceutical price controls, 102–109
Sponsor, The: Notes on a Modern Potentate (Barnouw), 226
stakeholder theory of business, 95, 97, 104
Standard & Poor's 500 stock index, 146, 148, 153
Stearns, W. Joseph, 312, 318
Steffens, Lincoln, 281
Stevenson, Howard H., 40
Sting, 338, 339
stock index futures. See financial derivative instruments
stock options, 154
strategic alliances, 331
Subliminal Seduction (Key), 231
substance abuse. See drug testing
Supreme Court, 199, 240; and controversy over property rights and environmental issues, 290–296. See also individual cases
Survival International, 339–340
sustainable development, and controversy over the rain forest, 326–342
swap contracts, 153

swaptions, 142
sweatshops, controversy over, 278–283
sympathy, as market virtue, 61–62, 68, 72–73
synthetic securities, 142, 146–147

Tagua Initiative, 329–330
takings clause, of the Fifth Amendment, and controversy over property rights and environmental issues, 290–296
tariffs, import, 270, 273
Teamsters Union, 271
teens: casino gambling and, 121, 124, 128; controversy over tobacco advertising aimed at, 238–250
telephones, tapping of, 204
teratogens, fetal protection policies and, 162–175
Theory of Justice, A (Rawls), 105
Theory of Moral Sentiments (Smith), 72
third estate, 13
Thomas, Ambrose, 227–228
Thornton, Joe, 312; on industrial use of chlorine, 300–311
Thrasymachus, 40, 42, 48
Tiegs, Cheryl, 278
tit for tat strategy, prisoner's dilemma and, 43, 70
titanium dioxide, 319
tobacco industry, controversy over advertising by, 238–250
Tocqueville, Alexis de, 58
toluene, 302
totally chlorine-free (TCF) paper, 309–310
Trade Not Aid, The Body Shop International and, 337
traditional realism, 255–259
tranches, 153
Treadway Commission, 72
Treasury bonds, 142, 146, 148
Trillin, Calvin, 240
trustworthiness, as market virtue, 60–61, 68, 69–71
truth, as social virtue, 58
Turner, Donald F., 229
Tylenol poisoning crisis, 25–28, 241

unions, trade, 18, 271, 308
Urabazzo, Ignacio, 272
Usery v. Tamiami Trail Tours, Inc., 172
utilitarianism, 145

validity, principle of, in corporate codes of ethics, 29, 32
valium, 107
vassals, 12
Velasquez, Manuel, 49, 51; on business ethics, 40–48; on morality and international business, 254–259; reaction to views of, 260–262
Verespej, Michael A., on employee drug testing, 196–198
vinyl chloride, 303, 313

virtue, controversy over the market as a teacher of, 56–74
Volberg, Rachel, 123
voluntary hospitals, 84

Wakeman, Frederick, 225
Wal-Mart Stores, 278, 279, 281, 283
Walton, Clarence, 103
warning labels, on tobacco products, 239, 240
water pollution, and controversy over industrial use of chlorine, 300–321
Watt, James, 66
Waxman, Henry, 242
Wealth of Nations (Smith), 4–11, 66
Weeks v. Southern Bell Telephone & Telegraph Co., 171
Weinstein, Bernard, 272
Werhane, Pat, 35, 61, 72–73
Wheeler, Robert, 272

whistle-blowing, 33; controversy over, 180–192
White, Byron, 164
Wicks, Andrew C., on compatibility of business and medicine, 89–98
wildlife, controversy over industrial use of chlorine and, 300–321
Wilson, Donald, 334
Wilson, E. O., 334
"wind wheat," 143, 147–148
World Medical Organization, 80
Wrich, James, 205–206
Wynn, Steve, 121, 125

York, Dick, 225

zero discharge policy, on chlorine, 300, 306–307
zoning, and controversy over property rights and environmental issues, 290–296